Clinical Perspectives on Autobiographical Memory

Autobiographical memory plays a key role in psychological well-being, and the field has been investigated from multiple perspectives for more than thirty years. One large body of research has examined the basic mechanisms and characteristics of autobiographical memory during general cognition, and another body has studied what happens to it during psychological disorders, and how psychological therapies targeting memory disturbances can improve psychological well-being. This edited collection reviews and integrates current theories on autobiographical memory when viewed in a clinical perspective. It presents an overview of basic applied and clinical approaches to autobiographical memory, covering memory specificity, traumatic memories, involuntary and intrusive memories, and the role of self-identity. The book discusses a wide range of psychological disorders, including depression, posttraumatic stress disorder, borderline personality disorder, and autism, and how they affect autobiographical memory. It will be of interest to students of psychology, clinicians, and therapists alike.

LYNN A. WATSON is a Post-Doctoral Researcher at the DNRF Center on Autobiographical Memory Research in the Department of Psychology and Behavioural Sciences at Aarhus University.

DORTHE BERNTSEN is a Professor in the Department of Psychology and Behavioural Sciences at Aarhus University, where she is the Director of the DNRF Center on Autobiographical Memory Research.

Clinical Perspectives on Autobiographical Memory

Edited by
Lynn A. Watson and Dorthe Berntsen

CAMBRIDGE
UNIVERSITY PRESS

University Printing House, Cambridge CB2 8BS, United Kingdom

Cambridge University Press is part of the University of Cambridge.

It furthers the University's mission by disseminating knowledge in the pursuit of education, learning and research at the highest international levels of excellence.

www.cambridge.org
Information on this title: www.cambridge.org/9781107039872

© Cambridge University Press 2015

This publication is in copyright. Subject to statutory exception and to the provisions of relevant collective licensing agreements, no reproduction of any part may take place without the written permission of Cambridge University Press.

First published 2015

A catalogue record for this publication is available from the British Library

Library of Congress Cataloguing in Publication data
Clinical perspectives on autobiographical memory / Lynn A. Watson and Dorthe Berntsen (eds.).
   pages   cm
Includes bibliographical references and index.
ISBN 978-1-107-03987-2 (Hardback)
1. Autobiographical memory.   I. Watson, Lynn A., 1982-   II. Berntsen, Dorthe.
BF378.A87C55 2015
153.1'3–dc23   2014040306

ISBN 978-1-107-03987-2 Hardback

Cambridge University Press has no responsibility for the persistence or accuracy of URLs for external or third-party internet websites referred to in this publication, and does not guarantee that any content on such websites is, or will remain, accurate or appropriate.

Contents

List of figures	*page* viii
List of tables	ix
List of contributors	x
Preface	xiii
Acknowledgments	xiv

1 Introduction   1
LYNN A. WATSON AND DORTHE BERNTSEN

PART I   Trauma and autobiographical memory

2 The complex fabric of trauma and autobiographical memory   17
RICHARD A. BRYANT

3 A basic systems account of trauma memories in PTSD: is more needed?   41
DAVID C. RUBIN

4 Construing trauma as a double-edged sword: how narrative components of autobiographical memory relate to devastation and growth from trauma   65
ADRIEL BOALS, DARNELL SCHUETTLER, AND SHANA SOUTHARD-DOBBS

5 Child maltreatment and autobiographical memory development: emotion regulation and trauma-related psychopathology   85
DEBORAH ALLEY, YOOJIN CHAE, INGRID CORDON, ANNE KALOMIRIS, AND GAIL S. GOODMAN

PART II Intrusive and involuntary memories

6 Intrusive reexperiencing in posttraumatic stress disorder: memory processes and their implications for therapy 109
ANKE EHLERS

7 Mental imagery in psychopathology: from the lab to the clinic 133
IAN A. CLARK, ELLA L. JAMES, LALITHA IYADURAI, AND EMILY A. HOLMES

8 Intrusive, involuntary memories in depression 154
MICHELLE L. MOULDS AND JULIE KRANS

9 From everyday life to trauma: research on everyday involuntary memories advances our understanding of intrusive memories of trauma 172
DORTHE BERNTSEN

PART III Overgeneral autobiographical memories and their mechanisms

10 Overgeneral autobiographical memories and their relationship to rumination 199
EDWARD WATKINS

11 Overgeneral memory in borderline personality disorder 221
KRIS VAN DEN BROECK, LAURENCE CLAES, GUIDO PIETERS, DIRK HERMANS, AND FILIP RAES

12 Difficulties remembering the past and envisioning the future in people with trauma histories or complicated grief 242
RICHARD J. MCNALLY AND DONALD J. ROBINAUGH

PART IV Autobiographical memory, identity, and psychological well-being

13 A model of psychopathological distortions of autobiographical memory narratives: an emotion narrative view 267
TILMANN HABERMAS

14 Self-images and autobiographical memory in memory impairment 291
CLARE J. RATHBONE AND CHRIS J. A. MOULIN

15	Experimentally examining the role of self-identity in posttraumatic stress disorder ADAM D. BROWN, NICOLE A. KOURI, AMY JOSCELYNE, CHARLES R. MARMAR, AND RICHARD A. BRYANT	316
16	The role of self during autobiographical remembering and psychopathology: evidence from philosophical, behavioral, neural, and cultural investigations LYNN A. WATSON AND BARBARA DRITSCHEL	335

PART V Discussion

17	Autobiographical memory in clinical disorders: a final discussion DORTHE BERNTSEN	361

Index   377

Figures

3.1	A schematic of the basic system model	*page* 46
3.2	The three classes of mechanisms that affect stressful memories in PTSD	51
7.1	Pathway via which mental images of autobiographical memories can affect emotion	135
7.2	The general trauma film paradigm procedure used across studies	137
7.3	Mean percentage blood oxygen level dependent signal change for each brain region for flashback and potential scenes relative to control scenes	142
9.1	Faulty encoding and reduced voluntary memory access leading to involuntary intrusive memories according to the discontinuity view	176
9.2	The continuity view	180
9.3	The salience of the traumatic event in memory	189
14.1	The self-memory system	292
14.2	Distribution of memories around age of self-emergence	295
14.3	Distributions of PJM's and controls' memories around age of self-emergence	299

Tables

3.1	Autobiographical Memory Questionnaire variables	49
11.1	DSM-IV criteria for borderline personality disorder	223
11.2	Sample and autobiographical memory test characteristics of the studies on overgeneral memory in relation to borderline personality disorder (symptoms)	225
13.1	Homologous process structures of narratives and emotion	269
13.2	Five levels of narrative	271
13.3	Characteristic narrative distortions in some psychological disorders	277
14.1	Self-images and associated memories	294

Contributors

DEBORAH ALLEY, University of California, USA

DORTHE BERNTSEN, Aarhus University, Denmark

ADRIEL BOALS, University of North Texas, USA

ADAM D. BROWN, Sarah Lawrence College, USA

RICHARD A. BRYANT, University of New South Wales, Australia

YOOJIN CHAE, Texas Tech University, USA

LAURENCE CLAES, University of Leuven, Belgium

IAN A. CLARK, University of Oxford, United Kingdom

INGRID CORDON, University of California, USA

BARBARA DRITSCHEL, University of St. Andrews, United Kingdom

ANKE EHLERS, University of Oxford, United Kingdom

GAIL S. GOODMAN, University of California, USA

TILMANN HABERMAS, Frankfurt University, Germany

DIRK HERMANS, University of Leuven, Belgium

EMILY A. HOLMES, University of Cambridge, United Kingdom

LALITHA IYADURAI, University of Oxford, United Kingdom

ELLA L. JAMES, University of Oxford, United Kingdom

AMY JOSCELYNE, New York University School of Medicine, USA

ANNE KALOMIRIS, University of California, USA

NICOLE A. KOURI, New York University School of Medicine, USA

JULIE KRANS, University of Leuven, Belgium

CHARLES R. MARMAR, New York University School of Medicine, USA

RICHARD J. MCNALLY, Harvard University, USA

MICHELLE L. MOULDS, University of New South Wales, Australia

CHRIS J. A. MOULIN, Université de Bourgogne, France

GUIDO PIETERS, University of Leuven, Belgium

FILIP RAES, University of Leuven, Belgium

CLARE J. RATHBONE, Oxford Brookes University, United Kingdom

DONALD J. ROBINAUGH, Harvard University, USA

DAVID C. RUBIN, Duke University, USA

DARNELL SCHUETTLER, United States Air Force, USA

SHANA SOUTHARD-DOBBS, University of North Texas, USA

KRIS VAN DEN BROECK, University of Leuven, Belgium

EDWARD WATKINS, University of Exeter, United Kingdom

LYNN A. WATSON, Aarhus University, Denmark

Preface

Most chapters in this book were given as invited addresses at the conference "Clinical Perspectives on Autobiographical Memory," held in Aarhus, Denmark, on June 11–12, 2012. The conference was the third in a series of conferences held at Aarhus University dedicated to the study of autobiographical memory. The conference involved more than 100 participants from around fifteen different countries. It brought together some of the most outstanding researchers investigating autobiographical memory from a variety of clinically relevant perspectives with the aim of facilitating scientific exchange in the rapidly growing research area of autobiographical memory and psychopathology. The conference was hosted by the Center on Autobiographical Memory Research (CON AMORE) at Aarhus University and was sponsored by the Danish National Research Foundation's Center of Excellence Program (DNRF93).

Acknowledgments

The editors thank the Danish National Research Foundation for funding. We also thank Tine Bennedsen Gehrt and the editors at Cambridge University Press for valuable assistance.

1 Introduction

Lynn A. Watson and Dorthe Berntsen

> The remarkable thing was that, when I chanced to return to reality, I thought no more of these terrible moments. I did not forget them, but I did not think of them. And still, they were repeated very frequently, pervading a larger and larger segment of my life.
> (From *Autobiography of a Schizophrenic Girl*, Sechehaye, p.27, 1994)

It is human nature to think and reflect on our own personal past. Prior to the emergence of psychology as a scientific discipline, the study of personal recollections was conducted in the form of autobiographies, biographies, photography, and the writings of historians and philosophers. Today, through the use of social media networks, such as Facebook and Twitter, our need to record and share events from our own lives is more evident than ever. What stands out about our interest in autobiographical memory within the discipline of psychology is that, as psychologists, we are dedicated to using the scientific method to systematically investigate the mechanisms, characteristics, and functions of recalling past events in order to understand how and why our autobiographical memories play such an important role in daily functioning. Within clinical psychology our focus is even more specific. We want to understand how autobiographical memories are altered during psychopathology and to what extent these changes contribute to the onset and maintenance of clinical disorders. A central focus of this research endeavor is to facilitate prevention and treatment development.

In clinical psychology there is a strong tradition for investigating changes in autobiographical memory as a function of psychopathology. Central aims have been to understand the mechanisms underlying autobiographical memory disturbances in different clinical populations and to develop appropriate evidence-based treatments for autobiographical memory deficits and psychopathology. Cognitive psychologists, on the other hand, have typically investigated autobiographical memory during healthy cognition with the goal of understanding the basic structures and processes in autobiographical remembering more broadly. Nonetheless, there are a number of important similarities between the two approaches.

First, researchers in both fields are deeply concerned with the ecological validity of their research findings; for both approaches it is paramount that the findings generalize from the laboratory to real-life settings. Second, both fields deal with memory of complex real-life events rather than simplified verbal material often used in mainstream memory studies. Third, both approaches are concerned with emotional and functional aspects of remembering as well as their interaction with individual dispositions.

In spite of these important similarities and shared interests, there is a long history of a sparse scientific exchange and cross-fertilization between researchers examining autobiographical memory in clinical disorders and researchers studying autobiographical memory in everyday life. Consider as an example the work of two eminent early scholars: Sigmund Freud and Frederic C. Bartlett, respectively. Freud is a strong representative for the clinical tradition, whereas Bartlett is often viewed as a founding father of research on everyday memory. Freud used introspection and clinical observation techniques to obtain biographies from his patients in order to identify experiences in their past that might help explain their neuroses. Bartlett studied how people remembered stories and pictures and how motivational factors and higher order cognitive structures, termed schemata, influenced what they perceived and recalled. Both Freud and Bartlett studied memory in real-life settings. Both acknowledged that memory was error prone and, importantly, that the errors often were motivationally derived and thus a highly meaningful research topic. For Freud, errors would reflect unconscious desires and wishes. For Bartlett, they reflected the operations of underlying schemata, shaped by the person's attitude, which largely was a matter of feeling and interests. Thus, both scholars underscored constructive and motivational aspects of remembering, and both were in sharp contrast to the contemporary verbal learning tradition and its usage of impoverished verbal material. Yet it seems that they exchanged very few ideas, let alone words, with one another. In his seminal book on remembering, Bartlett (1932) does refer to Freud in a couple of places, but never with great respect or enthusiasm. Conversely, although Freud might have benefited from some of Bartlett's ideas, such as the notion of schema, and although several of Bartlett's books were published during Freud's lifetime, Bartlett's ideas and observations never seemed to have gained any real attention from Freud.

Despite differences in their methodologies and in their focus of study, both scholars were ultimately interested in some of the same phenomena (such as the interplay between culture and memory) and therefore might have benefited from sharing their observations and conceptions. The goal of the present book is to try to overcome some of these historical obstacles by bringing together autobiographical memory researchers and clinical researchers with an interest in autobiographical memory and have them reflect on similar phenomena in the same book. Our goal is to enhance scientific exchange between researchers with different backgrounds but with a shared interest in gaining a deeper understanding of autobiographical memory in psychopathology. The book will serve methodological and conceptual integration but also show real, and maybe even incommensurable, disagreements. We believe both outcomes are helpful in promoting science.

Although it is beyond the scope of this introduction to provide an extensive review of clinical research into autobiographical memory, a number of key findings will be discussed. These key findings have stimulated a great deal of research and debate over the last thirty years, causing research within this field to expand exponentially. A literature search using the database PsychInfo revealed that of the some 2,879 peer-reviewed journal articles that had been published on the topic of autobiographical memory by September 2013, more than one-third of these articles (1,141) concern autobiographical memory during clinical disorders. More specifically, the search revealed 595 articles on autobiographical memory and depression, 129 articles on autobiographical memory and posttraumatic stress disorder (PTSD), and 265 articles on autobiographical memory and trauma. Given the rapid expansion within this field, a review of current lines of research and the theoretical models and concepts employed is pertinent.

Current theoretical models of autobiographical memory make a distinction between voluntary memory retrieval, which occurs following a strategic memory search, and involuntary memory retrieval, which occurs spontaneously without any conscious attempt at memory retrieval (Berntsen, 1996; Brewin et al., 2010; Conway & Pleydell-Pearce, 2000; Williams et al., 2007). Historically, research into these two forms of memory retrieval has been divided. The study of involuntary memory during healthy or general cognition has received little attention up until recently, while involuntary memories, or more specifically, intrusive memories of negative or traumatic events, have been studied extensively within the clinical domain (see Berntsen, 2009 for a review). Conversely, the study of voluntary memory retrieval has received attention from both cognitive psychologists and clinicians alike. However, psychologists interested in general cognition have investigated a wide variety of autobiographical memory phenomena (such as childhood amnesia, the reminiscence bump, memory accuracy, and memory qualities), while the main focus of clinical psychologists and those interested in clinical cognition has been memory specificity – that is, whether or not the deliberately retrieved memory refers to a concrete event in the past (Williams et al., 2007). The following short review will provide the historical context for these research directions within the study of clinical perspectives on autobiographical memory and serve as a guide for the organization of the five parts into which the chapters in this book are divided.

Intrusive memories of traumatic or stressful events as a topic of investigation gained attention in the 1970s and 1980s due to a number of factors. First, a number of major events occurred across the twentieth century that had a worldwide impact and resulted in millions of human casualties: two world wars, the Vietnam War, and catastrophic disasters of human and natural origin. The high numbers of human casualties and survivors of war led to a growing interest within the medical-psychiatric profession to investigate the long-term impact of trauma on psychological well-being (Wilson, 1994). At this time, psychoanalytic theories of psychopathology were popular. Such theories were developed based on clinical observations of individuals returning from war who reported "traumatic neuroses." Clinicians, such as Freud, repeatedly observed that dreams and repetitive thinking about the trauma were prevalent in these populations (Freud, 1920; for a review, see Horowitz & Becker, 1972). Following the end of the Vietnam War in 1975 increasing numbers of soldiers were returning to the United States reporting similar posttraumatic stress symptoms. This then led to pressure from political and social rights activists to establish a formal diagnosis of posttraumatic reactions to allow war veterans to receive proper legal rights to medical care and disability benefits (Wilson, 1994).

The combination of these societal and political pressures and the psychoanalytic tradition dominating clinical psychology at that time strongly influenced the early work of Mardi J. Horowitz on traumatic stress reactions and the subsequent introduction of the disorder of posttraumatic stress into the third edition of the *Diagnostic and Statistical Manual of Mental Disorders* in 1980 (American Psychiatric Association, 1980). Based on clinical observations, Horowitz theorized that intrusive recollections and repetitive thinking occurred as a reaction following stressful events (Horowitz & Becker, 1972). To investigate this phenomenon more systematically Horowitz and colleagues conducted a series of experiments on college students using a trauma film paradigm (see Horowitz, 1986 and Horowitz & Becker, 1972 for reviews). These studies demonstrated that individuals reported higher levels of intrusive recollections and repetitive thinking following traumatic films when compared with films of emotionally neutral material.

The finding that intrusive recollections occur to a greater extent following exposure to traumatic stimuli and the clinical observations that such reactions were prevalent in individuals reporting psychopathology following traumatic events led to the conception of intrusive recollections as a clinical phenomenon rather than a common psychological process occurring during daily life. Since this seminal work, a number of other theoretical models of intrusive recollection and memory for traumatic events have been developed (Brewin et al., 1996; 2010; Ehlers, 2010; Ehlers & Clark, 2000; Rubin et al., 2008).

The stress response theory developed by Horowitz (1986) and more recent clinical theories of both PTSD and intrusive recollections take the view that intrusive memories persist during PTSD and other forms of psychopathology due to incomplete or ineffective processing of the initial trauma experience (Brewin et al., 1996; 2010; Ehlers, 2010; Ehlers & Clark, 2000). Such models state that traumatized individuals report frequent involuntary and highly distressing memories of the traumatic event, which come to mind with strong sensory images and strong physical and emotional reactions. Conversely, these models also state that when individuals with PTSD are explicitly asked to retrieve memories of the traumatic event, these memories are highly disjointed and poorly constructed. However, two more recent lines of research employing diary study methodologies have brought some of the assumptions of these theoretical models into question. First, research by Berntsen and colleagues identified that involuntary or spontaneous autobiographical memories following nontraumatic everyday life events are a common psychological occurrence (see Berntsen, 2009; 2010 for reviews). This now robust finding calls into question the view that intrusive or involuntary memories are the result of traumatic stress reactions resulting from the incomplete processing of traumatic experiences. Second, studies of traumatic and nontraumatic memories in individuals with and without a diagnosis of PTSD have shown that rather than reporting difficulties retrieving traumatic memories voluntarily, individuals with PTSD show enhanced processing of traumatic memories retrieved both involuntarily and voluntarily (Rubin et al., 2011). Although a relatively new area of research, this alternative perspective has generated debate within the study of intrusive memories and has also had implications regarding our understanding of trauma and the diagnosis of PTSD (Berntsen, 2009; Brewin et al., 2010; Ehlers, 2010; Monroe & Mineka, 2008; Rubin et al., 2008). Although relatively recent, these findings are worth mentioning as these two contrasting perspectives continue to be a point of discussion within current research (see Bryant, Chapter 2; Rubin, Chapter 3; Ehlers, Chapter 6; Moulds and Krans, Chapter 8; and Berntsen, Chapter 9).

Another highly influential finding within the research on autobiographical memory during psychopathology is that when asked to retrieve autobiographical memories to positive and negative cue words, suicide attempters (Williams & Broadbent, 1986) and individuals reporting a current major depressive episode (Williams & Scott, 1988) had difficulties retrieving specific memories, that is, memories of events that took place at a particular time and place and happened only once, for example, "I remember when I went to Kate's birthday party and her husband gave her a kitten." Instead, these individuals tended to report more general or categoric memories of repeated events, for example, "I have attended many birthday parties." In these early studies, this effect was strongest for memories retrieved following positive cues. However, an extensive review of the literature revealed that the overgeneral memory effect occurs following both positive and negative cues, using a wide variety of stimuli and methodologies in a number of different clinical populations (Williams et al., 2007).

One of the reasons this effect has received so much attention within the clinical literature is that it is associated with a number of other clinically relevant mental phenomena, such as impaired problem solving (Evans et al., 1992; Goddard et al., 1996) and difficulties imagining future events (Williams et al., 1996). Furthermore, the overgeneral memory effect is associated with delayed recovery from major depression (Brittlebank et al., 1993) and has been found to be associated with the onset and maintenance of major depression (see Williams et al., 2007 for a review of these findings).

Overall, autobiographical memories seem to play a fundamental role in the experience of psychopathology. Researchers have repeatedly identified that memories retrieved both involuntarily and voluntarily are altered during clinical disorders. In line with this observation, individuals who are experiencing these disorders report high levels of subjective distress during or following memory retrieval (Hackmann et al., 2004; Newby & Moulds, 2011). One final set of key findings, which continue to drive interest in autobiographical memories for clinicians and researchers alike, is a growing body of evidence showing that significant reductions in clinical symptoms and improvements in psychological well-being can be obtained by directly addressing changes in autobiographical memory occurring during psychopathology. Cognitive therapy for PTSD, which targets elements of intrusive recollections, has been found to be effective across a number of treatment trials (Duffy et al., 2007; Ehlers et al., 2003; 2005), and positive developments have also been seen in imagery rescripting (Brewin et al., 2009; Holmes et al., 2007) and therapies targeting memory specificity during depression (Raes et al., 2009;

Watkins et al., 2012; for current reviews of treatment related research, see Ehlers, Chapter 6; Clark and colleagues, Chapter 7; and Watkins, Chapter 10). These findings point toward exciting future developments within this field and highlight the value of this edited collection. As this field continues to grow and evidence-based therapeutic interventions are being developed, the need for greater integration between divergent strands of research on autobiographical memory during psychopathology is paramount.

All chapters in the book offer a review and theoretical integration of findings in a particular area within clinical perspectives on autobiographical memory research. The book consists of fourteen chapters, and introduction and a discussion. The fourteen chapters are grouped in four parts, each with its own overarching topic. The four sections are as follows: Part I: Trauma and Autobiographical Memory; Part II: Intrusive and Involuntary Memories; Part III: Overgeneral Autobiographical Memories and Their Mechanisms, and Part IV: Autobiographical Memory, Identity, and Psychological Well-Being. The following serves as a brief description of the contents of these sections.

Trauma and autobiographical memory

One of the most debated questions within clinical research is how trauma affects autobiographical memory. Part I provides an overview of recent developments in our understanding of the relationship between trauma and autobiographical memory from both general cognition and clinical cognition perspectives. In the first chapter in Part I, Richard A. Bryant provides a review of the more traditional theoretical accounts of autobiographical memory retrieval following trauma, which extend from a clinical perspective. In his chapter he discusses the influence of cognitive and biological factors during the retrieval of traumatic memories in both PTSD and complicated grief. In the second chapter in this part David C. Rubin presents contrasting views of autobiographical memories following trauma by looking at how cognitive factors that are known to influence the characteristics of everyday autobiographical recollections can also be used to further our understanding of the development and maintenance of traumatic autobiographical memories. He provides evidence from both behavioral and neural studies of nonclinical and clinical populations in support of this view, which challenges the commonly held view that special mechanisms are required to explain the characteristics of memories for traumatic events. Taken together, these two chapters provide a comprehensive review of the current theoretical perspectives on traumatic memory and demonstrate the diversity of research within this area across behavioral, neural, and biological levels. Adriel Boals and colleagues then provide a different approach to trauma and autobiographical memory by reviewing not only negative outcomes following trauma but also positive outcomes in the form of posttraumatic growth, with particular focus on event centrality, that is, the tendency to view a traumatic event as being central to one's life story and identity. The authors outline a number of ways in which both posttraumatic stress and posttraumatic growth are associated with event-centrality and discuss ways to improve our understanding of this concept and the ways individuals provide narratives for traumatic events that may have strong implications for therapeutic interventions for PTSD. In the final chapter in this part, Deborah Alley and colleagues review developmental research and theoretical accounts of how the occurrence of traumatic events during childhood may impact the emotion-regulation strategies employed by children and adults in later life. They end by describing a theoretical account of how an avoidant-coping style in parents may lead to distortions in the processing of autobiographical memories of children following negative or traumatic events and the emotion-regulation strategies they employ.

Intrusive and involuntary memories

As discussed above the study of involuntary or spontaneous memories during psychopathology has generally focused on the retrieval of negative or distressing memories and images. The first two chapters in Part II follow in this tradition. Anke Ehlers focuses on the experience of intrusive reliving during PTSD and describes how our understanding of this phenomenon can be employed to develop effective evidence-based psychological therapies for the treatment of PTSD. She directly addresses a number of key questions regarding intrusive memories such as how these memories are triggered and their nature, content, and persistence before going on to address directly how these issues can be targeted during therapy. Ian A. Clark and colleagues then consider autobiographical memory research within the broader context of mental imagery, how both autobiographical memories and autobiographical future imaginations are relevant for treatment purposes. They present research investigating both bottom-up and top-down cognitive processing and review how both lines of research can elucidate the mechanisms underlying memory retrieval during psychopathology. They then outline how paradigms that were developed to examine imagery within an experimental setting can be employed within a therapeutic context. The following chapter by Michelle L. Moulds and Julie Krans provides a parallel review of the clinical literature investigating characteristics of intrusive memories with a focus on major depression. The authors then end their chapter by presenting the similarities between intrusive memories during clinical disorders and involuntary memories in the general population and highlight the need for researchers within both areas to consider their models not as incompatible but complementary. They stress the need for both bottom-up disorder-specific and top-down general cognitive models of autobiographical memory research. Finally, following the discussion presented by Moulds and Krans, Dorthe Berntsen reviews the current literature investigating involuntary autobiographical memories during both healthy and disordered cognition. She considers the characteristics of these memories and the relationship between involuntary memories occurring during everyday life and intrusive memories commonly described in the clinical literature. The presentation of these chapters together allows the reader to make a comparison of the literature related to both intrusive and involuntary memories across a variety of clinical disorders. It also shows the extent to which these two initially separate literatures are becoming increasingly more integrated.

Overgeneral autobiographical memories and their mechanisms

Overgeneral memories are autobiographical memories lacking a reference to a specific time and place. They have been observed in several clinical disorders, notably in depression (Williams et al., 2007). In the first chapter in Part III, Edward Watkins reviews the current literature on the phenomenon of overgeneral autobiographical memories during psychopathology, in particular during depression. He discusses current theoretical models, with particular focus on the relationship between overgeneral memory retrieval and rumination, one of the key mechanisms known to be involved in the onset and maintenance of overgeneral memory (Williams et al., 2007). In his chapter Watkins outlines how habitual processing of information in an abstract and generic way can help us understand the complex interplay between rumination and overgeneral memory. Furthermore, he provides evidence to suggest that psychological therapies targeting this type of maladaptive processing lead to improvements in psychological well-being. In the next chapter Kris van den Broeck and colleagues extend our understanding of the phenomenon of overgeneral memory by applying current models of autobiographical memory retrieval to borderline personality disorder. Their work reviews recent research in this emerging area investigating the presence of overgeneral memory retrieval in this unique, yet diverse, clinical population. They highlight a number of methodological issues that may contribute to the mixed findings identified in their review before discussing these findings in reference to the current models employed to explain overgeneral memory retrieval and its underlying mechanisms in individuals experiencing psychopathology. In the final chapter in this section, Richard J. McNally and Donald J. Robinaugh discuss traumatic reactions and overgeneral memory, in relation not only to autobiographical memories for past events, but also to future episodic thinking. They discuss autobiographical memory distortions across a number of areas of clinical interest, such as posttraumatic stress disorder and trauma survival, childhood sexual abuse, dissociative identity disorder, complicated grief, and false memories. This extensive review and discussion illustrates how wide the study of overgeneral memory and autobiographical memory during clinical disorders has become.

Autobiographical memory, identity, and psychological well-being

Part IV provides an overview of studies investigating an established line of research looking at how the personal significance of autobiographical memories can contribute to the characteristics of these memories in relation to both clinical disorders and psychological well-being. First, Tilmann Habermas employs narrative theory within the psychoanalytic tradition to discuss how different features of memory processing can influence psychological well-being across a range of psychological disorders such as PTSD, panic disorder, depression, and borderline personality disorder. Clare J. Rathbone and Chris J. A. Moulin then review research into self-identity and autobiographical memory in a number of other clinical contexts. Their review discusses research investigating the relationship between autobiographical memory, identity formation, and self images before extending this line of discussion to cases of amnesia, schizophrenia, and autism. In the third chapter in this part Adam D. Brown and colleagues discuss the role of self-identity in relation to posttraumatic stress by considering how changes in self-identity can have implications for psychological interventions. The authors review recent experimental research investigating self-identity, in conjunction with, and distinct from, autobiographical memory, as an important factor in the pathogenesis of PTSD. They also examine recent work demonstrating that shifts in self-views and changes in self-efficacy correspond with changes in processes that influence onset and maintenance of PTSD. Finally, Lynn A. Watson and Barbara Dritschel discuss the relationship between self-identity and emotional processing during autobiographical memory retrieval in relation to current cognitive, social, neuroimaging, and cultural studies investigating self-identity across a number of other psychological domains.

Discussion

The discussion seeks to review the main points of the preceding chapters in order to better understand the current themes evident in clinical perspectives into autobiographical memory. The chapter aims to integrate ideas but also to highlight true disagreements and discuss their possible sources as well as potential new lines of research within the field.

REFERENCES

American Psychiatric Association (1980). *Diagnostic and Statistical Manual of Mental Disorders* (3rd ed.). Washington, DC, American Psychiatric Association.

Bartlett, F. C. (1932/1972). *Remembering: A Study in Experimental and Social Psychology*. Cambridge: Cambridge University Press.

Berntsen, D. (1996). Involuntary autobiographical memories. *Applied Cognitive Psychology*, 10, 435.

(2009). *Involuntary Autobiographical Memories: An Introduction to the Unbidden Past*. Cambridge: Cambridge University Press.

(2010). The unbidden past: involuntary autobiographical memories as a basic mode of remembering. *Current Directions in Psychological Science*, 19, 138–142.

Brewin, C. R., Dalgleish, T., & Joseph, S. (1996). A dual representation theory of posttraumatic stress disorder. *Psychological Review*, 103, 670–686.

Brewin, C. R., Wheatley, J., Patel, T., Fearon, P., Hackmann, A., Wells, A., & Myers, S. (2009). Imagery rescripting as a brief stand-alone treatment for depressed patients with intrusive memories. *Behaviour Research and Therapy*, 47, 569–576.

Brewin, C. R., Gregory, J. D., Lipton, M., & Burgess, N. (2010). Intrusive images in psychological disorders: characteristics, neural mechanisms, and treatment implications. *Psychological Review*, 117, 210.

Brittlebank, A. D., Scott, J., Williams, J. M. G., & Ferrier, I. N. (1993). Autobiographical memory in depression: state or trait marker? *British Journal of Psychiatry*, 162, 118–121.

Conway, M. A., & Pleydell-Pearce, C. W. (2000). The construction of autobiographical memories in the self-memory system. *Psychological Review*, 107, 261–288.

Duffy, M., Gillespie, K., & Clark, D. M. (2007). Post-traumatic stress disorder in the context of terrorism and other civil conflict in Northern Ireland: randomised controlled trial. *British Medical Journal*, 334, 1147–1150.

Ehlers, A. (2010). Understanding and treating unwanted trauma memories in posttraumatic stress disorder. *Journal of Psychology*, 218, 141–145.

Ehlers, A., & Clark, D. M. (2000). A cognitive model of posttraumatic stress disorder. *Behaviour Research and Therapy, 38,* 319–345.

Ehlers, A., Clark, D. M., Hackmann, A., McManus, F., & Fennell, M. (2005). Cognitive therapy for PTSD: development and evaluation. *Behaviour Research and Therapy, 43,* 413–431.

Ehlers, A., Clark, D. M., Hackmann, A., McManus, F., Fennell, M., Herbert, C., et al. (2003). A randomized controlled trial of cognitive therapy, self-help booklet, and repeated assessment as early interventions for PTSD. *Archives of General Psychiatry, 60,* 1024–1032.

Evans, J., Williams, J. M. G., O'Loughlin, S., & Howells, K. (1992). Autobiographical memory and problem-solving strategies of parasuicide patients. *Psychological Medicine, 22,* 399–405.

Freud, Sigmund (1920). *Beyond the Pleasure Principle: The Standard Edition of the Complete Psychological Works of Sigmund Freud, Volume XVIII (1920–1922).*

Goddard, L., Dritschel, B., & Burton, A. (1996). Role of autobiographical memory in social problem solving and depression. *Journal of Abnormal Psychology, 105,* 609–616.

Hackmann, A., Ehlers, A., Speckens, A., & Clark, D. M. (2004). Characteristics and content of intrusive memories in PTSD and their changes with treatment. *Journal of Traumatic Stress, 17,* 231–240.

Holmes, E. A., Crane, C., Fennell, M. J. V., & Williams, J. M. G. (2007). Imagery about suicide in depression: "flash-forwards"? *Journal of Behavior Therapy and Experimental Psychiatry, 38,* 423–434.

Horowitz, M. J. (1986). Stress-response syndromes: a review of posttraumatic and adjustment disorders. *Hospital and Community Psychiatry, 37,* 241–249.

Horowitz, M. J., & Becker, S. S. (1972). Cognitive response to stress: experimental studies of a "compulsion to repeat trauma." *Psychoanalysis and Contemporary Science, 1,* 258–305.

Monroe, S. M., & Mineka, S. (2008). Placing the mnemonic model in context: diagnostic, theoretical, and clinical considerations. *Psychological Review, 115,* 1084–1098.

Newby, J. M., & Moulds, M. L. (2011). Characteristics of intrusive memories in a community sample of depressed, recovered depressed and never-depressed individuals. *Behaviour Research and Therapy, 49,* 234–243.

Raes, F., Williams, J. M. G., & Hermans, D. (2009). Reducing cognitive vulnerability to depression: a preliminary investigation of MEmory Specificity Training (MEST) in inpatients with depressive symptomatology. *Journal of Behavior Therapy and Experimental Psychiatry, 40,* 24–38.

Rubin, D. C., Berntsen, D., & Bohni, M. K. (2008). A memory based model of posttraumatic stress disorder: evaluating basic assumptions underlying the PTSD diagnosis. *Psychological Review, 115,* 985–1011.

Rubin, D. C., Dennis, M. F., & Beckham, J. C. (2011). Autobiographical memory for stressful events: the role of autobiographical memory in posttraumatic stress disorder. *Consciousness and Cognition, 20,* 840–856.

Sechehaye, M. (1994). *Autobiographical of a Schizophrenic Girl: The True Story of Renee.* New York: Penguin Books.

Watkins, E. R., Taylor, R. S., Byng, R., Baeyens, C., Read, R., Pearson, K., ... & Hennessy, S. (2012). Guided self-help concreteness training as an intervention for major depression in primary care: a phase II randomized controlled trial. *Psychological Medicine, 42*, 1359–1371.

Williams, J. M., & Broadbent, K. (1986). Autobiographical memory in suicide attempters. *Journal of Abnormal Psychology, 95*, 144–149.

Williams, J. M. G., & Scott, J. (1988). Autobiographical memory in depression. *Psychological Medicine, 18*, 689–695.

Williams, J. M. G., Ellis, N. C., Tyers, C., Healy, H., Rose, G., & MacLeod, A. K. (1996). The specificity of autobiographical memory and imageability of the future. *Memory and Cognition, 24*, 116–125.

Williams, J. M. G., Barnhofer, T., Crane, C., Herman, D., Raes, F., Watkins, E., & Dalgleish, T. (2007). Autobiographical memory specificity and emotional disorder. *Psychological Bulletin, 133*, 122–148.

Wilson, J. P. (1994). The historical evolution of PTSD diagnostic criteria: from Freud to DSM-IV. *Journal of Traumatic Stress, 7*, 681–698.

Part I

Trauma and autobiographical memory

2 The complex fabric of trauma and autobiographical memory

Richard A. Bryant

There is agreement that traumatic experience and autobiographical memory are inextricably tied together. Remembering and forgetting aversive experiences have been well documented, and the manner in which memories plague people who are affected by trauma underscores the central role that autobiographical memory plays following trauma. Despite this, we are only just beginning to understand the complex role of personal memories in traumatic experiences. This chapter provides an overview of some key factors that moderate how we remember traumatic experiences, and also how these memories in turn influence our behavior, thoughts, and emotions.

The specificity of trauma memories

When asked to recall a memory that happened at a particular time and place and lasted no longer than a day (e.g., "I had a fight with my son on Saturday"), individuals with a psychopathological response to a traumatic experience tend to recall general memories (e.g., "I am always fighting with my son"). This pattern has been observed in individuals with post-traumatic stress disorder (PTSD) following combat (McNally et al., 1995), motor vehicle accidents (Harvey et al., 1998), and cancer diagnosis (Kangas et al., 2005). There is also evidence that overgeneral retrieval of autobiographical memories shortly after trauma exposure is predictive of subsequent PTSD (Harvey et al., 1998). Overgeneral memory retrieval is also observed in samples of adults reporting childhood abuse (Kuyken & Brewin, 1995). This overgenerality is also reported in people with prolonged grief (Maccallum & Bryant, 2010a). This pattern across post-traumatic disorders is relevant because it has been associated with increased vulnerability to developing symptoms following stressful life events (Bryant et al., 2007), poorer response to treatment in depression (Brittlebank et al., 1993), impaired social problem-solving ability (Williams et al., 2005), and deficits in the ability to imagine the future in a specific way (Williams et al., 1996). In prolonged grief, overgeneral retrieval has been associated with impaired social problem solving (Maccallum & Bryant, 2010b) and reduced ability to imagine specific positive events in the future (Maccallum & Bryant, 2011; for a review of these findings, see McNally & Robinaugh, Chapter 12).

Overgeneral retrieval is generally interpreted in terms of the CARFAX model that posits that overgeneral memory results from a combination of three factors: a desire to avoid painful memories and emotions; the tendency to ruminate, which leads people to focus on categoric level memories and general themes; and executive processing limitations that preclude adequate retrieval resources to locate a specific memory. There is growing evidence supporting the roles of rumination (and executive processing demands; for a review of this research and theoretical model, see Williams et al., 2007) in overgeneral memory. In terms of adapting to traumatic experiences, the ability to draw on specific past experiences is hypothesized to be a critical means by which individuals may regulate distress and can be key to resilient responding (Fredrickson, 2001). Accordingly, an impaired ability to retrieve specific events may negatively impact adjustment to the trauma because one is limited in the capacity to contextualize the experience with many other (nontraumatic) experiences of the past (for a full review, see Watkins, Chapter 10).

Intrusions

Intrusive thoughts and memories are a key symptom of most posttraumatic psychiatric disorders (PTSD) (Brewin, 1998; Bryant et al., 2011b). Intrusive memories are experienced as more vivid and distressing (Berntsen et al., 2003); are experienced as spontaneous, repetitive, and difficult to control (Clark & Rhyno, 2005); and interfere with ongoing task performance (Hellawell & Brewin, 2002). Intrusions have been noted, however, across a number of clinical disorders, including obsessive compulsive disorder, depression, social phobia, and agoraphobia. Intrusions have also been noted in nonclinical samples (for a review of research investigating intrusions in clinical and nonclinical samples, see Brewin et al., 2010), and many studies have found that stress or trauma is a frequent trigger for intrusions (for a review, see Bernsten, Chapter 9). Most theories of PTSD place considerable emphasis on intrusions and suggest that the reexperiencing nature of intrusions are particularly characteristic of PTSD (Brewin et al., 1996b; Ehlers & Clark, 2000). This aspect of reexperiencing in PTSD involves people feeling that they are reliving the traumatic experience in the here and now. Cognitive models posit that PTSD is distinguished from other disorders by this reliving aspect of the trauma memories, which purportedly maintains the sense of current threat (Ehlers & Clark, 2000; for a review, see Ehlers, Chapter 6). Consistent with this proposal is evidence that whereas other forms of intrusions are as common in other posttraumatic stress disorders after trauma exposure, flashbacks are particularly found in people with PSTD (Bryant et al., 2011b). Various explanations have been offered for intrusive thoughts and memories. These include (1) that encoded memories are not sufficiently embedded in one's autobiographical memory base, and this leads to unintentional occurrences of these thoughts (Conway & Pleydell-Pearce, 2000); (2) that certain events are encoded in fragmented and perceptually based modes that lead to their subsequent intrusion into awareness (Brewin et al., 2010); (3) that memories are unintentionally activated by internal or external triggers that were initially conditioned with encoded memory (Foa et al., 1989); (4) that attempted thought suppression results in monitoring of the unwanted thought, which results in its increased intrusion into consciousness (Wenzlaff & Wegner, 2000); (5) that thoughts that are consistent with immediate and emotionally salient concerns are more likely to intrude (Klinger, 1996); or (6) that a thought may be so out of the realm of normally expected cognition that the person seeks an explanation for it, thereby leading to involuntary occurrences of it (Clark & Rhyno, 2005).

Mode of processing

There is increasing evidence that the mode of processing of encoded traumatic information can influence how the experience is subsequently retrieved. The prevailing model in this regard is the dual representation theory, which proposes that the encoding of emotionally arousing events generates two memory representations: one that is verbally processed and another that is visually processed (Brewin et al., 1996b). One system, termed the verbally accessible memory (VAM) system, involves mental representations that are consciously processed in working memory prior to being stored in long-term memory. VAM memories purportedly require conscious encoding, and they can be retrieved intentionally. They contain information that the individual has attended to before, during, or after the traumatic event. In this way, VAM memories function as do any other autobiographical memories. In contrast, the dual representation theory holds that memories that involve a reliving of the experience reflect the operation of situationally accessible memories (SAM). These memories contain sensory information that was encoded in primarily perceptual form and was not consciously processed at the time of the traumatic experience. It is proposed that the SAM system contains information that has been obtained from more extensive, lower level perceptual processing of the experience, such as sights, sounds, and smells that were too briefly attended to receive considerable conscious attention. The theory posits several factors that influence the development of VAM and SAM memories. For example, it posits that visually consolidated, as distinct from verbally consolidated, memories are more likely to be stored as SAM memories. It also argues that during consolidation, recalling the memory from an observer (third-person) perspective decreases the likelihood of intrusive memories because it integrates greater contextual information and reduces the sensory, visual representation. This is supported by the evidence reviewed above that observer perspectives are associated with greater avoidance of memories (Kenny et al., 2009). The dual representation theory posits that the SAM system explains why intrusions are experienced as detailed, perceptual, and emotionally charged memories. Other cognitive models exist that converge on the importance of the nature of encoding of the event in a way that it is laid down in a distinctive manner that results in its intrusive memories. For example, Ehlers and Clark propose that data-driven processing at the time of trauma can enhance the perceptually based consolidation of trauma memories, which contributes to these memories being poorly integrated into the autobiographical memory base and therefore representing a greater cause of distress subsequent to the trauma (Ehlers & Clark, 2000).

Relevant to this model is the work of Holmes and colleagues, who have conducted a series of experiments in which participants viewed a traumatic film while concurrently performing either a visuospatial or a verbal task. Whereas the concurrent visuospatial task was found to interfere with the encoding of perceptual information, resulting in fewer intrusive memories, the verbal task resulted in an impoverished conscious representation and greater intrusive memories, relative to a no-task control condition (Holmes et al., 2004). This and other findings provide indirect empirical support for the assertion of dual representation theory that intrusive trauma images are supported by a distinct, independent memory system, one that is primarily visuospatial, rather than verbal, in nature. Other research suggests that visually processed stimuli (purportedly related to the SAM system) are associated with greater levels of emotional arousal, thereby resulting in a greater amount of intrusive images (Brewin et al., 2010; Holmes et al., 2005). These findings suggest that visually based processing may result in overconsolidation of trauma memories, potentially because intrusive memories are based in a SAM-style system, and this may interfere with the adaptive process of consolidating these memories in the contextual base of other autobiographical memories.

It is worth noting that the evidence for dual representation theory is limited at this time. Whereas there is some evidence that flashback memories are associated with specific activation of neural circuits involved in visual processing (e.g., Clark and colleagues, Chapter 7), this evidence is very limited and requires replication. In this context, other researchers have made strong cases for the proposal that the memory patterns observed in conditions such as PTSD can be explained by memory processes observed in nonclinical populations (for a review, see Rubin, Chapter 3). Consistent with this argument, many of the features of PTSD memory phenomena, including memory fragmentation, involuntary recall, and sensory dominance of memories, can be observed in experimental studies of nonclinical populations (Rubin et al., 2011). This evidence does question whether the notion of a distinct memory system is required to explain the strong reliving memories of trauma that characterize PTSD. Further, there is some evidence that, contrary to dual process accounts of intrusive memories, contextual information (Pearson et al., 2012) and verbal processing (Krans et al., 2009) increases intrusive memories.

Role of arousal

One common theme across a number of these explanations is that trauma results in memories being encoded under conditions of high threat and arousal, which predisposes them to poor integration into one's autobiographical memory; these memories are highly represented in memory networks, which can lead to subsequent intrusions. Interestingly, little work has focused on the role of arousal at the time of encoding in relation to subsequent intrusive memories. In contrast, much evidence has accumulated on the role of arousal at the time of encoding in intentionally retrieved emotional memories. For example, there is much evidence that noradrenergic activation at the time of encoding leads to stronger memory for events, and this pattern is particularly strong for emotional events. Adrenergic agonists result in memory enhancement (McGaugh & Roozendaal, 2009) and antagonists impair memory for emotional events (Cahill et al., 2000). Similarly, increases in norepinephrine immediately after a stressful task is associated with memory for that task (McIntyre et al., 2002). This pattern of findings has been interpreted to suggest that stress hormones during and after emotional events trigger noradrenergic activation in the basolateral nucleus of the amygdala (BLA), which leads to stronger memory for these emotional events. Human studies demonstrate that pharmacological modulation of the adrenergic system effectively alters memory for emotional events. Administration of adrenergic receptor blockers (i.e., propanolol) decreases memory for emotional events relative to placebo (Cahill et al., 1994). Importantly, there is recent evidence that memory for emotional, but not neutral, stimuli presented to humans is associated with endogenous noradrenergic activation at the time of encoding (Segal & Cahill, 2009).

Not surprisingly, glucocorticoids are also involved in memory of emotional experiences. Administration of hydrocortisone results in superior recall of subsequently presented emotional (rather than neutral) stimuli (Abercrombie et al., 2006). Further, evidence suggests that the interaction of noradrenergic and glucocorticoid systems may underlie the superior recall of emotional memories (McGaugh & Roozendaal, 2009). It appears that noradrenergic and glucocorticoid systems interact to enhance emotional memories because glucocorticoids are able to pass the blood–brain barrier, thereby facilitating noradrenergic effects in the amygdala. This is supported by evidence that infusion of glucocorticoid antagonists into the BLA reduces the effects of β-adrenoceptor agonist on emotional memory (Roozendaal et al., 2002).

We recently extended this work to determine the influence of stress hormones at the time of encoding and consolidation on subsequent intrusions (Bryant et al., 2013). Participants viewed negative and neutral images. Half the participants immediately underwent a cold pressor test (high stress), immersing their hands in ice water, while the remaining participants immersed their hands in warm water (low stress). Two days later participants completed a measure of intrusions of these images. Participants in the high stress condition reported more intrusions of negative images than participants in the low stress condition. Further, an interaction variable in a linear regression involving increased noradrenergic and cortisol values predicted intrusive memories of emotional stimuli for men but not women. These findings accord with recent evidence of the combined effects of noradrenaline and corticoid responses to stress on emotional memories, but extend them to show that levels of stress hormones in the consolidation phase of emotional events can contribute to intrusive memories.

Although models of intrusive memories imply that arousal at the time of encoding leads to fragmented integration of these memories into one's autobiographical memory base (Ehlers & Clark, 2000), there is no evidence directly making this link. That is, we have no studies that indicate whether high arousal at the time of encoding does in fact lead to fragmented encoding, which in turn results in greater occurrence of intrusive memories. Experiments are required that index the role of glucocorticoid and noradrenergic response to stressful experiences and that simultaneously measure how these relate to fragmented encoding of these memories; these data could then be indexed to subsequent intrusive memories to determine the extent to which this mechanism is associated with intrusions.

Neural mechanisms relevant to trauma memories

In terms of understanding the neural networks implicated in trauma memories, much evidence exists pertaining to the central role of the basolateral nucleus of the amygdala in associative learning of emotional memories and of the hippocampus and surrounding medial prefrontal cortex in retrieval of memories by activating networks involved in the original events (LeDoux, 1996; see Watson and Dritschel, Chapter 16). In attempting to explain intrusive memories, Brewin et al.'s dual representation theory argues that the VAM and SAM are mediated by different neural networks (Brewin et al., 2010). It is proposed that the VAM is strongly associated with hippocampal functions, which are involved in learning about the context in which fear is encoded and also in regulation of the emotional responses (LeDoux, 1996). In contrast, the SAM memories are thought to be mediated by hard-wired connections between sensory systems and the lateral nucleus of the amygdala. The amygdala receives sensory information from subcortical pathways and registers fear and activates defensive responses at a very early stage in processing (LeDoux, 1992). It is proposed that memories encoded under conditions of extreme emotion or stress can be "hard-wired" via the amygdala, and these memories are subsequently experienced as intrusive because of their greater memory trace, which results in involuntary activation by many internal and external cues that were conditioned with the encoding of the memory. More recent developments have also noted the role of the lateral nucleus of the amygdala in memory reconsolidation; that is, when the memory is reactivated via retrieval, the trace can be strengthened or weakened through factors occurring in the reconsolidation context (Schiller et al., 2010). In addition, cognitive (Brewin et al., 1996b) and fear conditioning models (LeDoux, 1996) posit that a core reason for intrusive memories is failure of the medial prefrontal cortex to inhibit emotional reactions. In terms of evidence, several studies have used neuroimaging techniques (positron emission tomography [PET] and *functional magnetic resonance imaging* [fMRI]) to study flashback memories. Flashbacks are one subset of intrusive memories in that they are defined as dissociative states in which the person temporarily believes they are reexperiencing the event in a vivid and realistic manner, and in this sense are not representative of most intrusive memories. Although these studies indicate evidence of reduced medial prefrontal cortex (MPFC), there is very little consistency in the outcomes (Lanius et al., 2006). It should be noted, however, that there is evidence suggesting that flashbacks are associated with amygdala activation in response to memories but not to externally generated fearful stimuli (Shin et al., 1997).

Role of sex

Women tend to have better recall of emotional information than men (Bloise & Johnson, 2007) and are more likely to develop disorders related to emotional memory, such as posttraumatic stress disorder, than males (Olff et al., 2007). Further, sex-related lateralization of amygdala activity has been shown to differentially mediate enhanced emotional memory in men and women (Cahill et al., 2004). Sex hormones also influence emotional memory. Administration of an estrogen antagonist or ovariectomy in rats prevents the impairing effects of pretraining stress on eyeblink conditioning (Wood & Shors, 1998) and reduces sex differences in a fear-conditioning task (Gupta et al., 2001). In humans, the luteal phase of the menstrual cycle is associated with higher levels of circulating estrogen and progesterone, which in turn heightens glucocorticoid release due to progesterone binding to receptor sites (Koubovec et al., 2005). Increased glucocorticoid release at encoding of an emotional experience may consolidate the memory (Pitman, 1989). In this context it is relevant that the mid-luteal phase is linked with stronger recall of emotional memories in healthy controls (Andreano et al., 2008). We recently conducted a study in which we presented women in the mid-luteal and nonluteal phases images of neutral and threatening images followed immediately by either a cold pressor stressor test (to induce arousal) or control condition (Felmingham et al., 2012a). We also indexed their sex hormone levels, and several days later administered a surprise recall test. High progesterone levels were associated with elevated stress-elicited cortisol levels. Further, progesterone increase was associated with enhanced memory when the stress was administered. This pattern suggests that progesterone may mediate the cortisol response to stress, which may account for the stronger memory for arousing emotional material in women in the luteal phase. This interpretation accords with evidence from other laboratories that progesterone levels at the time of encoding predict subsequent emotional memory for negative images (Ertman et al., 2011). An interesting trend in recent years has been the realization that stress responses appear to differ between men and women. Women have greater noradrenergic activation after stress than men (Segal & Cahill, 2009), and cortisol increases predict emotional memory in women but not men (Felmingham et al., 2012b). It is possible that this convergent evidence is pointing toward stronger emotional, and possibly traumatic, memories in women than men being a function (at least in part) of sex hormones influencing how stress hormones increase the consolidation of these memories.

Despite this accruing evidence of the relevance of sex differences in emotional memories, there is little research on the role of sex hormones in intrusive memories. Women experience more intrusive recollections of emotional stimuli than men (Ferree & Cahill, 2009), and females in the luteal phase are more likely to experience intrusions of experimentally generated negative stimuli (Ferree et al., 2011) and flashback memories if they experience trauma during the mid-luteal phase (Bryant et al., 2011a). To test this issue further, we conducted a study in which we presented participants with distressing images, and half the participants underwent a cold pressor stress procedure by immersing their hands in ice cold water while control participants immersed their hands in warm water (Cheung et al., 2013). Saliva samples were collected to index estrogen, progesterone, noradrenaline, and cortisol. When assessed several days later, we found that estrogen levels predicted increased intrusions in women. This finding is consistent with evidence that levels of ovarian hormones influence memory for emotionally arousing events, and provides some evidence of the influence of sex hormones on intrusive memories. There is a need to further consider how sex hormones contribute to intrusive memories because women have much greater risk of developing PTSD than men, and it is very possible that the hormonal bases for how women consolidate memories may be critical in explaining this vulnerability to PTSD. Further, if cycling hormonal changes are influential, it is then possible that women may be more susceptible to developing trauma-related disorders that involve memories that are formed at times when they experience greater levels of estrogen or progesterone.

Memory reconsolidation

Remembering traumatic events can be influenced markedly by *when* stress impacts on the memory process. Much evidence has shown that remembering a long-term memory causes it to enter an unstable active state whereby a process of reconsolidation is required to stabilize the memory trace again (Lewis, 1979). The reconsolidation hypothesis proposes that while a memory is rendered unstable, it is vulnerable to disruption via environmental or pharmacological manipulations (Nader et al., 2000). Although there have been numerous animal studies investigating the impact of stress on the reconsolidation of fear learning and retention, there are fewer human studies (Schiller & Phelps, 2011). One study examined the effects of propranolol (a beta-blocker that impedes noradrenergic release) on reconsolidation in an attempt to modify reactions to trauma reminders in PTSD patients (Brunet et al., 2008). This study found that administering propranolol *after* reactivation of traumatic memories led to decreased maladaptive physiological responses to trauma reminders compared with placebo. Another study assessed the relative effects of propranolol, placebo, and propranolol without reactivation in a healthy population using a fear-conditioning paradigm (Kindt et al., 2009). Only participants who received propranolol *prior* to memory reactivation showed a decline in conditioned fear at extinction, suggesting that blocking the noradrenergic stress response during reactivation and reconsolidation facilitated a reduction in fear. Another study examining the specific effects of stress and reactivation on emotional memory found that administering cortisol *prior* to memory retrieval of previously learned word pairs impaired recall compared with placebo and propranolol groups (Tollenaar et al., 2009). These findings are consistent with the well-demonstrated impairing effects of elevated stress hormones on the retrieval process (Roozendaal, 2002). Finally, a study that applied a psychosocial stressor *after* reactivation found enhanced memory for emotional but not neutral stories (Marin et al., 2010). Although no studies have yet investigated the influence of stress and reactivation on intrusive trauma memories, this is an important area for investigation considering the frequent manner in which trauma memories are retrieved. That is, trauma memories are often elicited by stress and conversely they typically elicit marked arousal; accordingly, if these memories are reconsolidated during this unstable state in the presence of marked arousal it may serve to compound the traumatic nature of the memories.

Given that intrusive memories tend to be more emotionally charged memories (Ferree & Cahill, 2009), this appears to be a likely outcome.

Role of rumination

Relevant to the role of memory reconsolidation, it is possible that cognitive processes that occur during postencoding elaboration of the memory can influence subsequent memory. One possible mechanism is rumination, which involves repetitive thinking about the causes and consequences of an event. Rumination is common after trauma as people attempt to make sense of the experience. Importantly, this cognitive style has been shown to predict subsequent PTSD (Michael et al., 2007). Rumination typically involves selective retrieval of some aspects of a trauma experience, and accordingly it is likely that it involves rehearsing only some aspects of the experience. It is possible that this process could lead to activation of inhibition mechanisms that result in relative forgetting of the associated trauma memory that is not the focus of the repeated rehearsal. From the perspective of cognitive psychology this phenomenon has been termed "retrieval-induced forgetting" (RIF). In conventional RIF paradigms, there are three distinct phases. Initially, participants learn category-exemplar word pairs (e.g., fruit-strawberry, instrument-violin) with several exemplars from at least two categories. Participants are then given repeated retrieval practice of half of the exemplars in half of the categories by completing category-exemplar word stem tests (e.g., fruit-st___). Following a distracter task, participants are given a cued-recall test of the exemplars related to each category cue. This design produces a test of memory for three types of words: (1) practiced, (2) unpracticed but related to practiced words through a common category cue, and (3) unpracticed and unrelated to practiced words. The cued-recall test typically reveals superior memory for practiced words compared with unpracticed words. Of particular interest is the finding that unpracticed words that are related to the practiced words through a shared category are recalled less frequently than unpracticed words from a different category. This finding may suggest memory inhibition processes that act, during the practice phase, to inhibit related yet irrelevant material that may be competing for retrieval (Anderson et al., 1994). Focusing retrieval of certain features of a traumatic experience may lead to inhibition of related material that is not the focus of initial rehearsal. Although two studies have employed the RIF paradigm for affective stimuli and did not find any evidence of a retrieval-induced forgetting effect (Amir et al., 2009; Hauer et al., 2007), the stimuli did not involve actual experiences of the experience.

To address this issue more fully, we conducted a study in which participants watched a video clip of a car crash and the immediate aftermath (Small et al., 2011). Following the film presentation, participants were randomly allocated either to a focused condition where they were instructed to think negatively about the effects of the accident on the victims or a control condition. This induction shared some similarities with rumination in that participants were instructed to think about the victim's experiences in a repetitive, focused, and negative manner. As expected, participants recalled the central better than the peripheral details of the film. The novel finding was that participants who subsequently focused attention on the victims had poorer cued-recall memory for peripheral details of the event relative to those who did not focus on these events. This pattern suggests that there was a cognitive cost of focusing on the victim, and may suggest that ruminating on certain aspects of a traumatic experience may result in impoverished retrieval of other features of the trauma.

Vantage point

A key element of all cognitive models of PTSD is how trauma survivors manage their memories. Most models converge on the proposition that PTSD is characterized by minimizing the emotional impact of the memory through various forms of avoidance. One way that trauma survivors can reduce aversive features of a trauma memory appears to be through altering the vantage point from which the memory is recalled. There is considerable evidence that survivors with PTSD can remember their traumatic experience from an observer perspective, that is, as if they were a spectator watching the event from a point of view different from that which they experienced at the time of its occurrence (Foa & Rothbaum, 1998). It is possible that recalling an experience from a distant perspective reduces the emotional impact of the memory. McIsaac and Eich (2004) found that individuals with observer memories reported less anxiety related to these memories than individuals who recalled their trauma from their own (field) perspective. This accords with evidence from nonclinical populations that field memories are associated with stronger emotional responses than observer memories (McIsaac & Eich, 2002).

The possibility that remembering traumatic events from an observer vantage point may act as a form of emotional avoidance is supported by evidence of an association between observer memories and other forms of cognitive and behavioral avoidance following trauma (Kenny & Bryant, 2007). Stronger support has come from a longitudinal study that asked 947 trauma survivors to identify the vantage point of their trauma memory within four weeks of the traumatic experience and again twelve months later (Kenny et al., 2009). They were also interviewed about PTSD symptoms in the initial month after trauma, at three months, and at twelve months after the trauma. Initially recalling the trauma from an observer vantage point was related to more severe PTSD symptoms at that time and twelve months later. Shifting from a field to an observer perspective over the year after trauma was predicted by PTSD severity at three months. Taken together, these data support the proposal that remembering trauma from an observer vantage point can represent a form of avoidance, may impede emotional processing of the experience, and can therefore be related to ongoing PTSD symptoms.

Narrowed attention and trauma memories

Dissociation models of trauma memory posit that traumatic memories are often restricted in order to limit the distressing emotional reactions they elicit (van der Kolk & van der Hart, 1989). This model posits that dissociative mechanisms are invoked to help reduce awareness of the distressing aspects of a trauma; proponents of this view cite reports that in the aftermath of trauma it is common for people to report emotional numbing, reduction in awareness of one's surroundings, derealization, depersonalization, and amnesia (Feinstein, 1989). Much attention has focused on this issue because of reports of strong relationships between these acute dissociative responses and subsequent PTSD (Ehlers et al., 1998).

One way to understand this response and how it affects trauma memory is the evidence that people encode distressing information preferentially; that is, they tend to encode more information that is central to the emotional focus of an emotional or threatening event relative to peripheral details (Christianson, 1992). It has been suggested that this may occur because arousal-inducing experiences place greater demands on cognitive resources such that they cannot be used in the processing of extraneous details (Kramer et al., 1990). This latter explanation accords with one explanation of dissociative responses that highlights the role arousal plays in underpinning the experiences often described as dissociative. It has been suggested that dissociation is an epiphenomenon of heightened peritraumatic arousal (Friedman, 2000). This view accords with evidence that dissociative phenomena (e.g., flashbacks) occur in PTSD individuals with yohimbine-induced arousal (yohimbine elicits panic-like reactions with associated elevation in noradrenergic activation; Southwick et al., 1993); dissociative reactions are commonly reported during panic attacks (Krystal et al., 1991); panic attacks are very common during trauma, with more than half of trauma survivors experiencing panic attacks during the trauma itself (Bryant & Panasetis, 2001); and dissociative responses can be induced in recently trauma-exposed individuals with hyperventilation (Nixon & Bryant, 2006). Further, in a longitudinal study of trauma survivors peritraumatic dissociation mediated the effect of panic reactions during trauma and subsequent PTSD symptoms, indicating that whereas peritraumatic dissociation is associated with later PTSD symptoms, this relationship is influenced by initial acute panic responses. Further, the impact of arousal on dissociative responses is very apparent in nonpathological populations. One study found high rates of dissociative responses, including narrowed attention and memory, in novice skydivers, and these were associated with elevated arousal (Sterlini & Bryant, 2002). Another study of skydivers found that these responses were associated with narrowed attention on skydiving-related stimuli, which was linked to preferential memory for these events at the expense of peripheral details (Cavenett & Nixon, 2006). Taken together, it appears that under conditions of very high arousal, such as a traumatic experience, attention can be narrowed to the point that encoding is restricted to information that is the focus of primary interest. Accordingly, there is a relative deficit in encoding of other information.

Role of identity

One of the influential theories of autobiographical memory involves the self-memory system (Conway & Pleydell-Pearce, 2000). This theory proposes that autobiographical memory for specific events is reconstructed from mental representations in the autobiographical knowledge base; retrieval of specific information about one's personal past is influenced by constructions of the self, including one's self-image and goals. The self-memory system preferentially allows memory representations of past events into consciousness if they accord with the goals and constructions that one holds about oneself. Numerous studies have supported the idea that there is a relationship between dominant goals and preferential access to related memories (Conway & Holmes, 2004; Moberly & MacLeod, 2006). In terms of traumatized individuals, those who perceive themselves as vulnerable to future harm may selectively recall memories involving harmful experiences. In contrast to the view that intrusive memories are indelible imprints that replay encoded experiences, this modified theory posits that intrusive memories may contain information that is consistent with self-constructs and can alter according to altering self-constructs. Supporting this view is evidence of the content of intrusive memories changing over time and in parallel with the concerns of the individual (Bryant, 1996). For example, one severely brain injured patient who was densely amnesic of his accident reported no intrusive memories of the accident. Over a year after the accident, he began driving again and was concerned that he would have another accident. At this point he suddenly developed distressing intrusive memories that involved images of himself badly injured in his car, which appears to have been reconstructions of newspaper photographs that he had seen of his wrecked car. As time progressed and he began driving, he was encouraged to drive with his family in the car. His concerns extended to him crashing his car and hurting his children; at this stage he developed intrusive "flashbacks" involving images of his children in the crashed car – even though they were never involved in the initial accident. This example highlights how people reconstruct their traumatic pasts, how these memories can be consolidated in ways that form subjectively compelling reexperiencing of events that may not actually have occurred, and how the content of these memories can change in accord with a person's changing concerns (see also Rathbone and Moulin, Chapter 14). This interpretation is consistent with evidence that personal memories, including memories of trauma, often concur with self-identity and reported goals (McNally et al., 1995; Singer & Salovey, 1993; Sutherland & Bryant, 2005).

The role of identity in memory for trauma can be readily described in the context of prolonged grief (PG). Although most bereaved individuals adapt in the initial months after the loss, approximately 10%–15% of bereaved individuals suffer persistent problems often called PG (Bonanno & Kaltman, 2001). This syndrome (alternately known as complicated grief) is characterized by a persistent sense of yearning for the deceased, difficulty accepting or believing the loss, bitterness, lack of trust, and loss of perceived meaning in life that is ongoing for at least six months after the death (Zhang et al., 2006). Maccallum and Bryant (2010a) found that individuals with PG were more likely to recall grief-related memories than individuals without PG and that holding grief-related goals was an independent predictor of recalling grief-related memories. Maccallum and Bryant (2008) also reported that individuals with PG were more likely to provide self-defining memories that involved the deceased. Relatedly, Boelen (2009; see also Boelen, 2012) found that the degree to which the loss was central to the person's life story was significantly associated with PG severity, even when controlling for other relevant personality-related variables, and was predictive of PG, depression, and PTSD one year later. Boelen et al. (2012) found that the death of a loved one coincided with an acute reduction in self-concept clarity, which, in turn, affected the severity of symptoms experienced immediately after loss. The self-memory system model would propose that there is a tension between maintaining a consistency between the self and real life experiences; that is, the jarring discrepancy between goals and reality following the loss of a loved one can produce memory and emotional disturbances. Supporting this proposition, a discrepancy between current life situations and one's goals has been linked to depression and anxiety (Strauman et al., 2001). It is not a surprise, therefore, that the need to revise the self to incorporate the reality of the loss is a central component of models of PG (Boelen et al., 2006; Shear et al., 2007). Extending these models to more explicitly recognize the interacting roles of identity and autobiographical memory, Maccallum and Bryant (2013) have suggested that a pivotal mechanism during bereavement is the revision of self-identity to incorporate the reality of the loss and enable the development of new goals, life roles, and attachments that are independent of the deceased; central to this model is how autobiographical memories are integrated into the changing sense of identity after one has experienced marked bereavement. This example highlights that the role of identity is key to any understanding of how autobiographical memory influences adaptation to a highly stressful experience (see also Boals and colleagues, Chapter 4).

One implication of the research emerging from the self-memory model is the reconstructive nature of autobiographical memories. This pattern has been demonstrated repeatedly across many clinical and nonclinical studies (for a review, see Rubin, Chapter 3). For example, in a longitudinal study of trauma survivors who sustained mild traumatic brain injury and were partially amnesic of the trauma because of lack of consciousness, a significant proportion reported two years later that they could recall their trauma in its entirety (Harvey & Bryant, 2001). The finding that both intrusive and nonintrusive memories can change over time raises interesting challenges for models that posit that trauma memories are "hard-wired" and immutable. The increasing evidence points to all memories being susceptible to reconstructive influences, and there is little reason to suspect that trauma memories are different.

Toward integration of a model of trauma memories

This review highlights that there are numerous, potentially interacting influences that lead to remembering trauma in particular ways. One outstanding feature of research to date is that it has predominantly investigated trauma memories from the perspective of single paradigms, and therefore it is limited by the lack of understanding trauma memories from an integrative perspective. The emerging evidence suggests, however, that this can lead to misleading conclusions about the mechanisms underpinning trauma memories because the role of many of these factors needs to be understood in relation to other factors. For example, there is good reason to suggest that the mode of processing of a traumatic experience would be influenced by the level of physiological arousal experienced by the person at the time of encoding. That is, heightened arousal generated by the visual processing of emotionally evocative stimuli may be associated with enhanced noradrenergic and glucocorticoid activity in the amygdala and reduced prefrontal cortical and hippocampal activity. Such a proposition would be suggested by the integration of Brewin's (1996b) dual representation theory and McGaugh's (2004) memory modulation hypothesis. Consistent with these predictions, fMRI studies demonstrate that visual processing of emotionally arousing images was associated with bilateral amygdala activation, while verbal processing of the same stimuli was related to an attenuation of this amygdala response and a correlated increase in activity in the right prefrontal cortex (Hariri et al., 2003). Similarly, there is increasing awareness of the need to understand most findings regarding memory in relation to sex and, more specifically, in terms of sex hormones. For example, the finding that progesterone can mediate the cortisol response to stress (Felmingham et al., 2012a) suggests that any model that incorporates the role of arousal needs to recognize that sex hormones can influence this mechanism. There is also an increasing awareness that we need to be aware of the stage of processing of the information, insofar as different factors operate at encoding, consolidation, and retrieval stages, and that the concurrence of stress at any of these stages can have differential impacts on how trauma memories are consolidated. These factors point to the need for optimal understanding of traumatic memories to adopt cross-paradigm investigations that can capture the complex interplay of mechanisms that influence trauma memories. These factors, to name but a few, include sex, sex and stress hormones, timing of stress in relation to trauma encoding and retrieval, mode of processing at encoding, and conditions under which reactivated memories may be modified. Although autobiographical memory has traditionally been the exclusive focus of cognitive psychologists, there is a need for cross-disciplinary research that combines expertise from cognitive and biological psychology, as well as from neuroscience, and perception. By adopting a comprehensive approach to trauma memories, we are more likely to determine the factors that influence how people remember their trauma experiences.

REFERENCES

Abercrombie, H. C., Speck, N. S., & Monticelli, R. M. (2006). Endogenous cortisol elevations are related to memory facilitation only in individuals who are emotionally aroused. *Psychoneuroendocrinology, 31*(2), 187–196.

Amir, N., Badour, C. L., & Freese, B. (2009). The effect of retrieval on recall of information in individuals with posttraumatic stress disorder. *Journal of Anxiety Disorders, 23*(4), 535–540.

Anderson, M. C., Bjork, R. A., & Bjork, E. L. (1994). Remembering can cause forgetting: retrieval dynamics in long-term memory. *Journal of Experimental Psychology: Learning, Memory, and Cognition, 20*(5), 1063–1087.

Andreano, J. M., Arjomandi, H., & Cahill, L. (2008). Menstrual cycle modulation of the relationship between cortisol and long-term memory. *Psychoneuroendocrinology, 33*(6), 874–882.

Berntsen, D., Willert, M., & Rubin, D. C. (2003). Splintered memories or vivid landmarks? Qualities and organization of traumatic memories with and without PTSD. *Applied Cognitive Psychology, 17*(6), 675–693.

Bloise, S. M., & Johnson, M. K. (2007). Memory for emotional and neutral information: gender and individual differences in emotional sensitivity. *Memory*, *15*(2), 192–204.
Boelen, P. A. (2009). The centrality of a loss and its role in emotional problems among bereaved people. *Behaviour Research and Therapy*, *47*(7), 616–622
(2012). A prospective examination of the association between the centrality of a loss and post-loss psychopathology. *Journal of Affective Disorders*, *137*(1–3), 117–124.
Boelen, P. A., van den Hout, M. A., & van den Bout, J. (2006). A cognitive-behavioral conceptualization of complicated grief. *Clinical Psychology: Science and Practice*, *13*(2), 109–128.
Boelen, P. A., Keijsers, L., & van den Hout, M. A. (2012). The role of self-concept clarity in prolonged grief disorder. *Journal of Nervous and Mental Disease*, *200*(1), 56–62.
Bonanno, G. A., & Kaltman, S. (2001). The varieties of grief experience. *Clinical Psychology Review*, *21*(5), 705–734.
Brewin, C. R. (1998). Intrusive memories, depression and PTSD. *Psychologist*, *11*(6), 281–283.
Brewin, C. R., Dalgleish, T., & Joseph, S. (1996b). A dual representation theory of posttraumatic stress disorder. *Psychological Review*, *103*(4), 670–686.
Brewin, C. R., Gregory, J. D., Lipton, M., & Burgess, N. (2010). Intrusive images in psychological disorders: characteristics, neural mechanisms, and treatment implications. *Psychological Review*, *117*(1), 210–232.
Brittlebank, A. D., Scott, J., Williams, J. M., & Ferrier, I. N. (1993). Autobiographical memory in depression: state or trait marker? *British Journal of Psychiatry*, *162*, 118–121.
Brunet, A., Orr, S. P., Tremblay, J., Robertson, K., Nader, K., & Pitman, R. K. (2008). Effect of post-retrieval propranolol on psychophysiologic responding during subsequent script-driven traumatic imagery in post-traumatic stress disorder. *Journal of Psychiatric Research*, *42*(6), 503–506.
Bryant, R. A. (1996). Posttraumatic stress disorder, flashbacks, and pseudomemories in closed head injury. *Journal of Traumatic Stress*, *9*(3), 621–629.
Bryant, R. A., & Panasetis, P. (2001). Panic symptoms during trauma and acute stress disorder. *Behaviour Research and Therapy*, *39*(8), 961–966.
Bryant, R. A., Sutherland, K., & Guthrie, R. M. (2007). Impaired specific autobiographical memory as a risk factor for posttraumatic stress after trauma. *Journal of Abnormal Psychology*, *116*(4), 837–841.
Bryant, R. A., Felmingham, K. L., Silove, D., Creamer, M., O'Donnell, M., & McFarlane, A. C. (2011a). The association between menstrual cycle and traumatic memories. *Journal of Affective Disorders*, *131*(1–3), 398–401.
Bryant, R. A., O'Donnell, M. L., Creamer, M., McFarlane, A. C., & Silove, D. (2011b). Posttraumatic intrusive symptoms across psychiatric disorders. *Journal of Psychiatric Research*, *45*(6), 842–847.
Bryant, R. A., McGrath, C., & Felmingham, K.L. (2013). The roles of noradrenergic and glucocorticoid activation in the development of intrusive memories. *PloS ONE*, *8*, e62675.

Cahill, L., Prins, B., Weber, M., & McGaugh, J. L. (1994). Beta-adrenergic activation and memory for emotional events. *Nature, 371*(6499), 702–704.

Cahill, L., Pham, C. A., & Setlow, B. (2000). Impaired memory consolidation in rats produced with beta-adrenergic blockade. *Neurobiology of Learning and Memory, 74*(3), 259–266.

Cahill, L., Uncapher, M., Kilpatrick, L., Alkire, M. T., & Turner, J. (2004). Sex-related hemispheric lateralization of amygdala function in emotionally influenced memory: an FMRI investigation. *Learning and Memory, 11*(3), 261–266.

Cavenett, T., & Nixon, R. D. (2006). The effect of arousal on memory for emotionally-relevant information: a study of skydivers. *Behaviour Research and Therapy, 44*(10), 1461–1469.

Cheung, J., Chervonsky, L., Felmingham, K. L., & Bryant, R. A. (2013). The role of estrogen in intrusive memories. *Neurobiology of Learning and Memory, 106,* 87–94.

Christianson, S. A. (1992). Emotional stress and eyewitness memory: a critical review. *Psychological Bulletin, 112*(2), 284–309.

Clark, D. A., & Rhyno, S. (2005). Unwanted intrusive thoughts in nonclinical individuals: implications for clinical disorders. In D. A. Clark (ed.), *Intrusive Thoughts in Clinical Disorders: Theory, Research, and Treatment* (pp. 1–29). New York: Guilford Press.

Conway, M. A., & Holmes, A. (2004). Psychosocial stages and the accessibility of autobiographical memories across the life cycle. *Journal of Personality, 72*(3), 461–480.

Conway, M. A., & Pleydell-Pearce, C. W. (2000). The construction of autobiographical memories in the self-memory system. *Psychological Review, 107*(2), 261–288.

Ehlers, A., & Clark, D. M. (2000). A cognitive model of posttraumatic stress disorder. *Behaviour Research and Therapy, 38*(4), 319–345.

Ehlers, A., Mayou, R. A., & Bryant, B. (1998). Psychological predictors of chronic posttraumatic stress disorder after motor vehicle accidents. *Journal of Abnormal Psychology, 107*(3), 508–519.

Ertman, N., Andreano, J. M., & Cahill, L. (2011). Progesterone at encoding predicts subsequent emotional memory. *Learning and Memory, 18*(12), 759–763.

Feinstein, A. (1989). Posttraumatic stress disorder: a descriptive study supporting DSM-III-R criteria. *American Journal of Psychiatry, 146*(5), 665–666.

Felmingham, K. L., Fong, W. C., & Bryant, R. A. (2012a). The impact of progesterone on memory consolidation of threatening images in women. *Psychoneuroendocrinology, 37*(11), 1896–1900.

Felmingham, K. L., Tran, T. P., Fong, W. C., & Bryant, R. A. (2012b). Sex differences in emotional memory consolidation: the effect of stress-induced salivary alpha-amylase and cortisol. *Biological Psychology, 89*(3), 539–544.

Ferree, N. K., & Cahill, L. (2009). Post-event spontaneous intrusive recollections and strength of memory for emotional events in men and women. *Consciousness and Cognition, 18*(1), 126–134.

Ferree, N. K., Kamat, R., & Cahill, L. (2011). Influences of menstrual cycle position and sex hormone levels on spontaneous intrusive recollections following emotional stimuli. *Consciousness and Cognition, 20*(4), 1154–1162.

Foa, E. B., & Rothbaum, B. O. (1998). *Treating the Trauma of Rape: Cognitive-Behavioral Therapy for PTSD.* New York: Guilford Press.

Foa, E. B., Steketee, G., & Rothbaum, B. O. (1989). Behavioral/cognitive conceptualizations of post-traumatic stress disorder. *Behavior Therapy, 20* (2), 155–176.

Fredrickson, B. L. (2001). The role of positive emotions in positive psychology: the broaden and build theory of positive emotions. *American Psychologist, 56* (3), 218–226.

Friedman, M. J. (2000). What might the psychobiology of posttraumatic stress disorder teach us about future approaches to pharmacotherapy? *Journal of Clinical Psychiatry, 61*(Suppl. 7), 44–51.

Gupta, R. R., Sen, S., Diepenhorst, L. L., Rudick, C. N., & Maren, S. (2001). Estrogen modulates sexually dimorphic contextual fear conditioning and hippocampal long-term potentiation (LTP) in rats(1). *Brain Research, 888* (2), 356–365.

Hariri, A. R., Mattay, V.S., Tessitore, A., Fera, F., & Weinberger, D.R. (2003). Neocortical modulation of the amygdala response to fearful stimuli. *Biological Psychiatry, 53*, 494–501.

Harvey, A. G., & Bryant, R. A. (2001). Reconstructing trauma memories: a prospective study of amnesic trauma survivors. *Journal of Traumatic Stress, 14*, 277–282.

Harvey, A. G., Bryant, R. A., & Dang, S. T. (1998). Autobiographical memory in acute stress disorder. *Journal of Consulting and Clinical Psychology, 66*(3), 500–506.

Hauer, B. J., Wessel, I., Merckelbach, H., Roefs, A., & Dalgleish, T. (2007). Effects of repeated retrieval of central and peripheral details in complex emotional slides. *Memory, 15*(4), 435–449.

Hellawell, S. J., & Brewin, C. R. (2002). A comparison of flashbacks and ordinary autobiographical memories of trauma: cognitive resources and behavioural observations. *Behaviour Research and Therapy, 40*(10), 1143–1156.

Holmes, E. A., Brewin, C. R., & Hennessy, R. G. (2004). Trauma films, information processing, and intrusive memory development. *Journal of Experimental Psychology-General, 133*(1), 3–22.

Holmes, E. A., Grey, N., & Young, K. A. (2005). Intrusive images and "hotspots" of trauma memories in posttraumatic stress disorder: an exploratory investigation of emotions and cognitive themes. *Journal of Behavior Therapy and Experimental Psychiatry, 36*(1), 3–17.

Kangas, M., Henry, J. L., & Bryant, R. A. (2005). A prospective study of autobiographical memory and posttraumatic stress disorder following cancer. *Journal of Consulting and Clinical Psychology, 73*(2), 293–299.

Kenny, L. M., & Bryant, R. A. (2007). Keeping memories at an arm's length: vantage point of trauma memories. *Behaviour Research and Therapy, 45*(8), 1915–1920.

Kenny, L. M., Bryant, R. A., Silove, D., Creamer, M., O'Donnell, M., & McFarlane, A. C. (2009). Distant memories: a prospective study of vantage point of trauma memories. *Psychological Science*, *20*(9), 1049–1052.
Kindt, M., Soeter, M., & Vervliet, B. (2009). Beyond extinction: erasing human fear responses and preventing the return of fear. *Nature Neuroscience*, *12*(3), 256–258.
Klinger, E. (1996). The contents of thoughts: interference as the downside of adaptive normal mechanisms in thought flow. In I. G. Sarason, G. R. Pierce, & B. R. Sarason (eds.), *Cognitive Interference: Theories, Methods, and Findings* (pp. 3–23). Mahwah, NJ: Erlbaum.
Koubovec, D., Geerts, L., Odendaal, H. J., Stein, D. J., & Vythilingum, B. (2005). Effects of psychologic stress on fetal development and pregnancy outcome. *Current Psychiatry Reports*, *7*(4), 274–280.
Kramer, T., Buckhout, R., & Eugenio, P. (1990). Weapon focus, arousal, and eyewitness memory: attention must be paid. *Law and Human Behavior*, *14*, 167–184.
Krans, J., Naring, G., & Becker, E.S. (2009). Count out your intrusions: effects of verbal encoding on intrusive memories. *Memory*, *17*, 809–815.
Krystal, J. H., Woods, S. W., Hill, C. L., & Charney, D. S. (1991). Characteristics of panic attack subtypes: assessment of spontaneous panic, situational panic, sleep panic, and limited symptom attacks. *Comprehensive Psychiatry*, *32*(6), 474–480.
Kuyken, W., & Brewin, C. R. (1995). Autobiographical memory functioning in depression and reports of early abuse. *Journal of Abnormal Psychology*, *104*(4), 585–591.
Lanius, R. A., Bluhm, R., Lanius, U., & Pain, C. (2006). A review of neuroimaging studies in PTSD: heterogeneity of response to symptom provocation. *Journal of Psychiatric Research*, *40*(8), 709–729.
LeDoux, J. E. (1992). Emotion as memory: anatomical systems underlying indelible neural traces. In S. A. Christianson (ed.), *Handbook of Emotion and Memory* (pp. 269–288). Hillsdale, NJ: Erlbaum.
LeDoux, J. E. (1996). *The Emotional Brain: The Mysterious Underpinnings of Emotional Life*. New York: Simon & Schuster.
Lewis, D. J. (1979). Psychobiology of active and inactive memory. *Psychological Bulletin*, *86*(5), 1054–1083.
Maccallum, F., & Bryant, R. A. (2008). Self-defining memories in complicated grief. *Behaviour Research and Therapy*, *46*(12), 1311–1315.
  (2010a). Impaired autobiographical memory in complicated grief. *Behaviour Research and Therapy*, *48*(4), 328–334.
  (2010b). Social problem solving in complicated grief. *British Journal of Clinical Psychology*, *49*(4), 577–590.
  (2011). Imagining the future in complicated grief. *Depression and Anxiety*, *28* (8), 658–665.
  (2013). A cognitive attachment model of prolonged grief: integrating attachments, memory, and identity. *Clinical Psychology Review*, *33*, 713–727.

Marin, M. F., Pilgrim, K., & Lupien, S. J. (2010). Modulatory effects of stress on reactivated emotional memories. *Psychoneuroendocrinology*, *35*(9), 1388–1396.

McGaugh, J. L. (2004). The amygdala modulates the consolidation of memories of emotionally arousing experiences. *Annual Review of Neuroscience*, *27*, 1–28.

McGaugh, J. L., & Roozendaal, B. (2009). Drug enhancement of memory consolidation: historical perspective and neurobiological implications. *Psychopharmacology (Berlin)*, *202*(1–3), 3–14.

McIntyre, C. K., Hatfield, T., & McGaugh, J. L. (2002). Amygdala norepinephrine levels after training predict inhibitory avoidance retention performance in rats. *European Journal of Neuroscience*, *16*(7), 1223–1226.

McIsaac, H. K., & Eich, E. (2002). Vantage point in episodic memory. *Psychonomic Bulletin and Review*, *9*, 409–420.

(2004). Vantage point in traumatic memory. *Psychological Science*, *15*(4), 248–253.

McNally, R. J., Lasko, N. B., Macklin, M. L., & Pitman, R. K. (1995). Autobiographical memory disturbance in combat-related posttraumatic stress disorder. *Behaviour Research and Therapy*, *33*(6), 619–630.

Michael, T., Halligan, S. L., Clark, D. M., & Ehlers, A. (2007). Rumination in posttraumatic stress disorder. *Depression and Anxiety*, *24*(5), 307–317.

Moberly, N. J., & MacLeod, A. K. (2006). Goal pursuit, goal self-concordance, and the accessibility of autobiographical knowledge. *Memory*, *14*(7), 901–915.

Nader, K., Schafe, G. E., & Le Doux, J. E. (2000). Fear memories require protein synthesis in the amygdala for reconsolidation after retrieval. *Nature*, *406*(6797), 722–726.

Nixon, R. D. V., & Bryant, R. A. (2006). Dissociation in acute stress disorder after a hyperventilation provocation test. *Behavioural and Cognitive Psychotherapy*, *34*(3), 343–349.

Olff, M., Langeland, W., Draijer, N., & Gersons, B. P. R. (2007). Gender differences in posttraumatic stress disorder. *Psychological Bulletin*, *133*(2), 183–204.

Pearson, D.G., Ross, F.D., & Webster, V.L. (2012). The importance of context: evidence that contextual representations increase intrusive memories. *Journal of Behavior Therapy and Experimental Psychiatry*, *43*, 573–580.

Pitman, R. K. (1989). Post-traumatic stress disorder, hormones, and memory. *Biological Psychiatry*, *26*(3), 221–223.

Roozendaal, B. (2002). Stress and memory: opposing effects of glucocorticoids on memory consolidation and memory retrieval. *Neurobiology of Learning and Memory*, *78*(3), 578–595.

Roozendaal, B., Quirarte, G. L., & McGaugh, J. L. (2002). Glucocorticoids interact with the basolateral amygdala beta-adrenoceptor–cAMP/cAMP/PKA system in influencing memory consolidation. *European Journal of Neuroscience*, *15*(3), 553–560.

Rubin, D. C., Dennis, M. F., & Beckham. J. C. (2011). Autobiographical memory for stressful events: the role of autobiographical memory in posttraumatic stress disorder. *Consciousness and Cognition*, *20*, 840–856.

Schiller, D., & Phelps, E. A. (2011). Does reconsolidation occur in humans? *Frontiers in Behavioral Neuroscience*, 5, 24.

Schiller, D., Monfils, M. H., Raio, C. M., Johnson, D. C., Ledoux, J. E., & Phelps, E. A. (2010). Preventing the return of fear in humans using reconsolidation update mechanisms. *Nature*, 463(7277), 49–53.

Segal, S. K., & Cahill, L. (2009). Endogenous noradrenergic activation and memory for emotional material in men and women. *Psychoneuroendocrinology*, 34(9), 1263–1271.

Shear, M. K., Monk, T., Houck, P., Melhem, N., Frank, E., Reynolds, C., & Sillowash, R. (2007). An attachment-based model of complicated grief including the role of avoidance. *European Archives of Psychiatry and Clinical Neuroscience*, 257(8), 453–461.

Shin, L. M., Kosslyn, S. M., McNally, R. J., Alpert, N. M., et al. (1997). Visual imagery and perception in posttraumatic stress disorder: a positron emission tomographic investigation. *Archives of General Psychiatry*, 54(3), 233–241.

Singer, J. A., & Salovey, P. (1993). *The Remembered Self: Emotion and Memory in Personality*. New York: Free Press.

Small, L., Kenny, L., & Bryant, R.A. (2011). The cost in remembering of ruminating on negative memories. *Emotion*, 6, 1434–1438.

Southwick, S. M., Krystal, J. H., Morgan, C. A., Johnson, D., et al. (1993). Abnormal noradrenergic function in posttraumatic stress disorder. *Archives of General Psychiatry*, 50(4), 266–274.

Sterlini, G. L., & Bryant, R. A. (2002). Hyperarousal and dissociation: a study of novice skydivers. *Behaviour Research and Therapy*, 40(4), 431–437.

Strauman, T. J., Kolden, G. G., Stromquist, V., Davis, N., Kwapil, L., Heerey, E., & Schneider, K. (2001). The effects of treatments for depression on perceived failure in self-regulation. *Cognitive Therapy and Research*, 25(6), 693–712.

Sutherland, K., & Bryant, R. A. (2005). Self-defining memories in posttraumatic stress disorder. *British Journal of Clinical Psychology*, 44, 591–598.

Tollenaar, M. S., Elzinga, B. M., Spinhoven, P., & Everaerd, W. (2009). Immediate and prolonged effects of cortisol, but not propranolol, on memory retrieval in healthy young men. *Neurobiology of Learning and Memory*, 91(1), 23–31.

van der Kolk, B., & van der Hart, O. (1989). Pierre Janet and the breakdown of adaptation in psychological trauma. *American Journal of Psychiatry*, 146(12), 1530–1537.

Wenzlaff, R. M., & Wegner, D. M. (2000). Thought suppression. *Annual Review of Psychology*, 51, 59–91.

Williams, J. M. G., Ellis, N. C., Tyers, C., Healy, H., Rose, G., & MacLeod, A. K. (1996). The specificity of autobiographical memory and imageability of the future. *Memory and Cognition*, 24(1), 116–125.

Williams, J. M. G., Barnhofer, T., Crane, C., & Beck, A. T. (2005). Problem solving deteriorates following mood challenge in formerly depressed patients with a history of suicidal ideation. *Journal of Abnormal Psychology*, 114(3), 421–431.

Williams, J. M. G., Barnhofer, T., Crane, C., Hermans, D., Raes, F., Watkins, E., & Dalgleish, T. (2007). Autobiographical memory specificity and emotional disorder. *Psychological Bulletin, 133,* 122–148.

Wood, G. E., & Shors, T. J. (1998). Stress facilitates classical conditioning in males, but impairs classical conditioning in females through activational effects of ovarian hormones. *Proceedings of the National Academy of Sciences, 95*(7), 4066–4071.

Zhang, B., El-Jawahri, A., & Prigerson, H. G. (2006). Update of bereavement research: evidence-based guidelines for the diagnosis and treatment of complicated grief. *Journal of Palliative Medicine, 9,* 1188–1203.

3 A basic systems account of trauma memories in PTSD: is more needed?

David C. Rubin

The purpose of this chapter is to provide a summary of our current knowledge of autobiographical memory at the behavioral and neural level and how it can be applied to posttraumatic stress disorder (PTSD), a disorder whose diagnostic criteria and symptoms depend on autobiographical memory. I start with everyday memories in nonclinical populations because it is unlikely on theoretical and empirical grounds that changes in autobiographical memory in PTSD occur for just trauma-related memories rather than for autobiographical memories in general (Rubin et al., 2008a; 2008b; 2011). In addition, based on just the diagnostic symptoms of PTSD, there is good reason to examine general changes in autobiographical memory. The reliving, avoidance, and arousal symptoms of PTSD are not exclusive to the memory of the index trauma on which diagnosis is made. Rather, they extend to memories related to the index trauma in various ways from low-level direct perceptual matches to very abstract and symbolic similarities. Even repetitive intrusive memories do not have to repeat verbatim but can relate to different aspects of a trauma (Berntsen & Rubin, 2008). Avoidance symptoms include avoiding situations a neutral observer may not think would be reminders of the trauma. Arousal symptoms involving hypervigilance extend to more than appropriate trauma-related vigilance, and the increased startle response symptom results from stimuli unrelated to the trauma.

The section immediately following this brief introduction is titled "Autobiographical Memories are Constructed." Memories are constructed in the sense that processes create the memories anew each time they are recalled rather than retrieving a stored fixed version of the past. The constructive nature of memory is generally accepted by clinical and cognitive psychology, but for highly emotional events including flashbulb memories and trauma there has also been the conflicting proposal that an accurate image of at least fragments of the event remains unaffected by constructive processes or the passage of time, a proposal that I argue against. The next section, titled "The Basic System Model as an Account of the Construction of Autobiographical Memory," includes a review of everyday autobiographical memories in nonclinical populations using a model that considers the component systems needed to construct an autobiographical memory. The section following that, titled "Differences in the Construction of Voluntary and Involuntary Memories of Trauma in PTSD," contains a review of what is known about the differences that exist among three clinically relevant dimensions whose extremes are (1) whether the autobiographical memory is for a trauma or an everyday event, (2) whether the person having the autobiographical memory has PTSD or not, and (3) whether the autobiographical memory is involuntary or voluntary (see Berntsen, Chapter 9). The basic findings for everyday voluntary memories in nonclinical populations can serve as a comparison for these three clinically relevant dimensions. I report on basic findings in key areas that have been of concern to PTSD, including sensory imagery, emotional intensity, the sense of reliving involved in flashbacks, involuntary memories and their relation to voluntary memories, and the role of the narrative coherence of memories.

The final section before the conclusion is titled "Are Special Autobiographical Memory Mechanisms Needed?" These have been called special mechanisms in the literature because it is claimed that there is something special about trauma memories in PTSD. I focus on four special mechanisms that are explicit or implied in the DSM-IV-TR and continued in the DSM-5 (American Psychiatric Association, 2000; 2013) and in some, but not all, theories of PTSD. The first is that there exists a fixed, accurate, though perhaps fragmented memory of the traumatic event. The second is that dissociation is common and is especially strong for trauma memories in individuals with PTSD. The third is the fragmentation and incoherence of trauma memories in individuals with PTSD. The fourth is that involuntary memory has privileged access to trauma memories in individuals with PTSD. To counter the first special mechanism I examine the active construction of memories and their similarity to imagining future events. To counter the second, third, and fourth special mechanisms, I examine the independent contributions of the three clinically relevant dimensions discussed earlier. Support for the second, third, and fourth special mechanisms requires an interaction of these dimensions that should lead to marked differences in memories of traumatic events (or just involuntary memories of traumatic events) in people with PTSD when they are compared with relevant comparison memories. Thus, support for special mechanisms would come from differences that cannot be explained as additive effects of the three dimensions of whether the event was traumatic, the diagnosis of the person, and the voluntary versus involuntary nature of the recall.

Autobiographical memories are constructed

As with all memories, autobiographical memories are not stored and recalled; they are constructed anew at each recall (Bartlett, 1932). Both cognitive and clinical researchers believe this at a general level; in practice clinicians use the constructive nature of memory in therapies that change the evaluation and even the basic observations of their clients' memories. However, there are additional pressures on clinicians that purely academic researchers do not have. Clinicians must work within legal systems, diagnostic systems, and their clients' belief systems, which at times view memories as fixed and accurate representations of the past. I therefore stress a fully constructive view of memory here to counteract the nonconstructive views that are present in the cognitive and clinical literature. It may seem odd to have or to make claims about such a highly constructive autobiographical memory when accuracy would seem to be of value. It is especially odd to assume such a constructive memory for a crime or trauma when both the legal system and the diagnostic system assume that memory for such events can be recalled accurately enough a month or more after they occurred for testimony in court or for the basis of meeting the criterion for PTSD. For trauma, even in cases where the memory cannot be recalled, many theories assume the memory remains hidden in the individual as an accurate picture of the event waiting to be cued or uncovered. This is discussed later in the chapter (for general reviews, see Bryant, Chapter 2, and Dalgleish, 2004; for reviews more critical of the inclusion of nonconstructed memory, see Frankel, 1994; McNally, 2003; Rubin et al., 2008a; Smith, 2011). In contrast to the allure of photographic memories, there is a long and well-supported intellectual history arguing for constructive memory at the behavioral and neural level going back at least to Bartlett (1932). Moreover, how the memory is constructed and the person's reaction to it may play a more important role than the objective severity of the actual event (Rubin & Feeling, 2013; Rubin et al., 2008a). Therefore, before describing the constructive process in the next section, I provide two nonclinical examples, disputed memory ownership and future negative events, which illustrate in as radical fashion as I can find many of the points to be made later.

Twins often have similar memories of the same event, in which both twins remember the event in similar ways, except that each twin remembers that the event happened to them. When we first documented this phenomenon, we called it disputed memory ownership (Sheen et al., 2001). In it, the basic facts about the event are not disputed; only the "self" is in dispute. To ensure demand characteristics were not producing the effect, we first presented twins with cue words and asked for memories. Seventy percent of the twins produced disputed memories. For example, to the cue word *birthday*, in one set of twins each recalled having her ear glued to her head by a guest. In another set, both thought he was the one not invited to a friend's birthday party. Next, a different sample of twins who indicated they had disputed memories were asked to produce both disputed and nondisputed memories and to rate them on scales similar to those described later in the section on behavioral measures. The disputed memories were recalled with more reliving, emotion, and sensory vividness involving vision, audition, and spatial layout, even though for some events one twin may not have been present. Disputing to whom an event occurred is interesting for autobiographical memories in which the self is a defining feature, and could be seen as a form of out-of-body experience, extreme dissociation, or confabulation. For current purposes, it argues strongly for the constructive nature of memory in a nonclinical and less controversial way.

In recent years, both cognitive and clinical psychologists have noted with increased frequency that the same processing used to reconstruct events to examine the past can also be used to construct future events, to plan the future in realistic situations, and to imagine the future in more creative ones (see McNally and Robinaugh, Chapter 12). In such situations, construction is not in doubt because there is no event to remember. The basic finding from the existing literature on future episodic thought is that the behavioral and neural processes involved are generally similar to those used in the recall of past events (for reviews, see D'Argembeau, 2012; Miles, 2013; Rasmussen, 2013; Schacter & Addis, 2007; 2009; Szpunar, 2010).

For examples of events that must be imagined and how they compare to remembered events, I consider future negative events and undergraduates' reactions to them because this will be the most relevant to the negative memories to be considered here (Rubin, 2014). Undergraduates were asked to describe three negative events that would affect them that might occur in the near future or that did occur in the recent past; to rate the events on the scales of reliving, emotion, sensory vividness, and other measures; and to complete a widely used self-report test of PTSD symptom severity, the Posttraumatic Checklist (PCL; Weathers et al., 1994). Several findings are of interest. First, undergraduates' expectations of future events were generally consistent with culturally shared schemata. In particular, academic problems were reported by 58% of the students; own, family member, or friends' injury or illness by 42%; family member or friend's death by 39%; application rejected by 21%; and end of a romantic relationship by 21%. Together these categories accounted for 60% of the undergraduates' three responses. Second, PTSD symptom severity scores on the PCL for past events were typical of these students, but for future events PTSD symptom severity scores were well into the clinical range and would clearly be of concern if they were reporting actual reactions to remembered past events. The high PTSD severity scores were especially surprising because many expected events were relatively mild in terms of those that cause PTSD and most would not qualify as a trauma for clinical purposes. Nonetheless, imagining future events allowed the participant to consider much more troubling events than had actually happened in the past. Third, in spite of the higher PTSD severity scores and consistent with the literature on constructing future events, future events had fewer sensory details than past events unless extra effort was devoted to developing the descriptions of the events. Fourth, the correlations between individuals' ratings of properties of these past and future events often approached their reliabilities, indicating that the extent to which individuals varied in the degree that they used the processes rated were the same for past and future events. For example, individuals who had high visual imagery ratings for past events also had them for future events.

Thus, the constructive processes were similar. The worst events for the future were expected to produce more severe PTSD symptoms than did the actual worst events of the past, and the contents reflected common cultural expectations. The ability to construct past events allows future events to be constructed and allows preparation in case they occur, but the processes used for autobiographical memory could also support worry, anxiety, and clinical disorders involving expectations for the future when done to excess.

The basic system model as an account of the construction of autobiographical memory

Having claimed that autobiographical memories are constructed, a theory of how is in order. The construction of such memories cannot be considered as a simple unitary process with a highly localized neural basis; rather, autobiographical memories are constructed using a host of standard cognitive and emotional systems. The basic systems model is a comprehensive theory that I summarize here only briefly, as it appears in more detail elsewhere (Greenberg & Rubin, 2003; Rubin, 2005; 2006; 2014). According to the model, all autobiographical memories are constructed through the interaction of basic systems. Stability and change in autobiographical memories are due to the schemata of each system (e.g., narrative schemata, visual schemata, auditory schemata) as well as how the various systems interact. Properties of autobiographical memories that are centered in a single system can be measured by self-reports and by neural activity in that system. Properties that depend on multiple systems, such as metacognitive judgments of reliving, can be predicted by the degree of activity in the multiple systems. That is, autobiographical memories are constructed not from an abstract, propositional cognitive structure, but rather from sensory, language, emotion, and other systems, each of which uses fundamentally different structures and processes for fundamentally different kinds of information. Each system has its own functions, processes, structures, kinds of schemata, and types of errors, which have been studied individually. Figure 3.1 is a simplified schematic of the model.

Each component system in the basic systems model has a long intellectual and experimental history. Most of the components date back as far as the recorded history of speculation about the mind (e.g., the five senses, narrative, and emotion). Exceptions are the separate components for language and narrative, a division that is based on current behavioral and neuropsychological data (Rubin & Greenberg, 2003); the search-and-retrieval system, a construct that in memory research has roots in Atkinson & Shiffrin's (1971) control processes and Baddeley's (1986) central executive; and the event memory system, which has been a subject of study at least since the 1960s. In earlier work (Rubin, 2006),

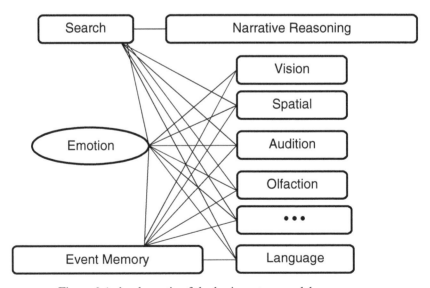

Figure 3.1 A schematic of the basic system model.

I called the hippocampus based event memory system the explicit memory system, but event memory is more accurate (Rubin & Umanath, in press).

It would be exceedingly difficult to deny that the basic systems are useful scientific concepts that describe components of the mind and brain. Perception, cognition, and neuroscience textbooks divide the mind and brain into these basic systems, including separate systems for each of the senses, language, emotion, and motor output (Rubin, 2006). The scientists who study the mind and the brain divide their journals and societies along these lines. Each system can be supported by results from (1) neuroanatomy, (2) neuropsychology, (3) neuroimaging, (4) cognitive-experimental psychology, and (5) individual differences research. Knowledge from all five sources sharpens and constrains predictions regarding memory functions of all the basic systems. Moreover, each system, with the possible exception of the event memory system, is used for tasks other than memory. Thus, each system is the only system of its kind in a model that could be extended to explain cognition in general, and so the considerable amount already known about each system from its nonmnemonic functions further constrains its functioning as a component system of memory (see Barsalou, 1999, for a similar approach to semantic memory).

Neuropsychological results

If the basic systems model is to be supported by and offer insight into the effects of neuropsychological damage, then damage to different systems should have different effects on autobiographical memory (Greenberg & Rubin, 2003; see also Rathbone and Moulin, Chapter 14). The three systems shown at the left of Figure 3.1 have long been known to affect autobiographical memory. The frontal lobe based search system is needed to find information relevant to a memory and inhibit information that is irrelevant to the memory. Its damage leads to confabulation. The hippocampus/medial temporal lobe based event memory system binds information that has been active at the same time in a relatively automatic fashion. Its damage leads to a general loss of autobiographical memory in the form of a general amnesia for events occurring after the damage and less loss for events before the damage. But neither of these systems stores the information that is used to construct an autobiographical memory; rather, they coordinate the storage and retrieval of information from the other systems. The emotions system is also placed to the left of the figure as its main function here is to modulate the other systems, affecting storage and retrieval of information from them. Of the systems on the right, damage to vision produces the most dramatic losses. Damage that results in visual memory loss, defined by the inability to identify an object by sight and to draw the object given its name or function (Farah, 1984), results in visual memory-deficit amnesia, which is marked by a dense general amnesia for all events that occurred before the damage and loss of visual information for events after the damage (Greenberg et al., 2005; Rubin & Greenberg, 1998). In contrast, damage to the other senses provides minimal loss to autobiographical memory beyond the loss of information in the memory related to the particular sense. Given the location of most of the lesions producing visual memory loss, it is likely that scenes as well as objects are affected. Loss of narrative reasoning has obvious effects on the organization of memories, whereas language loss does not seem to have major effects if extended time or other means are allowed to support the communication of the memory. Although this description is not the way the effects of neural damage on autobiographical memory are usually described, it is well documented and evolved from an early version of the conceptual model shown in Figure 3.1 (Greenberg & Rubin, 2003; Rubin 1995; 2006).

Neuroimaging results

Reviews of the neuroimaging literature on autobiographical memory converge on a network of brain regions involved in autobiographical memory retrieval that involve the search, narrative reasoning, emotion, event memory, and vision systems in a fashion that is generally consistent with the neuropsychological results (Cabeza & St. Jacques, 2007; St. Jacques 2012; Svoboda et al., 2006). They also include midline areas, especially in the anterior cingulate, that are involved in self-referential processing. The voluntary retrieval of an autobiographical memory can take on the order of 10 seconds. Because functional magnetic resonance imaging (fMRI) typically provides an image of the whole brain every 1.5 to 2 seconds, one can observe activity in the basic systems over time (Daselaar et al., 2008; St. Jacques et al., 2011b). There is less research on the changes in autobiographical memory in PTSD (St. Jacques et al., 2011a; 2013). However, there are consistent changes in script-driven imagery and a host of other procedures that indicate that the changes in PTSD are more widespread than in other anxiety disorders (Etkin & Wager, 2007).

Behavioral results

The way that we have measured the components of the model shown in Figure 3.1 behaviorally is to make rating scales intended to show how actively each system contributes to the underlying process. Table 3.1 shows a sample of the kind of scales chosen for their relevance to the

Table 3.1 *Autobiographical Memory Questionnaire (AMQ) Variables*

Variable	Brief Description of Rating Scales
	Emotions
Intensity	While remembering, the emotions that I feel are extremely intense.
Reaction	I had a physical reaction (laughed, felt tense, sweaty, heart pounding).
Mood Change	The memory changed my mood.
	Frequency with Which the Memory Comes to Mind
Rehearsal	Since it happened, I have thought or talked about this event.
Involuntary	This memory has come to me out of the blue, without my trying.
	Narrative Integration into Life Story
Life Story	The event in my memory is a central part of my life story.
	Narrative Integration Internal to Event
Story	It comes to me in words or in pictures as a coherent story.
Pieces	My memory comes to me in pieces with missing bits.
	Senses
See	While remembering the event, I can see it in my mind.
Setting	While remembering the event, I know the setting where it occurred.
Hear	While remembering the event, I can hear it in my mind.
Smell	While remembering the event, I can smell it.
	Metacognitive Judgments
Reliving	While remembering the event, I feel as though I am reliving it.
Belief	I believe the event in my memory really occurred – not imagined.

discussion of changes in the activity of the systems in PTSD and in the trauma memories. The emotion section provides intensity measures for the emotion circle on the left of Figure 3.1. The rehearsal section measures not a basic system but rather the availability of the memory for voluntary and involuntary recall. There are two sections on measures of narrative reasoning, measuring two levels of integration: how integrated the memory is to the broader life narrative and how internally coherent it is. The senses section of the table measures the systems in the right of Figure 3.1. Finally, there is a metacognitive judgments section to measure phenomenological judgments about the memories that play important roles in cognition and clinical issues. Reliving, which is a key aspect in cognitive theories of everyday autobiographical memory, appears in clinical theories of trauma memories, especially for intrusive memories where high levels are flashbacks (see Bryant, Chapter 2). The top three sections measure properties that show the greatest change for trauma memories and for PTSD.

Depending on the goals of the research we modify, add, and omit scales; thus they are public-domain attempts to capture many individual processes of interest rather than a normed single scale. Collectively, these scales are the Autobiographical Memory Questionnaire (AMQ). We have participants rate their voluntary and involuntary memories and future constructions while they are producing them, as this provides a more valid indication of the ongoing processes than retrospective reports (Ericsson & Simon, 1993). The rating scales have been used extensively in studies of autobiographical memory, so we know a great deal about how they normally function and relate to each other and to personality and other individual differences measures as well as in other cultures and in clinical populations; we know not only how the means on the scales vary with task, but also how they correlate with each other (Rubin, 2014; Rubin & Siegler, 2004; Rubin et al., 2003; 2004; 2007; 2008a; 2008b; 2011; Sheen et al., 2001).

Differences in the construction of voluntary and involuntary memories of trauma in PTSD

The cube shown in Figure 3.2 contains the mechanisms postulated to account for the general changes in autobiographical memory. Three cognitive and affective mechanisms on the vertical (*y*) axis are properties of the memory that increase the ease with which the memories come to mind, that is, their availability (Tversky & Kahneman, 1973) or accessibility (Tulving & Pearlstone, 1966). They are (1) the emotional intensity of the memory; (2) when and how often the memory has been retrieved in the past, as measured here by the retrospective reported frequency of voluntary and involuntary recall; and (3) the centrality of the memory to the person's life story and identity (see Boals and colleagues, Chapter 4). Because centrality involves how a memory fits into the core events of a person's life, it requires, but is more than, a normal integration with other autobiographical memories. These three mechanisms, which increase the encoding and maintenance of memories, are greater for extremely stressful events than for most other events (for reviews, see Rubin et al., 2008a; 2008b). They also work by augmenting each other. Independent of their valence, more emotionally intense events come to mind more frequently both voluntarily and involuntarily (Berntsen & Rubin, 2014; Hall & Berntsen, 2008), have more vividness and reliving (Talarico et al., 2004), and tend to be about current concerns and so become more integrated into a person's autobiographical memory and identity (Conway, 2005). Similarly, rehearsal and centrality help maintain the memory and its emotional intensity.

These three mechanisms, which vary across all memories, also vary across all people as indicated in the individual differences factor on the

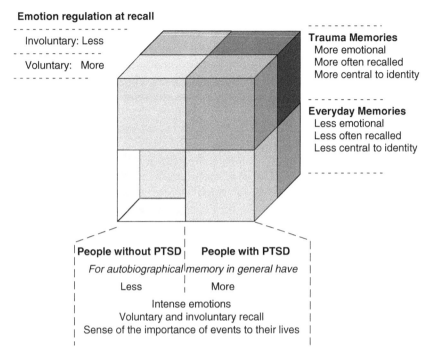

Figure 3.2 The three classes of mechanisms that affect stressful memories in PTSD are represented on the three axes: on the vertical axis, mechanisms that are more involved in stressful versus other memories; on the horizontal, characteristics more typical of people with PTSD; and on the front-to-back axis, emotion regulation. These mechanisms correspond, respectively, to stressful versus comparison memories, participants with and without PTSD, and voluntary versus involuntary memories.

horizontal (x) axis of Figure 3.2. In terms of individual differences, rather than the remembered event, people vary in the degree of emotional intensity with which they experience all kinds of events (Larsen & Diener, 1987) and in how central events are to their life stories (Berntsen & Rubin, 2007; Rubin et al., 2008b). Because emotional intensity and centrality to the life story affect availability, availability will also vary across people, causing differential rehearsal that results in differences in the retention of memories and their emotional impact. PTSD is associated with increases in these three mechanisms (Rubin et al., 2008b; 2011).

Emotion regulation is indicated on the front-to-back (z) axis of Figure 3.2. Because involuntary memories of all kinds, including those of traumatic events, come "unbidden" or "out of the blue," cued by thoughts or the environment in ways that are unexpected to the person instead of by a directed, voluntary search (Clark and colleagues, Chapter 7; Moulds and Krans, Chapter 8; Berntsen, Chapter 9; Berntsen, 2009), they benefit less from mechanisms of emotion regulation (Gross, 2001). Therefore, all involuntary memories will occur with more emotional reaction and mood change (Berntsen & Hall, 2004). For traumatic events they will be more "intrusive" than their voluntary counterparts, producing more of the reliving symptoms of PTSD than voluntary memories. Such involuntary memories can be especially disturbing because their unbidden nature can be interpreted as a lack of control. Thus, the arousal and avoidance symptoms of PTSD will result as an attempt to monitor and avoid situations and thoughts that might cue involuntary memories of the stressful event.

Starting in the lower left front cube, which is transparent, increases in emotional intensity, rehearsal, and centrality are illustrated by moving once up or to the right and are indicated by light gray. Two moves result in an even greater increase, as indicated by medium gray. A move to the back, which is from voluntary to involuntary memory, decreases emotion regulation, and thus the increases for moving in this direction involve only emotional intensity. Combining all three moves is indicated in the dark gray cube. Moderate changes on each dimension can add to substantial differences when the voluntary everyday memories of people without PTSD are compared with the involuntary trauma memories of people with PTSD. The next four sections examine the effects of behavioral changes in each of these three dimensions and of changes in more than one.

To pursue these three dimensions, I use a single study that allows all the comparisons illustrated in Figure 3.2 to be made in a clinical sample (Rubin et al., 2011), though the results changed in only minor ways when an analog sample of undergraduates that varied in PTSD symptom severity was measured (Rubin et al., 2008b). The clinical sample consisted of 117 community-dwelling participants, 75 with PTSD and 42 controls. Individuals in the control group were not required to have a trauma as defined by the DSM-IV-TR diagnosis, but 73% reported one during their clinical interview. Participants were excluded from the control group if they met criteria for lifetime PTSD or current subthreshold PTSD. All participants provided ratings for measures, including those in Table 3.1, for their three most-stressful or traumatic events, their three most-positive events, their seven most-important events not included in their most-stressful or most-positive events, and fifteen word-cued memories. The most-positive memories are the closest match for the most-stressful ones, being both important and of high emotional intensity. The most-important memories differed further from the most-stressful ones by having less intense emotions. The word-cued memories differed even further by also being less important. In addition, 90 of the participants agreed to carry a personal data assistant for a period of two weeks on which they could answer the questions in Table 3.1 as well as note whether the memory was related to one of their three most-stressful memories. Of these participants, 86 recorded seven or more involuntary memories (59 in the PTSD and 27 in the control group) and are included in the involuntary memory analyses. These participants also recorded and rated a comparison voluntary memory from the same period of life as each involuntary memory.

Behavioral differences in trauma memories

Compared with the most-positive memories, the most-stressful memories were higher on the *intensity, involuntary,* and *reliving* ratings. Compared with the most-important memories, the most-stressful memories were higher on these ratings and also *reaction, rehearsal, life story,* and *hear.* Compared with the word-cued memories, the most-stressful memories were higher on these ratings and also *see, setting,* and *story.* The only exception to this pattern for the scales listed in Table 3.1 was that the most-stressful memories came more in *pieces* when compared with the most-positive memories. Thus, the comparison memory is crucial to the amount of differences seen, with the differences increasing as the comparison memories become less emotional and less important. Overall, consistent with Figure 3.2, ratings associated with the mechanisms of more intense emotions, more prior voluntary and involuntary recall, and more centrality to identity were higher for the most-stressful memories in all people; ratings of the sensory variables and narrative differences internal to the memories showed fewer differences.

Behavioral differences in PTSD

When the ratings of participants with and without PTSD were examined, a similar pattern arose, though with larger differences. In particular, for all four kinds of memories, participants with PTSD rated their memories as higher on *intensity, reaction, rehearsal, involuntary, life story, hear, smell, reliving,* and *belief. See* and *setting* were higher on three of the types of memories but not for the most-positive memories. Ratings of *story* were higher for participants with PTSD for word-cued and most-important memories, and ratings of *pieces* were higher for participants with PTSD for their most-stressful memories. Consistent with Figure 3.2, ratings associated with the mechanisms or more intense emotions, more prior voluntary and involuntary recall, and more centrality to identity were higher for people with PTSD in all four kinds of memories; ratings of the narrative differences internal to the memories showed fewer differences.

Behavioral differences in involuntary memories

In this comparison involuntary memories were rated as they occurred for two weeks; comparison voluntary memories from the same period of life were obtained immediately after each involuntary memory. Involuntary memories had higher ratings on *intensity, reaction, mood change,* and *reliving*. Prior voluntary *rehearsal* was rated higher for voluntary memories. Thus, there were differences in ratings of associated emotions as noted in Figure 3.2 as well as in the metacognitive judgment of *reliving*. For these data we did not have three kinds of comparison memories but did have the participants' ratings of whether each memory was related to their three most-stressful memories. For this comparison, all the ratings associated with our three mechanisms (e.g., *intensity, reaction, mood change, life story, rehearsal,* and *involuntary*) were higher for memories related to most-stressful events, as was *hear, story,* and *reliving*. There were no interactions of being related to most-stressful memories and whether the memory was voluntary or involuntary for any of the measures listed in Table 3.1.

Behavioral differences when multiple dimensions are considered

The model proposed here and shown in Figure 3.2 does not require that all effects be additive; theoretically motivated interactions could exist, but it is simplest if there are no interactions. Moreover, alternative conceptions of the role of autobiographical memory in PTSD often rely on special mechanisms that apply to PTSD, and these often imply interactions when both differences in people and memories are considered. When a mechanism is postulated to account for an effect that occurs only in trauma memories in people diagnosed with PTSD, an interaction is always implied, as additive effects cannot make such a prediction. Thus, interactions play a key role here in testing the simplest form of the model to see if it needs modification.

When interactions with the most-stressful versus the other three kinds of memory as one factor and whether the participant had PTSD or not as the other were examined for all measures present in the main study, three interactions were found from 39 independent ANOVAs. They were for ratings of *reliving* for word-cued memories, of *involuntary* for word-cued memories, and of *pieces* for positive memories. In all cases, participants with PTSD had a larger difference for their most-stressful memories. None of these interactions was a "crossover" interaction in which people with PTSD were higher on a measure for one kind of memory and lower for another. For the online involuntary memory task, one factor corresponded to whether participants had PTSD or not; another corresponded to whether the memory was involuntary or voluntary; and a third factor corresponded to whether the memory was related to a stressful event or not. One of 56 possible interactions from 28 independent ANOVAs was observed. Memories related to a stressful event had a larger difference in their ratings of *smell* for participants with PTSD. All four interactions from both analyses were reasonable and did not indicate a pattern challenging the mechanism proposed here.

Behavioral difference: conclusions and implications

The main differences that were observed were additive and were in ratings related to the mechanisms shown in Figure 3.2. There were few differences in narrative measures internal to the memories, though there were large differences in narrative measures of whether the memories were important to the participants' life stories. Most clinical research focuses on trauma memories, so less is known about the substantial changes that occur in PTSD in nontrauma autobiographical memories even though these nontrauma memories also contribute to the general functioning of the individual. Such nontrauma autobiographical memories should be easier to probe in a therapeutic setting because they are less distressing, so relevant characteristics of nontrauma memories such as emotional intensity, availability, centrality, and reliving that are also impacted may also be of use in the therapeutic process.

Are special autobiographical memory mechanisms needed?

The purpose of reviewing the literature that argues that memories are constructed using the well-established cognitive and affective systems shown in Figure 3.1 and the mechanisms shown in Figure 3.2 has been to see if they could account for phenomena noted in the recall of trauma memories in people with PTSD. So far the chapter has argued that they can. However, other explanations of the same phenomena have been offered that directly contradict the theory and evidence presented here; they are special mechanisms in that they claim that there are special processes for trauma memories in PTSD. Four of these special mechanisms have generated considerable debate, and I address them here.

The first special mechanism is that there exists somewhere in the mind and brain an accurate memory of the traumatic event, perhaps etched indelibly by the high emotion of the trauma (Pitman, 1988). This memory could be accessible and of the "I will never forget it" variety, but more often it is hidden from conscious recall, with the exception of possible fragmentary versions that break through, often in dreams or involuntary memories. The idea can be seen as a particular version of repression or dissociation in which accuracy is preserved. It thus has a long intellectual tradition. There certainly can be mechanisms that could keep a memory from conscious recall, such as active inhibitory mechanisms, passive lack of effective cuing, or forgetting mechanisms. Most troubling, however, is the assumption of a fragmentary or intact accurate enduring memory that is often confounded with this view (e.g., Ehlers et al., 2004; Horowitz & Reidbord, 1992). For example, it is assumed that the memory of the trauma needed for a diagnosis of PTSD is accurate for at least a month after the event, and studies of repeated intrusive memories often assume that the exact same memory fragment returns without change. Much has been written on this issue (Berntsen, 2001; 2009; Berntsen & Rubin, 2008; Frankel, 1994; Kihlstrom, 2006; McNally, 2003; Rubin et al., 2008a), which is paralleled by debates within cognitive literature on flashbulb memories and in earlier debates on repressed memories of childhood abuse. Here I simply note that an accurate memory that is unaffected by the passage of time and changes in the person is counter to everything that is known from the scientific study of memory at the behavioral and neural level as reviewed, in part, earlier in the chapter. It is possible for some texts to remain stable for centuries over countless retellings through numerous individuals, but the stability is within limits and requires mnemonic systems; it is never unchanging (Lord, 1960; Rubin, 1995). In fact, the basic systems model shown in Figure 3.1 was first devised to account for such stability. In a situation of highly negative emotional intensity in which a person's life is in danger, and in which resources should be focused on survival, accurate memory would not be expected (Rubin et al., 2008a).

The second special mechanism is that dissociation is especially strong for trauma memories in individuals with PTSD (Ehlers et al., 2003; van der Kolk & van der Hart, 1989; see Bryant, Chapter 2, for a review). Without addressing the vexing question of exactly what dissociation is (Giesbrecht et al., 2008; Hacking, 1995), dissociative experiences such as those measured by the dissociative experiences scale (Bernstein & Putnam, 1986) are a personality trait that in the extreme can qualify as the basis of its own disorder and as well as a part of other clinical disorders. Dissociation and dissociative experiences may be increased by chronic childhood trauma, abuse, or neglect (e.g., Chu & Dill, 1990) or other factors, though Goodman et al. (2010) note that reduced memory for negative events has not been adequately demonstrated in maltreated children, and Giesbrecht et al. (2008, p. 617) found that "evidence for a link between dissociation and either memory fragmentation or early trauma based on objective measures is conspicuously lacking." Because dissociative experiences by definition exist for a wide variety of behaviors, it is not clear that any evidence indicates dissociation or dissociative experiences appear at especially high levels specifically for the index trauma leading to the diagnosis of PTSD. Specific dissociative-like behaviors, such as the traumatic event being seen from a third-person or out-of-body perspective, can be understood in terms of regular cognitive mechanisms such as tunnel memory (Bryant, Chapter 2; Rice & Rubin, 2009; 2011; Rubin et al., 2008a). The arguments about which dimensions in Figure 3.2 act as main effects and which act as interactions apply here as much for the theoretical claim of a special mechanism of dissociation as for the data for evaluating it. Although the DSM-5 allows for PTSD "with dissociative symptoms" (American Psychiatric Association, 2013, p. 272) if there is depersonalization and derealization in addition to the other symptoms, two of the general symptoms of PTSD and two of acute stress disorder are framed in terms of dissociation.

A third special mechanism, which is often seen as a part of dissociative behavior, but which I separate out here because it is often measured independently and need not require dissociation, is the fragmentation and incoherence of trauma memories in individuals with PTSD. Fragmentation and lack of coherence are observations made by PTSD researchers (e.g., Brewin et al., 1996; 2010; for reviews, see Bryant, Chapter 2; Brewin & Holmes, 2003; Dalgleish, 2004; Kihlstrom, 2006; McNally, 2003; 2009; Rubin et al., 2008a; Shobe & Kihlstrom, 1997). Fragmentation is also included as a PTSD symptom, described as an "inability to recall an important aspect of the trauma" (American Psychiatric Association, 2000, pp. 467–468). Again the arguments used for Figure 3.2 apply. Main effects of the form shown in Figure 3.2 abound for people with and without PTSD or who are high and low on PTSD symptom severity. Because the coherence with which a memory is given is related to education and general levels of stress, the interpretation of these data is unclear, though in any case they can be seen as a simple main effect in most studies, as comparison memories were not usually obtained. There are also studies showing that trauma memories are less (or more) coherent than nontrauma memories both in people in general and in those with PTSD, another main effect. There is only one study that appears to show the needed interaction, but it was found for only one of the three measures of coherence used in that study (Jelinek et al., 2009). In addition, there is one study that uses six measures of coherence and fails to find the interaction (Rubin, 2011). In all studies I have seen, there is no report of a level of real incoherence in any group or condition; the ratings obtained are all in levels that range from very coherent to slightly less coherent. For reviews of what has become a fairly substantial literature, see Berntsen and Rubin (2014) and Rubin (2011). Thus, when the logic used in Figure 3.2 is applied to the findings, the data do not support this special mechanism.

A fourth special mechanism is that involuntary memory has privileged access to trauma memories in individuals with PTSD. This idea is central to Horowitz's stress response syndromes (1976), which was the theoretical basis for the initial introduction of PTSD into the current diagnostic system. It is reflected in the current diagnostic listing of involuntary (intrusive) recollections as symptoms of PTSD with no mention of voluntary remembering except as being fragmented (Berntsen & Rubin, 2014). This view continues in current theories (Brewin et al., 1996; 2010; Ehlers & Clark, 2000; for reviews see Bryant, Chapter 2, and Berntsen, Chapter 9). In contrast to this view, the results reviewed here from Rubin et al. (2011) showed two additive effects with no interaction: the same ratings were higher for all voluntary and involuntary memories in participants with PTSD, and voluntary and involuntary memories related to very stressful and traumatic events in all participants. Thus, we reported no privileged status for trauma memories in PTSD beyond that which could be accounted for by additive effects. Four other studies show similar main effects in nonclinical populations (Berntsen & Rubin, 2014; Ferree & Cahill, 2009; Hall & Berntsen, 2008; Rubin et al., 2008b); I know of no exceptions. Thus, this special mechanism lacks support.

In all of these examples, the data and literature review presented here are inconsistent with the need for special mechanisms. Moreover, the use of the dimensions presented in Figure 3.2 helps to clarify the exact nature of some of these claims in terms of whether support for them requires just general properties of the person, the memory, or involuntary versus voluntary recall, or rather requires an interaction effect that should lead to a behavior being markedly higher with respect to memories of traumatic events (or just involuntary memories of traumatic events) in people with PTSD. Once this issue is clear, the existing studies can be more fairly reviewed, and future studies not subject to the critique of a lack of proper comparisons can be designed to test these mechanisms.

Conclusions

The purpose of this chapter was to review what we know about everyday autobiographical memory as it applies to behaviors that become symptoms of PTSD. As part of this exploration, I considered the properties of memories that are needed to produce the various behaviors considered as symptoms and how they change for traumatic events, for people with PTSD, for involuntary memories, and for these dimensions considered in combination. There were clear main effects of all dimensions that were consistent with proposed mechanisms, but few interactions. The results support the conclusion that involuntary and voluntary memories of traumatic events in people with PTSD can be understood in terms of standard mechanisms of cognition, emotion, and personality. There was no support for additional special mechanisms. This does not mean that such special mechanisms do not exist. It does mean that serious attempts to find them should demonstrate effects beyond the additive effects shown here by including appropriate comparisons on the dimensions needed for the claim.

Acknowledgments

I wish to thank Kaitlyn Batt, Dorthe Berntsen, Samantha Deffler, Christin Ogle, and Lynn Watson for comments and discussions, and National Institute of Mental Health grant R01 MH066079 and the Danish National Research Foundation grant DNRF93 for support.

REFERENCES

American Psychiatric Association (2000). *Diagnostic and Statistical Manual of Mental Disorders* (4th ed. text revision). Washington, DC: American Psychiatric Association.
  (2013). *Diagnostic and Statistical Manual of Mental Disorders* (5th ed.). Washington, DC: American Psychiatric Association.
Atkinson, R. C., & Shiffrin, R. M. (1971). The control of short-term memory. *Scientific American, 225*, 82–90.
Baddeley, A. D. (1986). *Working Memory*. Oxford: Oxford University Press.
Barsalou, L. W. (1999). Perceptual symbol systems. *Behavioral and Brain Sciences, 22*, 577–660.
Bartlett, F. C. (1932). *Remembering: A Study in Experimental and Social Psychology*. London: Cambridge University Press.
Bernstein, E. M., & Putnam, F. W. (1986). Development, reliability, and validity of a dissociation scale. *Journal of Nervous and Mental Disease, 174*, 727–735.

Berntsen, D. (2001). Involuntary memories of emotional events: do memories of traumas and extremely happy events differ? *Applied Cognitive Psychology*, *15*, 135–158.

(2009). *Involuntary Autobiographical Memories: An Introduction to the Unbidden Past*. Cambridge: Cambridge University Press.

Berntsen, D., & Hall, N. M. (2004). The episodic nature of involuntary autobiographical memories. *Memory and Cognition*, *32*, 789–803.

Berntsen, D., & Rubin, D. C. (2007). When a trauma becomes a key to identity: enhanced integration of trauma memories predicts posttraumatic stress disorder symptoms. *Applied Cognitive Psychology*, *21*, 417–431.

(2008). The reappearance hypothesis revisited: recurrent involuntary memories after traumatic events and in everyday life. *Memory and Cognition*, *36*, 449–460.

(2014). Involuntary memories and dissociative amnesia: assessing key assumptions in posttraumatic stress disorder research research. *Clinical Psychological Science*, *2*, 174–186.

Brewin, C. R., & Holmes, E. A. (2003). Psychological theories of posttraumatic stress disorder. *Clinical Psychology Review*, *23*, 339–376.

Brewin, C. R., Dalgleish, T., & Joseph, S. (1996). A dual representation theory of posttraumatic stress disorder. *Psychological Review*, *103*, 670–686.

Brewin, C. R., Gregory, J. D., Lipton, M., & Burgess, N. (2010). Intrusive images in psychological disorders: characteristics, neural mechanisms, and treatment implications. *Psychological Review*, *117*, 210–232.

Cabeza, R., & St. Jacques, P. (2007). Functional neuroimaging of autobiographical memory. *Trends in Cognitive Sciences*, *11*, 219–227.

Chu, J. A., & Dill, D. L. (1990). Dissociative symptoms in relation to childhood physical and sexual abuse. *American Journal of Psychiatry*, *147*, 887–892.

Conway, M. A. (2005). Memory and the self. *Journal of Memory and Language*, *53*, 594–628.

Dalgleish, T. (2004). Cognitive approaches to posttraumatic stress disorder: the evolution of multirepresentational theorizing. *Psychological Bulletin*, *130*, 228–260.

D'Argembeau, A. (2012). Autobiographical memory and future thinking. In D. Berntsen & D. C. Rubin (eds.), *Understanding Autobiographical Memory: Theories and Approaches* (pp. 311–330). Cambridge: Cambridge University Press.

Daselaar, S. M., Rice, H. J., Greenberg, D. L., Cabeza, R. LaBar, K. S., & Rubin, D. C. (2008). The spatiotemporal dynamics of autobiographical memory: neural correlates of recall, emotional intensity, and reliving. *Cerebral Cortex*, *18*, 217–229.

Ehlers, A., & Clark, D. M. (2000). A cognitive model of posttraumatic stress disorder. *Behaviour Research and Therapy*, *38*(4), 319–345.

Ehlers, A., Mayou, R. A., & Bryant, B. (2003). Cognitive predictors of posttraumatic stress disorder in children: results of a prospective longitudinal study. *Behaviour Research and Therapy*, *41*, 1–10.

Ehlers, A., Hackmann, A., & Michael, T. (2004). Intrusive reexperiencing in post-traumatic stress disorder: Phenomenology, theory, and therapy. *Memory, 12*, 403–415.

Ericsson, K. A., & Simon, H. A. (1993). *Protocol Analysis: Verbal Reports as Data* (Rev. ed.). Cambridge, MA: MIT (Bradford Books).

Etkin, A., & Wager, T. D. (2007). Functional neuroimaging of anxiety: a meta-analysis of emotional processing in PTSD, social anxiety disorder, and specific phobia. *American Journal of Psychiatry, 164*, 1476–1488.

Farah, M. J. (1984). The neurological basis of mental imagery: a componential analysis. *Cognition, 18*, 245–272.

Ferree, N. K., & Cahill, L. (2009). Post-event spontaneous intrusive recollections and strength of memory for emotional events in men and women. *Consciousness and Cognition, 18*, 126–134.

Frankel, F. H. (1994). The concept of flashback in historical perspective. *International Journal of Clinical and Experimental Hypnosis, 42*, 231–236.

Giesbrecht T., Lynn S. J., Lilienfield S., & Merckelbach, H. (2008). Cognitive processes in dissociation: an analysis of core theoretical assumptions. *Psychological Bulletin. 134*, 617–647.

Goodman, G. S., Quas, J. A., & Ogle, C. M. (2010). Child maltreatment and memory. *Annual Review of Psychology, 61*, 325–351.

Greenberg, D. L., & Rubin, D. C. (2003). The neuropsychology of autobiographical memory. *Cortex, 39*, 687–728.

Greenberg, D. L., Eacott, M. J., Brechin, D., & Rubin, D. C. (2005). Visual memory loss and autobiographical amnesia: a case study. *Neuropsychologia, 43*, 1493–1502.

Gross, J. J. (2001). Emotion regulation in adulthood: timing is everything. *Current Directions in Psychological Science, 10*, 214–219.

Hacking, I. (1995). *Rewriting the Soul: Multiple Personality and the Sciences*. Princeton, NJ: Princeton University Press.

Hall, N. M., & Berntsen, D. (2008). The effect of emotional stress on involuntary and voluntary conscious memories. *Memory, 16*, 48–57.

Horowitz, M. J. (1976). *Stress Response Syndromes*. New York: Jason Aronson.

Horowitz, M. J., & Reidbord, S. P. (1992). Memory, emotion, and response to trauma. In S.-Å. Christianson (ed.), *The Handbook of Emotion and Memory: Research and Theory* (pp. 343–357). Hillsdale, NJ: Erlbaum.

Jelinek, L., Randjbar, S., Seifert, D., Kellner, M., & Moritz, S. (2009). The organization of autobiographical and nonautobiographical memory in posttraumatic stress disorder (PTSD). *Journal of Abnormal Psychology, 118*, 288–298.

Kihlstrom, J. F. (2006). Trauma and memory revisited. In B. Uttl, N. Ohta, & A. L. Siegenthaler (eds.), *Memory and Emotions: Interdisciplinary Perspectives* (pp. 259–291). New York: Blackwell.

Larsen, R. J., & Diener, E. (1987). Affect intensity as an individual difference characteristic: a review. *Journal of Research in Personality, 21*, 1–39.

Lord, A. B. (1960). *The Singer of Tales*. Cambridge, MA: Harvard University Press.

McNally, R. J. (2003). *Remembering Trauma*. Cambridge, MA: Harvard University Press.

(2009). Can we fix PTSD in DSM-V? *Depression and Anxiety, 26,* 597–600.

Miles, A. N. (2013). Cuing methodologies in mental time travel. *Nordic Psychology, 65,* 120–136.

Pitman, R. K. (1988). Post-traumatic stress disorder conditioning, and network theory. *Psychiatric Annals 18,* 182–189.

Rasmussen, K.W. (2013). The role of the hippocampus and prefrontal cortex in imagining the future: insights from studies of patients with focal brain lesions. *Nordic Psychology, 65*(2), 166–188.

Rice, H. J., & Rubin, D. C. (2009). I can see it both ways: first- and third-person visual perspectives at retrieval. *Consciousness and Cognition, 18,* 877–890.

(2011). Remembering from any angle: the flexibility of visual perspective during retrieval. *Consciousness and Cognition, 20,* 658–577.

Rubin, D. C. (1995). *Memory in Oral Traditions: The Cognitive Psychology of Epic, Ballads, and Counting-Out Rhymes.* New York: Oxford University Press.

(2005). A basic-systems approach to autobiographical memory. *Current Directions in Psychological Science, 14,* 79–83.

(2006). The basic-systems model of episodic memory. *Perspectives on Psychological Science, 1,* 277–311.

(2011). The coherence of memories for trauma: evidence from posttraumatic stress disorder. *Consciousness and Cognition, 20,* 857–865.

(2014). Schema driven construction of future autobiographical traumatic events: the future is much more troubling than the past. *Journal of Experimental Psychology: General, 143*(2), 612–630.

Rubin, D. C., & Feeling, N. (2013). Measuring the severity of negative and traumatic events. *Clinical Psychological Science, 1,* 375–389.

Rubin, D. C., & Greenberg, D. L. (1998). Visual memory deficit amnesia: a distinct amnesic presentation and etiology. *Proceedings of the National Academy of Sciences, USA, 95,* 5413–5416.

(2003). The role of narrative in recollection: a view from cognitive and neuropsychology. In G. Fireman, T. McVay, & O. Flanagan (eds.), *Narrative and Consciousness: Literature, Psychology, and the Brain* (pp. 53–85). New York: Oxford University Press.

Rubin, D. C., & Siegler, I. C. (2004). Facets of personality and the phenomenology of autobiographical memory. *Applied Cognitive Psychology, 18,* 913–930.

Rubin, D. C., & Umanath, S. (in press). Event memory: a theory of memory for laboratory, autobiographical, and fictional events. *Psychological Review.*

Rubin, D. C., Schrauf, R. W., & Greenberg, D. L. (2003). Belief and recollection of autobiographical memories. *Memory and Cognition 31,* 887–901.

(2004). Stability in autobiographical memories. *Memory, 12,* 715–721.

Rubin, D. C., Schrauf, R. W., Gulgoz, S., & Naka, M. (2007). On the cross-cultural variability of component processes in autobiographical remembering: Japan, Turkey, and the U.S.A. *Memory, 15,* 536–547.

Rubin, D. C., Berntsen, D., & Bohni, M. K. (2008a). A memory-based model of posttraumatic stress disorder: evaluating basic assumptions underlying the PTSD diagnosis. *Psychological Review*, *115*, 985–1011.

Rubin, D. C., Boals, A., & Berntsen, D. (2008b). Memory in posttraumatic stress disorder: properties of voluntary and involuntary, traumatic and non-traumatic autobiographical memories in people with and without PTSD symptoms. *Journal of Experimental Psychology: General*, *137*, 591–614.

Rubin, D. C., Dennis, M. F., & Beckham, J. C. (2011). Autobiographical memory for stressful events: the role of autobiographical memory in posttraumatic stress disorder. *Consciousness and Cognition*, *20*, 840–856.

Schacter, D. L., & Addis, D. R. (2007). The cognitive neuroscience of constructive memory: remembering the past and imagining the future. *Philosophical Transactions of the Royal Society of London B: Biological Sciences*, *362*, 773–786.

(2009). On the nature of medial temporal lobe contributions to the constructive simulation of future events. *Philosophical Transactions of the Royal Society of London B: Biological Sciences*, *364*, 1245–1253.

Sheen, M., Kemp, S., & Rubin, D. C. (2001). Twins dispute memory ownership: a new false memory phenomenon. *Memory and Cognition*, *29*, 779–788.

Shobe, K. K., & Kihlstrom, J. F. (1997). Is traumatic memory special? *Current Directions in Psychological Science*, *8*, 70–74.

Smith, D. M. (2011). Diagnosing liability: the legal history of posttraumatic stress disorder. *Temple Law Review*, *84*, 1–69.

St. Jacques, P. L. (2012). Functional neuroimaging of autobiographical memory. In D. Berntsen & D. C. Rubin (eds.), *Understanding Autobiographical Memory: Theories and Approaches*. Cambridge: Cambridge University Press.

St. Jacques, P. L., Kragel, P. A., & Rubin, D. C. (2011a). Dynamic neural networks supporting memory retrieval. *NeuroImage*, *57*, 608–616.

St. Jacques, P. L., Botzung, A., Miles, A., & Rubin, D. C. (2011b). Functional neuroimaging of emotionally intense autobiographical memories in post-traumatic stress disorder. *Journal of Psychiatric Research*, *45*, 630–637.

St. Jacques, P. L., Kragel, P. A., & Rubin, D. C. (2013). Neural networks supporting autobiographical memory retrieval in post-traumatic stress disorder. *Cognitive, Affective, and Behavioral Neuroscience*. Advance online publication DOI 10.3758/s13415-013-0157-7.

Svoboda, E., McKinnon, M. C., & Levine, B. (2006). The functional neuroanatomy of autobiographical memory: a meta-analysis. *Neuropsychologia*, *44*, 2189–2208.

Szpunar, K. K. (2010). Episodic future thought: an emerging concept. *Perspectives on Psychological Science*, *5*, 142–162.

Talarico, J. M., LaBar K. S., & Rubin, D. C. (2004). Emotional intensity predicts autobiographical memory experience. *Memory & Cognition*, *32*, 1118–1132.

Tulving, E., & Pearlstone, Z. (1966). Availability versus accessibility of information in memory for words. *Journal of Verbal Learning and Verbal Behavior*, *5*, 381–391.

Tversky, A., & Kahneman, D. (1973). Availability: a heuristic for judging frequency and probability. *Cognitive Psychology*, 5, 207–232.

van der Kolk, B., & van der Hart, O. (1989). Pierre Janet and the breakdown of adaptation in psychological trauma. *American Journal of Psychiatry, 146*, 1530–1537.

Weathers, F. W., Litz, B. T., Huska, J. A., & Keane, T. M. (1994). The PTSD checklist (PCL), Unpublished scale available from the National Center for PTSD.

4 Construing trauma as a double-edged sword: how narrative components of autobiographical memory relate to devastation and growth from trauma

Adriel Boals, Darnell Schuettler, and Shana Southard-Dobbs

> The deeper that sorrow carves into your soul, the more joy you can contain. (Kahlil Gibran)

A large percentage of people experience a traumatic event at least once during their lifetimes. Examples of traumatic events include natural disasters, sexual or physical assaults, life-threatening illnesses, and severe car accidents. The 1995 National Comorbidity Study (Kessler et al., 1995) reported lifetime exposure rates of 60% for men and 51% for women, although other studies have found exposure rates varying from 39% to 92% (Breslau, 2002; Breslau et al., 1991; 1999; Norris, 1992). Given the high frequency of traumatic events, a great deal of research has been devoted to understanding the mental health consequences of experiencing such events. The overall picture is one of resilience (Bonanno, 2004). Although most people will experience at least some effects of the trauma, these effects typically subside within a reasonable amount of time, one month according to the *Diagnostic and Statistical Manual of Mental Disorders* (DSM-IV-TR; American Psychiatric Association, 2000). The fact that most who experience a traumatic event bounce back quickly is a testament to general human psychological resiliency.

However, a small percentage of individuals experience intense negative psychological symptoms resulting from the trauma over longer periods of time. The most common symptoms include recurrent, intrusive, and distressing thoughts, recollections, or dreams of the event; hyperarousal; and withdrawal from reminders of the event. When these symptoms are severe enough to cause disruption in everyday functioning, they demonstrate the core symptoms of posttraumatic stress disorder (PTSD). According to large-scale epidemiological studies, approximately 8% of individuals exposed to a traumatic event warrant a PTSD diagnosis, making PTSD one of the most common psychiatric disorders in the

United States (Kessler et al., 1995). These individuals who develop PTSD have received the most research attention.

Given that PTSD is not an inevitable result of trauma exposure, the etiology of PTSD symptoms has sparked a plethora of research. Since experimental methods are not a reasonable option, research on the etiology of PTSD symptoms has relied mostly on correlational data. The list of known correlates of PTSD is very long. These correlates can be split into three categories: pretrauma, the event itself, and posttrauma (Vogt et al., 2007). The simple fact that pretrauma variables predict PTSD symptoms in persons exposed to traumas is noteworthy. Such a finding suggests that some individuals are more vulnerable to developing pathological reactions before the trauma has taken place. One of the strongest pretrauma predictors of PTSD is sex. Even after controlling for type of event, females are twice as likely to develop PTSD as are males (Tolin & Foa, 2008). In addition, racial minorities, lower levels of education, a history of mental health issues (particularly any involving anxiety), and prior trauma history are also associated with higher levels of PTSD symptoms after trauma (see Brewin et al., 2000, for a meta-analysis). Personality traits, most notably neuroticism, also correlate with PTSD symptoms.

From the perspective of the DSM-IV-TR (American Psychiatric Association, 2000), the nature of the event is critical. PTSD is one of very few disorders that has a specific etiology. That is, not only must the individual experience the symptoms, but the symptoms must be attributable to a specific traumatic event. The DSM-IV-TR defines a traumatic event as an event that is both life-threatening (or potentially life-threatening) and evokes a response of fear, helplessness, and/or horror. However, a plethora of studies have found that stressful but not life-threatening events can result in PTSD symptoms at rates similar to events that do meet the DSM-IV-TR criteria (Anders et al., 2011; Boals & Schuettler, 2009). Nonetheless, there is evidence that severity of the event predicts PTSD symptoms, such that the more severe the event, the greater the probability of PTSD symptoms (Brewin et al., 2000; but see also Rubin & Feeling, 2013 for a counterexample). Another event-related predictor of PTSD symptoms is peritraumatic dissociation (Lensvelt-Mulders et al., 2008; Ozer et al., 2008), a feeling of being disconnected from one's body during the traumatic event. Posttrauma factors associated with PTSD levels include perceived social support (Brewin et al., 2000), coping styles, and cognitive construals or narratives individuals create in reference to their trauma experience (Foa et al., 1999; Rubin et al., 2008b; 2013). Certainly, this is not an exhaustive list of all PTSD correlates and there are numerous eloquent reviews (Brewin et al.,

2000; Ozer et al., 2008), so in keeping with the theme of this chapter, we focus on the cognitive construals and narratives that individuals create as trauma outcome predictors.

The role of cognition and autobiographical memory in PTSD

Though there are several known social, personality, and other predictors of PTSD, attention has recently focused on cognition and memory as key components in the development of PTSD. Ehlers and Clark (2000) proposed one of the first comprehensive cognitive models of PTSD, which emphasizes cognitive appraisals during and after the traumatic experience and the role of autobiographical memory in symptom maintenance. In their model, attention is focused on negative cognitive construals of the trauma event itself and subsequent experiences, including initial PTSD symptoms (e.g., intrusive thoughts about the trauma) and both positive and negative reactions from other people. Another key component of this model is the nature of autobiographical memory for the traumatic experience. Ehlers and Clark assert that poor encoding and integration of the trauma memory and enhanced sensory priming contribute to the difficult intentional recall of details of the trauma and the intrusive, unbidden reexperiencing that are common to PTSD (Ehlers & Clark, 2000).

Although there is now wide agreement that an individual's autobiographical memory for a traumatic experience plays a key role in determining the individual's response to the experience, other mechanisms beyond Ehlers and Clark's model have been proposed (e.g., Dalgleish, 2004; Rubin et al., 2008a; 2008b). For instance, Brewin and colleagues (Brewin, 2001; Brewin et al., 1996; 2010) outline in their dual representation theory of PTSD that there are two memory systems at work during and after a trauma: verbally based memories that can be intentionally recalled and that are integrated into the autobiographical narrative, and sensory-based memories that may be activated by unexpected exposure to an associated trigger. In individuals with PTSD, the verbally based memories are less prominent, leading to difficulty intentionally recalling details of the trauma, and the sensory-based memories are more prominent, leading to intrusive flashbacks (Brewin, 2001). There is also evidence that individuals with PTSD have a tendency toward overgeneral memories (for further discussion of this issue, see McNally and Robinaugh, Chapter 12).

In addition to the focus on the role of autobiographical memory in cognitive models of PTSD, there is a growing body of evidence supporting the role of peri- and posttrauma cognitions in the formation of posttrauma reactions. The individual's cognitive construal of the traumatic experience and its implications for beliefs regarding the self and the world (e.g., the world is no longer a safe place) play an integral role in determining posttrauma well-being (Foa et al., 1999). One other critical aspect of the individual's cognitive construal is the degree to which one perceives the event as central to his or her self-concept and life story, a construct identified as event centrality by Berntsen and Rubin (2006). The chapter by David C. Rubin in this book (Chapter 3) provides a nice context in which to understand the relevance and importance of event centrality in memories of stressful events. We now turn our discussion to this relatively recent addition to the literature on trauma and memory.

Event centrality and PTSD

To introduce the concept of event centrality, consider an example of two women who have both experienced a sexual assault. After the experience, the first woman begins to think of herself as a sexual assault victim or survivor and begins to view the experience as a key turning point in her life story. She may even frequently identify herself to others as a sexual assault victim or survivor. The second woman acknowledges the experience and its impact on her life, but she views it as just one entry in the timeline of her life's events, rather than an individually defining moment. For the first woman, the traumatic event has become central to her sense of self and a turning point in her life story (for further examples of self-defining events, see Brown and colleagues, Chapter 15).

Berntsen and Rubin (2006) developed the Centrality of Event Scale (CES) to assess the degree to which a traumatic event is construed as central to an individual's life story. The self-report measure includes items such as "I feel that this event has become part of my identity", "This event permanently changed my life," and "This event has become a reference point for the way I understand myself and the world" (Berntsen & Rubin, 2006); the measure is now frequently utilized in PTSD research.

Not surprisingly, high levels of event centrality for stressful life events have been linked with poor mental health outcomes, including depression and PTSD symptoms (Berntsen & Rubin, 2006; 2007) and poor physical health outcomes (Boals, 2010). The relationship between event centrality and PTSD symptoms has been demonstrated in combat veterans (Brown et al., 2010), community samples (Pinto-Gouveia & Matos, 2011), adult survivors of childhood sexual abuse (Robinaugh & McNally, 2011), older adults (Boals et al., 2012), college undergraduates

(Berntsen & Rubin, 2006; 2007; Boals, 2010; Schuettler & Boals, 2011), and adults experiencing prolonged grief after the death of a loved one (Boelen, 2012). Although most studies conducted thus far have relied on cross-sectional data, the correlation between event centrality and PTSD symptoms is consistently moderate to strong. Using a longitudinal design, Boelen (2012) demonstrated that for individuals who had recently (within the past twelve months) experienced the death of a close loved one, event centrality strongly predicted PTSD symptoms a year later. Given the growing evidence for the relationship between event centrality and PTSD symptoms, event centrality warrants a place in the discussion of factors contributing to the development of PTSD. But is event centrality just one of many in an already long list of known correlates of PTSD, or is it redundant with other known associates such as posttraumatic cognitions or event severity?

A number of studies have found that after controlling for depression, dissociation, and anxiety (three of the strongest correlates of PTSD symptoms), event centrality remains a significant predictor of PTSD symptoms (Berntsen & Rubin, 2007; Boals, 2010; Rubin et al., 2008b). But the construct of event centrality is very different from the constructs of depression, anxiety, and dissociation, so perhaps it is not surprising that event centrality was able to account for unique variance in the prediction of PTSD symptoms when these other three variables were considered.

The construct of event centrality in some ways is similar to the construct of posttraumatic cognitions, another known correlate of PSTD symptoms. Posttraumatic cognitions refer to the negative thoughts and beliefs that occur after a traumatic experience. The most commonly used measure of posttraumatic cognitions, the Posttraumatic Cognitions Inventory (PTCI), contains three subscales: negative cognitions about the self, negative cognitions about the world, and self-blame (Foa et al., 1999). These three types of cognitions are believed to be dysfunctional and maladaptive interpretations of trauma experiences that lead to the development and maintenance of PTSD. Event centrality and posttraumatic cognitions are both part of the cognitive construals, interpretations, and narratives individuals make about their traumatic experience. Lancaster et al. (2011) found in a sample of undergraduate students that both event centrality and posttraumatic cognitions uniquely predicted PTSD symptoms, suggesting these two variables independently contribute to PTSD symptoms. This finding was recently replicated in both an undergraduate sample and a sample of abused women recruited from a community outreach center (Barton et al., 2013). In fact, there was a small but significant additive effect such that the combination of high event centrality and high posttraumatic cognitions was associated with the highest levels of PTSD symptoms. Such findings underscore the role of cognitive conceptualizations and interpretations of trauma experiences in the progression of PTSD symptoms. In addition, the findings suggest that the construct of event centrality is not redundant with the construct of posttraumatic appraisals. These two constructs reflect different cognitive conceptualizations about the experience and can independently contribute to the prediction of PTSD symptoms.

In another study examining whether event centrality is redundant with other known predictors, Schuettler and Boals (2011) attempted to predict PTSD symptoms using a list of twenty common predictors. These predictors included event centrality, visceral reactions to the memory of the event, perceived stress, anxiety, depression, negative perspective of the event, psychological closure of the event, emotional intensity associated with the event, avoidant coping style, posttraumatic growth, forgiveness, and religious coping, all of which were shown to be significantly associated with PTSD symptoms in the sample. A large amount of overlap of predicted PTSD variance was expected between these variables, meaning there would likely be only a few unique predictors. The results of a forward stepwise regression analysis revealed five variables that accounted for unique variance in PTSD symptoms: avoidant coping, negative perspective of the event, two measures of visceral reactions, and, most notably, event centrality. Event centrality was the second strongest predictor, again demonstrating that event centrality uniquely contributes to the prediction of PTSD symptoms, even after controlling for numerous other predictors.

All of the evidence linking event centrality to trauma outcomes reviewed thus far has been based on correlational evidence. In a recent study, Boals and Murrell (2014) utilized an experimental design in which they manipulated event centrality. The manipulation was achieved using a therapist-led intervention based on Acceptance and Commitment Therapy (ACT) principles. ACT was chosen because some core ACT principles, such as self-as-context, are particularly relevant to the idea of event centrality. A group of women who experienced physical or sexual abuse and were seeking help at a community outreach center were recruited. Participants were assigned to either a control group (received treatment-as-usual from the outreach center) or to an experimental group (received treatment-as-usual plus four therapist-led ACT sessions). In comparison to the control group, the experimental group evidenced significant decreases in event centrality, PTSD symptoms, and depression. More important, decreases in event centrality significantly mediated decreases in PTSD symptoms. These results represent perhaps the strongest evidence to date of a causal relationship between event centrality and PTSD symptoms. Based on the collective body of growing evidence, we conclude that event centrality is not just another predictor. Although the construct was first published only six years ago (Berntsen & Rubin, 2006), it has proven to be one of the strongest and most consistent predictors of PTSD symptoms.

Positive trauma outcomes: posttraumatic growth

Although PTSD has received the lion's share of attention from trauma research, researchers are increasingly exploring possible positive benefits of trauma experiences. Beneficial effects of traumatic events may sound counterintuitive, but many individuals report positive changes after traumatic experiences (Calhoun & Tedeschi, 1999; Helgeson et al., 2006; Linley & Joseph, 2006; Park et al., 1996; Tedeschi et al., 1998). These benefits have been referred to by a variety of names, including benefit finding and adversarial growth, but perhaps the most commonly used term is posttraumatic growth (PTG). PTG represents personal growth as a direct result of experiencing a traumatic event (Tedeschi & Calhoun, 2008). Growth may be displayed as a greater sense of personal capability, greater appreciation of life, realignment of priorities, improved relationships, and/or recognition of new possibilities for one's life purpose or direction. PTG is associated with less depression, anxiety, and distress and with greater positive affect, quality of life, and physical health (Boals et al., 2010).

If growth is possible following traumatic experiences, then an important question trauma researchers must answer is what causes such growth to occur and why does not everyone experience such benefits of trauma? Moreover, some scholars hold that PTSD symptoms and PTG can co-occur (Linley et al., 2003). Similar to the approach taken with the etiology of PTSD, a first step is to examine correlates of PTG. In terms of demographics, many of the same variables that predict PTSD also predict PTG, and surprisingly some of these variables are associated with PTSD and PTG in the same direction (Denson et al., 2007; Gill & Page, 2006; Helgeson et al., 2006; Nemeroff et al., 2006). For example, in comparison to their counterparts, females, racial minorities, and younger adults report higher levels of PTSD symptoms and also report higher levels of PTG. Other characteristics of the individual that correlate with PTG include extraversion, openness to experience, agreeableness, and conscientiousness, all of which are also positively associated with PTSD (Linley & Joseph, 2004). Optimism is positively related with PTG (Helgeson, et al., 2006; Tedeschi & Calhoun, 1996; Wild &

Paivio, 2003), although some researchers disagree about optimism's predictive abilities for PTG (Davis et al., 1998; King et al., 2000). Higher levels of intelligence are associated with fewer PTSD symptoms and with lower levels of PTG (Schuettler & Boals, 2011). In terms of features of the traumatic event, subjective severity of trauma is a strong predictor of both PTSD symptoms and PTG, in the same direction (Morris et al., 2005).

Similar to PTSD, posttrauma factors also appear to play an important role in PTG. PTSD symptoms have long been linked to a poor social support system (Schlenger et al., 1992), whereas PTG is positively correlated with greater social support satisfaction (Linley & Joseph, 2004). Coping style also appears to play a role. A problem-focused coping style is associated with both higher reports of PTSD symptoms and higher reports of PTG (Linley & Joseph, 2004; Schnider et al., 2007). Religious coping is related to both PTSD symptoms and PTG, but the two types of religious coping affect PTSD symptoms and PTG differently. Negative religious coping methods (views of religious discontent and punishment) are related to greater PTSD symptoms (Witvliet et al., 2004), whereas positive religious coping (views of religious benevolence and forgiveness) is associated with greater PTG (Gerber et al., 2011; Linley & Joseph, 2004; Wild & Paivio, 2003). Stress positively correlates with both PTSD and PTG (Helgeson et al., 2006; Mason et al., 2006). Greater visceral reactions to and emotional intensity of the traumatic event are associated with greater PTSD symptoms and greater PTG (Schuettler & Boals, 2011).

In summary, many of the same variables associated with PTSD symptoms are also associated with PTG. Surprisingly, the majority of the variables associated with these two very different trauma outcomes correlate with PTSD and PTG in the same direction (e.g., sex, race, age, event severity, problem-focused coping, intelligence, visceral reactions, emotional intensity of the event), although a few variables evidence associations with PTSD symptoms and PTG in opposite directions (e.g., social support and optimism). Perhaps one of the reasons for the commonality among correlates is because an event has to have at least moderate (if not severe) levels of importance to the individual and emotional reactions.

The relationship between event centrality and posttraumatic growth

Considering that event centrality is one of the strongest and most reliable associates of PTSD symptoms, is event centrality also associated with PTG? And if so, what is the direction of this relationship? Considering

PTSD symptoms as a negative consequence and PTG as a positive consequence of trauma, one might expect the direction of relationship between event centrality and PTG to be opposite (negative relationship) that of event centrality and PTSD symptoms (positive relationship). Although one may assume that negative and positive consequences of trauma exposure are two opposite ends of a singular "consequences of trauma" construct, empirical evidence supports the possibility of independent negative and positive trauma consequences (Linley et al., 2003). In other words, even when an individual's struggle with a stressful event leads to PTG, this does not necessarily coincide with a subsequent decrease in negative symptoms.

Because PTG is believed to result from a challenge to and reexamination of core beliefs (Tedeschi et al., 2007), Boals and Schuettler (2011) hypothesized that PTG would be positively correlated with event centrality. They asked a large sample ($N=929$) of undergraduates to nominate their most stressful or traumatic event, then complete measures of event centrality, PTSD symptoms, and PTG in reference to this event. Participants also completed measures of depression, cognitive processing of the event, coping styles, and whether the event met DSM-IV-TR trauma criteria to be used as covariates. In terms of PTSD symptoms, event centrality was once again positively related, even after controlling for the covariates. Thus the results successfully replicated the consistent finding of a strong relationship between event centrality and PTSD symptoms. Also consistent with the hypotheses, event centrality was positively related to PTG. This relationship remained significant after controlling for the covariates. In both multiple regression analyses (one predicting PTSD symptoms, the other predicting PTG) using all variables measured in the study as predictors, event centrality was one of the two strongest predictors in both regression models, and the direction of both relationships was positive. Thus not only was event centrality found to be a very strong unique predictor of both PTSD symptoms and PTG, these two relationships were in the same direction. Another study (Schuettler & Boals, 2011) attempted to replicate the positive relationship between event centrality and PTG, controlling for a large number of other correlates including visceral reactions, perceived stress, anxiety, depression, negative perspective of the event, psychological closure of the event, emotional intensity, coping styles, forgiveness, and religious coping. Once again, event centrality continued to be a unique predictor of PTG after controlling for these other trauma-related variables. Thus in multiple studies and with a wide range of trauma-related covariates, event centrality has consistently been one of the strongest unique predictors of not only PTSD symptoms, but also PTG.

A double-edged sword: event centrality predicts both PTSD and PTG

The finding that event centrality is associated with PTSD symptoms and PTG in the same direction is noteworthy. It suggests that construing a stressful event as central to identity is like a double-edged sword: on the one hand, high event centrality appears detrimental in that it is associated with greater depression and levels of PTSD symptoms, and yet on the other hand, it is related to more growth after trauma. Event centrality appears to have the power to both debilitate and foster growth. How is this possible? One possibility is that construing a stressful event as central to one's identity transforms the event into what has sometimes been referred to as an "anchor event" (Pillemer, 1998) or a "self-defining memory" (Brown and colleagues, Chapter 15; Singer, 1995). Such memories become a reference point to interpret new information as well as generate expectations for future events. These event memories often mark the beginning and end of lifetime periods (Conway & Pleydell-Pearce, 2000) and give meaning and continuity to one's sense of self and life story (McAdams et al., 2006). In fact, an inability of the autobiographical memory system to allow important events to alter the self can be pathological (Crane et al., 2010). But when a negative or traumatic event becomes an anchor event, this scenario presents a new set of challenges. It keeps the memory highly available, leading to further rehearsal. The rehearsal in turn maintains and strengthens the memory and its emotional impact over long periods of time.

It is difficult to imagine that a relatively minor stressful event, such as being stuck in a traffic jam or getting a speeding ticket, could result in clinical-level PTSD symptoms (if it does, the symptoms may be more so due to an enduring adjustment disorder). Because the event is not likely severe enough to cause PTSD symptoms, it is similarly difficult to imagine such events also leading to significant levels of growth such as a new appreciation of life or newfound personal strength. Alternatively, it seems more plausible that the experience of a rape or a life-threatening war experience could result in clinically significant PTSD or PTG. The noteworthy point is that, regardless of the event type (seemingly traumatic or not), the event's impact must be capable of inflicting psychological damage on an individual for any type of psychological growth to occur. The research reviewed thus far suggests construing a stressful or traumatic event as central to one's identity is one of the most potent ways for an event to inflict psychological damage great enough to result in PTSD or PTG. Thus it should be no surprise that event centrality is similarly positively related with PTG. This idea is summed up nicely by the quote from poet Khalil Gibran at the start of this chapter: "The deeper that sorrow carves into your soul, the more joy you can contain."

Not every person who experiences a traumatic event and subsequent PTSD symptoms will experience PTG. If an individual does experience a traumatic event and construes that event as a core part of identity, which factors lead to PTG? Tedeschi et al. (2007) stated that "growth follows a challenge to and re-examination of core beliefs, not every bad experience" (p. 403). The results of this reexamination appear to be critical. Thus, as with PTSD research, PTG research should also not be based simply on whether an individual had a "bad experience" or a DSM-defined traumatic event. Rather, the event should challenge the individual's core beliefs and view of the world. Once this challenge has occurred, the individual is confronted with reanalyzing and making revisions to his or her views of the self and world. This shattering of beliefs can cause a major reexamination of one's view of and place in the world. In this sense, it is not the objective nature of the event that matters, but rather the individual's subjective interpretation of the experience. Across many cultures, most people expect that defining events in their lives will be positive (Rubin & Berntsen, 2003). For instance, many people expect to finish school, get married, have children, and retire comfortably. When major traumas occur, such as a major accident, a sexual assault, death, or unexpected illness, there can be a major shattering of one's assumptions and beliefs about the nature of the world, one's self, and one's life story (Janoff-Bulman, 1989). For instance, being suddenly sexually assaulted by a trusted friend or family member can violate core world assumptions about trust, safety, and the self. A heart-wrenching romantic breakup or divorce can cause a person to question his or her own self-worth and life path. This major reexamination and path to restoring views of the self and the world takes time and effort.

Some believe that intrusive thoughts and dreams are a common human response to trauma because intrusive thoughts are attempts to process the trauma experience, reexamine core assumptions about the self and the world, and attempt to restore them (Horowitz, 1975). This allows individuals to find meaning, value, and purpose in one's life, a core human motive (Baumeister, 1991). This is often achieved through narrative. Narrative is the linguistic means through which individuals express autobiographical memories and reflect how they think about, understand, and make meaning of their past. Some forms of narratives may be more adaptive than others (Ramírez-Esparza & Pennebaker, 2006). The result of this rethinking of core beliefs and subsequent development of narrative is likely crucial to the development of PTSD and/or PTG. Certainly, one path these revisions could take is one of newfound negative, degrading beliefs of self and the world. For example, after a sexual assault it is not uncommon for victims to believe that they are weak, inadequate, and responsible for the assault; that the world is dangerous; and that people cannot be trusted. Thus it is not surprising that posttraumatic cognitions, negative beliefs about the self and world as a result of trauma experience, are strongly associated with PTSD symptoms (Foa et al., 1999). However, another possible result is a more positive, optimistic view of the self and the world, such as beliefs that one has overcome extreme adversity. For example, the person believes that because he or she survived the traumatic event, he or she has been given a second chance in life and may have new motivation or purpose for living. These newfound beliefs can include but are certainly not limited to newfound personal strength, spiritual growth, and appreciation of life. Such positive construals of the self and the world as a result of a traumatic experience are the bedrock of PTG. Future studies are needed to further elucidate the trajectories of PTSD and PTG, for instance, whether prior PTSD symptoms are necessary to experience PTG or whether they can develop concurrently.

Recall the study described earlier that identified unique predictors of PTSD symptoms and PTG (Schuettler & Boals, 2011). Using the same group of individuals for both regression analyses allowed the simultaneous examination of PTSD symptoms and PTG as a result of stressful or traumatic events. Also relevant regarding this study is a measure of positive and negative trauma perspectives, which taps into the extent to which individuals created positive or negative narratives of their experiences. Stepwise regression analyses revealed that one of the two strongest unique predictors of both PTSD symptoms and PTG was event centrality. After event centrality, the remaining variables that accounted for unique variance in PTSD symptoms and PTG differed. For PTSD symptoms, additional unique predictors included avoidant coping, visceral reactions, and a negative perspective of the traumatic experience (e.g., "The pain I have felt has not been worth it"). For PTG, the additional unique predictors included problem-focused coping and a positive perspective of the traumatic experience (e.g., "Calling to mind painful experiences is part of healing"). Thus coping styles and having a positive or negative perspective of the experience appear to be key determinants in PTG development. These results support the idea that construing an event as high in event centrality sets the stage for PTSD and/or PTG. The subsequent narratives that followed then influenced whether the individuals experienced PTSD and/or PTG.

As another illustration of relationships between stressful event construals and PTSD and/or PTG, Groleau and colleagues (2013) measured challenge to core beliefs, intrusive rumination, deliberate rumination, search for meaning, and finding meaning, along with event centrality. These variables were used to predict PTSD symptoms and PTG separately. Two variables emerged as significant predictors of both PTSD symptoms and PTG in the same direction: event centrality and core beliefs. From there, the other variables differed greatly in relation to PTSD symptoms and PTG. Intrusive event-related rumination was positively associated with PTSD symptoms but was negatively associated with PTG. Further, deliberate event-related rumination was unrelated to PTSD symptoms but was positively related to PTG. Being engaged in a search for meaning in life versus a sense that one has found meaning in life also differed in its relation to PTSD symptoms and PTG. Search for meaning was positively associated with PTSD symptoms, whereas found meaning was related to PTG. This latter finding is consistent with the notion that PTG is a type of meaning resultant from the meaning-making process (Park, 2010; Park & Ai, 2006). Collectively, these various cognitive construals that make up a narrative after experiencing a trauma play a key role in the psychological impact of a traumatic experience.

Conclusions: the role of narrative in posttrauma outcomes

In summary, we posit that the narrative an individual creates regarding a traumatic experience plays a key role in the types of trauma outcomes experienced. If the event is construed as having low centrality and does not challenge one's core views and beliefs, the event will have a limited psychological impact on the individual. But if a negative event is construed as central to one's identity and life story, it causes a reexamination of values and beliefs. This reexamination sets the stage for the possibility of devastation. For instance, subsequent construals such as a negative perspective of the event, negative posttrauma cognitions of the self and world, and intrusive ruminations likely contribute to the development of PTSD symptoms. However, the reexamination also sets the stage for the possibility of growth. Subsequent construals such as positive perspectives of the event, a lack of negative posttraumatic cognitions about the self and world, and deliberate rumination likely contribute to PTG. There are no doubt numerous other construals and narrative components playing key roles that are yet to be identified and examined. Future research should continue to address various aspects of narrative and the role they play in trauma outcomes.

Narrative constructs such as event centrality and posttraumatic cognitions typically remain significant predictors in multiple regression models of PTSD symptoms and PTG, while other predictors such as personality traits and demographic features become nonsignificant. This consistent finding warrants further discussion. One possibility is that nonnarrative predictors of PTSD symptoms significantly correlate because they predict the extent to which different types of narratives are formed. For example, neuroticism is a very strong and consistent associate of PTSD symptoms. Perhaps the reason for this relationship is that neuroticism plays a key role in which types of narratives individuals are more likely to construct. After experiencing a stressful event, highly neurotic individuals may be more likely to create toxic narratives that include negative perspectives and negative posttraumatic cognitions of the self and the world. In contrast, individuals low in neuroticism are less likely to form these types of narratives. Sex is another strong correlate of both PTSD symptoms and PTG (Tolin & Foa, 2008). These relationships may exist because females are more likely to construe events as central to identity (Boals, 2010). Optimism may be related to PTG because highly optimistic individuals are likely to create narratives that include positive perspectives and fewer negative posttraumatic cognitions. This is not to say that narrative features are the only constructs that matter. Certainly, there are other factors that contribute to PTSD symptoms independent of narrative. For instance, biological, hippocampus functioning, hormone levels, social support levels, and classical conditioning likely have direct impacts on psychological functioning in the wake of trauma. The possibility that narrative plays a mediating role between many known predictors and PTSD symptoms should be explored in longitudinal studies.

The theory that narrative plays a central role in trauma-related psychological outcomes has important implications for treatment. Therapists cannot control whether people experience traumatic events, but a skilled therapist may be able to influence the narrative that follows. Narrative therapies are designed to change the narratives of those who have experienced traumatic events. There is some empirical evidence that changes in narratives are related to better outcomes (Foa et al., 1995). A leading explanation for the salutary benefits of the well-known expressive writing intervention is that through expressive writing, narratives are revised such that a coherent story emerges (Graybeal et al., 2002; Smyth et al., 2001). Indeed, increased use of cognitive processing words in writing samples is associated with better outcomes (Klein & Boals, 2001; Pennebaker et al., 1997). Use of cognitive processing words is believed to be a part of the meaning-making process, a precursor to formation of a coherent narrative (Boals, 2012; Boals et al., 2011). The facilitation of a healthy narrative should be a primary goal of therapies designed to help individuals cope with traumatic experiences. Understanding the narrative features that differentiate pathways to PTSD symptoms and PTG can help therapists not only reduce negative trauma outcomes such as PTSD symptoms, but also assist the individual to go beyond mere symptom reduction by also fostering growth.

REFERENCES

American Psychiatric Association. (2000). *Diagnostic and Statistical Manual of Mental Disorders* (4th ed., text revision). Washington, DC: American Psychiatric Association.

Anders, S. L., Frazier, P. A., & Frankfurt, S. B. (2011). Variations in criterion A and PTSD rates in a community sample of women. *Journal of Anxiety Disorders*, 25(2), 176–184.

Barton, S., Boals, A., & Knowles, L. (2013). Thinking about trauma: the unique contributions of event centrality and posttraumatic cognitions in predicting PTSD and posttraumatic growth. *Journal of Traumatic Stress*, 26, 718–726.

Baumeister, R. (1991). *Meanings of Life*. New York: Guilford Press.

Berntsen, D., & Rubin, D. C. (2006). The centrality of event scale: a measure of integrating a trauma into one's identity and its relation to post-traumatic stress disorder symptoms. *Behaviour Research and Therapy*, 44(2), 219–231.

(2007). When a trauma becomes a key to identity: enhanced integration of trauma memories predicts posttraumatic stress disorder symptoms. *Applied Cognitive Psychology*, 21(4), 417–431.

Boals, A. (2010). Events that have become central to identity: gender differences in the centrality of events scale for positive and negative events. *Applied Cognitive Psychology*, 24(1), 107–121.

(2012). The use of meaning making in expressive writing: when meaning is beneficial. *Journal of Social and Clinical Psychology*, 31(4), 393–409.

Boals, A., & Murrell, A. R. (2014). I am > trauma: the use of modified acceptance and commitment therapy to reduce event centrality and PTSD symptoms in a pseudo-randomized clinical trial. Manuscript submitted for publication.

Boals, A., & Schuettler, D. (2009). PTSD symptoms in response to traumatic and non-traumatic events: The role of respondent perception and the A2 criterion. *Journal of Anxiety Disorders*, 23, 458–462.

(2011). A double-edged sword: event centrality, PTSD and posttraumatic growth. *Applied Cognitive Psychology*, 25(5), 817–822.

Boals, A., Steward, J., & Schuettler, D. (2010). Advancing our understanding of posttraumatic growth by considering even centrality. *Journal of Loss and Trauma*, 15(6), 518–533.

Boals, A., Banks, J. B., Hathaway, L. M., & Schuettler, D. (2011). Coping with stressful events: use of cognitive words in stressful narratives and the meaning-making process. *Journal of Social and Clinical Psychology*, 30(4), 378–403.

Boals, A., Hayslip, B. Jr., Knowles, L. R., & Banks, J. B. (2012). Perceiving a negative event as central to one's identity partially mediates age differences in posttraumatic stress disorder symptoms. *Journal of Aging and Health, 24*(3), 459–474.

Boelen, P. A. (2012). A prospective examination of the association between the centrality of a loss and post-loss psychopathology. *Journal of Affective Disorders, 137*(1–3), 117–124.

Bonanno, G. (2004). Loss, trauma, and human resilience: have we underestimated the human capacity to thrive after extremely aversive events? *American Psychologist, 59*(1), 20–28.

Breslau, N. (2002). Epidemiologic studies of trauma, posttraumatic stress disorder, and other psychiatric disorders. *Canadian Journal of Psychiatry, 47*(10), 923–929.

Breslau, N., Davis, G., Andrewski, P., & Peterson, E. (1991). Traumatic events and posttraumatic stress disorder in an urban population of young adults. *Archives of General Psychiatry, 48*, 216–222.

Breslau, N., Chilcoat, H., Kessler, R., Peterson, E., & Lucia, V. (1999). Vulnerability to assaultive violence: further specification of the sex difference in post-traumatic stress disorder. *Psychological Medicine, 29*, 813–821.

Brewin, C. R. (2001). A cognitive neuroscience account of posttraumatic stress disorder and its treatment. *Behaviour Research and Therapy, 39*(4), 373–393.

Brewin, C. R., Dalgleish, T., & Joseph, S. (1996). A dual representation theory of posttraumatic stress disorder. *Psychological Review, 103*(4), 670–686.

Brewin, C. R., Andrews, B., & Valentine, J. D. (2000). Meta-analysis of risk factors for posttraumatic stress disorder in trauma-exposed adults. *Journal of Consulting and Clinical Psychology, 68*(5), 748–766.

Brewin, C. R., Gregory, J.D., Lipton, M., & Burgess, N. (2010). Intrusive images in psychological disorders: Characteristics, neural mechanisms, and treatment implications. *Psychological Review, 117*, 210–232.

Brown, A. D., Antonius, D., Kramer, M., Root, J. C., & Hirst, W. (2010). Trauma centrality and PTSD in veterans returning from Iraq and Afghanistan. *Journal of Traumatic Stress, 23*(4), 496–499.

Calhoun, L. G., & Tedeschi, R. G. (1999). *Facilitating Posttraumatic Growth: A Clinician's Guide*. Mahwah, NJ: Lawrence Erlbaum Associates.

Conway, M. A., & Pleydell-Pearce, C. W. (2000). The construction of autobiographical memories in the self-memory system. *Psychological Review, 107*(2), 261–288.

Crane, L., Goddard, L., & Pring, L. (2010). Brief report: self-defining and everyday autobiographical memories in adults with autism spectrum disorders. *Journal of Autism and Developmental Disorders, 40*(3), 383–391.

Dalgleish, T. (2004). Cognitive approaches to posttraumatic stress disorder: the evolution of multirepresentational theorizing. *Psychological Bulletin, 130*(2), 228–260.

Davis, C., Nolen-Hoeksema, S., & Larson, J. (1998). Making sense of loss and benefiting from the experience: two construals of meaning. *Journal of Personality and Social Psychology, 75*, 561–574.

Denson, T., Marshall, G., Schell, T., & Jaycox, L. (2007). Predictors of posttraumatic distress 1 year after exposure to community violence: the

importance of acute symptom severity. *Journal of Consulting and Clinical Psychology, 75*(5), 683–692.
Ehlers, A., & Clark, D. M. (2000). A cognitive model of posttraumatic stress disorder. *Behaviour Research and Therapy, 38*(4), 319–345.
Foa, E. B., Molnar, C., & Cashman, L. (1995). Change in rape narratives during exposure therapy for posttraumatic stress disorder. *Journal of Traumatic Stress, 8*, 675–690.
Foa, E. B., Ehlers, A., Clark, D. M., Tolin, D. F., & Orsillo, S. M. (1999). The posttraumatic cognitions inventory (PTCI): Development and validation. *Psychological Assessment, 11*(3), 303–314.
Gerber, M. M., Boals, A., & Schuettler, D. (2011). The unique contributions of positive and negative religious coping to posttraumatic growth and PTSD. *Psychology of Religion and Spirituality, 3*(4), 298–307.
Gill, J. M., & Page, G. G. (2006). Psychiatric and physical health ramifications of traumatic events in women. *Issues in Mental Health Nursing, 27*(7), 711–734.
Graybeal, A., Seagal, J. D., & Pennebaker, J. W. (2002). The role of story-making in disclosure writing: the psychometrics of narrative. *Psychology and Health, 17*, 571–581.
Groleau, J. M., Calhoun, L. G., Cann, A., & Tedeschi, R. G. (2013). The role of centrality of events in posttraumatic distress and posttraumatic growth. *Psychological Trauma: Theory, Research, Practice, and Policy, 5*(5), 477–483.
Helgeson, V., Reynolds, K., & Tomich, P. (2006). A meta-analytic review of benefit finding and growth. *Journal of Consulting and Clinical Psychology, 74*(5), 797–816.
Horowitz, M. J. (1975). Intrusive and repetitive thoughts after experimental stress. *Archives of General Psychiatry, 32*, 1457–1463.
Janoff-Bulman, R. (1989). Assumptive worlds and the stress of traumatic events: applications of the schema construct. *Social Cognition, 7*(2), 113–136.
Kessler, R., Sonnega, A., Bromet, E., Hughes, M., & Nelson, C. (1995). Posttraumatic stress disorder in the National Comorbidity Survey. *Archives of General Psychiatry, 52*, 1048–1060.
King, L., Scollon, C., Ramsey, C., & Williams, T. (2000). Stories of life transition: subjective well-being and ego development in parents of children with Down syndrome. *Journal of Research in Personality, 34*(4), 509–536.
Klein, K., & Boals, A. (2001). Expressive writing can increase working memory capacity. *Journal of Experimental Psychology: General, 130*(3), 520–533.
Lancaster, S. L., Rodriguez, B. F., & Weston, R. (2011). Path analytic examination of a cognitive model of PTSD. *Behaviour Research and Therapy, 49*(3), 194–201.
Lensvelt-Mulders, G., van der Hart, O., van Ochten, J. M., van Son, M. J. M., Steele, K., & Breeman, L. (2008). Relations among peritraumatic dissociation and posttraumatic stress: a meta-analysis. *Clinical Psychology Review, 28*, 1138–1151.
Linley, P., & Joseph, S. (2004). Positive change following trauma and adversity: a review. *Journal of Traumatic Stress, 17*(1), 11–21.

(2006). The positive and negative effects of disaster work: a preliminary investigation. *Journal of Loss and Trauma*, *11*, 229–245.

Linley, P., Joseph, S., Cooper, R., Harris, S., & Meyer, C. (2003). Positive and negative changes following vicarious exposure to the September 11 terrorist attacks. *Journal of Traumatic Stress*, *16*, 481–485.

Mason, S., Turpin, G., Woods, D., Wardrope, J., & Rowlands, A. (2006). Risk factors for psychological distress following injury. *British Journal of Clinical Psychology*, *45*, 217–230.

McAdams, D. P., Josselson, R., & Lieblich, A. (eds.). (2006). *Identity and Story: Creating Self in Narrative*. Washington, DC: American Psychological Association.

Morris, B. A., Shakespeare-Finch, J., Rieck, M., & Newbery, J. (2005). Multidimensional nature of posttraumatic growth in an Australian population. *Journal of Traumatic Stress*, *18*(5), 575–585.

Nemeroff, C., Bremner, J., Foa, E., Mayberg, H., North, C., & Stein, M. (2006). Posttraumatic stress disorder: a state-of-the-science review. *Journal of Psychiatric Research*, *40*, 1–21.

Norris, F. (1992). Epidemiology of trauma: frequency and impact of different potentially traumatic events on different demographic groups. *Journal of Consulting and Clinical Psychology*, *60*, 409–418.

Ozer, E. J., Best, S. R., Lipsey, T. L., & Weiss, D. S. (2008). Predictors of posttraumatic stress disorder and symptoms in adults: a meta-analysis. *Psychological Trauma: Theory, Research, Practice, and Policy*, *S*(1), 3–36.

Park, C. L. (2010). Making sense of the meaning literature: an integrative review of meaning making and its effects on adjustment to stressful life events. *Psychological Bulletin*, *136*, 257–301.

Park, C. L., & Ai, A. L. (2006). Meaning making and growth: new directions for research on survivors of trauma. *Journal of Loss and Trauma*, *11*, 389–407.

Park, C., Cohen, L., & Murch, R. (1996). Assessment and prediction of stress-related growth. *Journal of Personality*, *64*(1), 71–105.

Pennebaker, J. W., Mayne, T. J., & Francis, M. E. (1997). Linguistic predictors of adaptive bereavement. *Journal of Personality and Social Psychology*, *72*(4), 863–871.

Pillemer, D. B. (1998). What is remembered about early childhood events? *Clinical Psychology Review*, *18*(8), 895–913.

Pinto-Gouveia, J., & Matos, M. (2011). Can shame memories become a key to identity? The centrality of shame memories predicts psychopathology. *Applied Cognitive Psychology*, *25*(2), 281–290.

Ramírez-Esparza, N., & Pennebaker, J. W. (2006). Do good stories produce good health?: Exploring words, language, and culture. *Narrative Inquiry*, *16*(1), 211–219.

Robinaugh, D. J., & McNally, R. J. (2011). Trauma centrality and PTSD symptom severity in adult survivors of childhood sexual abuse. *Journal of Traumatic Stress*, *24*(4), 483–486.

Rubin, D. C., & Berntsen, D. (2003). Life scripts help to maintain autobiographical memories of highly positive, but not highly negative, events. *Memory and Cognition*, *31*(1), 1–14.

Rubin, D.C. & Feeling, N. (2013). Measuring the severity of negative and traumatic events. *Clinical Psychological Science*, *1*, 375-389.

Rubin, D. C., Berntsen, D., & Bohni, M. K. (2008a). A memory-based model of posttraumatic stress disorder: evaluating basic assumptions underlying the PTSD diagnosis. *Psychological Review*, *115*, 985–1011.

Rubin, D. C., Boals, A., & Berntsen, D. (2008b). Memory in posttraumatic stress disorder: Properties of voluntary and involuntary, traumatic and nontraumatic autobiographical memories in people with and without posttraumatic stress disorder symptoms. *Journal of Experimental Psychology: General*, *137*(4), 591–614.

Rubin, D.C., Boals, A., & Hoyle, R. H. (2013). Narrative centrality and negative affectivity: Independent and interactive contributors to stress reactions. *Journal of Experimental Psychology: General*. Advance online publication.

Schlenger, W., Kulka, R., Fairbank, J., Hough, R., Jorda, B., & Marmar, C. (1992). The prevalence of post-traumatic stress disorder in the Vietnam generation: a multimethod, multisource assessment of psychiatric disorder. *Journal of Traumatic Stress*, *5*, 333–363.

Schnider, K., Elhai., J., & Gray, M. (2007). Coping style use predicts posttraumatic stress and complicated grief symptoms severity among college students reporting a traumatic loss. *Journal of Counseling Psychology*, *54*(3), 344–350.

Schuettler, D., & Boals, A. (2011). The path to posttraumatic growth versus PTSD: contributions of event centrality and coping. *Journal of Loss and Trauma*, *16*(2), 180–194.

Singer, J. A. (1995). Seeing one's self: locating narrative memory in a framework of personality. *Journal of Personality*, *63*(3), 429–457.

Smyth, J., True, N., & Souto, J. (2001). Effects of writing about traumatic experiences: the necessity for narrative structure. *Journal of Social and Clinical Psychology*, *20*, 161–172.

Tedeschi, R. G., & Calhoun, L. G. (1996). The posttraumatic growth inventory: measure the positive legacy of trauma. *Journal of Traumatic Stress*, *9*, 455–471.

(2008). Beyond the concept of recovery: Growth and the experience of loss. *Death Studies*, *32*, 27–39.

Tedeschi, R. G., Park, C. L., & Calhoun, L. G. (1998). Posttraumatic growth: conceptual issues. In R. Tedeschi & L. Calhoun (eds.), *Posttraumatic Growth: Positive Changes in the Aftermath of Crisis* (pp. 1–22). Mahwah, NJ: Lawrence Earlbaum Associates.

Tedeschi, R. G., Calhoun, L. G., & Cann, A. (2007). Evaluating resource gain: understanding and misunderstanding posttraumatic growth. *Applied Psychology: An International Review*, *56*(3), 396–406.

Tolin, D. F., & Foa, E. B. (2008). Sex differences in trauma and posttraumatic stress disorder: a quantitative review of 25 years of research. *Psychological Trauma: Theory, Practice, and Policy*, *1*, 37–85.

Vogt, D. S., King, D. W., & King, L. A. (2007). Risk pathways for PTSD: making sense of the literature. In M. J. Friedman, T. M. Keane, & P. A.

Resick (eds.), *Handbook of PTSD: Science and Practice* (pp. 99–115). New York: Guilford Press.

Witvliet, C., Phipps, K., Feldman, M., & Beckham, J. (2004). Posttraumatic mental and physical health correlates of forgiveness and religious coping in military veterans. *Journal of Traumatic Stress, 17*(3), 269–273.

Wild, N., & Pavio, S. (2003). Psychological adjustment, coping, and emotional regulation as predictors of post-traumatic growth. *Journal of Aggression, Maltreatment and Trauma, 8*, 97–122.

5 Child maltreatment and autobiographical memory development: emotion regulation and trauma-related psychopathology

Deborah Alley, Yoojin Chae, Ingrid Cordon, Anne Kalomiris, and Gail S. Goodman

> The conflict between the will to deny horrible events and the will to proclaim them aloud is the central dialectic of psychological trauma.
> (Herman, *Trauma and Recovery*, 1992)

Our chapter concerns child maltreatment and autobiographical memory development. Specifically, we address how memory development can be influenced by the trauma of child abuse and by the emotion regulation problems and trauma-related psychopathology that can ensue. Research reveals that individuals with childhood abuse histories, like those without such histories, typically have particularly accurate memories for stressful life events. However, autobiographical memory deficits are observed in a subset of individuals who experienced childhood maltreatment. Although further research is needed, studies indicate that these deficits are not due to maltreatment per se, but are rather predicted by individual differences in emotion regulation strategies, likely honed in response to maltreatment, which are often associated with trauma-related psychopathology.

In this chapter, a selective review of research that links child maltreatment with trauma-related psychopathology in children and adults is provided, with a special focus on posttraumatic stress disorder (PTSD), dissociation, and depression, followed by a brief discussion of the neurobiological effects of trauma as related to autobiographical memory development. Then, we describe theoretical reasons as to why child abuse victims typically have particularly accurate memories of trauma-related information, followed by a review of theories pertaining to why a subset of child maltreatment victims show impaired memories for such information. Next, we present our autobiographical memory development model that places the role of attachment at the forefront of understanding emotion regulation for negative life experiences. We then turn to our own research findings on maltreatment experiences and memory development. Several of the ideas we propose are admittedly speculative. We hope that these ideas can nevertheless help move the field forward in a positive direction.

Childhood maltreatment and trauma-related psychopathology

Childhood maltreatment (e.g., physical or sexual abuse) can have far-reaching negative effects on development (Cicchetti & Toth, 2004) and increase the lifetime risk of trauma-related psychopathologies, including PTSD (Berntsen et al., 2012; Leeson & Nixon, 2011; Macfie et al., 2001; Widom, 1999; Widom et al., 2007). The risk is especially great when children experience multiple types of childhood maltreatment that start early in life, leading to cumulative adversity (e.g., Finkelhor et al., 2009).

The resulting trauma-related psychopathologies are associated with emotion regulation strategies and dysregulations (Shields & Cicchetti, 1998), some of which likely affect autobiographical memory. Emotion regulation refers to the approaches taken by an individual to deal with arousing emotions, ideally in flexible and adaptive ways, as opposed to less flexible and less adaptive ways, such as attempting to avoid thinking about the trauma later as a means to reduce negative feelings (Bowlby, 1980; Gross & Thompson, 2007; Shields & Cicchetti, 1998; Shipman & Zeman, 2001).

PTSD

A history of childhood abuse increases the chance of developing PTSD in childhood and in adulthood (e.g., Berntsen et al., 2012; Perry & Azad, 1999; Silva et al., 2000; Widom et al., 2007). PTSD is a chronic psychiatric disorder characterized by anxiety and memory problems (e.g., Rubin et al., 2008). Approximately one-third of maltreatment victims are diagnosed with PTSD in their lifetimes, and many more have PTSD symptoms, even if not reaching criteria for the diagnosis (Vranceanu et al., 2007; Widom, 1999). Family violence in childhood is the strongest predictor of developing military deployment-related PTSD in adulthood (Berntsen et al., 2012). Some of PTSD's most characteristic features include involuntary intrusions (i.e., "flashbacks") of traumatic memories and avoidance of reminders of the precipitating trauma. The involuntary intrusion of memories may reflect the evolutionarily based need to remember traumatic events in vivid detail so as to avoid the events in the future. The avoidance component of PTSD can be viewed as an (unsuccessful) emotion regulation strategy to limit the processing and memory (including the involuntary memory) of traumatic experiences. Further discussions of involuntary intrusive memories are provided by Ehlers, Chapter 6; Moulds and Krans, Chapter 8; and Berntsen, Chapter 9.

Dissociative disorders

Dissociative disorders have also been attributed to childhood trauma (e.g., Putnam, 1997; but see Giesbrecht et al., 2008). Victims of child maltreatment demonstrate more dissociative symptoms than nonmaltreated individuals (e.g., Eisen et al., 2007). Dissociative disorders are characterized by a wide range of aberrations to typical integrative roles of memory, consciousness, and identity, which can result in amnesia, depersonalization, and general confusion (Eisen & Lynn, 2001). Dissociation can become a stable emotion coping mechanism among child maltreatment victims, who may use dissociation to escape negative affect by preventing potentially haunting memories of abuse from reaching cognitive awareness or from intruding on daily functioning (Becker-Blease et al., 2004; Hulette et al., 2008). Dissociation can therefore also be viewed as an avoidant emotion regulation strategy.

Depression

Depression is often comorbid with PTSD and dissociation. Although depression can result from many causes, childhood maltreatment has consistently emerged as a predictive factor (Jaffee et al., 2002). Younger age at onset of maltreatment is related to greater likelihood of depressive symptoms in childhood and adulthood (Kaplow & Widom, 2007; Toth et al., 1992; Widom et al., 2007). Depression may be further exacerbated by aberrations in interpersonal functioning and poor emotion regulation (Kim & Cicchetti, 2010; Levendonsky et al., 1995). Depression is associated with lack of specific recall, which may result from avoidance of autobiographical memories (Williams et al., 2007). Thus, avoidant emotion regulation strategies are implicated in depression.

Conclusion

Childhood maltreatment can potentially contribute to the development of PTSD, dissociation, and depression. These trauma-related disorders involve maladaptive emotion regulation strategies, such as avoidance of trauma memories, which at least in theory can result in memory problems.

Neurobiological perspectives on trauma and autobiographical memory development

There is considerable interest at present in the possible neural underpinnings of trauma-related disorders and memory functioning throughout development. Thus, we provide a selective review of research concerning neurobiological perspectives on trauma, development, and autobiographical memory.

As it turns out, autobiographical memories are distributed over many neural systems (Rubin, 2005). Regions throughout the brain, from frontal regions involved in retrieving episodic memories to posterior regions involved in sensory processing, are activated during autobiographical recall (Addis et al., 2011; Conway et al., 2002; Maguire, 2001; Svoboda et al., 2006). In addition, for emotional autobiographical memories, right hemisphere regions (Winston et al., 2002), including the amygdala, are recruited (Greenberg et al., 2005; McGaugh, 2002). Protracted development of the core structures of autobiographical memory results in potential vulnerability of these neural areas. As a result, trauma and/or prolonged stress may disrupt brain development and the neurobiological systems concerned with brain maturation and function (Watts-English et al., 2006). Because of the prolonged development of core autobiographical memory structures, the timing of trauma may have differential consequences for brain development and function, and subsequently for autobiographical memory development (Andersen et al., 2008; Teicher et al., 2003; 2004; 2006).

Neuroscience research of particular interest here has focused on PTSD. One neurocircuitry model of adult PTSD posits that the amygdala is hyperresponsive; the medial prefrontal cortex is hyporesponsive; and the medial prefrontal cortex and the hippocampus fail to inhibit the amygdala (Shin et al., 2006). These trauma-related brain effects may influence (or reflect) behavioral functioning, such as decrement in the efficiency and flexibility of cognitive processing, deficits in memory and learning, and alterations in emotion processing (Behen et al., 2009; Chugani et al., 2001; Cicchetti et al., 2010; Shackman et al., 2007). However, although brain imaging studies of adults with trauma histories suggest that PTSD symptoms may adversely affect the volume and function of core brain structures of the autobiographical memory network (e.g., Behen et al., 2009; Bremner et al., 2003; Hanson et al., 2010; Tomada et al., 2009), these findings have not been consistently observed among maltreated children, including those with PTSD (Watts-English et al., 2006; but see Andersen et al., 2008; Teicher et al., 2012). It is possible that the adverse effects of trauma on brain structures, for example, on the hippocampus, are not evident until later in development after prolonged exposure to glucocorticoids (e.g., Saplosky, 2000; see Bryant, Chapter 2). However, given that there is some indication that children's hippocampal and prefrontal cortex activity may indeed be adversely affected by trauma-related PTSD (Carrion et al., 2010; De Bellis et al., 2010; Garrett et al., 2012; Richert et al., 2006), there is still reason to seriously consider this possibility. In any case, because of the paucity of research, it is unclear how these adverse neurobiological effects relate to the development of autobiographical memory (e.g., overgeneral autobiographical memory [Valentino et al., 2009; Williams, 1996] or impaired semantic autobiographical memory [Meesters et al., 2000]). It is possible that, across development, amygdala hyperactivity coupled with lack of hippocampal and prefrontal cortex inhibition contributes to heightened memory for trauma-related information, whereas hyporesponsiveness of the medial prefrontal cortex contributes to greater memory error. Of importance for our thesis, most of the findings identify PTSD, rather than maltreatment per se, as contributing to the effects uncovered.

Theoretical issues related to emotion regulation, trauma-related psychopathology, and autobiographical memory in maltreated children and adults

The associations between child maltreatment and later mental health problems, such as PTSD, dissociation, and depression, are well documented, as are associations for adults between childhood trauma and neurobiological changes; however, conclusive scientific inferences as to the effects of child maltreatment on memory are less straightforward. Research indicates that maltreated children's basic memory processes are not significantly different from those of nonmaltreated children (Howe et al., 2011). There are observed differences between maltreated and nonmaltreated children's and adults' memory *performance*, but those performance differences do not always suggest poorer autobiographical memory abilities in maltreated individuals; at times they suggest equal if not better performance in victims of child abuse (Eisen et al., 2007; Goodman et al., 2009). In this section, we first discuss several prominent theories, psychological mechanisms, and empirical findings that indicate heightened autobiographical memory for negative experiences in individuals with histories of trauma and/or trauma-related psychopathology. We then turn to several prominent theories, psychological mechanisms, and empirical findings that indicate impaired autobiographical memory for negative experiences in a subset of child maltreatment victims.

Heightened autobiographical memory for negative experiences

There is reason to believe that children who suffer trauma, especially chronic abuse, will have particularly accurate memory for negative autobiographical experiences. In fact, there are a host of basic memory mechanisms that may contribute to accurate memory for trauma-related information in child abuse victims. These include the positive effects on memory of such factors as distinctiveness, arousal, familiarity and "expertise," self-schema processing, and elaboration and rehearsal (e.g., see Howe, 2006; Howe & Otgaar, 2013; McWilliams et al., 2013). These processes are undoubtedly related to autobiographical memory for traumatic incidents in child abuse victims as well as individuals with no such histories. Several of the theories mentioned below rely on some of these basic memory process notions, but add a level of analysis specific to traumatic experiences. As we (and others) have argued previously, traumatic events may often have a special robustness in memory because of their bolstering by neural circuits or structures, such as by the amygdala, specifically evolved to ensure robust memory for traumatic threats (Cordon et al., 2004; Cordon et al., 2013).

Survival processing Nairne (2010) proposed that humans evolved to prioritize survival-related information with adaptive significance. Indeed, information processed for its relevance to survival is remembered better than the same information processed in other contexts (Nairne et al., 2008; Otgaar et al., 2010). In regard to child maltreatment victims' memory, survival processing may be activated repeatedly throughout childhood. According to Nairne's theory, one would expect children (perhaps even into adulthood) to have particularly robust and accurate memories for abusive experiences because these experiences are relevant not only to current survival but also to survival in our ancestral past.

Christianson's model Christianson (1992) proposed that during a traumatic experience attention is acutely focused on the main features of the stressor, and attention to peripheral details is diminished. As such, memory for the central details of an emotional event should be particularly robust.

Christianson's model is based primarily on studies of adults' memories for a single stressful event. Rather than facing a single traumatic incident, child maltreatment victims are likely to experience chronic abuse or multiple forms of maltreatment (Cicchetti & Toth, 2004). The studies on which Christianson relied did not concern child maltreatment victims or traumatized individuals. However, expanding on Christianson's ideas, it can be proposed that the acute focus on trauma-related information becomes crystallized in abuse victims, resulting in greater processing of and memory for trauma-related experiences. Indeed, more severe childhood abuse has been associated with better memory for the abuse in adolescents and adults (Alexander et al., 2005; see also Quas et al., 2010).

Foa's "fear network" theory Foa's theory, aimed at explaining PTSD, can be construed to predict memory for emotional stimuli in child abuse victims. For example, to the extent that childhood trauma victims have developed "fear networks" (i.e., mental structures that link and keep active trauma and fearful information), an overfocus on trauma cues that signal threat to safety or serve as reminders of past threats may lead to particularly accurate memory for such information (Foa et al., 1991). According to Foa's theory, people who develop anxiety disorders such as PTSD following traumatic events form mental networks of fear-related information that are activated by the presentation of relevant information.

Indeed, a heightened sensitivity to threat cues has been observed in maltreated children. For instance, in a selective attention task, physically abused children compared with nonmaltreated children were slower to disengage from angry faces (Pollak & Tolley-Schell, 2003). In addition, among traumatized individuals with PTSD, an increased Stroop interference effect was uncovered for trauma-related material as compared with neutral words (e.g., Dubner & Motta, 1999). Such an attentional bias may lead to accurate memory for traumatic or negative information and impaired memory for neutral or positive information (Moradi et al., 1999; 2000). To the extent that negative experiences are retained with particular accuracy (e.g., Berntsen et al., 2011; Christianson, 1992; Goodman et al., 1991), when asked to recall past experiences, child maltreatment victims should produce a relatively high percentage of negative autobiographical memories, especially those child victims with emotional disorders such as PTSD (for review, see Berntsen et al., 2011).

Impaired autobiographical memory for negative experiences

Some individuals show memory deficits about childhood events, including maltreatment experiences (Edelstein et al., 2005; Greenhoot et al., 2005; Ogle et al., 2011; Valentino et al., 2009). In our view, these deficits may reflect, at least in part, avoidant emotion regulation strategies. Below, we review several theories that explain inaccurate or incomplete autobiographical memory of childhood trauma victims.

Dissociation and repression Some theorists suggest that memories for traumatic experiences are particularly inaccurate or even absent. For example, van der Kolk and Fisler (1995) asserted that at the time of encoding, traumatic memories are "dissociated" and encoded as sensory fragments without cohesion, resulting in incomplete memory traces. Their ideas harken back to Janet's (1919/1976) theory of dissociation and memory. Others (e.g., Freud, 1909/1995; Terr, 1991) theorized that traumatic memories are "repressed" from conscious awareness to avoid reliving psychologically painful experiences. In support of this view, based on the findings that a significant number of women failed to disclose their childhood sexual abuse histories, Williams (1994) concluded that childhood abuse experiences could be completely forgotten, possibly through the "special memory mechanism" of repression. Although the participants might have been reluctant to disclose painful or embarrassing memories with strangers, they did disclose many other painful and embarrassing experiences, including ones of a sexual nature. Similarly, Goodman et al. (2003) found that dissociation predicted lack of memory for childhood sexual abuse, whereas abuse severity predicted more accurate memory. Thus, dissociation may play a key role in "lost memory" of abuse. However, it is difficult to scientifically test dissociation and repression theories, and the theories have been challenged (e.g., Giesbrecht et al., 2008; Loftus, 1993; Rubin et al., 2008). Moreover, there is evidence that traumatic memories are particularly coherent rather than disjointed (Berntsen et al., 2011; Rubin, 2005). Still, the notion of avoidance of painful memory as an emotion regulation strategy is implicit in dissociation and repression theories.

Orienting versus defensive responses Deffenbacher et al. (2004) also proposed that highly stressful events are poorly remembered. Specifically, they argued that less stressful events are remembered with greater accuracy than are more stressful events because the former involve orienting responses (activation mode of processing), whereas the latter involve defensive responses (arousal mode of processing). Defensive responses could be conceived as a failure in successful emotion regulation such that the organism becomes overly aroused and then cannot process information to form a rich memory. To support their proposal, a meta-analysis was performed. Included in the meta-analysis were studies such as that by Morgan et al. (2004), who examined eyewitness capabilities of active-duty military personnel enrolled in a survival school program. After twelve hours of confinement in a mock prisoner-of-war camp, participants experienced a high-stress interrogation and a low-stress interrogation by different interrogators (order was counterbalanced). A day after release from the prisoner-of-war camp, participants viewed a fifteen-person live lineup regarding the interrogator. For the low-stress condition, the hit and false alarm rates were 0.62 and 0.35, respectively, but comparable rates for the high stress condition were 0.27 and 0.73, respectively. Thus, memory accuracy for the high-stress interrogators suffered.

Overall, Deffenbacher et al. provide provocative evidence that memory for traumatic experiences may be disrupted or reduced. However, their model does not explicitly consider individual differences, although, to their credit, Deffenbacher et al. mention that individual differences likely play an important role.

Overgeneral memory Because severely abused children have likely also been maltreated repeatedly, an enduring schematic representation of abuse can be formed that blends specific instances and limits access to detailed memories (Greenhoot et al., 2005). Moreover, "functional avoidance" of painful memories can take place, in which child victims regulate their affect by not accessing details of life experiences. This effect is referred to as overgeneral memory (Valentino et al., 2009; Williams, 1996). Williams (1996) proposed that traumatized children learn to truncate autobiographical memory retrieval at an overgeneral stage to avoid experiencing negative affect.

Numerous studies reveal the overgeneral memory effect in traumatized individuals (e.g., Greenhoot et al., 2005; Johnson et al., 2005; see Williams et al., 2007). For instance, adolescents with more recent exposure to high levels of family violence produce shorter autobiographical memory reports about positive, negative, and neutral experiences, in addition to fewer negative memories in response to neutral cues (Greenhoot et al., 2005). For additional findings related to overgeneral memory during trauma, see McNally and Robinaugh (Chapter 12). Overgeneral memory may seem to be an adequate emotion regulation strategy for avoiding negative emotions. However, it is in the long term linked to impaired problem-solving abilities, delayed psychological recovery, and increased depression (Williams et al., 2007).

Our approach

We recently proposed a model that sheds light on the contradictory theories and empirical findings concerning child maltreatment and autobiographical memory development. This model reviewed below features the fundamental role of negative life events, attachment orientations, and emotion regulation in autobiographical memory development (Chae et al., 2011a; Goodman & Melinder, 2007).

Attachment and autobiographical memory model From an evolutionary perspective, the emergence of autobiographical memory has adaptive value and helps humans survive. Particularly negative experiences are well retained in memory, because individuals may need to recount, consider, and reflect on their past to avoid encountering dangerous situations again. Moreover, negative events are attachment related, given that children learn to look to their main caretakers (e.g., parents) for both protection from and understanding of such events.

Based on a concept from attachment theory coined "defensive exclusion" (Bowlby, 1980; 1987), attachment styles and associated internal working models likely act as affective and cognitive filters that influence attention to, processing of, and memory for distressing information. As one example, avoidantly attached children whose bids for care have been rejected or belittled may regulate the processing of (i.e., defend against) emotionally negative, attachment-eliciting information with the goal of preventing the negative affect associated with reminders of attachment-related loss. When defensive strategies are employed and potentially upsetting information is not fully processed, the attachment system is less likely to be activated, thus reducing psychological pain or discomfort but at the same time impairing memory. In contrast, securely attached children who have expectations of a supportive caregiver may cope with stress by directing attention toward and thinking coherently about negative experiences.

Also, parents' attachment may affect their behaviors toward their children in distressing situations (e.g., providing support or comfort, discussing the event afterward). Secure parents are more likely to discuss negative life experiences elaborately and openly and provide children with reminders, words, and emotion regulation that facilitate coherent, accurate memories, compared with more avoidant parents who may eschew discussion of negative events.[1] Therefore, children's own and their parents' attachment orientations have profound implications for the development of autobiographical memory and further create individual differences in recollections of negative experiences (Alexander et al., 2002). Research on adult attachment indicates that these early interactions with parents create emotion regulation strategies that are likely to follow an individual into adulthood, both for children who experience trauma and for those who do not (Mikulincer & Shaver, 2007), and therefore these strategies may affect autobiographical memory not only in childhood but also in the adult years.

---

[1] For effects of attachment anxiety (e.g., and possible rumination) on parent–child conversations about negative events, see Fivush and Sales (2006).

Because child maltreatment constitutes a negative life event, this model would be effective in predicting autobiographical memory development in maltreated populations. Experiencing repeated childhood traumas, especially if coupled with parental or child avoidant attachment tendencies, may lead to defensive coping and avoidant emotion-regulation strategies that affect the quality and quantity of later recollections (Maughan & Cicchetti, 2002; Williams et al., 2007). We thus emphasize important individual differences in emotion regulation strategies that are employed by traumatized (and some nontraumatized) individuals (Goodman et al., 2009). In the next section, we present research from our own laboratory that examined autobiographical memory in children and adults with documented maltreatment histories.

Research on emotion regulation, trauma-related psychopathology, and autobiographical memory in child maltreatment victims

Our research primarily aims to examine the circumstances under which individuals can provide accurate and complete autobiographical memory about childhood experiences. Of particular importance to the topic of the present chapter, emotion regulation and associated psychopathology have proven to be better predictors of autobiographical memory errors, rather than maltreatment status per se (e.g., Eisen et al., 2007).

We recently examined overgeneral memory and avoidant coping in adolescents and adults with or without histories of child sexual abuse (Harris et al., 2009). A measure of avoidant coping was included to assess emotion regulation. Results showed that participants with or without child sexual abuse histories were equally likely to evince overgeneral memory. However, avoidant coping was a robust, significant predictor of lack of memory specificity about childhood events, even when numerous other factors (e.g., age, gender, trauma symptoms) were controlled statistically. These findings thus fit with our proposal that emotion regulation is the better predictor of memory than maltreatment status.

The role of emotion regulation in autobiographical memory is also a possible explanation for our research findings on maltreated children's autobiographical memory for trauma-related experiences (Eisen et al., 2002; 2007). In this series of studies, we directly tested autobiographical memory abilities in maltreatment victims in relation to trauma-related psychopathology and cognitive functioning. Our participants included 328 three- to sixteen-year-olds who were admitted to an inpatient unit, to take part in a five-day comprehensive forensic evaluation for suspected child maltreatment. As part of the evaluation, a clinical psychologist assessed for PTSD and general psychological functioning. Trauma symptoms, including dissociation, and basic cognitive functioning were also assessed.

In addition, children received a complete physical examination, including an anogenital examination, by a physician to detect signs of abuse. Because the examination involved genital contact, it could be viewed as an analog for sexual abuse. We also had access to records related to the children's past involvement with social services and to interviews conducted with parents and caretakers. Thus, we could obtain in-depth information on each child's history and test the influences of maltreatment and psychopathology on the children's memory for various events that occurred during the five-day assessment (e.g., see Chae et al., 2011b).

With regard to memory for the standardized anogenital examination, abuse status was generally not significantly related to memory performance. An important exception was that the sexual abuse group showed particularly accurate memory about the anogenital exam. This finding is in accordance with the notion of fear networks and a heightened sensitivity to perceived trauma-related information. It might alternatively be explained by greater knowledge concerning genital touch.

Dissociation can be conceived as an avoidant emotion regulation strategy. In our study, more dissociative tendencies combined with higher self-reported trauma symptoms and higher physiological stress responses (as indexed by cortisol response) were related to more memory errors. High dissociators with more trauma symptoms may have been more stressed by the anogenital examination, thereby evoking emotion regulation strategies that are maladaptive for accurate memory performance. If so, this would provide some support for our theory on emotion regulation and memory. Overall, findings from this research again lend credence to the notion that maltreatment, in and of itself, is generally insufficient for predicting deficits in autobiographical memory.

A second line of research from our laboratory has been fruitful in elucidating the effects of development, trauma-related psychopathology, and emotion regulation on long-term memory for documented child sexual abuse. We followed a sample of 218 child sexual abuse victims who were originally studied when they were between the ages of four and seventeen (Goodman et al., 1992). For each child we obtained details of the abuse (e.g., duration, severity, perpetrator identity) from several sources (e.g., victim statements, prosecution files), and measured psychological and behavioral functioning. Starting approximately thirteen years following the original study, the participants were recontacted, and information was obtained about current mental health status, past and current victimizations, and memory for the abuse.

We successfully contacted 175 victims who ranged in age from 16.7 to 30.3 years at the time of the interview. Of those contacted, 81% disclosed the documented abuse (Goodman et al., 2003), which suggests that, contrary to repression theories, for the majority of this sample child sexual abuse memories were not subject to special memory mechanisms that make the victims keep traumatic memories away from awareness. To identify individual difference variables associated with child sexual abuse disclosure, we examined the age when abuse ended, gender, abuse severity, ethnicity, relationship to perpetrator, legal involvement, and maternal support at the time of the original disclosure. Being older when the abuse ended (six years or older), experiencing more severe abuse (e.g., more force used, longer duration), and receiving maternal support significantly predicted disclosure. Some theories might have implied that participants who experienced the most severe abuse would fail to disclose documented child sexual abuse due to those memories being "lost." However, our results suggest that memory for child sexual abuse largely operates similarly to memory for other personally significant life experiences.

Nonetheless, for a subset of the victims, lack of disclosure could have reflected lack of memory for the abuse. Moreover, by some accounts, dissociation should be related to nondisclosure because of the inability to form a cohesive memory and narrative of the event (e.g., van der Kolk & Fisler, 1995). In our study, high dissociation scores were associated with lack of memory of the past abuse (or, at least, nondisclosure). Dissociation is a prevalent form of emotion regulation after traumatic experiences (e.g., Hulette et al., 2011). This pattern is consistent with ideas of generally better memory for trauma in most victims, but not in the subset of victims who utilize certain (e.g., avoidant) emotion regulation strategies.

In this longitudinal study, we also examined the role of PTSD symptoms in memory for childhood sexual abuse experiences. Foa et al.'s theory (1991) suggests that PTSD should be associated with a greater tendency to remember the abuse given the trend toward hypervigilance to trauma-related stressors. We evaluated the accuracy of long-term memories for the abuse (Alexander et al., 2005) by comparing the memory reports with the original abuse documentation (Goodman et al., 1992). Additionally, we examined individual difference variables theorized to be associated with memory accuracy, such as nominating the documented child sexual abuse as the most traumatic experience in one's life. Results revealed that individuals who reported the documented child sexual abuse as their most traumatic life event had especially accurate memories for the abuse. This finding suggests that memories of childhood sexual abuse, like memories for other traumatic events, are often relatively well retained over time. Also of importance is that, for victims who indicated other events as their most traumatic life experiences, PTSD symptomology predicted more accurate memory for the documented child sexual abuse. This finding is in line with the theory that individuals with PTSD pay particular attention to trauma-related information encountered in their lives. In addition, abuse severity positively predicted memory accuracy.

Finally, in this same sample of victims, we examined attachment-related differences in memory for childhood sexual abuse and found that avoidantly attached individuals showed worse long-term memory for more severe abuse (Edelstein et al., 2005; see also Melinder et al., 2013). They may limit the processing of stressful information in an attempt to avoid activating their attachment systems ("defensive exclusion"). In addition, for less avoidant individuals, more severe abuse was associated with better long-term recall, as consistent with our thesis and also suggested by the theory that posits enhanced memory for core features of stressful experiences (e.g., Christianson, 1992).[2]

Overall, our results indicate that many adults do remember and disclose childhood sexual abuse, in particular, severe experiences, even after long delays. It is notable that more traumatic responses, as evidenced by PTSD, were associated with particularly accurate memory. However, some individuals with more dissociative tendencies or avoidant attachment orientations display an apparent loss of or reduction in painful memories. Our studies, however, did not directly assess facets of memory monitoring that might be more problematic for trauma victims with PTSD symptoms (e.g., Goodman, et al., 2011).

---

[2] Research on attachment and child maltreatment indicates that child abuse victims are particularly likely to form disorganized attachments (called "fearful avoidant attachments" in the adult attachment literature), which can be viewed as scoring high on both attachment avoidance and attachment anxiety dimensions (Mikulncer & Shaver, 2007). The avoidant dimension, as opposed to the anxiety dimension, appears to drive the memory effects we discuss in the present chapter. Moreover, attachment has been interpreted from the perspective of emotion regulation (Mikulncer & Shaver, 2007). From this perspective, although internal working models of attachment are formed early in life through interactions with one's caretaker and influence emotion regulation strategies, such internal working models and strategies can be influenced by events throughout life. Thus, although early experience is particularly important, such that early child abuse would be especially problematic, abusive experiences in childhood generally can influence internal working models and also have an effect on emotion regulation tendencies.

Conclusion

Autobiographical memory advantages and deficits exist in children and adults who experienced childhood maltreatment. The advantages may largely result from evolutionary forces that promote particularly accurate and robust memory for negative, trauma-related information and provide "the will to proclaim horrible events aloud." However, important individual differences exist, particularly in regard to emotion regulation strategies, which are also often associated with trauma-related psychopathology. Specifically, avoidant emotion regulation strategies (e.g., functional avoidance, defensive exclusion, avoidant coping) that provide "the will to deny horrible events" are associated with poor autobiographical memory for childhood experiences. "The conflict between the will to deny horrible events and the will to proclaim them aloud," as described by Judith Herman, is not only "the central dialectic of psychological trauma" (Herman, 1992), but also a key to understanding individual differences in the effects of trauma on autobiographical memory development.

REFERENCES

Addis, D. R., Roberts, R. P., & Schacter, D. L. (2011). Age-related neural changes in autobiographical remembering and imagining. *Neuropsychologia*, *49*, 3656–3669.

Alexander, K. W., Goodman, G. S., Schaaf, J. M., Edelstein, R. S., Quas, J. A., & Shaver, P. R. (2002). The role of attachment and cognitive inhibition in children's memory and suggestibility for a stressful event. *Journal of Experimental Child Psychology*, *83*, 262–290.

Alexander, K. W., Quas, J. A., Goodman, G. S., Ghetti, S., Edelstein, R. S., Redlich, A. D., Cordon, I. M., & Jones, D. P. H. (2005). Traumatic impact predicts long-term memory for documented child sexual abuse. *Psychological Science*, *16*, 33–40.

Andersen, S. L., Tomada, A., Vincow, E. S., Valente, E., Polcari, A., & Teicher, M. H. (2008). Preliminary evidence for sensitive periods in the effect of childhood sexual abuse on regional brain development. *Journal of Neuropsychiatry and Clinical Neuroscience*, *20*, 292–301.

Becker-Blease, K. A., Freyd, J. J., & Pears, K. C. (2004). Preschoolers' memory for threatening information depends on trauma history and attentional context: implications for the development of dissociation. *Journal of Trauma and Dissociation*, *5*, 113–131.

Behen, M. E., Muzik, O., Saporta, A. S. D., Wilson, B. J., Pai, D., Hua, J., & Chugani, H. T. (2009). Abnormal fronto-striatal connectivity in children with histories of early deprivation: a diffusion tensor imaging study. *Brain Imaging and Behavior*, *3*, 292–297.

Berntsen, D., Rubin, D. C., & Siegler, I. C. (2011). Two versions of life: emotionally negative and positive life events have different roles in the organization of life story and identity. *Emotion, 11,* 1190–1201.

Berntsen, D., Johannessen, K. B., Thomsen, Y. D., Bertelsen, M., Hoyle, R. H., & Rubin, D. C. (2012). Peace and war: trajectories of posttraumatic stress disorder symptoms before, during and after military deployment in Afghanistan. *Psychological Science, 23,* 1557–1565.

Bowlby, J. (1980). *Attachment and Loss.* Vol. 3: *Loss: Sadness and Depression.* New York: Basic Books.

— (1987). Defensive processes in the light of attachment theory. In J. L. Sacksteder, D. P. Schwart, & Y. Akabane (eds.), *Attachment and the Therapeutic Process: Essays in Honor of Otto Allen Will, Jr.* (pp. 63–79). Madison, CT: International Universities Press.

Bremner J. D., Vythilingam, M., Vermetten, E., Southwick, S. M., McGlashan, T., Nazeer, A., & Charney, D. S. (2003). MRI and PET study of deficits in hippocampal structure and function in women with childhood sexual abuse and posttraumatic stress disorder. *American Journal of Psychiatry, 160,* 924–932.

Carrion, V. G., Haas, B. W., Garrett, A., Song, S., & Reiss, A. L. (2010). Reduced hippocampal activity in youth with posttraumatic stress symptoms: an fMRI study. *Journal of Pediatric Psychology, 35,* 559–569.

Chae, Y., Goodman, G. S., & Edelstein, R. S. (2011a). Autobiographical memory development from an attachment perspective: the special role of negative events. In J. B. Benson (ed.), *Advances in Child Development and Behavior* (Vol. 40, pp. 1–49). Burlington, VT: Academic Press.

Chae, Y., Goodman, G. S., Eisen, M., & Qin, J. (2011b). Event memory and suggestibility in abused and neglected children: trauma-related psychopathology and cognitive functioning. *Journal of Experimental Child Psychology, 110,* 520–538.

Christianson, S.-Å. (1992). Emotional stress and eyewitness memory: a critical review. *Psychological Bulletin, 112,* 284–309.

Chugani, H. T., Behen, M. E., Muzik, O., Juhász, C., Nagy, F., & Chugani, D. C. (2001). Local brain functional activity following early deprivation: a study of postinstitutionalized Romanian orphans. *Neuroimage, 14,* 1290–1301.

Cicchetti, D., & Toth, S. (2004). Child maltreatment. *Annual Review of Clinical Psychology, 1,* 409–438.

Cicchetti, D., Rogosch, F. A., Gunnar, M. R., & Toth, S. L. (2010). The differential impacts of early physical and sexual abuse and internalizing problems on daytime cortisol rhythm in school-aged children. *Child Development, 81,* 252–269.

Conway, M. A., Pleydell-Pearce, C. W., Whitecross, S., & Sharpe, H. (2002). Brain imaging autobiographical memory. *Psychology of Learning and Motivation, 41,* 229–264.

Cordon, I., Pipe, M.-E., Sayfan, L., Melinder, A., & Goodman, G. S. (2004). Memory for traumatic events in early childhood. *Developmental Review, 24,* 101–132.

Cordon, I. M., Melinder, A. M., Edelstein, R. S., & Goodman, G. S. (2013). Children's and adults' memory for emotional pictures: differentiating valence and arousal using the Developmental Affective Photo System. *Journal of Experimental Child Psychology, 114,* 339–356.

De Bellis, M. D., Hooper, S. R., Woolley, D. P., & Shenk, C. E. (2010). Demographic, maltreatment, and neurobiological correlates of PTSD symptoms in children and adolescents. *Journal of Pediatric Psychology, 35,* 570–577.

Deffenbacher, K. A., Bornstein, B. H., Penrod, S. D., & McGorty, E. K. (2004). A meta-analytic review of the effects of high stress on eyewitness memory. *Law and Human Behavior, 28,* 687–706.

Dubner, A. E., & Motta, R. W. (1999). Sexually and physically abused foster care children and posttraumatic stress disorder. *Journal of Consulting and Clinical Psychology, 67,* 367–373.

Edelstein, R. S., Ghetti, S., Quas, J. A., Goodman, G. S., Alexander, K. W., Redlich, A. D., & Cordon, I. M. (2005). Individual differences in emotional memory: adult attachment and long-term memory for child sexual abuse. *Personality and Social Psychology Bulletin, 31,* 1537–1548.

Eisen, M. L., & Lynn, S. J. (2001). Dissociation, memory, and suggestibility in adults and children. *Applied Cognitive Psychology, 15,* 49–73.

Eisen, M. L., Qin, J., Goodman, G. S., & Davis, S. L. (2002). Memory and suggestibility in maltreated children: age, stress arousal, dissociation, and psychopathology. *Journal of Experimental Child Psychology, 83,* 167–212.

Eisen, M. L., Goodman, G. S., Qin, J., Davis, S., & Crayton, J. (2007). Maltreated children's memory: accuracy, suggestibility, and psychopathology. *Developmental Psychology, 43,* 1275–1294.

Finkelhor, D., Ormrod, R. K., Turner, H. A., & Holt, M. A. (2009). Pathways to poly-victimization. *Child Maltreatment, 14,* 316–329.

Fivush, R., & Sales, J. M. (2006). Coping, attachment, and mother-child narratives of stressful events. *Merrill-Palmer Quarterly, 52,* 125–150.

Foa, E. B., Feske, U., Murdock, T. B., Kozak, M. J., & McCarthy, P. R. (1991). Processing of threat-related information in rape victims. *Journal of Abnormal Psychology, 100,* 156–162.

Freud, S. (1909/1995). *Five Lectures on Psycho-analysis.* New York: Penguin.

Garrett, A. S., Carrion, V., Kletter, H., Karchemskiy, A., Weems, C. F., & Reiss, A. (2012). Brain activation to facial expressions in youth with PTSD symptoms. *Depression and Anxiety, 29,* 449–459.

Giesbrecht, T., Lynn, S. J., Lilienfeld, S. O., & Merckelbach, H. (2008). Cognitive processes in dissociation: an analysis of core theoretical assumptions. *Psychological Bulletin, 134,* 617–647.

Goodman, G. S., & Melinder, A. M. (2007). The development of autobiographical memory: a new model. In S. Magnussen & T. Helstrup (eds.), *Everyday Memory* (pp. 111–134). London: Psychology Press.

Goodman, G. S., Hirschman, J. E., Hepps, D., & Rudy, L. (1991). Children's memory for stressful events. *Merrill-Palmer Quarterly, 37,* 109–157.

Goodman, G. S., Pyle-Taub, E., Jones, D. P. H., England, P., Port, L., Rudy, L., & Prado, L. (1992). Testifying in criminal court: emotional effects on child

sexual assault victims. *Monographs of the Society for Research in Child Development, 57* (5, Serial No. 229).
Goodman, G. S., Ghetti, S., Quas, J. A., Edelstein, R. S., Alexander, K. W., Redlich, A. D., Cordon, I. M., & Jones, D. P. H. (2003). A prospective study of memory for child sexual abuse: new findings to the repressed-memory controversy. *Psychological Science, 14,* 113–118.
Goodman, G. S., Quas, J. A., & Ogle, C. M. (2009). Child maltreatment and memory. *Annual Review of Psychology, 61,* 26.1–26.27.
Goodman, G. S., Ogle, C. M., Block, S. D., Harris, L. S., Larson, R. P., Augusti, E.-M., & Urquiza, A. (2011). False memory for trauma-related Deese–Roediger–McDermott lists in adolescents and adults with histories of child sexual abuse. *Development and Psychopathology, 23,* 423–438.
Greenberg, D. L., Rice, H. J., Cooper, J. J., Cabeza, R., Rubin, D. C., & LaBar, K. S. (2005). Co-activation of the amygdala, hippocampus and inferior frontal gyrus during autobiographical memory retrieval. *Neuropsychologia, 43,* 659–674.
Greenhoot, A. F., McCloskey, L., & Glisky, E. (2005). A longitudinal study of adolescents' recollections of family violence. *Applied Cognitive Psychology, 19,* 719–743.
Gross, J. J., & Thompson, R. A. (2007). Emotion regulation: conceptual foundations. In J. J. Gross (ed.), *Handbook of Emotion Regulation* (pp. 3–24). New York: Guilford Press.
Hanson, J. L., Chung, M. K., Avants, B. B., Shirtcliff, E. A., Gee, J. C., Davidson, R. J., & Pollak, S. D. (2010). Early stress is associated with alterations in the orbitofrontal cortex: a tensor-based morphometry investigation of brain structure and behavioral risk. *Journal of Neuroscience, 30,* 7466–7472.
Harris, L., Block, S., Ogle, C. M., Pineda, A., Urquiza, A., Timmer, S., & Goodman, G. S. (2009, May). Coping and memory in adolescents and adults with maltreatment histories. In A. Greenhoot & G. S. Goodman (chairs), *Does Trauma Adversely Affect Autobiographical Memory?* Symposium presented at the Association of Psychological Science, San Francisco, CA.
Herman, J. L. (1992). *Trauma and Recovery.* New York: Basic Books.
Howe, M. L. (2006). Developmental invariance in distinctiveness effects in memory. *Developmental Psychology, 42,* 1193–1205.
Howe, M. L., & Otgaar, H. (2013). Proximate mechanisms and the development of adaptive memory. *Current Directions in Psychological Sciences, 22,* 16–22.
Howe, M. L., Toth, S. L., & Cicchetti, D. (2011). Can maltreated children inhibit true and false memories for emotional information? *Child Development, 82,* 967–981.
Hulette, A. C., Fisher, P. A., Kim, H. K., Ganger, W., & Landsverk, J. L. (2008). Dissociation in foster preschoolers: a replication and assessment study. *Journal of Trauma Dissociation, 9,* 173–190.
Hulette, A. C., Freyd, J. J., & Fisher, P. A. (2011). Dissociation in middle childhood among foster children with early maltreatment experiences. *Child Abuse & Neglect, 35,* 123–126.

Jaffee, S. R., Moffitt, T. E., Caspi, A., Fombonne, E., Poulton, R., & Martin, J. (2002). Differences in early childhood risk factors for juvenile-onset and adult-onset depression. *Archives of General Psychiatry, 59*, 215–221.

Janet, P. (1976). *Psychological Healing: A Historical and Clinical Study.* 2 vols. E. & C. Paul (Trans.). (Originally published in 1919.)

Johnson, R. J., Greenhoot, A. F., Glisky, E., & McCloskey, L. A. (2005). The relation among abuse, depression, and adolescents' autobiographical memory. *Journal of Clinical Child and Adolescent Psychology, 34*, 235–247.

Kaplow, J. B., & Widom, C. S. (2007). Age of onset of child maltreatment predicts long-term mental health outcomes. *Journal of Abnormal Psychology, 116*, 176–187.

Kim, J., & Cicchetti, D. (2010). Longitudinal pathways linking child maltreatment, emotion regulation, peer relations, and psychopathology. *Journal of Child Psychology and Psychiatry, 51*, 706–716.

Leeson, F., & Nixon, R. D. V. (2011). The role of children's appraisals on adjustment following psychological maltreatment: a pilot study. *Journal of Abnormal Child Psychology, 39*, 759–771.

Levendonsky, A. A., Okun, A., & Parker, J. G. (1995). Depression and maltreatment as predictors of social competence and social problem solving skills in school age children. *Child Abuse & Neglect, 19*, 1183–1195.

Loftus, E. F. (1993). The reality of repressed memory. *American Psychologist, 48*, 518–537.

Macfie, J., Cicchetti, D., & Toth, S. L. (2001). Dissociation in maltreated versus nonmaltreated preschool aged children. *Child Abuse & Neglect, 25*, 1253–1267.

Maguire, E. A. (2001). Neuroimaging studies of autobiographical event memory. *The Royal Society: Philosophical Transactions: Biological Sciences, 356*(1413), 1441–1451.

Maughan, A., & Cicchetti, D. (2002). Impact of child maltreatment and interadult violence on children's emotion regulation abilities and socioemotional adjustment. *Child Development, 73*, 1525–1542.

McGaugh, J. L. (2002). Memory consolidation and the amygdala: a systems perspective. *Trends in Neurosciences, 25*, 456–461.

McWilliams, K., Narr, R., Goodman, G. S., Mendoza, M., & Ruiz, S. (2013). Children's memory for their mother's murder: accuracy, suggestibility, and resistance to suggestion. *Memory, 21*, 591–598.

Meesters, C., Merckelbach, H., Muris, P., & Wessel, I. (2000). Autobiographical memory and trauma in adolescents. *Journal of Behavior Therapy and Experimental Psychiatry, 31*, 29–39.

Melinder, A. M., Baugerud, G. A., Ovenstad, K. S., & Goodman, G. S. (2013). Children's memory of removal: a test of attachment theory. *Journal of Traumatic Stress, 26*, 125–133.

Mikulincer, M., & Shaver, P. R. (2007). *Attachment in Adulthood: Structure, Dynamics, and Change.* New York: Guilford Press.

Moradi, A. R., Taghavi, M. R., Neshat-Doost, H. T., Yule, W., & Dalgleish, T. (1999). Performance of children and adolescents with PTSD on the Stroop colour-naming task. *Psychological Medicine, 29*, 415–419.

(2000). Memory bias for emotional information in children and adolescents with posttraumatic stress disorder: a preliminary study. *Journal of Anxiety Disorders, 14*, 521–534.

Morgan, C. A. III, Hazlet, G., Doran, A., Garrett, S., Hoyt, G., Thomas, P., Baranoski, M., & Southwick, S. M. (2004). Accuracy of eyewitness memory for persons encountered during exposure to highly intense stress. *International Journal of Psychiatry and Law, 27*, 265–279.

Nairne, J. S. (2010). Adaptive memory: evolutionary constraints on remembering. *Psychology of Learning and Motivation, 53*, 1–32.

Nairne, J. S., Pandeirada, J. N. S., & Thompson, S. R. (2008). Adaptive memory: the comparative value of survival processing. *Psychological Science, 19*, 176–180.

Ogle, C. M., Block, S. D., Harris, L., Goodman, G. S., Pineda, A., Timmer, S., & Saywitz, K. S. (2011). Autobiographical memory specificity in child sexual abuse victims. *Development and Psychopathology, 23*, 423–428.

Otgaar, H., Smeets, T., & van Bergen, S. (2010). Picturing survival memories: enhanced memory after fitness-relevant processing occurs for verbal and visual stimuli. *Memory & Cognition, 38*, 23–28.

Perry, B. D., & Azad, I. (1999). Posttraumatic stress disorders in children and adolescents. *Current Opinion in Pediatrics, 11*, 310–316.

Pollak, S. D., & Tolley-Schell, S. A. (2003). Selective attention to facial emotion in physically abused children. *Journal of Abnormal Psychology, 112*, 323–338.

Putnam, F. (1997). *Dissociation in Children and Adolescents: A Developmental Perspective*. New York: Guilford Press.

Quas, J. A., Alexander, K. W., Goodman, G. S., Ghetti, S., Edelstein, R. S., & Redlich, A. (2010). Long-term autobiographical memory for legal involvement: individual and sociocontextual predictors. *Cognitive Development, 25*(4), 394–409.

Richert, K. A., Carrion, V. G., Karchemskiy, A., & Reiss, A. L. (2006). Regional differences of the prefrontal cortex in pediatric PTSD: an MRI study. *Depression and Anxiety, 23*, 17–25.

Rubin, D. C. (2005). A basic-systems approach to autobiographical memory. *Current Directions in Psychological Science, 14*, 79–83.

Rubin, D. C., Berntsen, D., & Johansen, M. (2008). A memory based model of posttraumatic stress disorder: evaluating basic assumptions underlying the PTSD diagnosis. *Psychological Review, 115*, 995–1011.

Sapolsky, R. M. (2000). Glucocorticoids and hippocampal atrophy in neuropsychiatric disorders. *Archives of General Psychiatry, 57*, 925–935.

Shackman, J. E., Shackman, A. J., & Pollak, S. D. (2007). Physical abuse amplifies attention to threat and increases anxiety in children. *Emotion, 7*, 132–140.

Shields, A., & Cicchetti, D. (1998). Reactive aggression among maltreated children: the contributions of attention and emotion dysregulation. *Journal of Clinical Child and Adolescent Psychology, 27*, 381–395.

Shin, L. M., Rouch, S., & Pittman, R. K. (2006). Amygdala, prefrontal cortex, and hippocampal functioning in PTSD. *Annals of the New York Academy of Sciences, 1071*, 67–79.

Shipman, K. L. & Zeman, J. (2001). Socialization of children's emotion regulation in mother-child dyads: a developmental psychopathology perspective. *Developmental Psychopathology, 13*, 317–336.

Silva, R. R., Alpert, M., Munoz, D. M., Singh, S., Matzner, F., & Dummit, S. (2000). Stress and vulnerability to posttraumatic stress disorder in children and adolescents. *American Journal of Psychiatry, 157*, 1229–1235.

Svoboda, E., McKinnon, M. C., & Levine, B. (2006). The functional neuroanatomy of autobiographical memory: a meta-analysis. *Neuropsychologia, 44*, 2189–2208.

Teicher, M. H., Andersen, S. L., Polcari, A., Andersen, C.M., Navalta, C. P., & Kim, D. M. (2003). The neurobiological consequences of early stress and childhood maltreatment. *Neuroscience and Biobehavioral Reviews, 27*, 33–44.

Teicher, M. H., Dumont, N. L., Ito, Y., Vaituzis, C., Giedd, J. N., & Andersen, S. L. (2004). Child neglect is associated with reduced corpus callosum area. *Biological Psychiatry, 56*, 80–85.

Teicher, M. H., Tomodoa, A., & Andersen, S. L. (2006). Neurobiological consequences of early stress and childhood maltreatment: are results from human and animal studies comparable? *Annals of the New York Academy of Sciences, 1071*, 313–323.

Teicher, M. H., Anderson, C. M., & Polcari, A. (2012). Childhood maltreatment is associated with reduced volume in the hippocampal subfields CA3, dentate gyrus, and subiculum. *Proceedings of the National Academy of Sciences of the United States of America, 109*, 563–572.

Terr, L. C. (1991). Childhood trauma: an outline and overview. *American Journal of Psychiatry, 148*, 10–20.

Tomoda, A., Suzuki, H., Rabi, K., Sheu, Y. S., Polcari, A., & Teicher, M. H. (2009). Reduced prefrontal cortical gray matter volume in young adults exposed to harsh corporal punishment. *Neuroimage, 47*, T66–T71.

Toth, S. L., Manly, J. T., & Cicchetti, D. (1992). Child maltreatment and vulnerability to depression. *Development and Psychopathology, 4*, 97–112.

Valentino, K., Toth, S. L., & Cicchetti, D. (2009). Autobiographical memory functioning among abused, neglected, and nonmaltreated children: the overgeneral memory effect. *Journal of Child Psychology and Psychiatry, 50*, 1029–1038.

van der Kolk, B. A., & Fisler, R. (1995). Dissociation and the fragmentary nature of traumatic memories: overview and exploratory study. *Journal of Traumatic Stress, 8*, 505–525.

Vranceanu, A. M., Hobfoll, S. E., & Johnson, R. J. (2007). Child multi-type maltreatment and associated depression and PTSD symptoms: the role of social support and stress. *Child Abuse & Neglect, 31*, 71–84.

Watts-English, T., Fortson, B. L., Gibler, N., Hopper, S. R., & De Bellis, M. D. (2006). The psychobiology of maltreatment in childhood. *Journal of Social Issues, 62*, 717–735.

Widom, C. S. (1999). Posttraumatic stress disorder in abused and neglected children grown up. *American Journal of Psychiatry, 156*, 1223–1229.

Widom, C. S., Dumont, K., & Czaja, S. J. (2007). A prospective investigation of major depressive disorder and comorbidity in abused and neglected children grown up. *Archive of General Psychiatry, 64,* 49–65.

Williams, J. M. G. (1996). Depression and the specificity of autobiographical memory. In D. C. Rubin (ed.). *Remembering Our Past: Studies in Autobiographical Memory* (pp. 244–267). Cambridge: Cambridge University Press.

Williams, J. M. G., Barnhofer, T., Crane, C., Hermans, D., Raes, F., Watkins, E., & Dalgleish, T. (2007). Autobiographical memory specificity and emotional disorder. *Psychological Bulletin, 133,* 122–148.

Williams, L. M. (1994). Recall of childhood trauma: a prospective study of women's memories of child sexual abuse. *Journal of Consulting Clinical Psychology, 62,* 1167–1176.

Winston, J. S., Strange, B. A., O'Doherty, J., & Dolan, R. J. (2002). Automatic and intentional brain responses during evaluation of trustworthiness of faces. *Nature Neuroscience, 5,* 277–283.

Part II

Intrusive and involuntary memories

6 Intrusive reexperiencing in posttraumatic stress disorder: memory processes and their implications for therapy

Anke Ehlers

Posttraumatic stress disorder (PTSD) may develop after traumatic events such as sexual or physical assault, severe accidents, bombings, disasters, or war zone experiences. A core symptom of this distressing condition is reexperiencing, which can take the form of intrusive memories, dissociative flashbacks, nightmares, or emotional and/or physiological responding to trauma reminders. Reexperiencing is common in the immediate aftermath of trauma and thus not a sign of psychopathology (e.g., Creamer et al., 1992; Ehlers & Steil, 1995). For most trauma survivors, the frequency and intensity of reexperiencing decrease in the following weeks. Those who develop PTSD, however, may be haunted by recurrent, distressing reexperiencing symptoms for years.

The question of why reexperiencing persists in some people is important for understanding and treating PTSD. This chapter reviews research on cognitive processes that may contribute to its persistence. It focuses on findings that led to the development of a cognitive model and treatment program for PTSD (cognitive therapy for PTSD [CT-PTSD], Ehlers & Clark, 2000). A core idea of this approach is the hypothesis that PTSD persists because trauma survivors perceive a *current* threat, which has two sources: (1) characteristics of trauma memories that lead to reexperiencing and (2) excessively negative appraisals about the meaning of the trauma and its sequelae. The sense of current threat is maintained by maladaptive strategies that people use to control the perceived threat or symptoms. The chapter discusses these factors in turn and outlines how they are addressed in treatment. It is beyond the scope of this chapter to review alternative models of reexperiencing (see Brewin et al., 2010; Foa & Riggs, 1993).

The chapter describes how systematic observations of reexperiencing symptoms in clinical samples of people with PTSD led to hypotheses about possible cognitive mechanisms that may explain core characteristics of these symptoms, studies testing these hypotheses, and the development of treatment techniques that target these mechanisms. The author sees this approach as complementary to the approach described in chapters focusing on the application of research on voluntary and involuntary autobiographical memories to memories of trauma (Rubin, Chapter 3; Berntsen, Chapter 9). However, this chapter takes a somewhat broader view as not all reexperiencing symptoms in PTSD fit the definition of autobiographical memories. Nevertheless, both approaches share the basic assumption that trauma memories and reexperiencing symptoms in PTSD can be understood by general memory processes identified in cognitive psychology and neuroscience. However, it is also hypothesized here that there are systematic individual differences in how the trauma is laid down in memory and how people respond to these memories that are important for explaining the nature and persistence of reexperiencing in PTSD and for informing treatment.

The chapter addresses the following questions:

- What is reexperiencing?
- Do traumatized people with and without PTSD differ in their reexperiencing symptoms?
- Why do so many stimuli trigger reexperiencing in PTSD?
- Why does the content of reexperiencing appear to be happening *now*?
- How do characteristics of trauma memories contribute to distressing meanings of the trauma?
- Why does reexperiencing persist in PTSD?

What is reexperiencing?

Range of reexperiencing symptoms

Reexperiencing in PTSD includes a range of different experiences. Most research to date has concentrated on intrusive memories of the trauma (see also Rubin, Chapter 3; Berntsen, Chapter 9). This form of reexperiencing commonly takes the form of vivid and distressing sensory impressions from certain moments of the trauma (Ehlers et al., 2002). For example, a car crash survivor may reexperience the sight of headlights coming toward him, just like before the crash, or an assault survivor may reexperience a glimpse of the assailant standing before her with a knife before she was attacked.

Interestingly, and importantly for treatment, reexperiencing also includes phenomena that are not recognized as memories by the trauma survivor but can be identified by an observer as signs of memory. This includes reexperiencing affect or physiological reactions from the trauma without awareness that these stem from a memory, a phenomenon named *affect without recollection* (Ehlers & Clark, 2000). For example, Anna,[1] whose trauma involved being chased by a bull, felt an overwhelming urge that she had to "get out of here" when going for a walk in the country and jumped into an icy river. She was not aware of what had triggered this urge. Her partner realized that she had responded to a cow grazing at a distance. Clare, who had been raped by someone who was drunk, subsequently felt sick and sometimes vomited whenever she smelled alcohol, but she did not have memories of the trauma when experiencing these physical responses.

Furthermore, in the presence of idiosyncratic triggers, people with PTSD may lose *all* awareness of current reality and feel and behave as if the trauma was happening in the present, a phenomenon often called dissociative *flashback* (note that some authors use the term "flashback" in a broader sense, namely, as a very vivid involuntary memory; see Clark and colleagues, Chapter 7; Berntsen, 2009). For example, Tom, whose trauma involved being knocked off his motorbike by a car, was walking down a street when he suddenly felt that his body was light as a feather and that he was about to fly through the air. This was accompanied by vivid images of his body being shattered in pieces, just like during his accident. He clung to a lamppost to "save his life." In such flashbacks, memory content and current reality may merge to the extent that people have hallucinatory experiences in that they actually "see," "hear," "smell," or "taste" aspects of the trauma and react to them accordingly. For example, Linda, who had been traumatized in a riot, saw flames coming out of the milk bottle when she was making tea. In the trauma, she had seen petrol bombs flying toward her. Understandably, such experiences are very frightening and puzzling to the individual.

Although both *affect without recollection* and *dissociative flashbacks* stem from an autobiographical experience, they do not neatly fit with the definition of autobiographical memories. They appear to lack a feature of autobiographical memories termed "autonoetic awareness" by Tulving (2002), the awareness of the self in the past. While many intrusive memories after trauma are comparable to other involuntary autobiographical memories (see Rubin, Chapter 3; Berntsen, Chapter 9), "phenomena in which the involuntary mental contents overrule reality more or less completely" are usually considered outside the scope of involuntary autobiographical memory research (Berntsen, 2009, p. 15). Theories and treatments of PTSD, however, need to address these frightening

---

[1] Names and some details have been changed to preserve anonymity.

experiences alongside other involuntary memories. As discussed below, research on associative learning of emotional responses may help explain some of these phenomena and their triggers.

Which moments from the trauma are reexperienced?

Although traumatic events may extend over long periods of time, and many things happen during such events, systematic interviews with patients with PTSD suggest that their recurrent intrusive memories were about a small number of relatively brief moments from the trauma. Examples were "the sound of the impact," "hearing footsteps behind me," or "the eyes of the perpetrator peering through the letterbox" (Ehlers et al., 2002; Hackmann et al., 2004). The content of the recurrent intrusions may give clues about possible mechanisms and targets for treatment. Several studies reported that involuntary trauma memories are related to the most emotional parts of the trauma (e.g., Berntsen & Rubin, 2008; Holmes et al., 2005), which is congruent with what would be expected from autobiographical memory research. Ehlers et al. (2002) noticed that while this also applied to recurrent memories in PTSD, the content was more specific than just a simple replaying of the most distressing moments. They observed that the intrusions were usually about perceptions that the person had experienced just before the onset of the trauma (such as hearing footsteps before being attacked or seeing headlights before a head-on car crash) or its worst moments (e.g., a car crash survivor had intrusive memories of seeing policemen standing by his bed when he woke up in hospital; this was just before they told him that someone had died in the accident). Thus, although *linked* to the most emotional parts of the trauma, the recurrent intrusions usually did not include the moment when the traumatic outcome itself occurred, but rather something the person perceived just before this moment. This contributed to the impression that something terrible was about to happen (current threat) rather than something terrible had happened in the past. For example, Michael, who developed PTSD after surviving a tsunami, reported that one of the worst moments was when a friend that he had been trying to help drowned. Although Michael had witnessed the friend being swept away and disappearing in the water, his intrusive memories did not include these extremely distressing moments but were about hands slipping away just before he could no longer hold onto his friend. Other examples suggested that stimuli that were reexperienced included even those that had no meaningful association with the trauma (such as certain colors, visual patterns, sounds, or smells). On the basis of these observations, Ehlers et al. (2002) hypothesized that the perceptions that were reexperienced had functional significance in that they represented stimuli that *predicted* the onset of the trauma or its worst moments and suggested that intrusive memories are about stimuli that "through temporal association with the trauma acquired the status of warning signals, i.e., stimuli that if encountered again would indicate impending danger" – consistent with associative learning models that highlight the information value of conditioned stimuli in predicting the unconditioned stimuli (Rescorla, 1988). Further interview studies of the content of intrusive memories found evidence consistent with this interpretation (Evans et al., 2007a; Hackmann et al., 2004). The majority of intrusions were about warning signals predicting the onset of the trauma or one of the moments where the meaning of the situation changed for the worse. Berntsen and Rubin (2008) found that few tsunami survivors reported intrusions of the wave itself before they escaped and interpreted this finding as evidence against the warning signal hypothesis. However, the hypothesis states that in prolonged trauma there are usually several moments when the meaning changes for the worse, and each of them may be represented in reexperiencing and follow the warning signal pattern (see Michael's example). Thus, the findings are not inconsistent with the hypothesis. Note also that the hypothesis does not mean that the warning stimulus needs to be *finished* before trauma onset. Consistent with what is known about conditioned stimuli in Pavlovian conditioning (Rescorla, 1988), the hypothesis concerns sensory impressions that *started* just before the worst moment and thus had *predictive* information value. Two studies experimentally induced intrusive memories of such warning signals, using a paradigm developed by Sündermann et al. (2013). Participants saw picture stories that were either traumatic or neutral. Pictures of neutral objects that were unrelated to the stories were interspersed in the intervals between the story pictures. Participants later reported more intrusive memories of the neutral objects they had seen during the trauma stories than those interspersed into the neutral stories (Sündermann et al., in preparation). Work on triggers of reexperiencing reviewed below also points to a role of associative learning.

Alternative hypotheses about the content of reexperiencing are conceivable. The finding that recurrent intrusive memories are about perceptions that preceded the traumatic outcome may indicate avoidance or a premature interruption in the construction of the full memory of the worst moments (on the importance of memory construction, see Rubin, Chapter 3). Important for the treatment of PTSD is the observation that reexperiencing the stimuli that led up to the trauma or its worst moments contributes to a sense of current threat.

Conclusions and implications for therapy

Reexperiencing includes both experiences that are recognized by the individual as memories of parts of the trauma (and thus can be compared with other autobiographical memories) and emotional and behavioral responses that replicate the individual's responses during the trauma but are perceived as reactions to the present situation. Both groups of reexperiencing symptoms need to be explained by theories of PTSD and addressed in treatment.

The phenomenology of reexperiencing has implications for therapy. First, it is helpful to explore the content of the main intrusive memories and what followed with the patient, as this is informative about the subjectively most distressing moments of the trauma (and as discussed below, individuals may leave out these moments when giving a narrative account of the trauma; Evans et al., 2007b). Therapists need to be aware that patients may show affect without recollection and dissociative reactions in response to idiosyncratic triggers.

Do traumatized people with and without PTSD differ in their reexperiencing symptoms?

Intrusive memories are common in the immediate aftermath of trauma and are thus not unique to PTSD (e.g., Rubin, Chapter 3; Berntsen, Chapter 9; Creamer et al., 1992; Ehlers & Steil, 1995). This raises the question of whether some features of intrusive memories predict who is at risk of PTSD. Systematic questionnaire and interview studies found many similarities in the characteristics of intrusive memories reported by traumatized people with and without PTSD, for example, in sensory modalities and duration (e.g., Hellawell & Brewin, 2004; Michael et al., 2005b; Rubin et al., 2011; see also Rubin, Chapter 3). However, some intrusion features were associated with a greater risk of PTSD:

- a wider range of triggers (Halligan et al., 2003)
- the degree to which the content of intrusive memories is experienced as if it was happening in the "here and now" (e.g., Michael et al., 2005b; Rubin et al., 2011)
- the extent to which the content of intrusive memories is experienced as disconnected from its context (e.g., Michael et al., 2005b)
- the strength of emotional reactions to the memories (e.g., Michael et al., 2005b; Rubin et al., 2011).

While many of the studies in this area relied on retrospective reports, other studies found similar patterns of results with concurrent recordings of intrusive memories of negative personal experiences (Rubin, Chapter 3; Kleim et al., 2013b) or aversive films (Clark and colleagues, Chapter 7).

Why do so many stimuli trigger reexperiencing in PTSD?

A very wide range of situations can trigger intrusive memories and other reexperiencing symptoms such as affect without recollection in people with PTSD (e.g., Brewin et al., 2010; Ehlers & Clark, 2000; Foa & Riggs, 1993). Ehlers and Clark (2000) suggested that the ease with which reexperiencing is triggered in PTSD can be explained by (1) what is encoded in memory and (2) a combination of memory processes that facilitate (or fail to inhibit) cue-driven retrieval. This section focuses on how strong associative learning, strong perceptual priming, and perceptual processing may contribute to the ease and persistence with which reexperiencing is triggered.

Associative learning of memory triggers

Triggers of reexperiencing include stimuli that do not have an obvious meaningful connection with the trauma and those that the individual does not recognize as triggers. This points to a role of associative retrieval processes (see also Berntsen, Chapter 9). If strong associations between certain stimuli and emotional reactions are formed during trauma, this would increase the chances that people later show similar reactions to matching cues in the environment.

Systematic observation of patients treated for PTSD showed that triggers of reexperiencing often have *sensory* similarities with stimuli present shortly before or during the trauma (e.g., similar color, shape, smell, or body sensation; Ehlers et al., 2002). Importantly, overlap in a single sensory dimension appears to be sufficient in PTSD. For example, Jane, who was traumatized during incomplete anesthesia, collapsed on the floor when she entered the reception area of a building and felt unable to move. It emerged during subsequent discussions that she had responded to a vase of the same color as the surgeon's coat. Further systematic behavioral tests showed that she reacted strongly to all objects of this color. This example suggests that during trauma learned associations between emotional reactions and one perceptual feature (e.g., the color green) may be formed, rather than with complex conditioned stimuli (e.g., the surgeon wearing the green coat). This would facilitate cue-driven retrieval of the memories in a wide range of situations that are dissimilar to the trauma in most respects, but overlap in this particular perceptual feature. It also makes it harder for the individual to spot the triggers.

Individual differences in the ease with which such associations are extinguished or generalize to related stimuli may play a role in the persistence of reexperiencing. Heart rate responses to trauma-related pictures that the participants rated as very dissimilar to their own trauma taken at one month after the trauma predicted the severity of PTSD symptoms at six months (Ehlers et al., 2010; Sündermann et al., 2010). There is evidence for impaired extinction learning in PTSD (e.g., Blechert et al., 2007; Peri et al., 2000). In a prospective study of firefighters, Guthrie and Bryant (2006) found that reduced extinction learning predicted later PTSD symptoms. Another study further points to a possible impairment in discrimination learning in PTSD (Mauchnik et al., 2010).

Perceptual priming

Perceptual priming is a well-established elementary learning process that facilitates identification of stimuli after previous exposure (Schacter et al., 2004). If stimuli that are present during trauma are strongly primed, this would lead to a lower perceptual threshold and thus a processing advantage for similar stimuli in the aftermath of trauma, with the consequence that these are more likely to be noticed than other stimuli in the environment and to trigger reexperiencing through unintentional, cue-driven memory retrieval (Ehlers & Clark, 2000).

Results from experimental analog studies support the role of perceptual priming in reexperiencing. Participants watched trauma and neutral picture stories, and later completed a picture identification task assessing perceptual priming for visual stimuli that had appeared in these stories. Stimuli that had been embedded in the traumatic picture stories were more strongly primed than those that had been part of the neutral stories (e.g., Arntz et al., 2005; Ehlers et al., 2006; 2012b; Michael & Ehlers, 2007). The degree of priming for objects from the trauma stories predicted the number of intrusive memories about the picture stories that were experienced in the weeks following the session (Ehlers et al., 2006; 2012b; Michael & Ehlers, 2007). Further support for the perceptual priming hypothesis comes from two studies with trauma survivors (Kleim et al., 2012b). Accident survivors with PTSD identified blurred trauma-related pictures, but not general threat pictures, with greater likelihood than neutral pictures. These results were replicated in a second study with assault survivors, and the relative processing advantage for trauma-related pictures additionally predicted PTSD six months later.

Some trauma survivors may also show enhanced priming for trauma-related cues that they encounter in the aftermath of trauma. Such *post-trauma* priming of trauma-related cues may be involved in the development of chronic PTSD, as it would extend the range of trauma-related cues that are preferentially processed and serve as generalized potential triggers for PTSD-related symptoms. This hypothesis was tested with a range of different paradigms. In most of these studies, trauma survivors with PTSD showed greater posttrauma priming for trauma-related stimuli than for neutral stimuli, whereas trauma survivors without PTSD did not show differential priming (e.g., Amir et al., 2010; Michael et al., 2005a; for a review, see Ehlers et al., 2012a).

Perceptual processing during trauma

Building on Roediger's (1990) transfer appropriate processing account, Ehlers and Clark (2000) suggested that data-driven processing (i.e., primarily processing perceptual cues rather than conceptual information) during trauma puts people at risk for subsequent reexperiencing, as it facilitates perceptual priming and thus later cue-driven retrieval. It may also facilitate associations of emotional reactions with isolated perceptual features. In line with this hypothesis, several studies showed that self-reports of peritraumatic data-driven processing assessed shortly after the trauma predicted subsequent PTSD (e.g., Ehring et al., 2008; Halligan et al., 2003). Similarly, self-reported dissociation during trauma has repeatedly been found to predict PTSD (for a review, see Ozer et al., 2003).

Self-reports of cognitive processing during trauma are retrospective, even if taken soon after the trauma, and rely on people's introspective abilities. To address these limitations, researchers studied the effect of individual differences in cognitive processing styles and attempted to experimentally manipulate cognitive processing during analog traumatic stressors. Halligan et al. (2002) found that participants who reported more data-driven processing while watching a videotape of traffic accidents and those who scored high on habitual data-driven processing subsequently developed more frequent intrusive memories of the video and other analog PTSD symptoms than those with low data-driven processing scores. Similar results were obtained by Kindt et al. (2008). Further experimental studies found a similar pattern of results for dissociation during exposure to an aversive film (e.g., Kindt & van den Hout, 2003). Holmes and colleagues (e.g., Bourne et al., 2010; for a review, see Clark and colleagues, Chapter 7) showed that performing a distracting verbal task that interfered with conceptual processing of a trauma film predicted poor intentional recall but more frequent unintentional retrieval.

Conclusions and clinical implications

There is empirical support that perceptual processing during trauma, associative learning, and perceptual priming play a role in the development of reexperiencing symptoms and help explain the wide range of triggers of reexperiencing observed in PTSD. Neuroimaging studies are in line with these results. Sartory et al. (2013) conducted a meta-analysis of functional neuroimaging studies and concluded that people with PTSD showed greater activation than controls in response to trauma-related stimuli in the retrospenial cortex, an area that is involved in priming and associative learning.

In CT-PTSD, patients learn to respond differently to trauma reminders. The first step in therapy is to identify their idiosyncratic triggers of reexperiencing. Patients are encouraged to carefully observe situations where intrusive memories occur and identify any possible overlap with the traumatic situation, with particular attention to sensory similarities. In addition, therapists carefully observe patients for emotional or behavioral signs that reexperiencing is being triggered (e.g., startle responses, sudden change in affect or posture). This helps identify triggers of reexperiencing symptoms that the patient does not recognize as memories. The next step is for patients to learn that their emotions or physical reactions during reexperiencing are signs that a memory has been triggered rather than signs of current danger. They then learn to direct their attention to the differences between the harmless trigger and its present context ("now") and the stimulus configuration that occurred in the context of trauma ("then") (*stimulus discrimination training*).

Why does the memory content appear to happen in the "here and now"?

One of the most consistently replicated differences between intrusive memories in people with and without PTSD is the degree to which the memory content appears to happen in the "here and now" (e.g., Hellawell & Brewin, 2004; Kleim et al., 2013b; Michael et al., 2005b; Rubin et al., 2008b). A large-scale study found that whereas intrusive phenomena were common across psychiatric disorders after trauma, only flashback memories that involved a sense of reliving the experience were distinctive of PTSD (Bryant et al., 2011). Thus, like other reexperiencing symptoms, intrusive memories in PTSD appear to show a compromised awareness of experiencing a memory from a past event. There are several explanations for this difference (see also Rubin, Chapter 3; Berntsen, Chapter 9; Brewin et al., 2010). Ehlers and Clark (2000) explain this "nowness" of intrusive memories as the result of poor integration of the moments of trauma that are reexperienced (e.g., a moment when the person thought he or she was going to be paralyzed or believed that he or she was to blame for the event) with other relevant information in autobiographical memory that puts the meaning of these moments into perspective (such as the knowledge that he or she can still walk or that the event was not his or her fault). This *disjointedness* of the memories for the worst parts of the trauma is seen as central to recurrent reexperiencing (Ehlers et al., 2004). Until the respective moment in memory is elaborated, that is, the updating information is integrated with the memory of this particular moment, the original threatening meaning will be retrieved and appear to happen in the here and now. In line with this hypothesis, some patients with PTSD report having intrusions of different moments from the trauma that have contradictory meanings (Ehlers & Clark, 2000).

Kleim et al. (2008) used an autobiographical memory retrieval task during script-driven imagery to test the hypothesis of disjointed memories. Assault survivors with and without PTSD imagined (1) the assault and (2) an unrelated negative event. When listening to a taped imagery script of the worst moment of their assault, survivors with PTSD took longer to retrieve unrelated nontraumatic autobiographical information than those without PTSD, but not when listening to a taped script of the worst moment of another negative life event. The effects were not due to differences in arousal or general retrieval latencies. Some self-report findings are also in line with a disjointed memory (e.g., Halligan et al., 2003). For example, Rubin et al. (2011) found that people with PTSD were more likely than those without PTSD to endorse the statement "My memory comes to me in pieces with missing bits" (see also review of other findings on memory disorganization below; for an alternative view, see Rubin, Chapter 3).

Different definitions and hypotheses about the role of trauma memory elaboration in PTSD have been proposed in the literature. While Ehlers and Clark (2000) and Ehlers et al. (2004) refer to the poor elaboration of the worst moments of trauma with other autobiographical information that updates their meanings, Rubin et al. (2008a) suggested an *enhanced* elaboration of trauma memories such that the trauma becomes a central component of identity and reference point for other autobiographical experiences (for reviews of this work, see Boals and colleagues, Chapter 4; Berntsen, Chapter 9). These hypotheses are not mutually exclusive. Several studies showed that both memory disorganization/disjointedness and appraisals of being permanently changed by the trauma predict PTSD (e.g., Dunmore et al., 2001; Ehlers et al., 2000; Halligan et al.,

2003). The permanent change concept has similarities with Rubin et al.'s (2008a) centrality of event concept (see Berntsen, Chapter 9, for an alternative view) and correlates highly (Ehlers et al., in preparation), but is understood as an appraisal rather than a memory characteristic.

Conclusions and clinical implications

There is evidence from self-report and experimental data consistent with the hypothesis that in PTSD memories of the worst moments of the trauma are disjointed from information that gives these a less threatening meaning. CT-PTSD addresses this problem with the *Updating Trauma Memories* procedure. This includes (1) identifying the moments during the trauma that create the greatest distress and sense of "nowness" during recall ("hotspots") through imaginal reliving or writing a narrative and discussion of intrusive memories; (2) identifying the personal meaning of these moments; (3) identifying information that updates the impression the patient had at the time or the problematic meanings either by identifying relevant details from the course, circumstances, and outcome of the trauma or by cognitive restructuring of problematic meanings; and (3) actively linking the updating information to the hot spots in memory, for example, by bringing the hotspot vividly to mind and simultaneously using verbal reminders, images, incompatible actions, or incompatible sensations to remind the patient of the new meanings.

Autobiographical memories and distressing meanings of trauma

Recall of trauma memories

What people remember about a traumatic experience determines what meaning the trauma has for them. Clinical observations suggest that trauma survivors with PTSD are often confused about details of what happened during the trauma and have problems with giving a coherent narrative account of the traumatic event (e.g., Foa et al., 1995). Problems in recalling details of the experience can contribute to problematic appraisals of the trauma such as unfounded self-blame or inflated perceptions of risk. For example, Sue, who was raped, had intrusive memories of moments when she complied with the requests of the perpetrator, which made her feel very ashamed, as she believed she should have resisted more. She did not access memories of other parts of the trauma that made her behavior very understandable, namely, when the perpetrator had threatened her with a knife and said he would kill her if she did not do what he wanted. Bruce, who was assaulted by a group of people, believed that he was very likely to be attacked again, gave up work, and rarely left his home. In therapy, he reconstructed the sequence of events and remembered that he had hit one of the assailants first during a verbal dispute. This realization made him reevaluate the perceived risk, and he felt much less anxious about leaving his home.

The extent and specificity of problems in the intentional recall of trauma memories in PTSD has been a matter of considerable debate. There is very little evidence for complete psychogenic amnesia (Berntsen, 2009; Evans et al., 2009; McNally, 2003). Unless there are organic causes for poor memory (e.g., head injury, drugs, starvation), trauma survivors usually remember most of what happened.

There is some evidence, however, that people with PTSD show more subtle problems with intentional recall of what happened during the trauma (often termed *memory disorganization*), for example, gaps in memory, lack of coherence, and/or problems remembering the temporal order of events (e.g., Foa et al., 1995; Halligan et al., 2003) (for alternative views of this literature, see Rubin, Chapter 3; Berntsen, Chapter 9). Investigating *self-reported* memory characteristics, some, but not all, studies found that people with PTSD report greater trauma memory disorganization than those without PTSD (e.g., Engelhard et al., 2003; Halligan et al., 2003; Jelinek et al., 2009; for negative results, see, e.g., Rubin et al., 2008b). Halligan et al. (2003) also found evidence for specificity; trauma memories were described as more disorganized than other unpleasant memories; and this difference was more pronounced in assault survivors with PTSD compared with those without PTSD. Another study showed main effects of PTSD and event type, no significant interaction for self-reports (and an interaction for objective measures of disorganization, Jelinek et al., 2009), and two studies found neither significant main effects nor interactions (Megías et al., 2007; Rubin et al., 2008b).

Other studies used objective measures such as the analysis of *trauma narratives* by trained raters and repeatedly found that trauma survivors with acute stress disorder (Harvey & Bryant, 1999; Jones et al., 2007), PTSD (e.g., Hagenaars et al., 2009; Halligan et al., 2003, study 1; Jones et al., 2007), or intrusive memories (Evans et al., 2007a) gave more disorganized trauma narratives than nonsymptomatic participants. Furthermore, results of five prospective longitudinal studies showed that objective measures of trauma memory disorganization taken in the initial weeks after the trauma predicted the severity of PTSD symptoms at follow-up, using either a coding system for each meaningful unit of the narrative (Ehring, 2004; Halligan et al., 2003, study 2; Jones et al., 2007) and/or a global observer rating of the whole narrative (Buck et al., 2007;

Ehring, 2004; Halligan et al., 2003, study 2; Murray et al., 2002). Again, it is less clear whether the observed memory disorganization is specific to trauma narratives in PTSD. Jelinek et al. (2009) reported that participants with PTSD showed significantly greater trauma narrative disorganization than those without PTSD, whereas no group difference emerged for a nontrauma control narrative. Ehring (2004) found that trauma narratives were more disorganized than narratives of another very unpleasant life event, and participants with PTSD showed greater disorganization than those without PTSD, but there was no interaction between PTSD group and event type. Rubin (2011) did not find any significant main effects or interactions in a sample of undergraduates.

Thus, while there is some evidence for disorganized recall of trauma memories in PTSD, there are also negative findings, and the specificity to trauma memories in PTSD is unclear.

One reason why this research has generated contradictory findings may be that overall judgments about the memory for the whole trauma were investigated. Ehlers et al. (2004) suggested that in order to explain reexperiencing in PTSD, it is helpful to consider trauma as a series of experiences rather than a single experience. Even relatively short traumas comprise a sequence of events. For example, while a car accident happens very quickly, survivors may have protracted frightening experiences afterward, such as being trapped in the car and fearing that the car will explode, or feeling abandoned in hospital while waiting for treatment. Disorganization and disjointedness from other autobiographical information may not necessarily be characteristic of the memory for the whole trauma. The theoretical prediction is that memory disjointedness helps explain cue-driven reexperiencing, and thus refers to the memory for moments of the trauma that are reexperienced.

In line with this more focused hypothesis, Evans et al. (2007b) found that narratives of the moments that were reexperienced were more disorganized than other segments of trauma narratives that were not part of intrusive memories. In 23% of the cases these moments were not even included in the narrative at all. This finding was replicated in Ehring (2004) and partly replicated by Jelinek et al. (2010). These findings point to a relationship between poor intentional recall and reexperiencing for the worst moments of the trauma.

Perceived permanent change and overgeneral autobiographical memory

Many people with PTSD describe a changed sense of self after trauma. A perceived permanent change for the worse is a good predictor of PTSD (e.g., Dunmore et al., 2001; Ehlers et al., 2000). In a prospective study, a short self-report measure of perceived permanent change completed two weeks after experiencing physical assault predicted the severity of PTSD symptoms six months later with $r = 0.58$ (Kleim et al., 2007).

People's autobiographical memories influence how they perceive themselves. Perceived permanent change in PTSD is associated with difficulties in retrieving specific autobiographical memories (Schönfeld & Ehlers, 2006; Schönfeld et al., 2007), a cognitive bias known as *overgeneral memory* (for reviews, see McNally and Robinbaugh, Chapter 12; Williams et al., 2007).

Several studies reported that trauma survivors with PTSD or acute stress disorder (ASD) show less specific autobiographical memory retrieval than those without PTSD or ASD (e.g., Bryant et al., 2007; Harvey & Bryant, 1999; McNally et al., 1995; Schönfeld & Ehlers, 2006; Schönfeld et al., 2007). Kleim and Ehlers (2008) found that assault survivors with ASD or major depression at two weeks, but not those with phobia, retrieved fewer specific autobiographical memories than those without the respective disorder. Reduced autobiographical memory specificity at two weeks also predicted subsequent PTSD and major depression at six months over and above what could be predicted from initial diagnoses and symptom severity. This study also found that perceived permanent change in part mediates the effects of overgeneral autobiographical memory on PTSD.

Conclusions and implications for therapy

While there is some evidence that people with PTSD recall their traumas in a more disorganized way than those without PTSD, there are also negative findings. Memories of the worst moments of the trauma (that are most relevant for explaining reexperiencing) appear to be more disorganized than the memory for other parts of the trauma. Studies on the specificity of memory disorganization to trauma memories showed inconsistent results and, together with the results on disorganized and overgeneral memory recall for other events, may point to a general problem in recalling specific details of autobiographical memories in PTSD.

Regardless of whether memory disorganization is specific to trauma memories in PTSD, difficulties in retrieving important details or the order of events can contribute to distressing negative meanings of the trauma. In CT-PTSD, patient and therapist use imaginal reliving, narrative writing, and a visit to the site of the trauma to access relevant details and reconstruct the sequence of events, with particular attention to the worst moments. This enables the patient to identify information that updates the meaning of these moments.

The compromised access to specific autobiographical memories from before the trauma makes it harder for people with PTSD to put the trauma into perspective and reconnect with their former sense of self. Some patients even describe that they cannot remember the person they were before the trauma. In CT-PTSD, patients are encouraged to "reclaim" their former lives by reinstating significant activities or social contacts that they have given up since the trauma, usually in a series of homework assignments that are agreed on in the session. In each session, patient and therapist review *reclaiming your life* assignments and agree on the next step. These assignments contribute to change in negative cognitions about the self, such as permanent change (Kleim et al., 2013a). Furthermore, Sutherland and Bryant (2007) reported that with successful treatment of PTSD, autobiographical memory specificity increased.

Why does reexperiencing persist?

People with PTSD show negative appraisals of their reactions to the trauma, including their reexperiencing symptoms (e.g., "My reactions since the event show that I am going crazy"; Ehlers & Steil, 1995). These appraisals are thought to motivate maladaptive coping strategies such as effortful suppression of intrusive memories ("thought suppression"), rumination about the trauma (which can be distinguished from intrusive memories; e.g., Evans et al., 2007a; Hagenaars et al., 2010; Speckens et al., 2007), excessive precautions ("safety behaviors"), or substance abuse, which in turn contribute to the maintenance of PTSD by preventing updating of the trauma memory as well as a disconfirmation of excessively negative appraisals, thus inhibiting natural recovery and maintaining a sense of current threat (Ehlers & Clark, 2000; for a discussion of similar mechanisms during depression, see Moulds and Krans, Chapter 8).

Prospective studies supported these hypotheses. Negative appraisals of PTSD symptoms, rumination, thought suppression, and safety behaviors predicted chronic PTSD over and above what could be predicted from initial symptom levels (e.g., Dunmore et al., 2001; Ehlers et al., 1998; Ehring et al., 2008; Engelhard et al., 2002; Halligan et al., 2003; Kleim et al., 2007). Kleim et al. (2012a) further showed that the effects of early appraisals two weeks after assault on PTSD symptoms six months later 4 were mediated by cognitive responses to reexperiencing such as rumination and thought suppression.

Experimental studies investigated whether thought suppression and rumination play a causal role in maintaining PTSD symptoms. Most of the results are consistent with this hypothesis (for a review, see Ehlers et al., 2012a).

Conclusions and implications for therapy

There is consistent evidence that negative interpretations of PTSD symptoms, rumination, suppression of intrusive memories, and excessive precautions contribute to the maintenance of PTSD. In CT-PTSD, negative interpretations of intrusive memories and other PTSD symptoms are addressed through information, cognitive restructuring, and behavioral experiments. A thought suppression experiment (using a neutral image) is conducted early in therapy to introduce the idea that the patient's efforts to keep the symptoms under control may not be helpful in the long term. The patient is encouraged to experiment with dropping his or her idiosyncratic behaviors such as thought suppression, rumination, hypervigilance, and excessive precautions.

Conclusions and future directions

Systematic study of characteristics of reexperiencing symptoms and reactions to these symptoms led to novel therapeutic procedures used in CT-PTSD (Ehlers & Clark, 2000). The treatment program has been shown to be effective in adults and children, for acute and chronic PTSD, in clinical trials, outreach programs, and routine clinical settings (Duffy et al., 2007; Ehlers et al., 2003; 2005; 2013; 2014; Gillespie et al., 2002; Smith et al., 2007).

The work reviewed in this chapter also raised some questions for future theoretical and empirical work on reexperiencing. First, while there has been progress in understanding memories of trauma and other events in PTSD from an autobiographical memory perspective (see also Rubin, Chapter 3; Berntsen, Chapter 9; and McNally and Robinbaugh, Chapter 12), reexperiencing symptoms that are not recognized as memories are less well understood. More empirical research on reexperiencing symptoms besides intrusive memories is needed, for example, by investigating physiological and neural responses to trauma reminders. Second, there are clinical and empirical grounds for considering trauma as a series of events that is encoded as a series of episodic memories rather than as one memory. A clearer distinction of moments during the trauma that are persistently reexperienced and other parts of the trauma may help explain some of the inconsistencies reported in the literature. Third, evidence is emerging that reexperiencing symptoms are linked to the subjectively most distressing moments of the trauma. It therefore appears important to identify these moments, which may be different from what an objective observer would identify as the worst moment, when researching trauma memory characteristics in PTSD. Fourth, research on trauma memory characteristics using self-reports would benefit from a clearer distinction between memory features and appraisals.

Acknowledgment

The work described in this chapter was funded by the Wellcome Trust grant 069777.

REFERENCES

Amir, N., Leiner, A. S., & Bomyea, J. (2010). Implicit memory and posttraumatic stress symptoms. *Cognitive Therapy and Research, 34,* 49–58.

Arntz, A., de Groot, C., & Kindt, M. (2005). Emotional memory is perceptual. *Journal of Behavior Therapy and Experimental Psychiatry, 36,* 19–34.

Berntsen, D. (2009). *Involuntary Autobiographical Memories.* Cambridge: Cambridge University Press.

Berntsen, D., & Rubin, D. C. (2008). The reappearance hypothesis revisited: recurrent involuntary memories after traumatic events and in everyday life. *Memory and Cognition, 36,* 449–460.

Blechert, J., Michael, T., Vriends, N., Margraf, J., & Wilhelm, F. (2007). Fear conditioning in posttraumatic stress disorder: evidence for delayed extinction of autonomic, experiential, and behavioural responses. *Behaviour Research and Therapy, 45,* 2019–2033.

Bourne, C., Frasqilho, F., Roth, A. D., & Holmes, E. A. (2010). Is it mere distraction? Peri-traumatic verbal tasks can increase analogue flashbacks, but reduce voluntary memory performance. *Journal of Behavior Therapy and Experimental Psychiatry, 41,* 316–324.

Brewin, C. R., Gregory, J. D., Lipton, M., & Burgess, N. (2010). Intrusive images in psychological disorders: characteristics, neural mechanisms, and treatment implications. *Psychological Review, 117,* 210–232.

Bryant, R. A., Sutherland, K., & Guthrie, R. M. (2007). Impaired specific autobiographical memory as a risk factor for posttraumatic stress after trauma. *Journal of Abnormal Psychology, 116,* 837–841.

Bryant, R. A., O'Donnell, M. L., Creamer, M., McFarlane, A. C., & Silove, D. (2011). Posttraumatic intrusive symptoms across psychiatric disorders. *Journal of Psychiatric Research, 45,* 842–847.

Buck, N., Kindt, M., van Den Hout, M., Steens, L., & Linders, C. (2007). Perceptual memory representations and memory fragmentation as predictors of post-trauma symptoms. *Behavioural and Cognitive Psychotherapy, 35,* 259–272.

Creamer, M., Burgess, P., & Pattison, P. (1992). Reaction to trauma: a cognitive processing model. *Journal of Abnormal Psychology*, *101*, 165–174.
Duffy, M., Gillespie, K., & Clark, D. M. (2007). Post-traumatic stress disorder in the context of terrorism and other civil conflict in Northern Ireland: randomised controlled trial. *BMJ*, *334*, 1147.
Dunmore, E., Clark, D. M., & Ehlers, A. (2001). A prospective investigation of the role of cognitive factors in persistent posttraumatic stress disorder (PTSD) after physical or sexual assault. *Behaviour Research and Therapy*, *39*, 1063–1084.
Ehlers, A., & Clark, D. M. (2000). A cognitive model of posttraumatic stress disorder. *Behaviour Research and Therapy*, *38*, 319–345.
Ehlers, A., & Steil, R. (1995). Maintenance of intrusive memories in posttraumatic stress disorder: a cognitive approach. *Behavioural and Cognitive Psychotherapy*, *23*, 217–249.
Ehlers, A., Mayou, R. A., & Bryant, B. (1998). Psychological predictors of chronic posttraumatic stress disorder after motor vehicle accidents. *Journal of Abnormal Psychology*, *107*, 508–519.
Ehlers, A., Maercker, A. & Boos, A. (2000). PTSD following political imprisonment: the role of mental defeat, alienation, and permanent change. *Journal of Abnormal Psychology*, *109*, 45–55.
Ehlers, A., Hackmann, A., Steil, R., Clohessy, S., Wenninger, K., & Winter, H. (2002). The nature of intrusive memories after trauma: the warning signal hypothesis. *Behaviour Research and Therapy*, *40*, 995–1002.
Ehlers, A., Clark, D. M., Hackmann, A., McManus, F., Fennell, M., Herbert, C., & Mayou, R. (2003). A randomized controlled trial of cognitive therapy, self-help booklet, and repeated early assessment as early interventions for PTSD. *Archives of General Psychiatry*, *60*, 1024–1032.
Ehlers, A., Hackmann, A., & Michael, T. (2004). Intrusive re-experiencing in post-traumatic stress disorder: phenomenology, theory, and therapy. *Memory*, *12*, 403–415.
Ehlers, A., Clark, D. M., Hackmann, A., McManus, F., & Fennell, M. (2005). Cognitive therapy for post-traumatic stress disorder: development and evaluation. *Behaviour Research and Therapy*, *43*, 413–431.
Ehlers, A., Michael, T., Chen, Y. P., Payne, E., & Shan, S. (2006). Enhanced perceptual priming for neutral stimuli in a traumatic context: a pathway to intrusive memories? *Memory*, *14*, 316–328.
Ehlers, A., Sündermann, O., Böllinghaus, I., Vossbeck-Elsebusch, A., Gamer, M., Briddon, E., Walwyn Martin, M., & Glucksman, E. (2010). Heart rate responses to standardized trauma-related pictures in acute posttraumatic stress disorder. *International Journal of Psychophysiology*, *78*, 27–34.
Ehlers, A., Ehring, T., & Kleim, B. (2012a). Information processing in posttraumatic stress disorder. In J. G. Beck & D. M. Sloan (eds.), *The Oxford Handbook of Traumatic Disorders* (pp. 191–218). New York: Oxford University Press.
Ehlers, A., Mauchnik, J., & Handley, R. (2012b). Reducing unwanted trauma memories by imaginal exposure or autobiographical memory elaboration: an

analogue study of memory processes. *Journal of Behavior Therapy and Experimental Psychiatry, 43*, S67–S75.

Ehlers, A., Grey, N., Wild, J., Stott, R., Liness, S., Deale, A., Handley, R., Albert, I., Cullen, D., Hackmann, A., Manley, J,. McManus, F., Brady, F., Salkovskis, P., & Clark, D. M. (2013). Implementation of cognitive therapy for PTSD in routine clinical care: effectiveness and moderators of treatment outcome. *Behaviour Research and Therapy, 51*(11), 742–752.

Ehlers, A., Hackmann, A., Grey, N., Wild, J., Liness, S., Albert, I., Deale, A., Stott, R., & Clark, D. M. (2014). A randomized controlled trial of intensive and weekly cognitive therapy for PTSD and emotion-focused supportive psychotherapy. *American Journal of Psychiatry, 171*, 294–304.

Ehlers, A., Böllinghaus, I., Sündermann, O., & Kleim, B. (in preparation). Memory disorganization, permanent change and centrality of events in the prediction of PTSD after trauma.

Ehring, T. (2004). Psychological consequences of road traffic accidents: the prediction of PTSD, phobias and depression. Ph.D. thesis, King's College London.

Ehring, T., Ehlers, A., & Glucksman, E. (2008). Do cognitive models help in predicting the severity of posttraumatic stress disorder, phobia, and depression after motor vehicle accidents? A prospective longitudinal study. *Journal of Consulting and Clinical Psychology, 76*, 219–230.

Engelhard, I. M., van den Hout, M. A., Arntz, A., & McNally, R. J. (2002). A longitudinal study of "intrusion-based reasoning" and posttraumatic stress disorder after exposure to a train disaster. *Behaviour Research and Therapy, 40*, 1415–1424.

Engelhard, I. M., van den Hout, M. A., Kindt, M., Arntz, A., & Schouten, E. (2003). Peritraumatic dissociation and posttraumatic stress after pregnancy loss: a prospective study. *Behaviour Research and Therapy, 41*, 67–78.

Evans, C., Ehlers, A., Mezey, G., & Clark, D. M. (2007a). Intrusive memories and ruminations related to violent crime among young offenders: phenomenological characteristics. *Journal of Traumatic Stress, 20*, 183–196.

(2007b). Intrusive memories in perpetrators of violent crime: emotions and cognitions. *Journal of Consulting and Clinical Psychology, 75*, 134–144.

Evans, C., Mezey, G., & Ehlers, A. (2009). Amnesia for violent crime. *Journal of Forensic Psychiatry and Psychology, 20*, 85–106.

Foa, E. B., & Riggs, D. S. (1993). Posttraumatic stress disorder and rape. In J. M. Oldham, M. B. Riba & A. Tasman (eds.), *American Psychiatric Press Review of Psychiatry* (pp. 273–303). Washington, DC: American Psychiatric Press.

Foa, E. B., Molnar, C., & Cashman, L. (1995). Change in rape narratives during exposure therapy for posttraumatic stress disorder. *Journal of Traumatic Stress, 8*, 675–690.

Gillespie, K., Duffy, M., Hackmann, A., & Clark, D. M. (2002). Community based cognitive therapy in the treatment of post-traumatic stress disorder following the Omagh bomb. *Behaviour Research and Therapy, 40*, 345–357.

Guthrie, R. M., & Bryant, R. A. (2006). Extinction learning before trauma and subsequent posttraumatic stress. *Psychosomatic Medicine, 68*, 307–311.

Hackmann, A., Ehlers, A., Speckens, A., & Clark, D. M. (2004). Characteristics and content of intrusive memories in PTSD and their changes with treatment. *Journal of Traumatic Stress, 17*, 231–240.

Hagenaars, M. A., van Minnen, A., Hoogduin, C. A. L., & Verbraak, M. (2009). A transdiagnostic comparison of trauma and panic memories in PTSD, panic disorder, and healthy controls. *Journal of Behavior Therapy and Experimental Psychiatry, 40*, 412–422.

Hagenaars, M. A., Brewin, C. R., van Minnen, A., Holmes, E., & Hoogduin, K. A. L. (2010). Intrusive images and intrusive thoughts as different phenomena: two experimental studies. *Memory, 18*, 76–84.

Halligan, S. L., Clark, D. M., & Ehlers, A. (2002). Cognitive processing, memory, and the development of PTSD symptoms: two experimental analogue studies. *Journal of Behavior Therapy and Experimental Psychiatry, 33*, 73–89.

Halligan, S. L., Michael, T., Clark, D. M., & Ehlers, A. (2003). Posttraumatic stress disorder following assault: the role of cognitive processing, trauma memory, and appraisals. *Journal of Consulting and Clinical Psychology, 71*, 419–431.

Harvey, A. G., & Bryant, R. A. (1999). A qualitative investigation of the organization of traumatic memories. *British Journal of Clinical Psychology, 38*, 401–405.

Hellawell, S. J., & Brewin, C. R. (2004). A comparison of flashbacks and ordinary autobiographical memories of trauma: content and language. *Behaviour Research and Therapy, 42*, 1–12.

Holmes, E. A., Grey, N., & Young, K. A. D. (2005). Intrusive images and "hotspots" of trauma memories in post-traumatic stress disorder: an exploratory investigation of emotions and cognitive themes. *Journal of Behavior Therapy and Experimental Psychiatry, 36*, 31.

Jelinek, L., Randjbar, S., Seifert, D., Kellner, M., & Moritz, S. (2009). The organization of autobiographical and nonautobiographical memory in posttraumatic stress disorder (PTSD). *Journal of Abnormal Psychology, 118*, 288–298.

Jelinek, L., Stockbauer, C., Randjbar, S., Kellner, M., Ehring, T., & Moritz, S. (2010). Characteristics and organization of the worst moment of trauma memories in posttraumatic stress disorder. *Behaviour Research and Therapy, 48*, 680–685.

Jones, C., Harvey, A. G., & Brewin, C. R. (2007). The organisation and content of trauma memories in survivors of road traffic accidents. *Behaviour Research and Therapy, 45*, 151–162.

Kindt, M., & Van den Hout, M. (2003). Dissociation and memory fragmentation: experimental effects on meta-memory but not on actual memory performance. *Behaviour Research and Therapy, 41*, 167–178.

Kindt, M., Van den Hout, M., Arntz, A., & Drost, J. (2008). The influence of data-driven versus conceptually-driven processing on the development of

PTSD-like symptoms. *Journal of Behavior Therapy and Experimental Psychiatry, 39*, 546–557.

Kleim, B., & Ehlers, A. (2008). Reduced autobiographical memory specificity predicts depression and posttraumatic stress disorder after recent trauma. *Journal of Consulting and Clinical Psychology, 76*, 231–242.

Kleim, B., Ehlers, A., & Glucksman, E. (2007). Early predictors of chronic posttraumatic stress disorder in assault survivors. *Psychological Medicine, 37*, 1457–1468.

Kleim, B., Wallott, F., & Ehlers, A. (2008). Are trauma memories disjointed from other autobiographical memories in posttraumatic stress disorder? An experimental investigation. *Behavioural and Cognitive Psychotherapy, 36*, 221–234.

Kleim, B., Ehlers, A., & Glucksman, E. (2012a). Investigating cognitive pathways to psychopathology: predicting depression and posttraumatic stress disorder from early responses after assault. *Psychological Trauma: Theory, Research, Practice, and Policy, 4*, 527–537.

Kleim, B., Ehring, T, & Ehlers, A. (2012b). Perceptual processing advantages for trauma-related visual cues in posttraumatic stress disorder. *Psychological Medicine, 42*, 173–181.

Kleim, B., Grey, N., Hackmann, A., Nussbeck, F., Wild, J., Stott, R., Clark, D.M., & Ehlers, A. (2013a). Cognitive change predicts symptom reduction in cognitive therapy for PTSD. *Journal of Consulting and Clinical Psychology, 81*, 383–393.

Kleim, B., Graham, B., Bryant, R.A., & Ehlers, A. (2013b). Capturing intrusive re-experiencing in trauma survivors' daily lives using ecological momentary assessment. *Journal of Abnormal Psychology, 122*, 998–1009.

Mauchnik, J., Ebner-Priemer, U. W., Bohus, M., & Schmahl, C. (2010). Classical conditioning in borderline personality disorder with and without posttraumatic stress disorder. *Zeitschrift für Psychologie, 218*, 80–88.

McNally, R. J. (2003). *Remembering Trauma*. Cambridge, MA: Harvard University Press.

McNally, R. J., Lasko, N. B., Macklin, M. L., & Pitman, R. K. (1995). Autobiographical memory disturbance in combat-related posttraumatic stress disorder. *Behaviour Research and Therapy, 33*, 619–630.

Megías, J. L., Ryan, E., Vaquero, J. M. M., & Frese, B. (2007). Comparisons of traumatic and positive memories in people with and without PTSD profile. *Applied Cognitive Psychology, 21*, 117–130.

Michael, T., & Ehlers, A. (2007). Enhanced perceptual priming for neutral stimuli occurring in a traumatic context: two experimental investigations. *Behaviour Research and Therapy, 45*, 341–358.

Michael, T., Ehlers, A., & Halligan, S. L. (2005a). Enhanced priming for trauma-related material in posttraumatic stress disorder. *Emotion, 5*, 103–112.

Michael, T., Ehlers, A., Halligan, S. L., & Clark, D. M. (2005b). Unwanted memories of assault: What intrusion characteristics are associated with PTSD? *Behaviour Research and Therapy, 43*, 613–628.

Murray, J., Ehlers, A., & Mayou, R. A. (2002). Dissociation and posttraumatic stress disorder: two prospective studies of motor vehicle accident survivors. *British Journal of Psychiatry, 180,* 363–368.

Ozer, E. J., Best, S. R., Lipsey, T. L., & Weiss, D. S. (2003). Predictors of posttraumatic stress disorder and symptoms in adults: a meta-analysis. *Psychological Bulletin, 129,* 52–73.

Peri, T., Ben-Shakar, G., Orr, S. P., & Shalev, A. (2000). Psychophysiologic assessment of aversive conditioning in posttraumatic stress disorder. *Biological Psychiatry, 47,* 512–519.

Rescorla, R. A. (1988). Pavlovian conditioning: it's not what you think it is. *American Psychologist, 43,* 151–160.

Roediger, H. L. (1990). Implicit memory: retention without remembering. *American Psychologist, 45,* 1043–1056.

Rubin, D. C. (2011). The coherence of memories for trauma: evidence from posttraumatic stress disorder. *Consciousness and Cognition, 20,* 857–865.

Rubin, D. C., Berntsen, D., & Bohni, M. K. (2008a). A memory-based model of posttraumatic stress disorder: Evaluating basic assumptions underlying the PTSD diagnosis. *Psychological Review, 115,* 985–1011.

Rubin, D. C., Boals, A., & Berntsen, D. (2008b). Memory in posttraumatic stress disorder: Properties of voluntary and involuntary, traumatic and nontraumatic autobiographical memories in people with and without posttraumatic stress disorder symptoms. *Journal of Experimental Psychology: General, 137,* 591–614.

Rubin, D. C., Dennis, M. F., & Beckham, J. C. (2011). Autobiographical memory for stressful events: the role of autobiographical memory in posttraumatic stress disorder. *Consciousness and Cognition, 20,* 840–856.

Sartory, G., Cwik, J., Knuppertz, H., Schürholt, B., Lebens, M., & Seitz, R. J. (2013). In search of the trauma memory: a meta-analysis of functional neuroimaging studies of symptom provocation in posttraumatic stress disorder (PTSD). *PLoS ONE, 8*(3), e58150.

Schacter, D. L., Dobbins, I. G., & Schnyer, D. M. (2004). Specificity of priming: a cognitive neuroscience perspective. *Nature Neuroscience, 5,* 853–862.

Schönfeld, S., & Ehlers, A. (2006). Overgeneral memory extends to pictorial retrieval cues and correlates with cognitive features in posttraumatic stress disorder. *Emotion, 6,* 611–622.

Schönfeld, S., Ehlers, A., Böllinghaus, I., & Rief, W. (2007). Overgeneral memory and suppression of trauma memories in posttraumatic stress disorder. *Memory, 15,* 339–352.

Smith, P., Yule, W., Perrin, S., Tranah, T., Dalgleish, T., & Clark, D.M. (2007). Cognitive-behavioral therapy for PTSD in children and adolescents: a preliminary randomized controlled trial. *Journal of the American Academy of Child and Adolescent Psychiatry, 46,* 1051–1061.

Speckens, A. E. M., Ehlers, A., Hackmann, A., Ruths, F. A., & Clark, D. M. (2007). Intrusive memories and rumination in patients with post-traumatic stress disorder: a phenomenological comparison. *Memory, 15,* 249–257.

Sutherland, K., & Bryant, R. B. (2007). Autobiographical memory in posttraumatic stress disorder before and after treatment. *Behaviour Research and Therapy*, *45*, 2915–2923.

Sündermann, O., Ehlers, A., Böllinghaus, I., Gamer, M., & Glucksman, E. (2010). Early heart rate responses to standardized trauma-related pictures predict posttraumatic stress disorder: a prospective study. *Psychosomatic Medicine*, *72*, 302–310.

Sündermann, O., Hauschildt, M., & Ehlers, A. (2013). Perceptual processing during trauma, priming and the development of intrusive memories. *Journal of Behavior Therapy and Experimental Psychiatry*, *44*, 213–220.

Sündermann, O., Sachschal, J. & Ehlers, A. (in preparation). Development of intrusive memories after single trial associative learning.

Tulving, E. (2002). Episodic memory. *Annual Review of Psychology*, *53*, 1–25.

Williams, J. M. G., Barnhofer, T., Crane, C., Hermans, D., Raes, F., Watkins, E., & Dalgleish, T. (2007). Autobiographical memory specificity and emotional disorder. *Psychological Bulletin*, *133*, 122–148.

7 Mental imagery in psychopathology: from the lab to the clinic

Ian A. Clark, Ella L. James, Lalitha Iyadurai, and Emily A. Holmes

Mental imagery is increasingly recognized as having an important role in relation to autobiographical memory and psychopathology. Autobiographical memories frequently take the form of mental images (Conway & Pleydell-Pearce, 2000; Tulving, 1984) and, as mentioned in Bernsten (Chapter 9) can be recalled both voluntarily or involuntarily as a normal part of everyday life (see also Berntsen, 1996; 2010). Autobiographical memory for most individuals demonstrates a positivity bias. For example, more positive memories are recalled than negative ones; individuals perceive a greater number of positive events than negative events as occurring in their lives; and the emotional affect of negative memories fades faster than for positive ones (Walker et al., 2003b). However, in psychopathology this bias can be disrupted. After trauma, involuntary mental images and memories, for example, of an intrusive image of a car crash or assault, can be distressing and disruptive. In depressed individuals it can become difficult to recall positive memories, creating an automatic bias toward more negative information and increasing negative affect. Mental imagery offers a possible route to alleviating distress in psychopathology by reducing the occurrence of negative imagery or boosting positive imagery and biases toward positive imagery and information.

Mental imagery, emotion, and autobiographical memory

Mental imagery has been described as the phenomenon of "seeing with the mind's eye," "hearing with the mind's ear," and so forth, by accessing sensory information from memory rather than from direct perception (Kosslyn et al., 2001). Neuroimaging studies have revealed that performing the same task either perceptually or via mental imagery activates predominantly the same brain regions, suggesting a high degree of overlap between these two systems (Ganis et al., 2004). In a sense, mental imagery can act as a substitute for perceiving real stimuli, to recollect past events and to simulate situations that have not yet happened. It even allows us to imagine situations that would be impossible to experience in real life.

Mental imagery can have a powerful impact on emotion (for a review, see Holmes & Mathews, 2010). Research into mental imagery suggests several reasons why this may be the case. First, mental imagery can evoke the same physiological reactions as experiencing an event itself, including increased heart rate, breathing rate, and skin conductance (Lang et al., 1993). Second, as discussed, visual mental imagery recruits similar brain areas as visual perception (Ganis et al., 2004). For example, when emotional faces are imagined, brain areas involved in emotion processing (e.g., the amygdala) are activated in the same way as when emotional faces are visually perceived (Kim et al., 2007). Third, autobiographical memories typically take the form of images (Rubin, 2006; Tulving, 1984) and there is a large overlap between the neural systems involved in recalling an autobiographical memory and those involved in imagining events (e.g., Schacter et al., 2007). Neural investigations of autobiographical memory show increased activation in emotion-related areas of the brain for autobiographical memory recall compared with semantic memory recall (Greenberg et al., 2005), and the extent of this activity has been positively correlated with self-reported levels of emotional intensity (Daselaar et al., 2008). Mental imagery can reactivate autobiographical memories containing similar content that bring with them the initial emotional response. Figure 7.1 provides an illustrative overview of the way in which imagery can impact on emotion. It suggests that relative to verbal processing, imagery has a greater overlap with perceived events and leads to heightened emotional states.

The involuntary recall of an autobiographical memory is often more emotional than voluntarily recalling an autobiographical memory (Rubin et al., 2008). A notable example in psychopathology is imagery-based flashbacks in posttraumatic stress disorder (PTSD; Ehlers et al., 2004; Hackmann et al., 2004). In PTSD the term "flashback" is sometimes used to describe an intense period of dissociation where the patient feels as though he or she is reliving a traumatic event. In clinical practice, however, these experiences are rare. We note that the new DSM-5 (American Psychiatric Association, 2013) makes a distinction between "recurrent, involuntary, and intrusive distressing memories of the traumatic event(s)" (Criterion B1) and "dissociative reactions (e.g., flashbacks) in which the individual feels or acts as if the traumatic event(s) were recurring" (Criterion B3). We use the term "flashback" throughout this chapter in an experimental psychopathology context (see Clark et al., 2014), that is, as an experimental analog of a broader clinically relevant memory phenomenon to encompass non dissociative intrusive memories of psychological trauma. Flashback-type mental images have also been identified in other psychological disorders. We refer the reader to Moulds

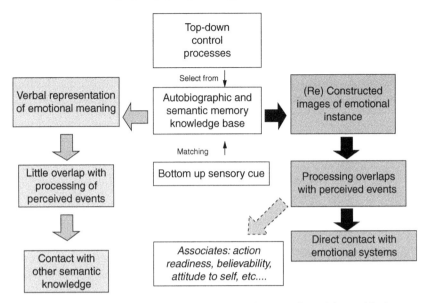

Figure 7.1 Pathway via which mental images of autobiographical memories, in comparison to verbal representations, can affect emotion (adapted from Holmes & Mathews, 2010; Pictet & Holmes, 2013).

and Krans (Chapter 8) for detail on intrusions across psychological disorders, but examples of psychological disorders with involuntary mental imagery include agoraphobia (Day et al., 2004), other phobias (Hackmann et al., 2000), bipolar disorder (Holmes et al., 2008b), and depression (Holmes et al., 2007a; Williams & Moulds, 2007). These involuntary mental images may be autobiographical, as reported in PTSD; may be of the future; or may have no time basis (e.g., Holmes et al., 2007a). They can also be positive for the individual as well as negative; in suicidal imagery an image of an event that might typically be constructed as negative is often perceived as being positive (Hales et al., 2011). Clinically, such involuntary mental images are thought to hold an important etiological role in psychopathology through their effect on emotion and behavior. As such they are a potential target for treatment.

Within the last decade there has been an expansion in translational research and clinical innovation targeting mental imagery in psychopathology. Imagery rescripting is an increasingly used technique within cognitive behavioural therapy and has been successfully used to target mental imagery in a range of psychological disorders (Giesen-Bloo et al., 2006; Hackmann et al., 2011; Holmes et al., 2007b). Within our research group we use an experimental psychopathology approach to develop interventions targeting mental imagery. Here we provide examples of two lines of research that aim to bridge cognitive science with clinical applications: flashback development and cognitive bias modification. We believe that this approach may help to develop evidence-based treatments for the future and can inform our theoretical understanding of autobiographical memory and mental imagery.

Flashbacks in the laboratory

A large body of research investigating flashbacks and flashback-type memories has been conducted in the context of patients with PTSD. Risk factors for PTSD consistently suggest that the subjective experience at the time of the trauma (i.e., peritraumatically) is important for predicting PTSD development (Brewin et al., 2000; Ozer et al., 2003). However, the very nature of a traumatic event makes real-world trauma difficult to study in controlled settings, particularly peritraumatically. Experimental designs using analog trauma offer an opportunity to investigate the development of flashbacks in controlled laboratory settings.

One way to study flashbacks in the laboratory is using the trauma film paradigm; a laboratory-based analog of trauma and its sequelae (for review, see Holmes & Bourne, 2008). On arrival at the laboratory, healthy volunteers complete questionnaires concerning their current moods and various participant characteristics (e.g., current depression levels and trait anxiety). Participants then watch a film with traumatic content designed to relate to the PTSD diagnostic criteria for a traumatic event, such as graphic scenes of human surgery, death, and real injury (DSM-5; American Psychiatric Association, 2013). Participants are asked to immerse themselves in the film and to imagine that the events being depicted are happening to them right at that present moment. During and after film viewing, questionnaires and tasks can be administered to study mood change, trait vulnerability, and other factors. Over the following week, participants are asked to record any flashbacks of the film in a simple diary, similar to those given to PTSD patients undergoing therapy (Grey et al., 2001; Holmes et al., 2004). In the diaries, participants record features of each flashback memory, including content (allowing it to be matched back to the film), emotion, and vividness. After one week participants return to the laboratory to perform a surprise memory test of the film content (see Figure 7.2 for an overview of the general procedure).

As an experimental analog of trauma, the trauma film paradigm is used across a variety of research groups (e.g., Dunn et al., 2009; Morina et al.,

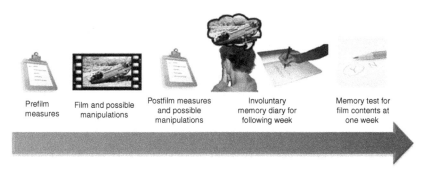

Figure 7.2 The general trauma film paradigm procedure used across studies.

2013; Verwoerd et al., 2011). The following section describes a series of experiments from our group that used the trauma film paradigm to systematically investigate the effect of cognitive tasks on subsequent flashback memory development for an analog trauma. It goes on to describe two broad approaches that seek to explain how cognitive tasks may help to influence negative memory development.

Memory encoding: cognitive tasks during a trauma film

Initial studies investigated whether playing a cognitive task during film viewing (i.e., memory encoding) could reduce flashback frequency. A series of trauma film paradigm experiments found that completing visuospatial cognitive tasks (such as practicing a complex, predetermined tapping sequence on a keypad held out of sight or modeling clay into geometric shapes) decreased flashback frequency after film viewing relative to no-task control conditions (Deeprose et al., 2012; Holmes et al., 2004; Stuart et al., 2006). In contrast, certain nonvisuospatial tasks (such as counting backward in 3s or 7s) when performed concurrently with film viewing did not decrease flashback frequency relative to a no-task control condition, and in some instances even *increased* flashback frequency (Bourne et al., 2010; Holmes et al., 2004).

Memory consolidation: cognitive tasks soon after a trauma film

Performing tasks to reduce flashback frequency during traumatic events is not practical in terms of real-world application. Memory formation, however, is not an immediate process, suggesting there may be a window of opportunity to affect flashback formation *after* the traumatic event has occurred. Following memory acquisition the brain undergoes a time-dependent process of stabilization (a cascade of molecular processes involving protein synthesis and the development of new synaptic connections) necessary for the memory to persist, referred to as "consolidation" (McGaugh, 2000). The neurobiology of memory suggests there is up to a six-hour time frame while memory consolidates, during which memory is labile and vulnerable to modification (Nader et al., 2000; Walker et al., 2003a). Performing cognitive tasks up to six hours posttrauma may therefore still reduce flashback frequency.

A series of experiments were performed to test this prediction. In the first experiment, playing the visuospatial computer game "Tetris" thirty minutes after watching a traumatic film reduced flashback frequency over one week compared with a no-task control condition in healthy volunteers (Holmes et al., 2009a). This finding was replicated in a second experiment, which also found that a verbal-based computer pub quiz game *increased* flashback memories despite being rated as equally enjoyable and challenging to play (experiment 1; Holmes et al., 2010). A third experiment extended the time frame between film viewing and game play to show that the protective effects of Tetris were still apparent when played four hours following film viewing (experiment 2; Holmes et al., 2010).

These experiments, by systematically building on previous laboratory work, were able to demonstrate that (1) ecologically valid tasks, such as Tetris, with visuospatial properties can be successfully exploited to reduce the buildup of flashbacks following (analog) trauma and (2) the effectiveness of such tasks is apparent when harnessed up to four hours following an event, consistent with the idea that memory is still labile and undergoing consolidation. Emerging research into memory *re*consolidation – the idea that a previously consolidated memory may become transiently labile, and therefore modifiable, following memory retrieval (Lee et al., 2006; Nader et al., 2000; Schiller et al., 2010) – offers a possible extended time frame for clinical intervention.

Mechanisms of flashback reduction

Models of memory differentiate between distinct memory systems in the brain (Henson & Gagnepain, 2010). Baddeley's model of working memory suggests a visuospatial system (the visuospatial sketchpad), a verbal system (the phonological loop), and a governing central executive (Baddeley, 1986; 1990; 2003). Studies using dual-task paradigms indicate that these systems are indeed modality specific (Cocchini et al., 2002) and have limited cognitive capacity to process information (Marois & Ivanoff, 2005).

Accordingly, findings from trauma film paradigm studies suggest that visuospatial cognitive tasks *selectively* compete for those resources needed to generate sensory-perceptual flashback memories, resulting in fewer flashbacks being experienced over the subsequent week (e.g., Holmes et al., 2010). Furthermore, nonvisuospatial (verbal-based) tasks may be ineffective at reducing flashback memories because they fail to occupy the type of image-based resources involved in flashback development. Such a shift toward more sensory-perceptual processing following a traumatic event is implicated in cognitive theories of PTSD for the development of reexperiencing symptoms (Ehlers & Clark, 2000). Subsequently, during flashback formation, reducing the power of mental imagery by occupying visuospatial cognitive resources may help to reduce flashback frequency.

These findings may be placed in the context of the model of mental imagery and autobiographical memory in Figure 7.1. We may hypothesize that using visuospatial cognitive tasks offers a "bottom up" approach to reducing flashbacks by occupying visuospatial resources, reducing the construction of emotional mental images of autobiographical events. This is in contrast to therapeutic approaches such as talking therapies, which may offer a more "top down" approach to reducing flashbacks.

However, there is also opposing evidence to such a "modality specific" hypothesis. An alternative theory is a "distraction hypothesis" (Bourne et al., 2010), which suggests that cognitive tasks may reduce flashbacks through a task's capability to sufficiently tap the resources of the central executive of short-term working memory, rather than a modality-specific subsystem. Thus, any task that sufficiently competes with the resources needed for an unpleasant memory to be held in mind will result in the degrading of that memory image (Gunter & Bodner, 2008; 2009).

In keeping with a distraction hypothesis, task complexity can also influence subsequent negative memory development. Complex tasks (e.g., complex tapping sequences) performed concurrently while holding a negative memory in mind are more effective at reducing later vividness and emotionality of the memory compared with performing more simplistic cognitive tasks (e.g., single key tapping; Engelhard et al., 2010; Gunter & Bodner, 2009). However, if the task is too complex, beneficial effects are no longer observed, possibly due to the task preventing the memory from being held in mind (Engelhard et al., 2011).

Thus an interesting dilemma exists as to whether it is the visuospatial properties of a specific task or the attentional demand of the task at a central executive level of working memory that impacts flashback memory development. However, it would seem that within the trauma film paradigm literature there is a consistent effect of visuospatial imagery-based tasks on reducing the frequency of flashback memories. Additionally, a modest relationship has been found between the vividness of emotional memories and participants' ratings of the memory emotionality after cognitive task performance (Engelhard et al., 2011). Theoretically, we can hypothesize how this may be placed in the context of the model in Figure 7.1; greater vividness of the memory, that is, stronger mental imagery, increases the overlap in processing with the original perceived event and increases emotion. Subsequently, reducing this relationship, either directly, by using visuospatial tasks to occupy resources in the visuospatial sketch pad, or possibly indirectly, by using complex tasks to occupy resources in the central executive, may help to reduce the imagery and frequency of the memory.

Clinical implications and future directions

Laboratory and analog studies provide a foundation for understanding the development of involuntary mental images in psychopathology and for developing novel interventions to treat, or even prevent, these symptoms. The next step is to begin translating these laboratory paradigms to clinical populations and clinical settings. We note that within PTSD there are already successful treatments for the full-blown disorder: eye-movement desensitization and reprocessing (EMDR; Shapiro, 1989) and trauma focused cognitive behavioral therapy (CBT; Ehlers & Clark, 2000; Foa & Rothbaum, 1998). The research in our laboratory aims to complement these successful treatments.

Studies are currently underway with the aim of translating treatment approaches for flashbacks from the laboratory to more clinical settings. Lilley et al. (2009) investigated the effects of a visuospatial task on mental images of trauma in patients with PTSD. They tested the effect of an eye-movement task in comparison to a verbal counting task or a no-task control on image vividness and emotionality, while participants held a traumatic mental image in mind. Consistent with studies using a trauma analog with healthy volunteers, a visuospatial eye-movement task reduced the vividness and emotionality of the image relative to both the verbal task and the no-task control condition. This provides preliminary evidence for the beneficial effect of visuospatial tasks in alleviating traumatic imagery in a clinical population, at least within the therapy session itself. Longer term effects remain to be explored. The current findings also support the possibility that the eye-movement techniques used in EMDR are effective due to their use of visuospatial resources, which reduces available resources for image-based memory formation. This is being examined further in an elegant body of experimental work by van den Hout and colleagues (2010; 2011; 2012).

Laboratory studies using the trauma film paradigm have also opened up new possibilities for preventing the development of posttraumatic stress symptoms in the immediate aftermath of trauma. At present, preventative treatments for PTSD are lacking (Roberts et al., 2009; Rothbaum et al., 2012). Critically, early reexperiencing symptoms (such as flashbacks) may predict later PTSD (O'Donnell et al., 2007). Findings from laboratory studies (as described above) showing that Tetris reduces flashbacks in the week after traumatic footage may hold potential as a preventative intervention after real-world trauma. Our team plans to test whether Tetris can be used with patients in an emergency department to reduce the development of flashbacks and posttraumatic stress symptoms after a road-traffic accident. If successful, further work may begin to develop this approach as a low-intensity, language-free preventative intervention to deliver in the immediate aftermath of trauma. For a discussion of other psychological interventions for PTSD, we refer the reader to Ehlers (Chapter 6).

Adaptations to the trauma film paradigm

The trauma film paradigm was recently adapted for use with functional magnetic resonance imaging (fMRI) to investigate the brain activity involved at the time of flashback memory encoding (Bourne et al., 2013). Brain activation was compared between "flashback scenes" (scenes remembered involuntarily in the seven-day diary), "potential" scenes (scenes that caused flashbacks in others, but not in that individual), and "control" scenes (scenes that never caused flashbacks). A widespread increase in activation was found for flashback scenes compared with both potential and control scenes, in regions including the amygdala (emotional processing), rostral anterior cingulate cortex (threat detection and attentional salience), and ventral occipital cortex (visual processing and mental imagery). Additionally, decreased activation for potential scenes compared with both flashback and control scenes was found in the left inferior frontal gyrus, an area typically associated with language processing, but also with selective attention, emotion, and autobiographical memory (see Figure 7.3). These results provide the first prospective evidence that the brain may react differently when encoding emotional memories that are later recalled involuntarily compared with emotional and nonemotional memories that are recalled only deliberately.

Not all involuntary images in psychopathology are negative. Individuals with bipolar disorder are thought to have an excess of positive

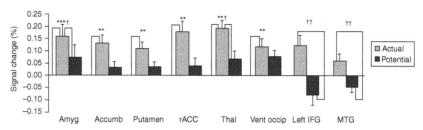

Figure 7.3 Mean percentage blood oxygen level dependent (BOLD) signal change for each brain region for flashback and potential scenes relative to control scenes. Actual scenes were those recalled as a flashback by that individual. Potential scenes were those scenes that caused flashbacks in other participants, but not in that individual. Mean value significantly different from that for the control scenes: ** $p < 0.01$, *** $p < 0.001$. Mean value significantly different from that for the potential scenes: † $p < 0.05$, †† $p < 0.01$. Amyg, amygdala; Accumb, accumbens; rACC, rostral anterior cingulate cortex; Thal, thalamus; Vent occip, ventral occipital cortex; IFG, inferior frontal gyrus; MTG, middle temporal gyrus.

(involuntary) mental imagery during (hypo)manic stages (Holmes et al., 2008b). Recently, the trauma film paradigm was adapted to look at responses to elated mood (as a result of viewing a positive film) and the occurrence of subsequent involuntary memories (Davies et al., 2012). Scenes included the excitement of a rollercoaster ride and the jubilation of finishing university final examinations. As with negative involuntary memories, playing Tetris reduced the occurrence of involuntary memories following the positive film. Further work suggests that positive involuntary memory frequency is associated with the individual's emotional response at the time of viewing the positive footage (Clark et al., 2013). Understanding positive imagery may be useful not only for disorders such as bipolar disorder, where the presence of positive images can facilitate hypomanic symptoms, but also for understanding how to increase positive imagery, for example, in depression, where positive imagery is lacking (Werner-Seidler & Moulds, 2011).

These adaptations to the trauma film paradigm continue to support the relationship between mental imagery, autobiographical memory, and emotion. Further, the relationship may be bidirectional: heightened emotions leading to more frequent involuntary autobiographical memories and flashbacks (Clark et al., 2014). Tailoring treatments to target mental imagery components of autobiographical memories in psychopathology may therefore help to reduce their effects on emotion.

Cognitive bias modification

Flashbacks to trauma provide a concrete target for mental imagery in autobiographical memory. However, across most psychological disorders there is not a distinct memory that can be targeted. Manipulating mental imagery even without an index event can still be effective. Cognitive bias modification (CBM; Koster et al., 2009) is designed to target information processing biases to investigate their direct effects on emotion and behavior. It has long been established that cognitive biases exist in autobiographical memory and typically do not represent a problem. However, there are some clinical disorders where certain cognitive biases may represent a causal factor. For example, biases in autobiographical memory have been implicated in clinical anxiety (Burke & Mathews, 1992), social phobia (Hirsch & Clark, 2004), social anxiety (Morgan, 2010), and depression (Kuyken & Dalgleish, 1995). Given that autobiographical memories often take the form of images and that mental imagery has a strong effect on emotion (Holmes & Mathews, 2010), targeting cognitive biases in autobiographical memory with mental imagery may be an avenue for treatment development within cognitive therapies for emotional disorders.

In depression, maladaptive appraisals are thought to maintain negative involuntary memories and depressive symptoms. Recent work adapted the trauma film paradigm to use a depressive film to induce involuntary images of an analog depression-related event. The study investigated the effect of altering an individual's cognitive bias toward involuntary memories on involuntary memory frequency (Lang et al., 2009). Participants were trained using cognitive bias modification to have either maladaptive appraisals about involuntary memories, for example, "Having an involuntary memory means *something* is wrong with me," or positive appraisals, for example, "Having an involuntary memory means *nothing* is wrong with me." In the week following film viewing, participants in the positive appraisal group experienced fewer involuntary memories of the depressive film compared with the negative appraisal group. These results suggest that maladaptive appraisals of involuntary memories may be a maintaining factor for depression and that promoting more positive, normalizing appraisals using simple computerized techniques may help to alleviate involuntary memories and other depressive symptomatology. Thus, by targeting cognitive appraisals we may be able to alter individuals' cognitive thinking styles and biases toward more positive information and memories.

How can we most effectively alter cognitive appraisals? Using mental imagery within cognitive bias modification has been shown to have stronger effects compared with using just verbal thinking. Holmes and Mathews (2005) asked participants to listen to initially ambiguous events that were resolved negatively under either imagery instructions (participants were asked to imagine the event happening) or verbal instructions (participants were asked to focus on the meaning of the words). In the imagery group, state anxiety scores significantly increased over the course of the experiment, while in the verbal group they did not. These results are not unique to negative emotions. When participants were given ambiguous sentences that resolved positively, those in the imagery group showed a greater increase in positive affect than those in the verbal group (Holmes et al., 2006; 2009b; Nelis et al., 2012).

A possible limitation of using ambiguous verbal sentences is that emotional differences may be due to the recruitment of additional cognitive resources in the imagery condition (imagery plus verbal resources) compared with the verbal condition (verbal resources only). To overcome this, picture–word pairs have been used in replacement of ambiguous sentences. Participants are asked to combine a picture and a word presented to them, therefore using equal imagery and verbal resources regardless of condition. When no specific instructions were given to participants concerning how to combine negative picture–word pairs, reports of imagery use positively correlated with the resulting emotional intensity, while no association was seen for verbal combinations (Holmes et al., 2008a). Additionally, when participants were given explicit instructions about using verbal or imagery techniques, imagery instructions led to greater increases in anxiety following negative picture–word pairs and greater reductions in anxiety following benign pairs. Further, positive picture–word pairs have been found to increase positive mood in dysphoric participants and their performance on a motivational behavioral task (a fishing game; Pictet et al., 2011).

The imagery and verbal distinction may be considered similar to that of "concrete" and "abstract" definitions of thinking styles as defined by Watkins et al. (e.g., Watkins et al., 2008). When a concrete thinking style is used, participants are instructed to focus their attention on the experience of their feelings, similar to when participants experience imagery. When using an abstract thinking style, participants are asked to think about the causes, meaning, and consequences, similar to that of a verbal condition. Interestingly, concrete thinking styles have been found to have a stronger effect on emotion than abstract thinking, similar to imagery and verbal conditions (Rimes & Watkins, 2005; Watkins & Moulds, 2005). For more details we refer the reader to Watkins (Chapter 10). Overall, it may be suggested that targeting appraisals using mental imagery has a greater effect than using more verbal thinking styles.

Cognitive bias modification and the clinic

The use of mental imagery in CBM has recently been extended to clinical studies. Blackwell and Holmes (2010) conducted a case series with seven patients with depression to test the effect of a CBM paradigm promoting positive imagery. Participants were asked to complete seven sessions of CBM over a one-week period with the first session guided by a researcher. The training involved repeated presentation of ambiguous scenarios, presented aurally through headphones, which were resolved positively. Crucially, participants were required to imagine themselves in the scenarios as they listened. Four of the seven participants showed improvements in interpretation bias and mood after one week, and improvements in depression symptoms were maintained at two weeks. Of the three participants who did not show improvements, one did not fully engage with the sessions and the other two reported using a verbal processing style, continuing to suggest that the use of mental imagery (as opposed to verbal processing) is important.

Lang et al. (2012) extended Blackwell & Holmes's (2010) study to a larger sample. Twenty-eight participants with depression completed a positive imagery-focused CBM condition or a control condition daily for one week. Participants in the positive imagery condition showed significant improvements in depression symptoms and interpretation bias compared with participants in the control condition. These studies therefore provide early clinical evidence for the potential of an imagery-based CBM paradigm as a novel computerized intervention for depression.

The next step in developing positive imagery-based CBM as a treatment for depression is to evaluate the intervention in a larger randomized controlled trial. In addition further experimental work is warranted. It is not yet clear how training positive imagery might improve mood and cognitive bias and thus reduce symptoms of depression (Browning et al., 2013). Future laboratory studies may begin to elucidate the mechanism of this emerging intervention. Nonetheless, it seems that cognitive bias modification using mental imagery may help train individuals to restore their positivity bias and improve their mood, offering a more "top down" approach to target emotions (see Figure 7.1).

Discussion and conclusions

This chapter has focused on the effects of mental imagery and autobiographical memories in psychopathology. Concentrating on two paradigms, we have reviewed work from our group progressing from the laboratory to more clinical settings. The trauma film paradigm has been used as an analog of trauma to further our understanding of flashback development and possible intervention approaches. Cognitive bias modification has been used in small-scale studies to demonstrate the potential of CBM to improve mood in depression, and it is hoped that larger scale clinical trials will be able to add to this evidence base.

Manipulating mental imagery has consequences for autobiographical memory and emotion in psychopathology. Figure 7.1 presented at the beginning of this chapter suggests that recalling an autobiographical memory in the form of a mental image leads to direct contact with emotional systems and increases in emotional processing. The research presented here focusing on flashbacks after trauma demonstrates that by directly engaging systems implicated in mental imagery we can reduce the frequency of emotional involuntary-based memories via a simple "bottom up" method using visual interference. On the other hand, rather than reducing images, we can seek to boost imagery in the context of depression via CBM. Using CBM we can encourage individuals to focus more on the (positive) emotional response to a situation or memory in repeated imagery exercises. Although these techniques are working in opposite directions – reducing negative imagery flashbacks versus boosting positive imagery in depression – they both harness the power and potential of mental imagery to manipulate emotion within the individual, demonstrating the strength and flexibility of mental imagery as an avenue for treatment for a range of psychological disorders.

Psychological science may be able to help answer clinical questions in regard to the treatment of psychological disorders. Understanding which treatments work, when they work, and how they work is essential for effective intervention (e.g., McNally et al., 2003; van den Hout et al., 2012). Further, psychological treatments for many disorders, including both anxiety and depression, have reached a plateau. The application of cognitive neuroscience to clinical treatments may help elucidate the active mechanisms of therapy and enhance current psychological treatments (e.g., Browning et al., 2010; McNally, 2007).

This chapter has restricted itself to two strands of work from our laboratory. The reader is strongly encouraged to look at the wider literature surrounding these topics, including other chapters in the current book and recent journal special issues (Hagenaars & Holmes, 2012; Holmes & Hackmann, 2004; Krans, 2011). Mental imagery in clinical autobiographical memory is a young and emerging field, and the future holds promise for exciting developments, especially those bridging basic and clinical science.

Acknowledgments

Ian Clark is supported by a United Kingdom Medical Research Council Centenary Early Career Award. Ella L. James is supported by the United Kingdom Medical Research Council intramural programme (MC-A060-5PR50) and the Colt Foundation. Lalitha Iyadurai is supported by the National Institute for Health Research (NIHR; DRF-2011-04-076). Emily Holmes is supported by the United Kingdom Medical Research Council intramural programme (MC-A060-5PR50), a Wellcome Trust Clinical Fellowship (WT088217), and the National Institute for Health Research Oxford Biomedical Research Centre Programme. The views expressed are those of the authors and not necessarily those of the National Health Service, the NIHR, or the Department of Health.

REFERENCES

American Psychiatric Association (2013). *Diagnostic and Statistical Manual of Mental Disorders* (5th ed.). Washington, DC: American Psychiatric Association.

Baddeley, A. D. (1986). *Working Memory*. Oxford: Clarendon Press.

(1990). *Human Memory: Theory and Practice*. Needham Heights, MA: Allyn & Bacon.

(2003). Working memory: looking back and looking forward. *Nature Reviews Neuroscience, 4*, 829–839.

Berntsen, D. (1996). Involuntary autobiographical memory. *Applied Cognitive Psychology, 10*, 435–454.

(2010). The unbidden past. *Current Directions in Psychological Science, 19*(3), 138–142.

Blackwell, S. E., & Holmes, E. A. (2010). Modifying interpretation and imagination in clinical depression: a single case series using cognitive bias modification. *Applied Cognitive Psychology, 24*(3), 338–350.

Bourne, C., Frasquilho, F., Roth, A. D., & Holmes, E. A. (2010). Is it mere distraction? Peri-traumatic verbal tasks can increase analogue flashbacks but reduce voluntary memory performance. *Journal of Behavior Therapy and Experimental Psychiatry, 41*(3), 316–324.

Bourne, C., Mackay, C. E., & Holmes, E. A. (2013). The neural basis of flashback formation: the impact of viewing trauma. *Psychological Medicine, 43* (7), 1521–1533.

Brewin, C. R., Andrews, B., & Valentine, J. D. (2000). Meta-analysis of risk factors for posttraumatic stress disorder in trauma-exposed adults. *Journal of Consulting and Clinical Psychology, 68*(5), 748–766.

Browning, M., Holmes, E. A., Murphy, S. E., Goodwin, G. M., & Harmer, C. J. (2010). Lateral prefrontal cortex mediates the cognitive modification of attentional bias. *Biological Psychiatry, 67*(10), 919–925.

Browning, M., Blackwell, S. E., & Holmes, E. (2013). The use of cognitive bias modification and imagery in the understanding and treatment of depression. *Current Topics in Behavioral Neurosciences, 14,* 243–260.

Burke, M., & Mathews, A. (1992). Autobiographical memory and clinical anxiety. *Cognition and Emotion, 6*(1), 23–35.

Clark, I. A., Mackay, C. E., & Holmes, E. A. (2013). Positive involuntary autobiographical memories: you first have to live them. *Consciousness and Cognition, 22*(2), 402–406.

(2014). Low emotional response to traumatic footage is associated with an absence of analogue flashbacks: an individual participant data meta-analysis of 16 trauma film paradigm experiments. *Cognition and Emotion,* advance online publication.

Cocchini, G., Logie, R. H., Sala, S. D., MacPherson, S. E., & Baddeley, A. D. (2002). Concurrent performance of two memory tasks: evidence for domain-specific working memory systems. *Memory and Cognition, 30,* 1086–1095.

Conway, M. A., & Pleydell-Pearce, C. W. (2000). The construction of autobiographical memories in the self- memory system. *Psychological Review, 107*(2), 261–288.

Daselaar, S. M., Rice, H. J., Greenberg, D. L., Cabeza, R., LaBar, K. S., & Rubin, D. C. (2008). The spatiotemporal dynamics of autobiographical memory: neural correlates of recall, emotional intensity, and reliving. *Cerebral Cortex, 18*(1), 217–229.

Davies, C., Malik, A., Pictet, A., Blackwell, S. E., & Holmes, E. A. (2012). Involuntary memories after a positive film are dampened by a visuospatial task: unhelpful in depression but helpful in mania? *Clinical Psychology and Psychotherapy, 19,* 341–351.

Day, S. J., Holmes, E. A., & Hackmann, A. (2004). Occurrence of imagery and its link with early memories in agoraphobia. *Memory, 12*(4), 416–427.

Deeprose, C., Zhang, S., Dejong, H., Dalgleish, T., & Holmes, E. A. (2012). Imagery in the aftermath of viewing a traumatic film: using cognitive tasks to modulate the development of involuntary memory. *Journal of Behavior Therapy and Experimental Psychiatry, 43*(2), 758–764.

Dunn, B. D., Billotti, D., Murphy, V., & Dalgleish, T. (2009). The consequences of effortful emotion regulation when processing distressing material: a comparison of suppression and acceptance. *Behaviour Research and Therapy, 47*(9), 761–773.

Ehlers, A., & Clark, D. M. (2000). A cognitive model of posttraumatic stress disorder. *Behaviour Research and Therapy, 38*(4), 319–345.

Ehlers, A., Hackmann, A., & Michael, T. (2004). Intrusive re-experiencing in post-traumatic stress disorder: Phenomenology, theory, and therapy. *Memory, 12*(4), 403–415.

Engelhard, I. M., van Uijen, S. L., & van den Hout, M. A. (2010). The impact of taxing working memory on negative and positive memories. *European Journal of Psychotraumatology, 1,* 5623–5630.

Engelhard, I. M., van den Hout, M. A., & Smeets, M. A. M. (2011). Taxing working memory reduces vividness and emotional intensity of images about

the Queen's Day tragedy. *Journal of Behavior Therapy and Experimental Psychiatry*, *42*(1), 32–37.
Foa, E. B., & Rothbaum, B. (1998). *Treating the Trauma of Rape: Cognitive-Behavioral Therapy for PTSD*. New York: Guilford Press.
Ganis, G., Thompson, W. L., & Kosslyn, S. M. (2004). Brain areas underlying visual mental imagery and visual perception: an fMRI study. *Cognitive Brain Research*, *20*(2), 226–241.
Giesen-Bloo, J., van Dyck, R., Spinhoven, P., van Tilburg, W., Dirksen, C., van Asselt, T., et al. (2006). Outpatient psychotherapy for borderline personality disorder: a randomized clinical trial of schema focused therapy versus transference focused psychotherapy. *Archives of General Psychiatry 63*(6), 649–658.
Greenberg, D. L., Rice, H. J., Cooper, J. J., Cabeza, R., Rubin, D. C., & LaBar, K. S. (2005). Co-activation of the amygdala, hippocampus and inferior frontal gyrus during autobiographical memory retrieval. *Neuropsychologia*, *43*(5), 659–674.
Grey, N., Holmes, E. A., & Brewin, C. R. (2001). Peritraumatic emotional "hot spots" in memory. *Behavioural and Cognitive Psychotherapy*, *29*(3), 357–362.
Gunter, R. W., & Bodner, G. E. (2008). How eye movements affect unpleasant memories: support for a working memory account. *Behaviour Research and Therapy*, *46*(8), 913–931.
  (2009). EMDR works...but how? Recent progress in the search for treatment mechanisms. *Journal of EMDR Practice and Research*, *3*(3), 161–168.
Hackmann, A., Clark, D. M., & McManus, F. (2000). Recurrent images and early memories in social phobia. *Behaviour Research and Therapy*, *38*(6), 601–610.
Hackmann, A., Ehlers, A., Speckens, A., & Clark, D. M. (2004). Characteristics and content of intrusive memories in PTSD and their changes with treatment. *Journal of Traumatic Stress 17*(3), 231–240.
Hackmann, A., Bennett-Levy, J., & Holmes, E. A. (2011). *Oxford Guide to Imagery in Cognitive Therapy*. Oxford: Oxford University Press.
Hagenaars, M. A., & Holmes, E. A. (2012). Mental imagery in psychopathology: another step. Editorial for the special issue of *Journal of Experimental Psychopathology*. *Journal of Experimental Psychopathology*, *3*(2), 121–126.
Hales, S. A., Deeprose, C., Goodwin, G. M., & Holmes, E. A. (2011). Cognitions in bipolar disorder versus unipolar depression: imagining suicide. *Bipolar Disorders*, *13*(7–8), 651–661.
Henson, R. N., & Gagnepain, P. (2010). Predictive, interactive multiple memory systems. *Hippocampus*, *20*(11), 1315–1326.
Hirsch, C. R., & Clark, D. M. (2004). Information-processing bias in social phobia. *Clinical Psychology Review*, *24*(7), 799–825.
Holmes, E. A., & Bourne, C. (2008). Inducing and modulating intrusive emotional memories: a review of the trauma film paradigm. *Acta Psychologica*, *127*(3), 553–566.

Holmes, E. A., & Hackmann, A. (2004). A healthy imagination? Editorial for the special issue of *Memory*: mental imagery and memory in psychopathology. *Memory*, *12*(4), 387–388.

Holmes, E. A., & Mathews, A. (2005). Mental imagery and emotion: a special relationship? *Emotion*, *5*(4), 489–497.

(2010). Mental imagery in emotion and emotional disorders. *Clinical Psychology Review*, *30*(3), 349–362.

Holmes, E. A., Brewin, C. R., & Hennessy, R. G. (2004). Trauma films, information processing, and intrusive memory development. *Journal of Experimental Psychology: General*, *133*(1), 3–22.

Holmes, E. A., Mathews, A., Dalgleish, T., & Mackintosh, B. (2006). Positive interpretation training: effects of mental imagery versus verbal training on positive mood. *Behavior Therapy*, *37*(3), 237–247.

Holmes, E. A., Crane, C., Fennell, M. J. V., & Williams, J. M. G. (2007a). Imagery about suicide in depression: "flash-forwards"? *Journal of Behavior Therapy and Experimental Psychiatry*, *38*(4), 423–434.

Holmes, E. A., Arntz, A., & Smucker, M. R. (2007b). Imagery rescripting in cognitive behaviour therapy: images, treatment techniques and outcomes. *Journal of Behavior Therapy and Experimental Psychiatry*, *38*(4), 297–305.

Holmes, E. A., Mathews, A., Mackintosh, B., & Dalgleish, T. (2008a). The causal effect of mental imagery on emotion assessed using picture-word cues. *Emotion*, *8*(3), 395–409.

Holmes, E. A., Geddes, J. R., Colom, F., & Goodwin, G. M. (2008b). Mental imagery as an emotional amplifier: application to bipolar disorder. *Behaviour Research and Therapy*, *46*(12), 1251–1258.

Holmes, E. A., James, E. L., Coode-Bate, T., & Deeprose, C. (2009a). Can playing the computer game "Tetris" reduce the build-up of flashbacks for trauma? A proposal from cognitive science. *PLoS ONE*, *4*(1), e4153.

Holmes, E. A., Lang, T. J., & Shah, D. M. (2009b). Developing interpretation bias modification as a "cognitive vaccine" for depressed mood: imagining positive events makes you feel better than thinking about them verbally. *Journal of Abnormal Psychology 118*(1), 76–88.

Holmes, E. A., James, E. L., Kilford, E. J., & Deeprose, C. (2010). Key steps in developing a cognitive vaccine against traumatic flashbacks: visuospatial Tetris versus verbal pub quiz. *PLoS ONE*, *5*(11), e13706.

Kim, S. E., Kim, J. W., Kim, J. J., Jeong, B. S., Choi, E. A., Jeong, Y. G., et al. (2007). The neural mechanism of imagining facial affective expression. *Brain Research*, *1145*, 128–137.

Kosslyn, S. M., Ganis, G., & Thompson, W. L. (2001). Neural foundations of imagery. *Nature Reviews Neuroscience*, *2*(9), 635–642.

Koster, E. H. W., Fox, E., & MacLeod, C. (2009). Introduction to the special section on cognitive bias modification in emotional disorders. *Journal of Abnormal Psychology*, *118*(1), 1–4.

Krans, J. (2011). Introduction to the special issue: intrusive imagery in psychopathology: new research findings, implications for theory and treatment, and future directions. *International Journal of Cognitive Therapy*, *4*, 117–121.

Kuyken, W., & Dalgleish, T. (1995). Autobiographical memory and depression. *British Journal of Clinical Psychology*, *34*(1), 89–92.

Lang, P. J., Greenwald, M. K., Bradley, M. M., & Hamm, A. O. (1993). Looking at pictures: affective, facial, visceral, and behavioral reactions. *Psychophysiology*, *30*(3), 261–273.

Lang, T. J., Moulds, M. L., & Holmes, E. A. (2009). Reducing depressive intrusions via a computerized cognitive bias modification of appraisals task: developing a cognitive vaccine. *Behaviour Research and Therapy*, *47*(2), 139–145.

Lang, T. J., Blackwell, S. E., Harmer, C. J., Davison, P., & Holmes, E. A. (2012). Cognitive bias modification using mental imagery for depression: developing a novel computerized intervention to change negative thinking styles. *European Journal of Personality*, *26*(2), 145–157.

Lee, J. L. C., Milton, A. L., & Everitt, B. J. (2006). Cue-induced cocaine seeking and relapse are reduced by disruption of drug memory reconsolidation. *Journal of Neuroscience*, *26*(22), 5881–5887.

Lilley, S. A., Andrade, J., Turpin, G., Sabin-Farrell, R., & Holmes, E. A. (2009). Visuospatial working memory interference with recollections of trauma. *British Journal of Clinical Psychology*, *48*(3), 309–321.

Marois, R., & Ivanoff, J. (2005). Capacity limits of information processing in the brian. *Trends in Cognitive Sciences*, *9*(6), 296–305.

McGaugh, J. L. (2000). Memory: a century of consolidation. *Science*, *287*, 248–251.

McNally, R. J. (2007). Mechanisms of exposure therapy: how neuroscience can improve psychological treatments for anxiety disorders. *Clinical Psychology Review*, *27*(6), 750–759.

McNally, R. J., Bryant, R. A., & Ehlers, A. (2003). Does early psychological intervention promote recovery from posttraumatic stress? *Psychological Science in the Public Interest*, *4*(2), 45–79.

Morgan, J. (2010). Autobiographical memory biases in social anxiety. *Clinical Psychology Review*, *30*(3), 288–297.

Morina, N., Leibold, E., & Ehring, T. (2013). Vividness of general mental imagery is associated with the occurrence of intrusive memories. *Journal of Behavior Therapy and Experimental Psychiatry*, *44*(2), 221–226.

Nader, K., Schafe, G. E., & LeDoux, J. E. (2000). The labile nature of consolidation theory. *Nature*, *1*(3), 216–219.

Nelis, S., Vanbrabant, K., Holmes, E. A., & Raes, F. (2012). Greater positive affect changes after mental imagery than verbal thinking in a student sample. *Journal of Experimental Psychopathology*, *3*(2), 178–188.

O'Donnell, M. L., Elliott, P., Lau, W., & Creamer, M. (2007). PTSD symptom trajectories: from early to chronic response. *Behaviour Research and Therapy*, *45*, 601–606.

Ozer, E. J., Best, S. R., Lipsey, T. L., & Weiss, D. S. (2003). Predictors of posttraumatic stress disorder and symptoms in adults: a meta-analysis. *Psychological Bulletin*, *129*(1), 52–73.

Pictet, A., & Holmes, E. A. (2013). The powerful impact of mental imagery in changing emotion. In B. Rimé, B. Mesquita, & D. Hermans (eds.), *Changing Emotions* (p. 256). London: Psychology Press.

Pictet, A., Coughtrey, A. E., Mathews, A., & Holmes, E. A. (2011). Fishing for happiness: the effects of generating positive imagery on mood and behaviour. *Behaviour Research and Therapy*, 49(12), 885–891.

Rimes, K. A., & Watkins, E. (2005). The effects of self-focused rumination on global negative self-judgements in depression. *Behaviour Research and Therapy*, 43(12), 1673–1681.

Roberts, N. P., Kitchiner, N. J., Kenardy, J., & Bisson, J. I. (2009). Multiple session early psychological interventions for the prevention of posttraumatic stress disorder. *Cochrane Database of Systematic Reviews*, Art. No. CD006869(3).

Rothbaum, B. O., Kearns, M. C., Price, M., Malcoun, E., Davis, M., Ressler, K. J., et al. (2012). Early intervention may prevent the development of posttraumatic stress disorder: a randomized pilot civilian study with modified prolonged exposure. *Biological Psychiatry*, 72(11), 957–963.

Rubin, D. C. (2006). The Basic-Systems Model of episodic memory. *Perspectives on Psychological Science*, 1(4), 277–311.

Rubin, D. C., Boals, A., & Bernsten, D. (2008). Memory in posttraumatic stress disorder: properties of voluntary and involuntary, traumatic and non-traumatic autobiographical memories in people with and without PTSD symptoms. *Journal of Experimental Psychology: General*, 137 (4), 591–614.

Schacter, D. L., Addis, D. R., & Buckner, R. L. (2007). Remembering the past to imagine the future: the prospective brain. *Nature Reviews: Neuroscience*, 8, 657–661.

Schiller, D., Monfils, M., Raio, C., Johnson, D. C., LeDoux, J. E., & Phelps, E. A. (2010). Preventing the return of fear in humans using reconsolidation update mechanisms. *Nature*, 463(7277), 49–53.

Shapiro, F. (1989). Efficacy of the eye movement desensitization procedure in the treatment of traumatic memories. *Journal of Traumatic Stress Studies*, 2, 199–223.

Stuart, A. D. P., Holmes, E. A., & Brewin, C. R. (2006). The influence of a visuospatial grounding task on intrusive images of a traumatic film. *Behaviour Research and Therapy*, 44(4), 611–619.

Tulving, E. (1984). Précis of elements of episodic memory. *Behavioral and Brain Sciences*, 7(2), 223–238.

van den Hout, M. A., Engelhard, I. M., Smeets, M. A. M., Hornsveld, H., Hoogeveen, E., de Heer, E., et al. (2010). Counting during recall: taxing of working memory and reduced vividness and emotionality of negative memories. *Applied Cognitive Psychology*, 24(3), 303–311.

van den Hout, M. A., Engelhard, I. M., Rijkeboer, M. M., Koekebakker, J., Hornsveld, H., Leer, A., et al. (2011). EMDR: eye movements superior to beeps in taxing working memory and reducing vividness of recollections. *Behaviour Research and Therapy*, 49(2), 92–98.

van den Hout, M. A., Rijkeboer, M. M., Engelhard, I. M., Klugkist, I., Hornsveld, H., Toffolo, M. J. B., et al. (2012). Tones inferior to eye movements in the EMDR treatment of PTSD. *Behaviour Research and Therapy*, 50(5), 275–279.

Verwoerd, J., Wessel, I., de Jong, P., Nieuwenhuis, M., & Huntjens, R. (2011). Pre-stressor interference control and intrusive memories. *Cognitive Therapy and Research*, *35*(2), 161–170.

Walker, M. P., Brakefield, T., Hobson, J. A., & Stickgold, R. (2003a). Dissociable stages of human memory consolidation and reconsolidation. *Nature*, *425*(6958), 616–620.

Walker, W. R., Skowronski, J. J., & Thompson, C. P. (2003b). Life is pleasant – and memory helps to keep it that way! *Review of General Psychology*, *7*(2), 203–210.

Watkins, E., & Moulds, M. (2005). Distinct modes of ruminative self-focus: impact of abstract versus concrete rumination on problem solving in depression. *Emotion*, *5*(3), 319–328.

Watkins, E., Moberly, N. J., & Moulds, M. L. (2008). Processing mode causally influences emotional reactivity: distinct effects of abstract versus concrete costrual on emotional response. *Emotion*, *8*, 364–378.

Werner-Seidler, A., & Moulds, M. L. (2011). Autobiographical memory characteristics in depression vulnerability: formerly depressed individuals recall less vivid positive memories. *Cognition and Emotion*, *25*(6), 1087–1103.

Williams, A. D., & Moulds, M. L. (2007). An investigation of the cognitive and experiential features of intrusive memories in depression. *Memory*, *15*, 912–920.

8 Intrusive, involuntary memories in depression

Michelle L. Moulds and Julie Krans

Human memory has a range of different forms and functions: we can recall events that happened to us in the past week at will, and we can draw on our long-term memory and recollect events that occurred twenty years ago as a means to help us to solve current problems or to make plans for the future. Sometimes, however, remembering is less under our control. Take, for example, the first time that you were in love. Perhaps you were at university at the time, and the memory of the first conversation with that person kept coming to mind, keeping you from focusing on the (perhaps less exciting) history lecture. While this example may be quite benign, memories that are similarly spontaneous and intrusive also often occur after highly negative experiences, for example, traumatic and other distressing life events. Many victims of assault, rape, and natural disasters, to name a few, reexperience the memory of their traumatic events repeatedly.

Intrusive memories of negative life events are reported by individuals with a range of clinical disorders (Moulds & Holmes, 2011). Most of our understanding of intrusive memories in clinical conditions comes from studies of individuals with posttraumatic stress disorder (PTSD). However, research over the past two decades has demonstrated that individuals with an array of clinical conditions experience intrusive autobiographical memories of events that typically reflect disorder-related concerns and experiences; among these are agoraphobia (Day et al., 2004), social phobia (Hirsch et al., 2003), bipolar disorder (Hales et al., 2011), grief (Boelen & Huntjens, 2008) and depression (Newby & Moulds, 2011a).

In this chapter, we focus on intrusive memories in depression. In so doing, we review studies that have taken the PTSD literature as the starting point from which to investigate intrusive memories in dysphoric and depressed individuals. First, we provide an overview of the findings of the initial series of studies that demonstrated that intrusive memories are experienced by depressed individuals. Next, we move on to describe the findings of research that has directly compared (first between, and then within studies) the nature and frequency of intrusive memories in PTSD and depression. Third, and drawing specifically from cognitive models of PTSD, we provide an overview of studies in which researchers have examined the cognitive strategies adopted by dysphoric and depressed individuals to manage intrusive memories, as well as the nature and impact of negative appraisals of such memories. We then take the opportunity to explore some common ground between the traditionally rather distinct literatures that have investigated "intrusive" and "involuntary" memories. We finish with some food for thought, and a call for crosstalk between researchers who study involuntary remembering in the clinical and cognitive psychology literatures in order to facilitate theoretical developments.

Intrusive memories as a shared feature of PTSD and depression

An important series of studies published in the mid-1990s provided the first evidence that individuals diagnosed with major depression reported experiencing intrusive memories of negative life events (Brewin et al., 1996; 1999; Kuyken & Brewin, 1994; 1995). In terms of prevalence, 86% (Kuyken & Brewin, 1994) and 87% (Brewin et al., 1996) of depressed participants in these studies reported the presence of an intrusive memory in the preceding week. More recent studies have yielded similar rates (96%; Newby & Moulds, 2011a).

Not only are intrusive memories reported by individuals with depression, there is evidence that the degree of *intrusiveness* of these memories (as measured by the Intrusions subscale of the Impact of Event Scale (IES; Horowitz et al., 1979)) and the extent to which these memories are avoided (indexed by the Avoidance subscale of the IES) is associated with level of depression symptoms (Kuyken & Brewin, 1994). Further, in depressed individuals with a history of abuse, ratings of memory intrusiveness were inversely associated with self-esteem and positively related to negative attribution style and avoidance coping (Kuyken & Brewin, 1999). Beyond these associations, prospective studies have demonstrated that levels of intrusion and avoidance of memories predict levels of depression (Brewin et al., 1999) and anxiety (Brewin et al., 1998) over a six-month period. Collectively, these studies provided initial evidence that intrusive memories – one of the key diagnostic features of PTSD – are commonly experienced by depressed individuals and suggest that they also play an important role in this disorder.

Taking this observation a step further, investigators have directly compared matched samples of individuals with PTSD (with or without comorbid depression) and depression alone, and found that participants with PTSD reported significantly more intrusive memories in the preceding week (Reynolds & Brewin, 1999). Furthermore, for their most prominent intrusion, individuals with PTSD reported higher IES-Intrusion subscale scores than did their depressed counterparts. With respect to the qualitative experience of memories, a greater proportion of participants with PTSD reported that their memories were accompanied by an out-of-body experience, and more participants with PTSD spontaneously referred to their memory as being associated with a sense of helplessness. Interestingly, the two groups did not differ in their endorsement of the other most common emotional correlates of their memories (e.g., anger, sadness, fear, guilt), ratings of intrusion-related distress, vividness of the intrusion, or sense of reliving the event in the memory. Further, there were no between group differences in the extent to which participants reported that they avoided their memories.

In a similar study, Birrer et al. (2007) compared three groups of participants: individuals with PTSD, individuals with depression who had experienced a traumatic event but did not meet criteria for PTSD, and individuals with depression who had never been exposed to a Criterion A traumatic event. Interestingly, the proportions of participants in these three groups who reported intrusive images did not significantly differ (100%, 100%, and 90%, respectively). Further, the groups did not differ in terms of their ratings of the frequency, duration, or vividness of their intrusions or intrusion-related distress, and rumination was the most commonly reported trigger of intrusions in all three groups. However, some differences emerged. For example, the PTSD group reported that their intrusions had a stronger "here and now" quality, and relative to participants with depression and no history of trauma, those with PTSD were more likely to experience their intrusions as a visual sensation.

Comparing intrusive memories in PTSD and depression: some methodological considerations

Together, the findings of these studies provided initial evidence of similarities and overlap in the frequency and phenomenological experience of intrusive memories in depression and PTSD. However, a consideration of these two studies also prompts us to acknowledge some important differences that require some thought when drawing comparisons between intrusive memories among the two disorders.

First, owing to the nature of the events experienced by individuals with PTSD, a variety of peritraumatic processes and states (e.g., significant levels of arousal, extreme anxiety, derealization, depersonalization, emotional numbing) can be experienced during and in the immediate aftermath of a trauma. Such factors have important implications for the encoding and consolidation of memory, which in turn influence the development of intrusive memories – although there is debate in the literature as to the consequences of peritraumatic processes for encoding in PTSD. That is, while some theorists have argued that such traumatic events are strongly encoded (McNally, 2003), others maintain that encoding is compromised by peritraumatic responses such as dissociation (van der Kolk & Fisler, 1995). In comparison, in depression, the cognitive and emotional conditions under which memories that are later experienced as intrusions are encoded have not been systematically studied. Nonetheless, the conditions under which the traumatic events experienced by individuals with PTSD (e.g., assault) and the nontraumatic life events reported by depressed individuals (e.g., relationship breakups) are encoded and the cognitive and emotional processes associated with the occurrence of such events are likely to be significantly different. Clearly, there are salient differences in several factors involved in the encoding of memories during traumatic versus nontraumatic (albeit negative) events that are later experienced as intrusive memories.

Related to this, a second critical difference that must also be kept in mind is the content of the intrusive memories experienced by individuals with PTSD and depression. The content of intrusions in PTSD is dictated by the *Diagnostic and Statistical Manual of Mental Disorders* (American Psychiatric Association, 2000), that is, the event that is persistently reexperienced must by definition involve the experience or witnessing of an event in which one's life, safety, or physical integrity was jeopardized (i.e., Criterion A of the PTSD diagnosis). In questioning depressed individuals about the presence of intrusive memories, there is some variability between studies in terms of how researchers define target events (an issue that we return to later). This issue aside, in our own work we have found substantial variability in the content of intrusive memories reported by depressed individuals – although we would add that many fall under the definition of interpersonal stressors (e.g., relationship breakups, arguments).

Another difference along these lines is that in PTSD, by definition, the event that is reexperienced in the form of intrusive memories is the event that marked the onset of the disorder. Although an individual with PTSD may experience a range of intrusive memories of aspects of their traumatic event (e.g., the moments before impact in a motor vehicle accident or seeing a loved one unconscious in the passenger's seat or the doctor's face on arrival in the emergency room) and may also experience intrusions of thematically similar yet distinct events (e.g., a motor vehicle accident that they witnessed ten years earlier), nonetheless, the intrusive memories emanate from the Criterion A–specified traumatic event. The same is not necessarily true in depression. Indeed, it is possible that an identifiable life event that served as the catalyst for a depressive episode may then become the content of intrusive memories. However, this may not always be the case: a depressed individual may recall intrusive memories of a difficult childhood experience (or a range of other, perhaps additional, stressful events), even though such events may not have occurred temporally as a clear trigger to his or her current episode. This is particularly true of depressed individuals who have experienced multiple episodes, given evidence that precipitating life events play an increasingly diminished role across the course of the disorder (Kendler et al., 2000). In sum, the content of intrusive memories in PTSD is by definition concerned with the traumatic event, whereas the content of intrusive memories in depression is much more variable. Clearly, the aforementioned differences in the content of intrusive memories have implications for interpreting the findings of these comparative studies.

There are important methodological issues that should also be borne in mind when drawing conclusions from the aforementioned studies and in designing future investigations of intrusive memories in depression. First, it is critical to differentiate individuals with major depression who experience intrusive memories of a Criterion A event from those with major depression who report nontraumatic (although negative) life events. A conservative approach (and one that we have taken in our work) would be to remove any participants in the former group from studies of intrusive memories in depression – to remove the possibility that PTSD symptoms, even if at only a subclinical level, might potentially confound the results. That said, there may be important differences between the intrusive recollections of traumatic versus nontraumatic memories in depressed individuals. Distinguishing participants on this basis is the necessary first step to take to examine such differences.

Another important methodological factor that varies significantly between studies is the nature of the instructions and questionnaire tools employed to gather information from participants about their intrusive memories. For example, in early studies in this literature, participants were presented with established checklists of life events (e.g., List of Threatening Experiences) and asked to indicate whether they had ever experienced any of the events. The events ranged in nature and severity, for example, the death of a close relative, such as your child or husband/wife; separation due to marital difficulties; any problems with the police and a court appearance. In contrast, other researchers have not used a prescriptive life events list but have opted instead to take a broader approach and simply question dysphoric and depressed participants as to whether they have experienced intrusive memories of *negative events* – irrespective of their nature. Another procedural difference is that while in most investigations in this line of work participants are asked to report about intrusive memories, in some instances other terms such as "intrusive images" are used. While "images" could feasibly refer to the sensory aspects in memories of past events, they could also refer to snapshots of prospective or imagined events (Holmes et al., 2007; Krans et al., 2010; 2011; see Clark and colleagues, Chapter 7). To facilitate meaningful comparisons of the findings across studies, researchers should be mindful about the way in which they define and elicit examples of intrusive memories, and also attempt to be consistent in the terminology that they employ in questioning participants about intrusive phenomena.

These points of difference aside, taken together with the studies described above, highlight that individuals with both PTSD and depression report experiencing memories of negative events that come to mind unbidden and cause distress. Although the conditions under which such memories are encoded and the content of these intrusions may differ in important ways between the two disorders, these data suggest that once memories do intrude, they share some features and elicit negative emotional responses in both clinical groups. Another (albeit less direct) approach to comparing intrusive memories in depression and PTSD is to consider the findings of studies in which researchers have drawn from dominant cognitive models of PTSD (Ehlers & Clark, 2000; see also Ehlers, Chapter 6) and investigated whether the problematic cognitive responses to intrusive memories that are characteristic of traumatized individuals are similarly observed in depression. We turn now to consider the findings of some of our own work in which we have taken this approach.

Drawing on models of PTSD to understand the nature and management of intrusive memories in depression

There is evidence that some of the key features of intrusive memories in PTSD are also characteristic of the intrusive memories experienced by individuals with depression. For example, individuals with PTSD report that their intrusions contain high levels of sensory experience and occur with a sense of "nowness" (e.g., Ehlers et al., 2002; Hackmann et al., 2004). Similarly, we have shown that sensory features (including nowness) account for unique variance in the prediction of depression, controlling for intrusion frequency (Williams & Moulds, 2007a). Specifically, we interviewed a sample of undergraduate students ($n = 250$) and assessed for the presence of an intrusive memory in the past week. Participants also completed a battery of measures that indexed their cognitive and affective responses to the memory. Consistent with prediction, intrusive memories contained high levels of sensory experience and were marked by a sense of nowness. Furthermore, sensory features accounted for unique variance in the prediction of depression severity, over and above the variance accounted for by intrusion frequency.

The visual vantage perspective (i.e., first-person field perspective or third-person observer perspective) from which intrusive memories are recalled is an aspect of intrusive memories that is linked to *avoidance* in both PTSD and depression. In PTSD, there is evidence that trauma memories are more likely to be recalled from a third-person observer perspective (McIsaac & Eich, 2004) and that recalling one's trauma from an observer perspective is associated with avoidance (Kenny & Bryant, 2007). We have shown that in high dysphoric individuals, the tendency to recall intrusive memories from an observer vantage perspective is associated with avoidant cognitive strategies such as rumination and thought suppression (Williams & Moulds, 2007b).

Autobiographical memory has been suggested to serve several important functions. For example, autobiographical memories provide us with knowledge that can help in problem solving, predicting future events, and understanding the outcomes of past and present events (e.g., Bluck et al., 2005; Pillemer, 2003). Another proposed function is that autobiographical memory supports self-continuity or, more broadly, provides information about the self (e.g., Bluck et al., 2005; Neisser, 1988). Similarly, several functions have been suggested for intrusive memories (for an overview, see Krans et al., 2009). For example, intrusive memories of trauma may serve as warning signals to prevent harm in a current situation that resembles the situation of the original trauma (Ehlers et al., 2002). More generally, the presence of intrusive memories may indicate a threat to the self that needs to be resolved (e.g., Conway et al., 2004a; 2004b). In psychopathology, the interpretation of the occurrence and content of intrusive memories is critical in the extent to which each of these potential functions becomes dysfunctional (Krans et al., 2009). In the clinical literature, these interpretations are more commonly referred to as "appraisals."

The way in which an individual appraises his or her intrusive memories has important implications in both disorders. In PTSD, maladaptive appraisals of intrusive memories (e.g., "Having this memory means that there is something wrong with me") are associated with PTSD severity, intrusion-related distress, and avoidance (Clohessy & Ehlers, 1999; Dunmore et al., 2001). Similarly, controlling for intrusion frequency and severity of intrusive memory content, we have reported that maladaptive appraisals are associated with higher levels of depression, intrusion-related distress, and avoidance (e.g., rumination, suppression) and that negative appraisals were the strongest predictor of depression concurrently (Starr & Moulds, 2006).

In an experimental study, Lang et al. (2009) manipulated appraisals and presented participants with either positive (e.g., "Having an intrusive memory means nothing is wrong with me") or negative (e.g., "Having an intrusive memory means something is wrong with me") appraisals, followed by a depressing film clip. At follow-up one week later, participants in the negative appraisals condition reported greater IES scores and more intrusive recollection of the film. We have also found that negative appraisals of intrusive memories prompt the use of unhelpful safety behaviors (Moulds et al., 2008). Together, these studies highlight the importance of appraisals of intrusive memories in the context of depression.

The abovementioned findings lead us to the preliminary conclusion that the presence and features of and responses to intrusive memories are transdiagnostic inasmuch as they are present in PTSD and depression. However, a couple of issues warrant mention. First, the studies reviewed in the previous section were conducted with nonclinical samples. In order to draw definitive conclusions about the extent to which these features and correlates of intrusive memories are important in depression, replication with clinically depressed samples is vital. Second, these data do not tell us whether the features and responses to intrusive memories outlined above are unique to depression. That is, there is a need to elucidate which of these variables are simply characteristic of intrusive memories in general and which are instead depression-specific. To tease this apart, studies can compare currently depressed individuals with both individuals who are formerly depressed as well as participants who have never experienced depression.

In one such study, we found that in samples of current, recovered, and never-depressed individuals, 96%, 80%, and 73.3% of participants, respectively, reported the presence of an intrusive memory in the previous week (Newby & Moulds, 2011a). Although this rate was highest in the currently depressed group, interestingly, the difference was not significant. In terms of memory features, currently depressed participants reported that their memories were more vivid and distressing and caused greater interference, and rated them as associated with more sadness, helplessness, and anger. Interestingly, the phenomenological experience of intrusive memories (e.g., here and now quality, reliving) was strikingly similar across the three groups – suggesting that these are basic qualities of intrusive memories rather than depression-specific features.

We have also investigated the appraisals of intrusive memories reported by these three groups (Newby & Moulds, 2010). Depressed individuals endorsed greater strength of beliefs about the need to control intrusive memories, beliefs that having intrusive memories indicates a psychological problem and leads to negative self-evaluation, and a trend toward stronger beliefs that experiencing an intrusive memory would interfere with functioning. Interestingly, the belief ratings of the recovered depressed participants fell midway, not differing from either of the other two groups. When we followed up with these participants six months later, the strength of belief of their negative appraisals predicted depression, controlling for baseline symptoms (Newby & Moulds, 2011b). In addition, participants in the depressed group reported engaging in more safety behaviors and passive strategies (e.g., dwelling, rumination) in response to their memories than did both recovered depressed and never-depressed participants.

Taken together, the findings of these studies suggest that it is not merely the occurrence or phenomenology of intrusive memories that distinguishes depressed, recovered, and never-depressed groups; rather, depressed individuals differ in the extent to which they engage in maladaptive interpretations and cognitive and behavioral responses when they experience intrusive memories. It follows from these data that the focus of clinical interventions should perhaps not be to reduce the occurrence of intrusive memories per se but, rather, to target unhelpful appraisals and cognitive responses to these memories. These studies highlight the need for more investigations in which researchers compare currently, formerly, and never-depressed groups. Without including the latter groups, we cannot be confident that the frequency, features, and responses to intrusive memories reported by depressed individuals are depression-specific, or whether instead they simply reflect the experience of intrusive memories more generally.

Intrusive and involuntary memories

Until this point in the chapter we have discussed *intrusive* memories. In using this term, we refer to distressing memories that come to mind unbidden and unwanted. The studies outlined earlier highlight that intrusive memories occur in the context of PTSD as well as depression and are experienced as distressing and are avoided in both disorders (e.g., Kuyken & Brewin, 1994; 1999). Further, they demonstrate that intrusive memories in PTSD and depression share many phenomenological features such as vividness, physical sensations, and a sense of reliving (Birrer et al., 2007; Williams & Moulds, 2007a).

The notion that memories can come to mind in the absence of a deliberate attempt at retrieval is not new. In fact, this type of memory was recognized by Ebbinghaus in 1885. Beyond the clinical studies described above, in the past two decades there has been a surge of interest in this form of recalling the past, commonly referred to as "involuntary memory" (Berntsen, Chapter 9; Berntsen, 2010; Mace, 2007). This traditionally cognitive literature has recently started to explore the extent to which basic principles of involuntary memory apply to clinical disorders, with a special focus on PTSD (e.g., Rubin, Chapter 3; Rubin et al., 2008).

Interestingly, the intrusive memory and involuntary memory literatures seem to have developed largely independently. It is only recently that an exchange of ideas and dialog between researchers in these two lines of work has begun to take place. The contributions in this book will likely further add to this dialog. One possible impediment to such dialog to date has been the use of different terminology and language to refer to spontaneously recalled memories in the clinical and cognitive literatures. As documented earlier, clinical researchers have primarily employed the term "intrusive memories" to refer to the unbidden recall of negative autobiographical experiences. The labeling of such memories as "intrusive" is perhaps reflective of the subjective experience of patients who report these types of memories. This term has a negative connotation, and its use very likely leads to the interpretation that such memories are always negative in content and are necessarily associated with distress. This is perhaps not surprising given that the core focus of clinical research is on cognitive processes that maintain psychopathology. However, one possible implication is that the connotations of the label "intrusive" have moved clinical researchers away from considering the possibility that intrusive memories of positive events, and problematic responses to them (e.g., rumination, avoidance), might also be important to explore in clinical disorders. That said, we acknowledge some emerging work in this area (Davies et al., 2012; Moulds et al., 2012). This point is even more salient in light of the established finding that involuntary memories of positive events are more frequent than those of negative events (for a review, see Berntsen, 2009).

In the cognitive literature, the term "involuntary memory" is commonly used to refer to "memories [that] come to mind with no preceding attempt directed at their retrieval" (Berntsen, 2010, p. 138). This term thereby emphasizes the contrast with voluntary memory retrieval, in which the individual actively engages in a memory search. In our view, the label "involuntary" does not carry with it the implication that such memories are necessarily distressing, disruptive, or even negative.

Rather, it simply refers to any autobiographical memory that comes to mind without a directed attempt at recall, without qualifying the specific subjective experience of such recall.

There is ongoing debate about whether "intrusive" and "involuntary" memories are different phenomena (e.g., Kvavilashvili & Schlagman, 2011). Although we recognize this debate, we align with the view that both terms refer to the same retrieval process and are therefore not separate phenomena. An "intrusive memory," then, refers to a memory that is recalled without any deliberate attempt at retrieval (i.e., an involuntary memory) *and* is associated with the subjective experience of distress, is unwanted, and is disruptive, as commonly reported by patients with depression or PTSD. Such a definition provides a starting point for a bridging of the two literatures that we hope will support communication between them.

Moving forward

It is an exciting time to be working in the field of involuntary memory as the research efforts of clinical and cognitive psychologists are beginning to merge. It is hoped this will result in a rich understanding of the nature and impact of involuntary memories in psychopathology via the use of methods and approaches employed to study such memories in the nonclinical literature (e.g., diary methods; Berntsen, 1998) and, conversely, result in advances in understanding of involuntary memory in everyday life by the adoption of approaches in the psychopathology literature (e.g., experimental manipulations such as cognitive bias modification; Lang et al., 2009). Indeed, a handful of studies have already set an example for this dialog in studies of depression (e.g., Kvavilashvili & Schlagman, 2011; Watson et al., 2012; 2013). To push this exciting convergence forward, we recommend that as a key starting point researchers adopt a common language with which to refer to involuntary memory, irrespective of the context or literature in which such memories are studied. In our view, intrusive memories in clinical disorders can be best defined as involuntary memories that are experienced as distressing, come to mind unwanted, and have the consequence of disrupting one's thought processes. Regardless of the definition that researchers adopt, our sense is that it is vital to adopt terminology with a consideration of both the clinical and cognitive traditions of empirical literatures.

From the research reviewed in this chapter it is clear that involuntary memory plays an important role in depression. However, there are many questions that remain to be addressed, and many gaps in our understanding of involuntary recall in depressive disorders. For example, the possibility that depression is associated with less frequent positive involuntary memories and/or maladaptive responses to involuntarily recalled positive memories warrants exploration. In addition, there is tremendous scope to draw on the methodologies that are commonly used in studies of involuntary memory in healthy samples (e.g., real-time monitoring using diary methods) in order to better understand the experience of involuntary memories in depressed individuals in everyday life, beyond the laboratory setting. Finally, and perhaps most notably, the literature lacks a comprehensive theoretical model that accounts for the emergence and maintenance of involuntary memories in depression. While conceptual models from the PTSD literature have critically informed and guided research on involuntary memories in depression, a depression-specific theoretical account is needed in order to provide a solid theoretical platform for future work in this area.

In the clinical literature, theoretical models of specific disorders are often developed in order to address the need to understand the maintenance of and, in turn, to better treat the disorder. This type of theory development can be referred to as a "bottom-up" approach. That is, empirical observations from the clinic fuel research investigations that are aimed at explaining these particular phenomena. In such an approach, theory is essentially developed on the basis of empirical observation. In the absence of a theoretical model of involuntary memory in depression, our proposed integration of empirical findings of studies with depressed participants (that were guided by Ehlers and Clark's PTSD model) into a theoretical model of involuntary recall in depression reflects such a bottom-up approach.

A different strategy is a "top-down" approach. Here, specific clinical phenomena are approached from a more general psychological framework. Empirical studies are often aimed at testing the explanatory power of a general model in the specific context of clinical disorders. The main rationale for this approach (although not always explicit) is one of redundancy, and its main hypothesis is that in clinical disorders the process under investigation is not qualitatively different from that of a "healthy" population. The main advantage of a top-down approach is its efficiency in explaining a similar phenomenon in many different contexts. That is, a top-down approach does not require a different model for each specific clinical disorder. From a clinical perspective a possible disadvantage is that relevant disorder-specific processes (e.g., avoidance, rumination, cognitive biases) are generally not specified in such a model. The top-down approach has already been adopted by some researchers to study involuntary memory in clinical disorders. For example, the memory-based model of PTSD (Berntsen, 2010; Rubin et al., 2008) has evolved from the cognitive literature and aims to explain involuntary memories of traumatic events.

In our view, these two approaches are complementary rather than incongruent. The most important requirements of studies conducted using either approach are a well-specified research question and scope for clinical translation. The ultimate integration of the approaches would be to develop a general model of involuntary memory that leaves room for specifications as appropriate for specific clinical disorders. That is, the general model would contain the outline of processes that are thought to "hold true" regardless of the circumstances. For example, an involuntary memory becomes activated when an individual encounters a trigger (excluding intentional memory search) that matches the memory representation to a sufficient threshold. The model should then allow room to specify the type of trigger that is thought to be relevant in the context of a specific disorder or even an individual. For example, in the context of PTSD, a trigger would often be a stimulus that resembles the physical features of the memory representation. This trigger can be further specified for an individual patient and his or her index trauma. In the context of depression, the trigger might be a depressive emotional state. Second, a general model may propose that the content of an involuntary memory is partially determined by what is encoded during the experience. Specifying this process in PTSD may include taking into account high levels of peritraumatic arousal and dissociation, which could enhance the richness of the sensory information in the memory representation. As a final example, a general model could postulate that appraisals about having involuntary memories can influence their occurrence. The "color" of these appraisals would again depend on the disorder and the individual (e.g., "I am going crazy" in PTSD and depression versus "This is a normal experience" in a healthy individual).

To summarize, a general model of involuntary memory would be essentially neutral and would describe processes that are known to be related to the experience of involuntary memory. The specific directions, valence, and content of these processes would be defined by the context of the disorder (for research purposes) and/or the individual involved (for clinical purposes). That is, they provide the "color" of the experience, be it a pleasant involuntary memory of a significant other when one is in love or a distressing involuntary memory of a negative experience when one is in a depressed state. Such a model would also allow, for example, further investigations of positive involuntary memories in depression that have recently begun to emerge (e.g., Watson et al., 2012; 2013).

Summary and conclusions

In this chapter we have provided an overview of the empirical literature on intrusive memories in depression. Overall, the findings demonstrate that the prevalence and experience of involuntarily recalled memories in this clinical condition appears to be strikingly similar to that in PTSD. While there are key differences between depression and PTSD in terms of the content of intrusive memories and the conditions under which these memories were encoded, the evidence is consistent with the conclusion that once memories do intrude, they share key features, prompt similar maladaptive responses (e.g., rumination, suppression), and elicit significant distress for individuals with both of these disorders. We also presented the findings of studies that compared currently, formerly, and never-depressed participants. Our preliminary conclusion from this work is that it is not the occurrence of intrusive memories per se that distinguishes depressed, recovered, and never-depressed groups, but rather that depressed individuals' maladaptive interpretations and cognitive and behavioral responses to their memories differentiate them from formerly and never depressed individuals.

We also described a parallel line of investigation that has examined involuntary recall in healthy (i.e., nonclinical) individuals (e.g., Berntsen, 1998; 2010). We proposed that although studied in separate literatures, both intrusive memories (as studied in the clinical literature) and involuntary memories (a topic of investigation in the general cognitive literature) in fact refer to the same retrieval process, rather than being separate phenomena. We highlighted the exciting promise for conceptual development that will arise from further dialog between researchers who study involuntary remembering in the clinical and cognitive psychology literatures, and we applaud the efforts of researchers who have already begun systematic work in this direction (e.g., Kvavilashvili & Schlagman, 2011; Watson et al., 2012; 2013).

Finally, we proposed that in order for these literatures to become better integrated, an important starting point will be for researchers to adopt common terminology. We suggested that the term "involuntary memory" may be most appropriate to refer to the recall of autobiographical memories in the absence of a deliberate retrieval attempt (Berntsen, 2010) – whether in clinical or nonclinical samples. Future research will also benefit from the exchange and thoughtful selection of methods that best address pressing research questions. Finally, as a result of focusing and combining research effort, we see value in the development of a general model of involuntary recall that allows for specifications of important clinical processes according to the specific disorder or individual. Such a model has the potential to focus research on involuntary memory in both healthy and clinical samples and also to function as a guide to case formulation for practitioners in the clinic.

Acknowledgments

Michelle Moulds is supported by an Australian Research Fellowship (DP0984791) from the Australian Research Council (ARC); Julie Krans was supported by a Rubicon Postdoctoral Fellowship awarded by the Netherlands Organisation of Scientific Research. We are grateful to Dorthe Berntsen and Clare Rathbone for their helpful comments and suggestions on an earlier draft of this chapter.

REFERENCES

American Psychiatric Association (2000). *Diagnostic and Statistical Manual of Mental Disorders* (4th ed., text revision). Washington, DC: American Psychiatric Association.

Berntsen, D. (1998). Voluntary and involuntary access to autobiographical memory. *Memory*, 6, 113–141.

(2009). *Involuntary Autobiographical Memories: An Introduction to the Unbidden Past.* Cambridge: Cambridge University Press.

(2010). The unbidden past: involuntary autobiographical memories as a basic mode of remembering. *Current Directions in Psychological Science*, 19, 138–142.

Birrer, E., Michael, T., & Munsch, S. (2007). Intrusive images in PTSD and in traumatised and non-traumatised depressed patients: a cross-sectional clinical study. *Behaviour Research and Therapy*, 45, 2053–2065.

Bluck, S., Alea, N., Habermas, T., & Rubin, D. C. (2005). A tale of three functions: the self-reported uses of autobiographical memory. *Social Cognition*, 23, 91–117.

Boelen, P. A., & Huntjens, R. J. C. (2008). Intrusive images in grief: an exploratory study. *Clinical Psychology and Psychotherapy*, 15, 217–226.

Brewin, C. R., Hunter, E., Carroll, F., & Tata P. (1996). Intrusive memories in depression: an index of schema activation? *Psychological Medicine*, 26, 1271–1276.

Brewin, C. R., Watson, M., McCarthy, S., Hyman, P., & Dayson, D. (1998). Memory processes and the course of anxiety and depression in cancer patients. *Psychological Medicine: A Journal of Research in Psychiatry and the Allied Sciences*, 28, 219–224.

Brewin, C. R., Reynolds, M., & Tata, P. (1999). Autobiographical memory processes and the course of depression. *Journal of Abnormal Psychology*, 108, 511–517.

Clohessy, S., & Ehlers, A. (1999). PTSD symptoms, response to intrusive memories and coping in ambulance service workers. *British Journal of Clinical Psychology*, 38, 251–265.

Conway, M.A., Meares, K., & Standart, S. (2004a). Images and goals. *Memory*, *12*, 525–531.
Conway, M.A., Singer, J.A., & Tagini, A. (2004b). The self and autobiographical memory: correspondence and coherence. *Social Cognition*, *22*, 491–529.
Davies, C., Malik, A., Pictet, A., Blackwell, S. E., & Holmes, E. A. (2012). Involuntary memories after a positive film are dampened by a visuospatial task: unhelpful in depression but helpful in mania? *Clinical Psychology and Psychotherapy*, *19*, 341–351.
Day, S. J., Holmes, E. A., & Hackmann, A. (2004). Occurrence of imagery and its link with early memories in agoraphobia. *Memory*, *12*, 416–427.
Dunmore, E., Clark, D. M., & Ehlers, A. (2001). A prospective investigation of the role of cognitive factors in persistent posttraumatic stress disorder (PTSD) after physical or sexual assault. *Behaviour Research and Therapy*, *39*, 1063–1084.
Ebbinghaus, H. (1885). *Über das Gedächtnis. Untersuchungen zur experimentellen Psychologie*. Leipzig: Duncker & Humblot.
Ehlers, A., & Clark, D. M. (2000). A cognitive model of posttraumatic stress disorder. *Behaviour Research and Therapy*, *38*, 319–345.
Ehlers, A., Hackmann, A., Steil, R., Clohessy, S., Wenninger, K., & Winter. (2002). The nature of intrusive memories after trauma: the warning signal hypothesis. *Behaviour Research and Therapy*, *20*, 995–1002.
Hackmann, A., Ehlers, A., Speckens, A., & Clark, D. M. (2004). Characteristics and content of intrusive memories and their changes with treatment. *Journal of Traumatic Stress*, *17*, 231–240.
Hales, S. A., Deeprose, C., Goodwin, G. M., & Holmes, E. A. (2011). Cognitions in bipolar affective disorder and unipolar depression: imagining suicide. *Bipolar Disorders*, *13*, 651–661.
Hirsch, C. R., Clark, D. M., Mathews, A., & Williams, R. (2003). Self-images play a causal role in social phobia. *Behaviour Research and Therapy*, *41*, 909–921.
Holmes, E. A., Crane, C., Fennell, M. J. V., & Williams, J. M. G. (2007). Imagery about suicide in depression: "flash-forwards"? *Journal of Behavior Therapy and Experimental Psychiatry*, *38*, 423–434.
Horowitz, M., Wilner, N., & Alvarez, W. (1979). Impact of Event Scale: a measure of subjective distress. *Psychosomatic Medicine*, *41*, 209–218.
Kendler, K. S., Thornton, L. M., & Gardner, C. O. (2000). Stressful life events and previous episodes in the etiology of major depression in women: an evaluation of the "kindling" hypothesis. *American Journal of Psychiatry*, *157*, 1243–1251.
Kenny, L. M., & Bryant, R. A. (2007). Keeping memories at an arm's length: vantage point of trauma memories. *Behaviour Research and Therapy*, *45*, 1915–1920.
Krans, J., Näring, G., Becker, E. S., & Holmes, E. A. (2009). Intrusive trauma memory: a review and functional analysis. *Applied Cognitive Psychology*, *23*, 1076–1088.
Krans, J., Näring, G., Holmes, E.A., & Becker, E.S. (2010). "I see what you're saying": intrusive images from an aversive verbal report. *Journal of Anxiety Disorders*, *24*, 134–140.

Krans, J., Näring, G., Speckens, A., & Becker, E.S. (2011). Eyewitness or earwitness: the role of mental imagery in intrusion development. *International Journal of Cognitive Therapy*, *4*, 145–153.

Kuyken, W., & Brewin, C. R. (1994). Intrusive memories of childhood abuse during depressive episodes. *Behaviour Research and Therapy*, *32*, 525–528.

(1995). Autobiographical memory functioning in depression and reports of early abuse. *Journal of Abnormal Psychology*, *104*, 585–591.

(1999). The relation of early abuse to cognition and coping in depression. *Cognitive Therapy and Research*, *23*, 665–677.

Kvavilashvili, L., & Schlagman, S. (2011). Involuntary autobiographical memories in dysphoric mood: a laboratory study. *Memory*, *19*, 331–345.

Lang, T. J., Moulds, M. L., & Holmes, E. A. (2009). Reducing depressive intrusions via a computerized cognitive bias modification of appraisals task: developing a cognitive vaccine. *Behaviour Research and Therapy*, *47*, 139–145.

Mace, J. H. (2007). Involuntary memory: concept and theory. In J. H. Mace (ed.), *Involuntary Memory* (pp. 1–9). Malden, MA: Blackwell.

McIsaac, H. K., & Eich, E. (2004). Vantage point in traumatic memory. *Psychological Science*, *15*, 248–253.

McNally, R. J. (2003). *Remembering Trauma*. Cambridge, MA: Belknap Press of Harvard University Press.

Moulds, M. L., & Holmes, E. A. (2011). Intrusive imagery in psychopathology: a commentary. *International Journal of Cognitive Therapy*, *4*, 197–207.

Moulds, M. L., Kandris, E., Williams, A. D., & Lang, T. J. (2008). The use of safety behaviours to manage intrusive memories in depression. *Behaviour Research and Therapy*, *46*, 573–580.

Moulds, M. L., Williams, A. D., Grisham, J. R., & Nickerson, A. (2012). A comparison of retrieval vantage perspective of positive and negative intrusive memories. *Journal of Experimental Psychopathology*, *3*, 168–177.

Neisser, U. (1988). Five kinds of self-knowledge. *Philosophical Psychology*, *1*, 35–59.

Newby, J. M., & Moulds, M. L. (2010). Negative intrusive memories in depression: the role of maladaptive appraisals and safety behaviours. *Journal of Affective Disorders*, *126*, 147–154.

(2011a). Characteristics of intrusive memories in a community sample of depressed, recovered depressed and never-depressed individuals. *Behaviour Research and Therapy*, *49*, 234–243.

(2011b). Do negative appraisals and avoidance of intrusive memories predict depression at six months? *International Journal of Cognitive Therapy*, *4*, 178–186.

Pillemer, D. B. (2003). Directive functions of autobiographical memory: the guide power of the specific episode. *Memory*, *11*, 193–202.

Reynolds, M., & Brewin, C. R. (1999). Intrusive memories in depression and posttraumatic stress disorder. *Behaviour Research and Therapy*, *37*, 201–215.

Rubin, D. C., Berntsen, D., & Bohni, M. K. (2008). A memory-based model of posttraumatic stress disorder: evaluating basic assumptions underlying the PTSD diagnosis. *Psychological Review*, *115*, 985–1011.

Starr, S., & Moulds, M. L. (2006). The role of negative interpretations of intrusive memories in depression. *Journal of Affective Disorders, 93,* 125–132.

van der Kolk, B. A., & Fisler, R. (1995). Dissociation and the fragmentary nature of traumatic memories: overview and exploratory study. *Journal of Traumatic Stress, 8,* 505–525.

Watson, L. A., Berntsen, D., Kuyken, W., & Watkins, E. R. (2012). The characteristics of voluntary and involuntary autobiographical memories in depressed and never depressed individuals. *Consciousness and Cognition, 21,* 1382–1392.

(2013). Involuntary and voluntary autobiographical memory specificity as a function of depression. *Journal of Behavior Therapy and Experimental Psychiatry, 44,* 7–13.

Williams, A. D., & Moulds, M. L. (2007a). An investigation of the cognitive and experiential features of intrusive memories in depression. *Memory, 15,* 912–920.

(2007b). Cognitive avoidance of intrusive memories: recall vantage perspective and associations with depression. *Behaviour Research and Therapy, 45,* 1141–1153

9 From everyday life to trauma: research on everyday involuntary memories advances our understanding of intrusive memories of trauma

Dorthe Berntsen

By the end of World War II, the Royal Air Force undertook the mission to bomb a Gestapo headquarters in central Copenhagen in order to destroy the Gestapo archives of the Danish resistance movement. The intention was to do so while hurting as few civilians as possible. Entering Danish airspace, the British bombers had to stay at a very low altitude in order not to be detected by the German radar systems. Poor weather conditions rendered this especially challenging. One of the planes hit a pole, crashed, and exploded with its load of bombs in a residential area in Copenhagen. To make things worse, some of the planes that followed mistook the heavy smoke from the crashing airplane to indicate the target and consequently dropped their load of bombs over the same neighborhood. A school and several apartment buildings were destroyed by the bombers. Almost a hundred children were killed. A seventy-seven-year-old woman who was a high school student at the time witnessed the collapse of apartment buildings next door:

> Suddenly, we heard a bomb, the alarm rang, we had to run to the basement. Our classroom was up high and we rushed down the back stairs. While we were running, we saw the apartment buildings on Maglekildevej crash. It looked like a movie, but it was real....

Fifty-six years later on September 11, 2001, this woman watched the collapse of the World Trade Center on television. She explains that she reacted "with very unpleasant physical symptoms: I was trembling, I had strong pains in my stomach and I was on the edge of a depression. I constantly saw the World Trade Center towers and [the apartment buildings on] Maglekildevej as one single event" (Berntsen, 2009, p. 144; see also Berntsen & Thomsen, 2005, on older Danes' memories from World War II).

People who have lived through traumatic or highly stressful events often have involuntary memories of the event. These memories are intrusive, in the sense that they are unwanted, stressful, and accompanied by attempts at avoidance. Such intrusive involuntary memories are observed in relation to many psychiatric disorders (see Ehlers, Chapter 6; Clark and colleagues, Chapter 7; Moulds and Krans, Chapter 8). Still, they have received most attention in relation to posttraumatic stress disorder (PTSD), for which they are considered as a distinctive symptom (American Psychiatric Association, 2000; 2013).

However, involuntary remembering is not limited to negative events. Over the last couple of decades an accumulating body of research has documented that involuntary autobiographical memories are common in daily life – that is, people often experience memories of past events that come to mind with no preceding attempts at retrieval (Berntsen, 1996). As in the case of the World War II memory quoted earlier, such everyday involuntary memories are usually accompanied by a sense of reliving the past event and are typically preceded by some feature overlap between the current situation and the remembered event that appears to have helped to trigger the memory. Also consistent with the World War II example, everyday involuntary memories tend to involve stronger emotional reactions than strategically retrieved personal memories (Berntsen, 2009). Such similarities between intrusive involuntary memories and everyday involuntary memories of more mundane events have led some researchers (including myself) to propose that a key to understanding stressful involuntary memories in psychopathological disorders are the mechanisms underlying everyday involuntary memories (e.g., Berntsen, 1996; 2001; 2009; Berntsen & Rubin, 2008; 2013). Normally, such mechanisms are functional and adaptive, but they may become dysfunctional when applied to extreme events, according to this position.

In this continuity view, intrusive involuntary memories are considered as a subclass of everyday involuntary memories – a subclass of memories that deal with stressful negative events and are accompanied by avoidance attempts (for further discussions of this view, see Clark and colleagues, Chapter 7; Moulds aand Krans, Chapter 8). This continuity view is an alternative to a prevalent and long-standing view going back to the infancy of PTSD research. According to this traditional and still dominant discontinuity view, intrusive memories of traumatic events constitute a separate category, which cannot be explained by standard theories of long-term memory and mechanisms of everyday involuntary remembering, but which requires explanations that may pertain specifically to memory for traumatic or stressful events, for example, by invoking distinctions or memory systems that are not well established in relation to memory for nontraumatic events (e.g., Brewin, 2014). The goal of the present chapter is to review and discuss these two views and their evidence. First I review the central tenets of the traditional view, its theoretical and historical origins, and its evidence. Then I review what we know about healthy involuntary remembering from naturalistic and experimental studies and discuss how these insights may help to provide a new understanding of stressful intrusive memories of traumatic or negative events.

Involuntary memories conceived as a stress response: theoretical origins and evidence

Involuntary, intrusive memories have not always been considered as a psychopathological response. They appear to have been introduced as a posttraumatic stress reaction through the psychiatrist Mardi J. Horowitz's seminal work in the late 1960s and 1970s (e.g., Horowitz, 1969b; 1975). Involuntary, intrusive memories played no central role in preceding theories of reactions to psychological traumas, such as in Freud's writings about posttraumatic reactions (e.g., Freud, 1919; 1920) or in accounts of war neuroses by River (1920) and Kardiner (1941). These scholars generally regarded nightmares, rather than intrusive memories in waking life, as the dominant way of reliving the traumatic experiences in consciousness. Even though Freud and Breuer stated that hysterics "suffer mainly from reminiscences" (Breuer & Freud, 1893–1895, p. 7), they meant not that hysterics had intrusive conscious recollections but that their symptoms were due to unconscious and repressed memories (Gammelgaard, 1992). In general, Freud was much more concerned with involuntary forgetting and unconscious memories reflecting themselves in dreams and behavioral symptoms than he was with involuntary conscious recollections (for a review, see Berntsen, 2009). Unlike his predecessors, Horowitz regarded involuntary intrusive memories as a key stress response category and placed them at the core of his theory. In this chapter I argue that Horowitz discovered a real and very important phenomenon but also that central tenets of his theory of these memories are incorrect. This argument is not interesting only for historical reasons. It is primarily interesting because these tenets are repeated in modern theories of intrusive memories of traumas as well as reflected in the diagnostic description of the symptoms of posttraumatic stress disorder (PTSD; American Psychiatric Association, 2000; 2013).

Horowitz's (1975; 1976) model for stress responses holds two main tenets concerning the role of memory. First, voluntary (strategic and controlled) remembering of the stressful or traumatic event is considerably reduced due to defense mechanisms serving to protect the person against reliving the emotional stress as well as due to a poor cognitive match between the trauma and preexisting schema structures, leading to faulty encoding of the event. Second, at the same time the memory of the stressful event tends to repeat itself in an involuntary and uncontrollable fashion. This leads to the paradoxical situation in which periods with vivid intrusive images of the event may be followed by partial or complete amnesia of the event. According to Horowitz, the underlying cause for both the enhanced involuntary remembering and the impaired voluntary access is incomplete cognitive processing of the traumatic event and defense mechanisms (e.g., repression and denial). Instead of a normal integration into the cognitive schemata of the person, the event is subsumed to an active memory storage – a hypothesized memory system that tends to repeat its own content until its processing has been completed.

Both ideas are reflected in the DSM-IV diagnosis for PTSD (American Psychiatric Association, 2000) as well as in the recently published revision of the diagnosis in the DSM-5 (American Psychiatric Association, 2013). First, the idea of reduced strategic recall is present in the C3 symptom of the DSM-IV describing an "inability to recall an important aspect of the trauma" (American Psychiatric Association, 2000, pp. 467–468) and in the D1 symptom of DSM-5, "inability to remember an important aspect of the traumatic event(s)" (American Psychiatric Association, 2013, p. 271). Second, the assumption of involuntary remembering having privileged access to traumatic and stressful material is reflected in the listing of involuntary (intrusive) recollection as a symptom of PTSD with no mentioning of voluntary remembering – except in terms of the statement of an inability to remember central aspects (for further discussion, see Berntsen & Rubin, 2013; Berntsen et al., 2008).

There are clear historical reasons for this overlap between Horowitz's theoretical conceptions and the PTSD diagnosis. In the middle of the 1970s, Horowitz joined a working group formed by Vietnam veterans and their advocates, struggling to convince the chief editor of DSM-III to include a diagnosis for combat-related disorders, what later became PTSD (Scott, 1990). At this time, Horowitz had just published his theory on stress response syndromes (Horowitz, 1976). As pointed out by Berntsen et al. (2008), substantial conceptual overlaps exist between the posttraumatic stress reactions identified by Horowitz (1976) and the symptoms of PTSD that were listed in the DSM-III four years later, as well as in subsequent revisions (American Psychiatric Association, 1980, 1986, 1994, 2000, 2013).

Given that these tenets from Horowitz's theory are reflected in the diagnosis, it may not be surprising that many modern theories of posttraumatic stress reactions share the assumptions that the encoding of the traumatic event is faulty and that voluntary memory access therefore is impaired. At the same time, this faulty encoding and reduced voluntary access is assumed to be the direct cause of intrusive involuntary memories of the traumatic event (see Figure 9.1).

The view illustrated by Figure 9.1 is widespread. It has been proposed by researchers with a clinical background as well as by researchers with a background in cognitive psychology. For example, citing an idea originally proposed by Conway and Pleydell-Pearce (2000), Halligan et al. (2003) observe: "Thus, if trauma memories are poorly elaborated within the autobiographical memory base (i.e., have relatively few associations with other stored information), in addition to impairing intentional retrieval, this will render memories more vulnerable to triggering by matching sensory cues, increasing the frequency of

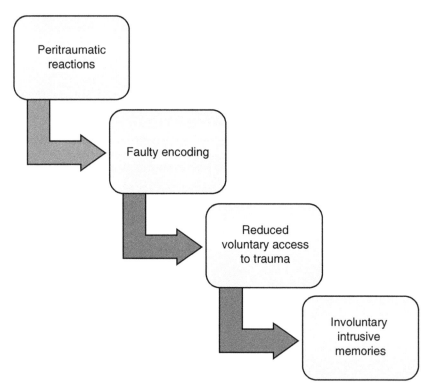

Figure 9.1. Faulty encoding and reduced voluntary memory access leading to involuntary intrusive memories according to the discontinuity view.

intrusive symptoms" (p. 419). Likewise in Brewin's dual representation theory (Brewin et al., 1996; 2010) a shallow encoding of the trauma, focusing on sensory, perceptual, and emotional aspects of the event at the cost of deeper conceptual processing and contextual integration, is claimed to cause poor intentional recall and, conversely, strong and vivid involuntary recollection. This view frequently has been repeated by other researchers. For example, Jelinek et al. (2009) observe that "distorted trauma memories of trauma survivors with PTSD manifest in vivid and highly emotional unintentional recall, as well as incoherent intentional recall" (p. 288). Thus, as in Horowitz's original theory (1975; 1976), the trauma is proposed to be incompletely processed and this lack of completion and integration leads to reduced intentional memory access and enhanced involuntary remembering. However, in spite of its popularity, very little evidence supports this theoretical view, as I argue below.

Poor intentional recall of trauma memories?

The idea of poor integration and fragmentation of trauma memories has been interpreted in many different ways. In one interpretation, it refers to the memory being poorly integrated into the cognitive structures supporting the person's life story and identity. For example, it has been assumed that traumatic experiences are encoded without adequate self-reference (Halligan et al., 2003) and that they are lacking reference to ongoing plans and goals, which normally would mediate encoding and cognitive integration (Conway & Pleydell-Pearce, 2000). For these reasons, the trauma memory is assumed to be poorly integrated and therefore difficult to access through a top-down strategic retrieval process, while at the same time frequently intruding on awareness. These assumptions are counter to a number of studies showing that schema-deviant and emotional events usually are highly accessible and vividly remembered compared with more mundane experiences (e.g., Hunt & Worthen, 2006; McGaugh, 2003). Memories for emotional events are rarely poorly integrated or lacking self-reference. Rather they are perceived as highly self-relevant and observed to become reference points for the organization of memories of less important events. For example, they tend to structure our life narratives by providing turning points and forming beginnings and ends of life time periods (e.g., Conway & Pleydell-Pearce, 2000; McAdams, 2001; Robinson, 1992; Thomsen & Berntsen, 2005) and they have been found to anchor and stabilize our conceptions of ourselves (Pillemer, 1998).

To disentangle these different possibilities for the integration – or lack of integration – of trauma memories, Berntsen and Rubin (2006) developed the Centrality of Event Scale (CES), which measures the extent to which an event is perceived as central to the person's life story and identity. The CES contains such questions as "I feel that this event has become part of my identity"; "This event has become a reference point for the way I understand myself and the world"; "I feel that this event has become a central part of my life story"; and "I often think about the effects this event will have on my future." Several studies have shown that the centrality score for traumatic events correlates positively with level of PTSD symptoms and other symptoms of distress, such as complicated grief (Berntsen & Rubin, 2006; 2007; 2008; Boelen, 2009, 2012; Brown et al., 2010; Lancaster et al., 2011; Robinaugh & McNally, 2010; Schuettler, & Boals, 2011; Smeets et al., 2010), counter to the idea of disintegration. This association remains even when controlling for factors such as depression and neuroticisms.

It might be suggested that the CES simply measures a dysfunctional "overintegration" of traumatic events that, in reality, *is* a form of disintegration. However, this interpretation is unlikely for a number of reasons. First, it would seem to predict a U-shaped functional relation between CES score and level of PTSD symptoms, which is inconsistent with the data (Berntsen & Rubin, 2007). Second, it agrees poorly with recent findings of the centrality of positive events. Consistent with a general positive self-bias (e.g., Ross & Wilson, 2002; Wilson & Ross, 2001), the centrality score for positive events has been found to be considerably higher than the centrality score for negative and traumatic events. Berntsen et al. (2011) asked more than 2,000 adults in their sixties to complete the CES for their most positive and most negative/traumatic life event, as well as measures of current PTSD symptoms, depression, well-being, and personality. Consistent with a positivity bias, the positive events were overall judged to be markedly more central to life story and identity than were the negative events. The positive events typically referred to normative life script events, such as getting married and having children, which are known to play a central role in the organization of life story and identity (Berntsen & Rubin, 2002; Bohn & Berntsen, 2008; 2013). The centrality for positive events was unrelated to measures of emotional distress (symptoms of depression and PTSD), whereas the centrality for the negative event showed clear positive correlations with such measures. Importantly, the centrality score for negative events increased systematically and even exceeded the centrality score for positive events with increasing levels of PTSD symptoms (Berntsen et al., 2011). This seems to suggest that with high levels of PTSD symptoms, memories of traumatic events may indeed become a key to identity and thereby replace, or at least challenge, standard positive life script events in the organization of life story and identity. This is counter to the idea that memory for such events is dissociated and disintegrated in PTSD. (For further discussions of this issue, see Boals and colleagues, Chapter 4; Ehlers, Chapter 6; Brown and colleagues, Chapter 15.)

Memory impairment can also refer to the remembered events being internally fragmented, for example, in terms of the remembered event having missing details and an unclear temporal order with the consequence that intentional recall of the traumatic event seems incoherent, fragmented, and with central details missing.

A number of studies have examined the level of fragmentation of trauma memories in people with PTSD (or acute stress disorder) versus individuals who have not developed PTSD in response to traumatic events in their past. Many of such studies have indeed found the trauma memories in the clinical group to be less coherent than in the control group (Amir et al., 1998; Harvey & Bryant, 1999; Jones et al., 2007; Murray et al., 2002). However, this may not be so surprising, since clinical groups often have more general cognitive disturbances compared with healthy controls. Unfortunately, none of the studies cited above included a nontrauma control memory in their comparisons, which leaves the possibility that any reduced coherence of the trauma memory observed in the clinical group reflects more general cognitive deficits in this group compared with controls (Berntsen & Rubin, 2013; Rubin, 2011). When studies have included mundane autobiographical memories as control memories they have generally found that a pattern of reduced coherence in the PTSD group is not specific to the trauma memory but generalizes to nontraumatic memories (for a review, see Berntsen & Rubin, 2013) and is therefore likely to reflect a broader cognitive deficit in the clinical (or subclinical) group compared with the control group (e.g., Gray & Lombardo, 2001).

The C3 symptom in the DSM-IV PTSD diagnosis (as well as the D1 symptom in the recent DSM-5 PTSD diagnosis) is consistent with the idea of impaired integration and fragmentation of trauma memories in PTSD because it describes an inability to recall an important aspect of the trauma, consistent with the idea of partial amnesia. However, meta-analyses of studies reported in the PTSD literature have demonstrated that this symptom does not correlate well with the other PTSD symptoms (Rubin et al., 2008a, Table 4). Recently, we have shown that a conceptual reversal of the C3 to having trouble *forgetting* important aspects of the trauma correlates significantly better with the remaining PTSD symptoms than does the original formulation of this symptom in terms of having trouble remembering important aspects (Berntsen & Rubin, 2013). In short, across a number of studies involving different samples and analyses, there is little evidence for the claim that intentional recall of trauma memories is impaired (for further discussion, see also Habermas, Chapter 13; Berntsen & Rubin, 2013; Kihlstrom, 2006; McNally, 2003).

Enhanced involuntary recall of trauma memories?

There is no doubt that individuals who have survived traumatic events or suffered severe losses often may have involuntary memories of the traumatic event. But is it the case that these involuntary memories come at the cost of voluntary retrieval, as the theoretical understanding illustrated by Figure 9.1 proposes? According to this view, peritraumatic reactions at the time of the traumatic event cause faulty encoding of the event, leading to poor intentional access and causing repeated intrusive memories of the traumatic event. The alternative view is illustrated in Figure 9.2. Because the traumatic event is highly emotional and distinctive it will be encoded very well and hold a privileged position in memory. This, in turn, leads to enhanced access to the event for both involuntary and voluntary retrieval (Hall & Berntsen, 2008; Berntsen & Rubin, 2008; Rubin et al., 2008b). As I review below, studies that have included both a voluntary and involuntary recall condition support this alternative view.

As mentioned in the beginning of this chapter, the idea of involuntary, intrusive memories as a stress response was introduced by Horowitz (1976) in his influential theory of stress response syndromes. His main evidence derived from an experimental paradigm that modern researchers call a trauma analog paradigm (see Clark and colleagues, Chapter 7) where aversive films or photographs are used as analog for real traumatic events.

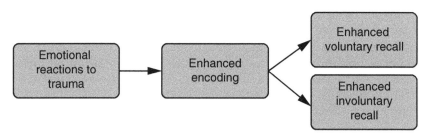

Figure 9.2. The continuity view: the emotionality and distinctiveness of the trauma leading to enhanced encoding, which enhances both voluntary and involuntary access to the traumatic event.

In a number of experiments reported by Horowitz (1975), groups of subjects saw either a stressful film (involving bodily injury threat) or a neutral film. Afterward, the subjects participated in a trivial signal detection task that demanded continuous attention. This task was frequently interrupted and the subject was asked to write a report of his or her mental contents during the preceding period. Subjects who had seen a stressful film reported significantly more intrusive thoughts than subjects who had been watching a neutral film. Horowitz concluded that the intrusive memories as observed clinically after traumatic life events should be regarded as extreme forms of the same stress response tendency. His theoretical explanation for the intrusive memories and thoughts about the stressful material was the idea described earlier in this chapter that the stressful events were difficult to process and integrate with existing cognitive structures, for which reason they become part of an "active memory storage" (p. 1461), which automatically repeats its own content until the information in question has become integrated with preexisting schemata of the self and the world.

One serious problem with Horowitz's studies was, however, that only involuntary, intrusive memories were examined, whereas voluntary recall of the stressful film was never measured. It therefore remained an unexamined question whether intentional access to the aversive film stimuli was similarly enhanced, as the alternative model depicted in Figure 9.2 would suggest. Only very recently has this question been examined empirically. As I review here, the findings contradict the claim that involuntary (compared with voluntary) remembering has privileged access to stressful/traumatic material as well as the related point that PTSD increases that privileged access. Instead, the findings reviewed in the following suggest that the memory enhancement associated with stressful/traumatic material concerns *both* involuntary and voluntary memory and that both involuntary and voluntary memories of the traumatic event are enhanced in PTSD, consistent with the understanding illustrated in Figure 9.2.

Some studies have compared involuntary memories of negative stimuli with (voluntary) recognition for the same stimuli. Such studies have generally found no correlations between these two measures (for review, see Brewin, 2014). However, this is hardly surprising since it is well established that recall and recognition form two different memory tasks, with the former generally considered more demanding than the latter. A more valid comparison is between involuntary and voluntary recall, for which robust positive correlations are seen.

Hall and Berntsen (2008) followed the leads of Horowitz and used emotionally upsetting photographs as a trauma analog. They obtained individual recordings of the participants' emotional reactions to these aversive pictures at the time of encoding. Afterward, the participants participated in a diary study where they made records of both involuntary and voluntary memories over the following five days. The findings showed that the emotional distress associated with the pictures at the time of encoding strongly predicted the frequency with which the memories were retrieved in the subsequent diary study, and this did interact with whether retrieval was involuntary or voluntary. Similar findings were reported by Ferree and Cahill (2009) in a study using emotional films as memory material. Ferree and Cahill showed that the number of intrusive memories of the film recorded in a diary study was highly correlated with the participants' performance on a voluntary recall task for the stressful film.

Do these findings using the trauma analog paradigm generalize to real-life traumatic events and individuals suffering from clinical or subclinical levels of PTSD in response to such traumas? The answer seems to be yes. Recent studies have shown that involuntary and voluntary remembering is similarly affected by real-life traumatic events and that the accessibility of the trauma increases for both types of recall with increasing levels of PTSD. In a diary study of undergraduates with a history of trauma and with either high or low levels of PTSD symptoms, Rubin et al. (2008b) found that undergraduates with high levels of PTSD symptoms recorded more memories related to their traumatic events than did participants with low symptom levels. Consistent with the understanding illustrated by Figure 9.2 (but counter to Figure 9.1), this effect was found to the same extent for both voluntary and involuntary recall. Similar findings were more recently obtained in a clinical sample (Rubin et al., 2011). Compared with a non-PTSD control group, individuals diagnosed with PTSD recorded more memories related to their trauma, but this effect was found to the same extent for both voluntary and involuntary recall (see also Rubin, Chapter 3).

In short, emotional stress at the time of encoding enhances subsequent accessibility of the memory for both involuntary and voluntary recall. This enhanced access is amplified with higher levels of PTSD symptoms. These findings are consistent with the view illustrated by Figure 9.2 but counter to the idea that emotional stress at encoding has differential effects on involuntary and voluntary remembering as well as the related idea that emotional stress leads to reduced voluntary recall of the event in terms of fragmented and disintegrated memories (Figure 9.1). In the next section, I discuss how intrusive memories of traumatic events may be explained based on what we generally know about mechanisms underlying involuntary autobiographical memories in everyday life.

Intrusive and everyday involuntary memories: how are they related?

Today we know much more about autobiographical memory in general and involuntary autobiographical memory in particular than Horowitz did when he launched his influential theory. Can this new knowledge help us to develop an explanation of the activation of intrusive memories in psychopathological disorders? In the remaining parts of this chapter I first describe what we know about the characteristics of involuntary autobiographical memories as they occur in daily life, including the mechanisms underlying their activation. I then try to apply this knowledge to the occurrence of intrusive memories after traumatic events.

The characteristics of everyday autobiographical involuntary memories

Over the last two decades, evidence has accumulated showing that involuntary autobiographical memories are common in everyday life and that such memories resemble voluntary autobiographical memories in a number of ways. First, diary studies and survey studies demonstrate that involuntary remembering of personal events happens at least as frequently as voluntary recollections (Rasmussen & Berntsen, 2011; Rubin & Berntsen, 2009). Second, both involuntary and voluntary memories are most frequently about emotionally positive events and do not differ concerning the emotional intensity of the remembered events, rated retrospectively in diary studies (for a review, see Berntsen, 2009). This agrees with the laboratory studies cited above showing that emotion at the time of encoding does not differentially affect subsequent involuntary versus voluntary recall; instead, both are equally enhanced by emotion at encoding. Third, both types of memories involve reliving of the remembered event so that the person may feel as if he or she is mentally transported back in time (Tulving, 2002), and both types of memories involves sensory, predominantly visual, imagery (Brewer, 1996; Rubin et al., 2008b; 2011). There is no evidence that level of reliving and imagery is more (or less) pronounced for involuntary than for voluntary remembering (although involuntary remembering tends to involve more emotional impact at the time of retrieval, as I shall return to shortly). Fourth, the two types of memories also do not seem to differ with regard to retention time, although there may be a tendency for involuntary memories to be slightly more recent when compared with word-cued voluntary memories. Both show the standard retention curve, and for both types of memory this curve is best described in terms of a power function (for a review, see Berntsen, 2009).

In spite of these similarities, some important differences between involuntary and voluntary autobiographical memories have been observed (for reviews, see Berntsen, 2009; 2012). First, compared with voluntary memories retrieved in response to verbal cues, involuntary memories are more frequently about specific events – that is, events that refer to a particular occasion in the past (e.g., the last time I gave a talk at a conference), in contrast to more abstract representations of recurrent activities (e.g., giving talks in general). This dominance of specific episodes has been found across many studies (Berntsen, 1998; Berntsen & Hall, 2004; Berntsen & Jacobsen, 2008; Finnbogadottir & Berntsen, 2011; Johannessen & Berntsen, 2010; Mace, 2006; Schlagman & Kvavilashvili, 2008; Schlagman et al., 2009; Watson et al., 2013). Second, involuntary autobiographical memories more frequently than voluntary memories exert a detectable impact on the person's mood at the time of retrieval (Berntsen & Hall, 2004; Berntsen & Jacobsen, 2008; Finnbogadottir & Berntsen, 2011; Johannessen & Berntsen, 2010; Rubin et al., 2008b; 2011; Watson et al., 2012) and tend to be more frequently followed by a behavioral or emotional reaction, such as smiling, laughing, crying, or feeling butterflies in one's stomach (Berntsen & Hall, 2004; Rubin et al., 2008b; 2011; Watson et al., 2012). This enhanced emotional impact of the involuntary memories is most likely due to their unbidden and uncontrollable retrieval, leaving little room for antecedent emotion regulation (Gross, 2001). As I have argued elsewhere (e.g., Berntsen, 2009; 2012), these differences between involuntary and voluntary autobiographical memories are most likely caused by differences in the way the two types of memories are retrieved – a topic to which I turn now.

How do involuntary autobiographical memories come to mind?

Diary studies yield consistent findings regarding the retrieval of involuntary autobiographical memories (for overviews, see Berntsen, 2009; 2012). Involuntary memories are generally triggered by some identifiable features of the ongoing situation that match parts of the memory. This cue is often peripheral to the ongoing activity in the retrieval situation (e.g., a song played on the radio while the person is studying) but central to the content of the memory (e.g., a school performance in the music class involving that particular song).

These findings suggest that involuntary autobiographical memories represent an associative, context-sensitive mode of constructing memories – a mode that is dependent on salient characteristics of the environment and the links they have formed to memory through the previous activities of the individual. There is some evidence to suggest that this mode is evolutionarily older and present in nonhuman animals (Martin-Ordas et al., 2013). But exactly how does this involuntary retrieval work?

Many theorists have invoked the notion of encoding specificity in order to explain the activation of involuntary episodic memories (e.g., Conway, 2005). According to this principle, the probability of successfully retrieving a memory increases by increasing overlap between the information present at retrieval (i.e., the cue) and the information stored in memory (Tulving & Thomson, 1973). Although this seems to be a straightforward explanation, the idea of an encoding-retrieval match leaves several questions unresolved. First, assuming that features in the retrieval context overlap with the content of several past events, why does one of these memories (but not the others) become activated? Second, explanations based on the encoding-retrieval match fail to explain why we are not constantly flooded by involuntary episodic memories. Any moment in our lives seems to include an almost endless number of potential memory cues in terms of features that were also part of our past experiences. When we dwell on such features in an ongoing situation, we are able to voluntarily generate memories in response to many of them (Berntsen & Hall, 2004; Galton, 1907). Thus, if having involuntary autobiographical memories were simply a matter of an encoding-retrieval match, it seems that we should be flooded by involuntary memories throughout our waking lives. But normally we are not.

One solution to this puzzle is that it is the *uniqueness*, not the size, of the encoding-retrieval match that is decisive for having an involuntary memory. This point may be illustrated by the following example. Assume that you are in a seminar room attending (or maybe teaching) a class on autobiographical memory. You are surrounded by the other participants in this class, as you have been at many other occasions during this semester. Being back in class today is unlikely to suddenly activate a spontaneous memory of one of the earlier occasions, although there is an extensive feature overlap. But assume something unusual happens. The projector does not work. You may then immediately remember an earlier occasion this semester where the projector also failed to work. If the projector has failed to work only once before during this semester's autobiographical memory class, this feature overlap between the current and this past situation is unique, which increases the probability that the memory of the first occasion will come to mind. This may even help you fix the problem (by reminding you how you solved the problem the previous time; e.g., Schank, 1982). Adhering to the uniqueness of the encoding-retrieval match does two things for us. First, it explains why we are not constantly flooded by involuntary memories. The answer is simply that it is relatively rare to find oneself in situations in which there is a feature overlap with a past event that is sufficiently distinct to activate a memory of this event. Second, a unique feature overlap increases the probability that the remembered event will bear some relevance to the retrieval situation. Of course, this does not mean that all involuntary memories are useful, only that the mechanisms underlying their activation increase the probability that they may be.

Ongoing experiments in our laboratory provide evidence that the uniqueness (not the size per se) of the associative link between the cue and the target (memory) is decisive for the activation of involuntary memories of neutral scenes. In these experiments, the participants are first presented with a series of visually presented scenes, each coupled with a sound (e.g., a scene with a dog and the sound of a dog barking). Some of these pairs are unique in that the sound and the scene derive from a category that is presented only once; others are repeated – that is, the same types of sounds (e.g., barking dogs) and the same types of scenes (e.g., scenes with dogs) are presented multiple times. After this encoding phase, the participants are presented with the sounds they just heard in a sound location task. They are told that spontaneously arousing images may interfere when they conduct the task. And they are instructed to press a button if this happens. As expected based on the idea that the uniqueness of the encoding-retrieval match is decisive, involuntary memories of the scenes predominantly arise in response to unique sounds that were coupled with unique scenes during encoding (Berntsen et al., 2013).

The idea that the uniqueness of the encoding-retrieval match is important for the retrieval of memories is not new; it is known from the verbal learning tradition and the concept of cue overload (Watkins & Watkins, 1975). The principle of cue overload states that "the probability of recalling an item declines with the number of items subsumed by its functional retrieval cue" (p. 442). This idea was further elaborated by Rubin (1995), who introduced the notion of cue-item discriminability according to which a cue, or cue configuration, associated with just one item (or event) would have a high ability to discriminate this particular item from other items in memory.

However, the discriminability of a situational cue is just one part of the story. The other part is the general salience of the past event in memory, irrespective of momentarily present cues. The strength of the memory itself is determined by factors at encoding, such as strong emotion that facilitates an elaborated encoding and consolidation, as well as by factors influencing the maintenance of the event in memory, such as the time since the event and the frequency of rehearsal. Such factors enhance the accessibility of both involuntary and voluntary memories (e.g., Berntsen, 2009) and are especially important to also take into consideration when considering intrusive memories after stressful events because of the high levels of emotion and self-relevance associated with such events.

How the findings may help us to understand intrusive memories

In the memory description that opened this chapter an older woman had an intrusive memory of a terrifying day fifty-six years earlier when she had run for shelter during a bomb attack. The intrusive memory was activated when she was watching the collapse of the World Trade Center on television on September 11, 2001. There was a clear and distinct feature overlap between the present and the past situation, and following the principle of cue-item discriminability it makes sense why this memory involuntarily came to her mind at that moment. After all, the sight of a big building collapsing due to a strike is rare, especially for a woman who has lived her life in a relatively peaceful country.

However, not all intrusive memories seem so easily explained with reference to this simple associative mechanism. In fact, many intrusive memories are recurrent and often come to mind in response to features that appear to have been associated with very many past events. Ehlers et al. (2004) describe an example where a bright patch of sunlight on the lawn appears to trigger an intrusion of approaching headlights in a survivor of a motor vehicle accident (example 10 in Ehlers et al., 2004). They also report a different example (example 11) where another survivor of a motor vehicle accident has an intrusive image of the bus that had hit her car. The intrusion came when she turned her head to the left to reach for a tea towel and thereby made a head movement similar to one she had made immediately after the crash.

To the extent these reports are adequate descriptions of the retrieval situation, the involuntary memories do not seem to have had a unique encoding-retrieval match. In each case the cue is a common feature that is likely to be associated with multiple events. Therefore, the cue suffers from cue overload and should be unlikely to activate any of the past events due to response competition, following the explanation in the previous section.

However, this explanation would be valid only if all the past events associated with the cue had equal salience in memory. As already mentioned, the accessibility of past events in memory is also determined by factors influencing encoding and maintenance, such as emotional arousal and subsequent rehearsal. Clearly, such factors are likely to play a central role in relation to traumatic events. As pointed out by Berntsen and Rubin (2008), such events would stand out because they satisfy multiple accessibility constraints of autobiographical memory, notably, distinctiveness and high emotional intensity, which are known to enhance memory access. Also due to frequent rehearsal and life impact, the traumatic event may become an enduring landmark for the person's life story and identity (Berntsen & Rubin, 2007).

As a consequence of the increased salience, a situational feature that is associated with many past events and that therefore under normal conditions would hold little discriminability nonetheless may be able to trigger a memory for the traumatic event. This point can be illustrated by an example from one of my own diary studies. A young female participant in a diary study (Berntsen, 2001) reported three involuntary memories of a traumatic event in which she had been physically assaulted by her former boyfriend. None of them appeared to have highly distinct cues. On the contrary, they were activated in response to features potentially matching many past events. For example, one memory came to her mind at a crowded birthday party with lots of noise and smoke around her. In this context she involuntarily remembered "what he looked like on that day when he came home, how he smelled of beer and smoke" (for further analyses, see Berntsen & Rubin, 2008).

Although the smell of beer and cigarette smoke is likely to have been associated with many past events in this woman's life, these mundane events do not have the same salience as the traumatic event. Because of its extraordinary distinctiveness and high emotionality the traumatic event stands out in memory and can thus be activated by cues that would normally be too indiscriminate to access any memories. Expressed in the language of the verbal learning tradition, the memory of the traumatic event breaks away from proactive and retroactive interference due to its inherent salience in memory, and therefore may be repeatedly activated even by indistinct cues (e.g., Bjork, 2003). This is illustrated by Figure 9.3.

In this view, the activation of involuntary memories in general and intrusive memories in particular reflects an interaction between the discriminability of the cues available in the present situation and, on the other hand, the general salience of the memories, as this is shaped by factors influencing encoding and memory maintenance – such as emotion, distinctiveness, rehearsal, and recency (Berntsen, 2009). This means that highly emotional events can be repeatedly activated by a variety of even vague situational cues, as illustrated by the examples above and by Figure 9.3. The explanation is also supported by the fact that typically the most emotional moments ("hot spots") are the ones that come repeatedly to mind (Berntsen & Rubin, 2008; e.g., Clark and

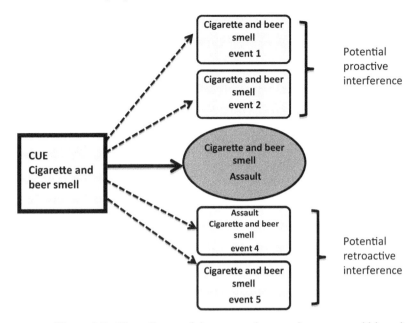

Figure 9.3. The salience of the traumatic event in memory. Although the cue (smell of beer and cigarette smoke) is associated with other events, both before and after the trauma, it is nonetheless capable of making the trauma discriminable on the basis of association. The memory of the traumatic event breaks away from proactive and retroactive interference due to its enhanced salience in memory.

colleagues, Chapter 7). Subjectively, it may seem as if these different temporal and narrative aspects of the traumatic memory take turns in presenting themselves in consciousness in response to random features of the environment or thought. This situation can indeed be very bothersome. In essence, the traumatic memory breaks away from the mechanisms that normally prevent us from being flooded by involuntary memories.

These mechanisms can explain the *recurrent* nature of intrusive trauma memories. How should we explain the extraordinary reliving, or "flashback" quality, which is sometimes associated with intrusive memories? Here it is important to remember that the notion of flashback originally was introduced by Horowitz (1969a) with reference to hallucinatory reliving of past psychedelic LSD trips – a reliving that happened after the physiological effect of the hallucinogens had ceased, and therefore appeared to be memory based (Frankel, 1994). Full-blown flashback states after traumatic events appear to be a rare phenomenon (e.g., Clark and colleagues, Chapter 7). For this reason, many authors use less extreme definitions of traumatic flashback, such as Clark and colleagues in Chapter 7 defining flashbacks more broadly as "distressing, image-based, involuntary autobiographical memories of trauma that hijack attention," also see the recent revision of the PTSD diagnosis (American Psychiatric Association, 2013). Such intense emotional reliving of traumatic memories may be caused by two additive factors. First, as mentioned earlier, compared with voluntary autobiographical memories, involuntary autobiographical memories are more often accompanied by detectable emotional impact and reaction. Second, the strongest predictor for such an impact is the emotional intensity associated with the remembered event (Berntsen, 2001). Since the latter is very high in the case of traumatic events, this may explain why intrusive memories of traumas often come with strong emotional reliving. But it is important to note that this mechanism is not limited to traumatic events. In addition, highly positive events can lead to involuntary memories with a "flashback-like" quality (Berntsen, 2001).

In summary, recurrent intrusive memories of traumatic events may be explained in terms of the mechanisms that govern involuntary memories in everyday life and that normally are functional. However, these same mechanisms may become dysfunctional in relation to traumatic events due to the distinctiveness and extraordinary emotion associated with this event. In this sense, Horowitz (1975) and his followers were right: recurrent intrusive memories are a response to stressful events. However, no trauma-specific mechanisms are needed to explain their existence. Instead, basic mechanisms of association and interference seem to be able to do this job together with our knowledge of emotional reactions in relation to involuntary autobiographical memories in general. These mechanisms are likely to interact with individual dispositions, such as variations in our ability to ignore or disengage from negative information (e.g., Moulds and Krans, Chapter 8; Ehlers & Clark, 2000; Koster et al., 2011). Examining how such individual dispositions affect involuntary remembering is an important task for future research. Future research should also study the mechanisms delineated here in relation to memory for other types of extreme events, such as memories of intensely pleasant, sexually arousing, or provoking experiences as well as in relation to disorders other than PTSD.

Acknowledgments

I thank David C. Rubin for comments and the Danish National Research Foundation (grant DNRF93) and the Danish Council for Independent Research: Humanities for support.

REFERENCES

American Psychiatric Association (1980). *Diagnostic and Statistical Manual of Mental Disorders* (3rd ed.). Washington, DC: American Psychiatric Association.
  (1986). *Diagnostic and Statistical Manual of Mental Disorders* (3rd ed. rev). Washington, DC: American Psychiatric Association.
  (1994). *Diagnostic and Statistical Manual of Mental Disorders* (4th ed.). Washington, DC: American Psychiatric Association.
  (2000). *Diagnostic and Statistical Manual of Mental Disorders* (4th ed. text revision). Washington, DC: American Psychiatric Association.
  (2013). *Diagnostic and Statistical Manual of Mental Disorders* (5th ed.). Washington, DC: American Psychiatric Association.
Amir, N., Stafford, J. Freshman, M. S., & Foa, E. B. (1998). Relationship between trauma narratives and trauma pathology. *Journal of Traumatic Stress, 11,* 385–392.
Berntsen, D. (1996). Involuntary autobiographical memories. *Applied Cognitive Psychology, 10,* 435–454.
  (1998). Voluntary and involuntary access to autobiographical memory. *Memory, 6,* 113–141.
  (2001). Involuntary memories of emotional events: do memories of traumas and extremely happy events differ? *Applied Cognitive Psychology, 15,* 135–158.
  (2009). *Involuntary Autobiographical Memories: An Introduction to the Unbidden Past.* Cambridge: Cambridge University Press.
  (2012). Spontaneous recollections: involuntary autobiographical memories as a basic mode of remembering. In D. Berntsen & D. C. Rubin (eds.), *Understanding Autobiographical Memory: Theories and Approaches* (pp. 290–310). Cambridge: Cambridge University Press.
Berntsen, D., & Hall, N. M. (2004). The episodic nature of involuntary autobiographical memories. *Memory and Cognition, 32,* 789–803.
Berntsen, D., & Jacobsen, A. S. (2008). Involuntary (spontaneous) mental time travel into the past and future. *Consciousness and Cognition, 17,* 1093–1104.
Berntsen, D., & Rubin, D. C. (2002). Emotionally charged autobiographical memories across the lifespan: the recall of happy, sad, traumatic, and involuntary memories. *Psychology and Aging, 17,* 636–652.
  (2006). The centrality of event scale: a measure of integrating a trauma into one's identity and its relation to post-traumatic stress disorder symptoms. *Behaviour Research and Therapy, 44,* 219–231.
  (2007). When a trauma becomes a key to identity: enhanced integration of trauma memories predicts posttraumatic stress disorder symptoms. *Applied Cognitive Psychology, 21,* 417–431.
  (2008). The reappearance hypothesis revisited: recurrent involuntary memories after traumatic events and in everyday life. *Memory and Cognition, 36,* 449–460
  (2013). Involuntary memories and dissociative amnesia: assessing key assumptions in PTSD research. *Clinical Psychological Science.* Preprint on-line publication.

Berntsen, D., & Thomsen, D.K. (2005). Personal memories for remote historical events. Accuracy and clarity for flashbulb memories related to WWII. *Journal of Experimental Psychology: General, 134,* 242–257.

Berntsen, D., Rubin, D. C., & Bohni, K. M. (2008). Contrasting models of PTSD. Reply to Monroe and Mineka. *Psychological Review, 115,* 1099–1107.

Berntsen, D., Rubin, D. C., & Siegler, I. C. (2011). Two versions of life: emotionally negative and positive life events have different roles in the organization of life story and identity. *Emotion, 11,* 1190–1201.

Berntsen, D., Staugaard, S. R., & Sørensen, L. M. T. (2013). Why am I remembering this now? Predicting the occurrence of involuntary (spontaneous) episodic memories. *Journal of Experimental Psychology: General, 142,* 426–444.

Bjork, R. A. (2003). Interference and forgetting. In J. H. Byrne (ed.), *Encyclopedia of Learning and Memory* (2nd ed.) (pp. 268–273). New York: Macmillan Reference USA.

Boelen, P. A. (2009). The centrality of a loss and its role in emotional problems among bereaved people. *Behaviour Research and Therapy, 47,* 616–622.

  (2012). A prospective examination of the association between the centrality of a loss and post-loss psychopathology. *Journal of Affective Disorders, 137,* 117–124.

Bohn, A., & Berntsen, D. (2008). Life story development in childhood: the development of life story abilities and the acquisition of cultural life scripts from late middle childhood to adolescence. *Developmental Psychology, 44,* 1135–1147.

  (2013). Cultural life scripts and the development of personal memories. In P. Bauer & R. Fivush (eds.), *Handbook of the Development of Children's Memory* (pp. 626–644). Wiley-Blackwell.

Breuer, J., & Freud, S. (1893–1895). Studies on hysteria. In *The Standard Edition of the Complete Psychological Work of Sigmund Freud,* vol. 2. London: Hogarth Press.

Brewer, W. F. (1996). What is recollective memory? In D. C. Rubin (ed.), *Remembering Our Past: Studies in Autobiographical Memory* (pp. 19–66). Cambridge: Cambridge University Press.

Brewin, C. R. (2014). Episodic memory, perceptual memory, and their interaction: foundations for a theory of posttraumatic stress disorder. *Psychological Bulletin, 140,* 98–104.

Brewin, C. R., Dalgleish, T., & Joseph, S. (1996). A dual representation theory of posttraumatic stress disorder. *Psychological Review, 103,* 670–686.

Brewin, C. R., Gregory, J. D., Lipton, M., & Burgess, N. (2010). Intrusive images in psychological disorders: characteristics, neural mechanisms, and treatment implications. *Psychological Review, 117,* 210–232.

Brown, A. D., Antonius, D., Kramer, M., Root, J. C., & Hirst, W. (2010). Trauma centrality and PTSD in veterans returning from Iraq and Afghanistan. *Journal of Traumatic Stress, 23,* 496–499.

Conway, M. A. (2005). Memory and the self. *Journal of Memory and Language, 53,* 594–628.

Conway, M. A., & Pleydell-Pearce, C. W. (2000). The construction of autobiographical memory in the self-memory system. *Psychological Review*, *107*, 261–288.
Ehlers, A., & Clark, D. M. (2000). A cognitive model of posttraumatic stress disorder. *Behaviour Research and Therapy*, *38*, 319–345.
Ehlers, A., Hackmann, A., & Michael, T. (2004). Intrusive re-experiencing in post-traumatic stress disorder: phenomenology, theory, and therapy. *Memory*, *12*, 403–415.
Ferree, N. K., & Cahill, L. (2009). Post-event spontaneous intrusive recollections and strength of memory for emotional events in men and women. *Consciousness and Cognition*, *18*, 126–134.
Finnbogadottir, H., & Berntsen, D. (2011). Involuntary mental time travel in high and low worriers. *Memory*, *19*, 625–640.
Frankel, F. H. (1994). The concept of flashback in historical perspective. *International Journal of Clinical and Experimental Hypnosis*, *42*, 321–336.
Freud, S. (1919). Introduction to "psycho-analysis and the war neurosis." *The Standard Edition of the Complete Psychological Works of Sigmund Freud*, vol. 17 (J. Strachey, ed.). London: Hogarth Press.
  (1920). Beyond the pleasure principle. In *The Standard Edition of the Complete Psychological Works of Sigmund Freud* (vol. 18, pp. 7–67). London: Hogarth Press.
Galton, F. (1907). *Inquiries into Human Faculty and Its Development*. London: J. M. Dent & Sons.
Gammelgaard, J. (1992). They suffer mainly from reminiscences. *Scandinavian Psychoanalytic Review*, *15*, 104–121.
Gray, M. J., & Lombardo, T. W. (2001). Complexity of trauma narratives as an index of fragmented memory in PTSD: a critical analysis. *Applied Cognitive Psychology*, *15*, S171–S186.
Gross, J. J. (2001). Emotion regulation in adulthood: timing is everything. *Current Directions in Psychological Science*, *10*, 214–219.
Hall, N. M., & Berntsen, D. (2008). The effect of emotional stress on involuntary and voluntary conscious memories. *Memory*, *16*, 48–57.
Halligan, S. L., Michael, T., Clark, D. M., & Ehlers, A. (2003). Posttraumatic stress disorder following assault: the role of cognitive processing, trauma memory, and appraisals. *Journal of Consulting and Clinical Psychology*, *71*, 419–431.
Harvey, A. G., & Bryant, R. A. (1999). A qualitative investigation into the organization of traumatic memories. *British Journal of Clinical Psychology*, *38*, 401–405.
Horowitz, M. J. (1969a). Flashbacks: recurrent intrusive images after the use of LSD. *American Journal of Psychiatry*, *126*, 565–569.
  (1969b). Psychic trauma: Return of images after stress film. *Archives of General Psychiatry*, *20*, 552–559.
  (1975). Intrusive and repetitive thought after experimental stress. *Archives of General Psychiatry*, *32*, 1457–1463.
  (1976). *Stress Response Syndromes*. New York: Jason Aronson.

Hunt, R. R., & Worthen, J. B. (eds.) (2006). *Distinctiveness and Memory.* New York: Oxford University Press.

Jelinek, L., Randjbar, S., Seifert, D., Kellner, M., & Moritz, S. (2009). The organization of autobiographical and nonautobiographical memory in posttraumatic stress disorder (PTSD). *Journal of Abnormal Psychology, 118,* 288–298.

Johannessen, K. B., & Berntsen, D. (2010). Current concerns in involuntary and voluntary autobiographical memories. *Consciousness and Cognition, 19,* 847–860.

Jones, C., Harvey, A. G., & Brewin, C. R. (2007). The organization and content of trauma memories in survivors of road traffic accidents. *Behaviour Research and Therapy, 45,* 151–162.

Kardiner, A. (1941). *The Traumatic Neuroses of War.* New York: Paul B. Hoeber.

Kihlstrom, J. F. (2006). Trauma and memory revisited. In B. Uttl, N. Ohta, & A. L. Siegenthaler (eds.), *Memory and Emotions: Interdisciplinary Perspectives* (pp. 259–291). New York: Blackwell.

Koster, E. H. W., Lissnyder, E. D., Derakshan, N., & Raedt, R. D. (2011). Understanding depressive rumination from a cognitive science perspective: the impaired disengagement hypothesis. *Clinical Psychological Review, 31,* 138–145.

Lancaster, S. L., Rodrigueza, B. F., & Westonb, R. (2011). Path analytic examination of a cognitive model of PTSD. *Behaviour Research and Therapy, 49,* 194–201.

Mace, J. H. (2006). Episodic remembering creates access to involuntary conscious memory: demonstrating involuntary recall on a voluntary recall task. *Memory, 14,* 217–224.

Martin-Ordas, G., Berntsen, D., & Call, J. (2013). Memory for distant past events in chimpanzees and orangutans. *Current Biology, 23,* 1–4.

McAdams, D. P. (2001). The psychology of life stories. *Review of General Psychology, 5,* 100–122.

McGaugh, J. L. (2003). *Memory and Emotion: The Making of Lasting Memories.* New York: Columbia University Press.

McNally, R. J. (2003). Progress and controversy in the study of posttraumatic stress disorder. *Annual Review of Psychology, 54,* 229–252.

Murray, J., Ehlers, A., & Mayou, R. A. (2002). Dissociation and post-traumatic stress disorder: two prospective studies of road traffic accident survivors. *British Journal of Psychiatry, 180,* 363–368.

Pillemer, D. B. (1998). *Momentous Events, Vivid Memories.* Cambridge, MA: Harvard University Press.

Rasmussen, A. S., & Berntsen, D. (2011). The unpredictable past: spontaneous autobiographical memories outnumber memories retrieved strategically. *Consciousness & Cognition, 20,* 1842–1846.

Rivers, W. H. R. (1920). *Instinct and the Unconscious: A Contribution of a Biological Theory of the Psycho-neuroses.* Cambridge: Cambridge University Press.

Robinaugh, D. J., & McNally, R. J. (2010). Autobiographical memory for shame and guilt provoking events: association with psychological symptoms. *Behaviour Research and Therapy, 48,* 646–665.

Robinson, J. A. (1992). First experiences: contexts and functions in personal histories. In M. A. Conway, D. C. Rubin, H. Spinnler, & W. Wagenaar (eds.), *Theoretical Perspectives on Autobiographical Memory* (pp. 223–239). Utrecht: Kluwer Academic.

Ross, M., & Wilson, A. E. (2002). It feels like yesterday: self-esteem, valence of personal past experiences, and judgments of subjective distance. *Journal of Personality and Social Psychology, 82*, 792–803.

Rubin, D. C. (1995). *Memory in Oral Traditions: The Cognitive Psychology of Epic, Ballads, and Counting-Out Rhymes*. New York: Oxford University Press.

(2011). The coherence of memories for trauma: evidence from posttraumatic stress disorder. *Consciousness and Cognition, 20*, 857–865.

Rubin, D. C., & Berntsen, D. (2009). The frequency of voluntary and involuntary autobiographical memories across the lifespan. *Memory and Cognition, 37*, 679–688.

Rubin, D. C., Berntsen, D., & Bohni, M. K. (2008a). A memory-based model of posttraumatic stress disorder: evaluating basic assumptions underlying the PTSD diagnosis. *Psychological Review, 115*, 985–1011.

Rubin, D. C., Boals, A., & Berntsen, D. (2008b). Memory in posttraumatic stress disorder: properties of voluntary and involuntary, traumatic and non-traumatic autobiographical memories in people with and without PTSD symptoms. *Journal of Experimental Psychology: General, 137*, 591–614.

Rubin, D. C., Dennis, M. F., & Beckham, J. C. (2011). Autobiographical memory for stressful events: the role of autobiographical memory in posttraumatic stress disorder. *Consciousness and Cognition, 20*, 840–856.

Schank, R. C. (1982). *Dynamic Memory*. New York: Cambridge University Press.

Schlagman, S., & Kvavilashvili, L. (2008). Involuntary autobiographical memories in and outside the laboratory: how different are they from voluntary autobiographical memories? *Memory and Cognition, 36*, 920–932.

Schlagman, S., Kliegel, M., Schulz, J., & Kvavilashvili, L. (2009). Effects of age on involuntary and voluntary autobiographical memory. *Psychology and Aging, 24*, 397–411.

Schuettler, D., & Boals, A. (2011). The path to posttraumatic growth versus PTSD: contributions of event centrality and coping. *Journal of Loss and Trauma, 16*,180–194.

Scott, W. J. (1990). PTSD in DSM-III. A case in the politics of diagnosis and disease. *Social Problems, 37*, 294–309.

Smeets, T., Giesbrecht, T., Raymaekers, L., Shaw, J., & Merckelbach, H. (2010). Autobiographical integration of trauma memories and repressive coping predict post-traumatic stress symptoms in undergraduate students. *Clinical Psychology and Psychotherapy.17*, 211–218.

Thomsen, D. K., & Berntsen, D. (2005). The end point effect in autobiographical memory: more than a calendar is needed. *Memory, 13*, 846–861.

Tulving, E. (2002). Episodic memory: from mind to brain. *Annual Review of Psychology, 53*, 1–25.

Tulving, E., & Thomson, D. M. (1973). Encoding specificity and retrieval processes in epsodic memory. *Psychological Review, 80*(5), 352–373.

Watkins, O. C., & Watkins, M. J. (1975). Build up of proactive inhibition as a cue-overload effect. *Journal of Experimental Psychology. Human Learning and Memory, 1,* 442–452.

Watson, L. A., Berntsen, D., Kuyken, W., & Watkins, E. R. (2012). The characteristics of involuntary and voluntary autobiographical memories in depressed and never depressed individuals. *Consciousness and Cognition, 21,* 1382–1392.

   (2013). Involuntary and voluntary autobiographical memory specificity as a function of depression. *Journal of Behaviour Therapy and Experimental Psychiatry, 44,* 7–13.

Wilson, A., & Ross, M. (2001). From chump to champ: people's appraisals of their earlier and present selves. *Journal of Personality and Social Psychology, 80,* 572–584.

Part III

Overgeneral autobiographical memories and their mechanisms

10 Overgeneral autobiographical memories and their relationship to rumination

Edward Watkins

Introduction

Overgeneral autobiographical memory (Williams et al., 2007) is the recall of categoric summaries of repeated events (e.g., "playing golf every week") even when asked to recall specific memories that are located at a particular place and time (e.g., "beating my friend Paul at golf last Saturday"). Overgeneral memory recall is clinically important because it is elevated in depressed patients (e.g., Kuyken & Brewin, 1995; Williams & Broadbent, 1986) and formerly depressed patients compared with controls (Brittlebank et al., 1993; Mackinger et al., 2000) and predicts poorer long-term outcomes including future depression (Brittlebank et al., 1993; Dalgleish et al., 2001; Mackinger et al., 2000; for review, see Williams et al., 2007). Thus, categoric autobiographical memory is either a marker for or itself a vulnerability factor for depression.

As research has sought to understand the mechanisms underpinning the development and maintenance of overgeneral autobiographical memory in depression, convergent evidence has increasingly implicated a key role for ruminative thinking. More recently, there is also preliminary evidence that manipulating the specificity of autobiographical memory recall may itself influence rumination. This chapter therefore briefly summarizes the rumination literature and then reviews the evidence that rumination causally influences overgeneral autobiographical memory, and vice versa. Through this chapter, the concept of abstract processing will emerge and be discussed as a unifying construct across rumination and overgeneral memory.

Rumination

Rumination is defined as "behaviours and thoughts that focus one's attention on one's depressive symptoms and on the implications of those symptoms" (Nolen-Hoeksema, 1991, p. 569). In practice, rumination involves repeated dwelling on the self, depressed symptoms, upsetting events, and personal problems, for example, "Why did this happen to me? Why do I feel like this? Why do I always react this way?"

Both prospective longitudinal and experimental studies have confirmed that rumination plays an important causal role in the onset, maintenance, and recurrence of depression. Rumination prospectively predicts the onset of major depressive episodes and the severity of depressive symptoms in nondepressed and currently depressed individuals, and mediates the effects of other risk factors on depression (e.g., Nolen-Hoeksema, 2000; Spasojević & Alloy, 2001; see meta-analysis by Mor & Winquist, 2002; reviews by Nolen-Hoeksema et al., 2008; Watkins, 2008). Rumination is elevated in women relative to men, and in currently depressed and recovered depressed patients relative to healthy controls.

Rumination also prospectively predicts symptoms of anxiety after controlling for baseline anxiety, as shown in numerous longitudinal studies (Watkins, 2008). For example, rumination predicts the onset and severity of posttraumatic stress symptoms and diagnosis of posttraumatic stress disorder (PTSD) up to three years after traumatic events (e.g., Ehlers et al., 1998). Moreover, two large-scale longitudinal studies found that rumination explained the concurrent and prospective associations between symptoms of anxiety and depression (McLaughlin & Nolen-Hoeksema, 2011). Rumination also prospectively predicts substance abuse (Nolen-Hoeksema et al., 2007; Skitch & Abela, 2008), alcohol abuse (Caselli et al., 2010), and eating disorders (Holm-Denoma & Hankin, 2010; Nolen-Hoeksema et al., 2007), after controlling for initial symptoms. These convergent data across studies have led to the proposal that rumination may be a transdiagnostic process, that is, a process present across multiple psychiatric diagnoses, and that causally contributes to those disorders (Ehring & Watkins, 2008; Harvey et al., 2004; Nolen-Hoeksema & Watkins, 2011).

Furthermore, there is extensive experimental evidence that manipulating rumination causally influences existing negative affect and negative cognition, suggesting that it may be a key driver in the activation of maladaptive patterns of information processing associated with an episode of depression. Studies have used a standardized rumination induction, in which participants are instructed to spend eight minutes concentrating on a series of sentences that involve rumination about themselves, their current feelings, and physical state and the causes and consequences of their feelings (e.g., "Think about the way you feel inside"; Lyubomirsky & Nolen-Hoeksema, 1995). As a control condition, a distraction induction is typically used, in which participants are instructed to spend eight minutes concentrating on a series of sentences that involve imagining visual scenes that are unrelated to the self or to current feelings (e.g., "Think about a fire darting round a log in a fireplace").

Compared with the distraction induction, the rumination induction is reliably found to have negative consequences on mood and cognition, but only when participants are already in a negative rather than a neutral mood (e.g., selected dysphoric or depressed participants, or following a sad mood induction). Thus, for participants in a sad mood, compared with distraction, rumination exacerbates negative mood, increases negative thinking about the self, increases negative autobiographical memory recall, increases negative thinking about the future, impairs concentration and central executive functioning, and impairs social problem solving (e.g., Lyubomirsky & Nolen-Hoeksema, 1995; Rimes & Watkins, 2004; Watkins & Brown, 2002; Watkins & Teasdale, 2001; see review in Watkins, 2008). Thus, ruminative thinking can act to fuel a negative spiral between cognition and emotion, resulting in depression.

This convergent evidence indicates the importance of rumination in depression, of understanding the mechanisms underpinning rumination, and of deriving tractable theoretical accounts of rumination. Experimental attempts to disentangle the mechanisms of rumination further revealed that there are distinct modes of processing within rumination, each with distinct functional effects (adaptive versus maladaptive, e.g., Watkins & Moulds, 2005; Watkins & Teasdale, 2001; 2004). These studies led to the elaboration of a processing mode theory, which distinguishes between abstract versus concrete processing modes within rumination (Watkins, 2008). An abstract processing mode involves focusing on general, superordinate, and decontextualized mental representations that convey the essential meaning, causes, and implications of goals and events, including the "why" aspects of an action and the ends consequential to it. Such abstract thinking is characteristic of the phenomenology of depressive rumination. In contrast, a concrete processing mode involves a focus on the direct, specific, and contextualized experience of an event and on the details of goals, events, and actions that denote the feasibility, mechanics, and means of "how" to do the action. The processing mode theory hypothesized that abstract processing of negative information is maladaptive relative to concrete processing. The rationale behind the processing mode theory and relevant evidence is described in more detail in the section titled "Abstract Processing Causally Influences Rumination and Its Consequences."

Rumination causally influences overgeneral autobiographical memory

When examined in patients with depression, the standard experimental manipulations of rumination versus distraction were found to influence overgeneral autobiographical memory recall: compared with distraction, rumination reduced the specificity of autobiographical memory retrieval (Kao et al., 2006; Park et al., 2004; Watkins & Teasdale, 2001; 2004; Watkins et al., 2000; see Williams et al., 2007 for discussion).

Watkins and Teasdale (2001) further distinguished between two components within the standard conceptualization of rumination: focus on the self and symptoms versus a particular processing style or mode characterized by analytical-evaluative thinking focused on meanings and implications (e.g., asking "Why me?"). To investigate hypothesized differential effects of self-focus versus the analytical processing mode, Watkins and Teasdale (2001) developed four alternative versions of the standard experimental manipulations to manipulate these different dimensions in a 2 × 2 design: high analytical, high self-focus (rumination); low analytical, low self-focus (distraction); low analytical, high self-focus (experiential self-focus); high analytical, low self-focus (abstraction). Thus, the two high self-focus manipulations were equivalent in focus on mood, symptoms, and self but differ in the mode of thinking, either encouraging an analytical, conceptual, abstract orientation (i.e., starting with the prompt "'Think about the causes, meanings and consequences of...") or an experiential orientation (starting with the prompt "Focus your attention on your experience of..."), each applied to the same self-related and feeling-focused items (e.g., "how happy or sad you feel," "how alert or tired you feel"). The abstraction condition involved focus on abstract non-self-related concepts, such as "Think about whether the ends justify the means." The distraction condition was the same as the previous distraction condition used by Lyubomirsky and Nolen-Hoeksema (1995).

This experiment found a double dissociation between the effects of self-focus and processing mode in patients with depression. First, self-focus but not processing mode influenced self-reported mood in depressed patients following the manipulations: sad mood increased in high self-focus conditions (rumination; experiential self-focus) relative to low self-focus conditions (distraction; abstraction). Second, processing mode but not self-focus influenced the proportion of overgeneral autobiographical memories recalled from before to after the manipulation: the proportion of categoric memories recalled increased in the high analytical/abstract conditions (rumination; abstraction) relative to the low analytical/abstract conditions (experiential self-focus; distraction).

Thus, the mode of processing adopted during rumination (analytical and abstract versus concrete and experiential) influenced the recall of overgeneral autobiographical memories, indicating that this recall was influenced by thinking style at retrieval. This pattern of findings was replicated by Watkins and Teasdale (2004), who compared analytical versus experiential self-focus in depressed patients. Again, these two manipulations had distinct functional effects on overgeneral autobiographical memory recall in depressed patients: conceptual-evaluative self-focus maintained overgeneral autobiographical memory recall, whereas experiential self-focus reduced overgeneral autobiographical memory recall (Watkins & Teasdale, 2004).

These results suggested that rumination can have a causal role in influencing overgeneral autobiographical memory. More specifically, they indicated that reducing rumination is associated with reductions in categoric memory recall and that the abstract processing element of rumination is important. However, this left open the question of whether overgeneral autobiographical memory can be experimentally induced in nondysphoric participants, that is, whether this effect generalizes to other individuals. Moreover, to date, studies had shown only that reducing rumination was associated with reductions in overgeneral autobiographical memory. Definitive evidence of the causal role of rumination in the recall of overgeneral autobiographical memories requires the demonstration that overgeneral memory recall can be induced in a sample that does not typically display it. To test this direction of causality, Barnard et al. (2006) induced setting conditions for rumination experimentally in a nonclinical sample. Phenomenologically, rumination involves perseverative thinking on repetitive and narrow themes about self-related material (typically on negative content). Theoretically, this can be conceptualized as the combination of an abstract processing mode focused on meanings and implications coupled with a relatively impoverished schematic model, such that there is limited scope for a wide range of thoughts, resulting in the same negative thoughts recurring again and again (Barnard et al., 2006).

To recreate this pattern of processing experimentally, Barnard et al. (2006) manipulated a category fluency task. In the "blocked" condition, participants repeatedly generated self-related information on the same theme across each block in the category fluency task to parallel perseverative thinking associated with an impoverished schematic model. In the contrasting "intermixed" condition, participants generated self-related information in the category fluency task within blocks that intermixed prompts across superordinate themes to minimize the recreation of perseverative thinking. Thus, while both conditions generated self-related information in the category fluency task to the same sets of stimuli arranged across blocks, in the "blocked" condition, self-related information was generated on the same theme repeatedly, whereas in the "intermixed" condition, self-related information moved rapidly across themes. As predicted, there were fewer specific autobiographical memories and more categoric memories generated in the blocked (ruminative) condition than in the intermixed condition, but only when the themes were self-related. No difference was found in a subsequent study when the themes related to the activities of animals. Thus, this study provides convergent evidence in a different population and with a different rumination induction that rumination causally contributes to the reduction in specific autobiographical memory recall.

In a further experimental study, Raes et al. (2008) examined whether inducing an abstract evaluative ruminative mode relative to a more concrete, process-focused mode could influence overgeneral memory recall in students. Previous studies had shown that participants trained to think in an abstract or concrete way, through repeated practice at either abstractly evaluating the causes, meanings, and implications of emotional scenarios or imagining the concrete details of how an event is occurring, responded differently to an unanticipated failure. Individuals trained to think about emotional events in a concrete way had reduced emotional reactivity to a subsequent experimental stressor relative to those who were trained to think abstractly (Moberly & Watkins, 2006; Watkins et al., 2008). Raes and colleagues adapted these approaches to examine whether training participants to adopt a more abstract mode would maintain overgeneral autobiographical memory recall in 195 undergraduates. Because the standard Autobiographical Memory Test utilized to assess overgenerality of memory is not sensitive in nonclinical populations, a more sensitive test, the Sentence Completion for Events from the Past Test (SCEPT), was used. This involves participants being provided with a written list of sentence stems (e.g., "I often…"), which they then complete. These completions are then rated on the standard autobiographical memory task categories for whether the completions reflect specific or categoric autobiographical memories.

Participants were exposed to training in the two different modes across twelve emotional scenarios, of which six were positive and six were negative (e.g., "car accident," "birthday surprise"), to match their effects on emotional valence. As predicted, the proportion of overgeneral memories recalled was significantly greater for participants who practiced in the abstract condition relative to participants who practiced in the concrete condition. Furthermore, the proportion of specific autobiographical memories recalled was significantly less for the abstract condition than the concrete condition (for more information on abstract and concrete self-images, see Rathbone and Moulin, Chapter 14).

In summary, multiple studies, with different methodologies, in clinical and nonclinical samples have found that manipulating rumination causally influences the specificity/generality of autobiographical memory recall. These results provide robust evidence consistent with the hypothesis that abstract rumination plays a causal role in the generation of overgeneral autobiographical memory. It is interesting to note, however, that self-reported trait rumination is not always found to be associated with level of memory specificity (see Smets et al., 2013, for evidence of null findings, although with the caveat that these studies were mainly in nonclinical populations). It may be that the relationship between rumination and overgeneral memory is dependent on increased clinical symptoms and/or activation of current state rumination.

These findings in turn informed the Capture and Rumination, Functional Avoidance, and Executive (CaRFAX) model of autobiographical memory (Williams et al., 2007). The CaRFAX model proposes three interacting mechanisms to account for overgeneral memory recall. First, information capture and rumination processes are hypothesized to contribute to the maintenance of overgeneral autobiographical memory retrieval. Williams et al. (2007) argued that the act of starting to retrieve autobiographical memories can activate ruminative thinking because such recall involves accessing information about the self and about personally relevant goals, which is likely to trigger rumination in those with negative self-image and/or unresolved personal goals (Watkins, 2008). Furthermore, because depressive rumination is characterized by abstract processing focused on evaluating the meanings and implications of events, it is likely to result in more abstract and generic mental representations, including the search terms used in autobiographical memory recall.

The CaRFAX model adopts the theoretical framework proposed by Conway and Pleydell-Pearce (2000) to explain the process of autobiographical memory retrieval. Key to this model is the assumption that autobiographical memory retrieval occurs in a generative way when deliberately recalling a memory in response to a request or cue, working through a hierarchy of stages of memory search. In response to a search attempt, general lifetime period information (e.g., "when I was at school") is interrogated first, which then informs the access to and search for categoric information (e.g., "when waiting for the bus"), which in turn can help to search for relevant specific perceptual and sensory detail, which needs to be added to generate a specific episodic autobiographical memory. Within this framework, the abstract processing that occurs during rumination would focus representations toward the categoric generic stage of the hierarchy of information retrieval and, thus, could interfere with moving toward the construction of a specific memory. Furthermore, the repeated elaboration of such generic descriptions, which would occur during rumination, would make this level of the hierarchy more easily accessible and build up a conceptual network of associated generic descriptions, such that when an individual sought to retrieve specific information with a generic search description, it may lead instead to activation of other generic descriptions, making it harder to access specific information. This process, called "mnemonic interlock," has been proposed as a central mechanism accounting for overgeneral autobiographical memory recall (Williams et al., 2007).

The CaRFAX model also proposes that functional avoidance may be a mechanism underpinning overgeneral autobiographical memory. There is some evidence that specific memories of negative events involve more intense affect. Thus, truncating the memory search at the more generic and categoric stage may be negatively reinforced by avoiding the more intense affect associated with specific memories (for further details, see Van den Broeck and colleagues, Chapter 11).

Finally, the CaRFAX model hypothesizes that impairments in executive capacity and control can underpin reduced specificity of autobiographical memory recall, by reducing the resources necessary for generative retrieval. Moving through the information hierarchy will require executive capacity and cognitive control to inhibit unwanted descriptions, to reduce unwanted emotional responses, and to focus on desired information. However, individuals with impaired executive control, whether due to a persistent individual difference or the consequence of state effects (e.g., depression, fatigue, alcohol) may find it more difficult to efficiently navigate the different stages of memory retrieval, causing them to be stuck at the generic level.

In sum, the CaRFAX model predicts that "overgeneral memory should shift in response to interventions that reduce the accessibility of negative self-schemas, break ruminative processing cycles, and/or train individuals in executive control of cognitive processing" (Williams et al., 2007, p. 143).

Rumination causally influences overgeneralization

In parallel to the evidence that rumination causally contributes to overgeneral autobiographical memory recall, there is evidence that implicates rumination in the generation of other forms of overgeneral thinking, such as overgeneralization. Overgeneralization has been defined as drawing a general rule or conclusion on the basis of an isolated incident that is applied across the board to related and unrelated situations. For example, a single negative event, such as doing poorly on a test, is interpreted as indicating a global, characterological inadequacy, such as being stupid. Overgeneralization is considered an important mental process because it is elevated in depression (Beck, 1976; Carver & Ganellen, 1983), appears to be specific to depression and not anxiety (Carver & Ganellen, 1983; Carver et al., 1988; Ganellen, 1988), and prospectively predicts subsequent depression (Carver, 1998; Dykman, 1996; Edelman et al., 1994), paralleling the observed properties of overgeneral autobiographical memory.

Experimental studies have shown that manipulating the processing mode during rumination influences overgeneralization. Rimes and Watkins (2005) found that the abstract-analytical rumination condition increased global self-devaluations, in the form of ratings of worthlessness and competence, relative to the experiential-concrete rumination condition, in depressed patients. Watkins and Moberly (in preparation) compared the effects of repeated training to adopt abstract versus concrete processing modes on overgeneralization in an undergraduate sample. Overgeneralization was assessed using a paradigm developed by Wenzlaff and Grozier (1988), in which each participant rates him- or herself on general trait adjectives (e.g., competence, friendliness) before and after an anagram stressor task described as an intelligence test. The extent to which failure on the task leads to increased endorsement of general trait adjectives unrelated to intelligence provides an index of overgeneralization in response to poor performance on the anagram task. As predicted, the abstract condition resulted in greater overgeneralization (reduced ratings of proficiency and friendliness) following the failure than did the concrete condition. These findings provide further evidence consistent with the processing mode theory and suggest that adoption of an abstract processing mode could account for the elevated tendency for overgeneralization found in depressed and low-self-esteem individuals.

Abstract processing causally influences rumination and its consequences

As noted earlier, Watkins (2008) proposed that the distinct consequences of rumination may depend on the processing mode (concrete versus abstract) adopted during ruminative thinking about self-related information. This theory was initially informed by the findings described above in which different variants of rumination manipulations had differential effects on mood versus specificity of autobiographical memory retrieval (Watkins & Teasdale, 2001; 2004) and was supported by further experimental studies (see below).

The processing mode theory proposes that the consequences of abstract versus concrete processing during rumination are determined by their relative sensitivity to contextual and situational detail. Relative to a concrete mode, an abstract mode (1) insulates an individual from the specific context, (2) makes the individual less distractible and less impulsive, (3) enables more consistency and stability of goal pursuit across time, and (4) allows gainful and unhelpful generalizations and inferences across different situations. However, it also (1) makes the individual less responsive to the environment and to any situational change and (2) provides fewer specific and contextual guides to action and problem solving because of its distance from the mechanics of action (Watkins, 2011). When faced with difficulties and negative events, concrete processing will be adaptive relative to abstract processing because it will result in (1) improved self-regulation focused on the immediate demands of the situation rather than its evaluative implications; (2) reduced negative overgeneralizations to emotional events, which contribute to increased emotional reactivity and vulnerability to depression; and (3) more effective problem solving.

Consistent with this theory, experimental studies have robustly found that abstract rumination causes negative consequences relative to concrete rumination, at least when focused on negative self-relevant information. As noted earlier, the standardized rumination induction was adapted into two variants that each retained the key original element of focus on self and mood, but with distinct instructions to induce concrete ("focus attention on the experience of") versus abstract ("think about the causes, meanings, and consequences of") processing. In depressed patients, compared with abstract rumination, concrete rumination reduced recall of overgeneral autobiographical memories (Watkins & Teasdale, 2001; 2004), reduced negative global self-judgments (Rimes & Watkins, 2005), improved recovery from prior negative events (Watkins, 2004), and improved social problem solving (Watkins & Moulds, 2005). Providing a conceptual replication to this finding, prompting abstract rumination (questions such as "Why did this problem happen?") impaired social problem solving in a recovered depressed group, who performed as well as never-depressed participants in a no-prompt control condition, whereas prompting concrete rumination ("How are you deciding what to do next?") ameliorated the problem-solving deficit found in currently depressed patients (Watkins & Baracaia, 2002).

Finally, repeated training to think in a concrete mode reduced subsequent emotional reactivity to analog loss and trauma events, relevant to training in an abstract mode (Watkins et al., 2008). Participants imagined thirty emotional scenarios (e.g., argument with best friend) in one or another mode of processing as training before a stressful anagram test. In the abstract training condition, for one minute per each scenario, participants were asked to "think about why it happened and to analyze the causes, meanings, and implications of this event." In the concrete training condition, for one minute per each scenario, participants were asked to "focus on how it happened and to imagine in your mind as vividly and as concretely as possible a 'movie' of how this event unfolded." The training mode was found to causally influence despondency after failure (Watkins et al., 2008).

Together, these studies provide convergent evidence that an abstract processing mode contributes to the negative consequences of rumination, relative to a more concrete mode. Because such abstract processing is characteristic of naturally occurring depressive rumination, it may be an important component of the negative effects of depressive rumination.

Because processing mode is observed to influence the consequences of rumination, a logical question is whether specificity of autobiographical memory retrieval also influences rumination. After all, overgeneral autobiographical memories are characterized by an abstract, generic form of mental representation, whereas specific autobiographical memories are characterized by recall of contextual and sensory-perceptual detail, necessarily involving more concrete representations. Thus, it is hypothesized that recall of categoric memories may causally contribute to rumination. To test this hypothesis, Raes et al. (2006) manipulated undergraduate students to recall either specific or overgeneral memories and then counted the number of sentences unscrambled with a ruminative meaning on a scrambled sentence task. In the specific retrieval style manipulation, participants were given word cues and asked to recall specific memories to the cues, whereas in the overgeneral retrieval style manipulation, participants were asked to recall categoric memories to the same cues. In high trait ruminators, relative to the specific retrieval condition, the overgeneral retrieval resulted in more ruminative completions. There was no effect of the memory manipulation in low trait ruminators. This study provides preliminary evidence that specificity of memory recall may influence ruminative processing, although it needs to be interpreted cautiously because the scrambled sentence task provided only an indirect measure of rumination and did not directly assess ongoing ruminative thinking.

Targeting abstract processing reduces rumination and depression

The experimental research reviewed above suggests that repeated and systematic targeting of abstract processing may be an efficacious intervention to reduce rumination and, thereby, treat depression. Consistent with the hypothesized causal relationship between processing mode and individual differences in rumination, a proof-of-principle randomized controlled treatment trial found that training stable dysphoric individuals (Beck Depression Inventory > 16 on two occasions separated by two weeks) to be more concrete when faced with difficulties reduced depression, anxiety, and rumination relative to a no-treatment control and a bogus training control (Watkins et al., 2009). The concreteness training involved repeated practice via direct instructions and guiding questions at (1) focusing on details in the moment (e.g., participants were asked to focus on and describe what they could see, hear, feel), (2) noticing what is specific and distinctive about the context of the event, (3) noticing the process of how events and behaviors unfolded (e.g., "imagine a movie of how events unfolded"), and (4) generating detailed step-by-step plans of how to proceed from here. Participants practiced audio-recorded exercises on a CD daily for one week.

In a follow-up phase II randomized controlled trial, concreteness training adapted as a facilitated self-help treatment was found to be superior to treatment-as-usual in reducing rumination, worry, and depression in 121 patients with major depression recruited in primary care (Watkins et al., 2012). The concreteness training involved one face-to-face session (ninety minutes), three thirty-minute phone sessions over six weeks, and daily practice on CD audio-recorded exercises. Patients were randomly allocated to treatment-as-usual as provided by general practitioners, concreteness training, and relaxation training, which was matched with concreteness training for structure, rationale, therapist contact, identification of warning signs, and active practice of CD exercises (in this case, progressive relaxation). There was no significant difference between relaxation training and concreteness training on reduction in depression, suggesting that identifying warning signs for rumination and practice at adopting an alternative coping strategy may be effective for reducing depression. Nonetheless, concreteness training outperformed relaxation training in reducing rumination and reducing negative attributional style.

One treatment designed specifically to target rumination is rumination-focused cognitive behavioral therapy (RFCBT). RFCBT is a manualized CBT treatment, consisting of up to twelve individual sessions scheduled weekly or fortnightly. RFCBT is theoretically informed by the research indicating that there are distinct constructive and unconstructive processing modes and is focused on inculcating the concrete processing mode in patients. Patients are coached to shift from the unconstructive abstract processing mode to the constructive concrete processing mode through the use of functional analysis, experiential/imagery exercises, and behavioral experiments. Functional analysis involves the close observation of behavior to establish the potential relationships between stimuli and responses within the principles of operant conditioning. Practically, it involves operationalizing a target behavior to be increased or decreased, and then identifying the antecedents and triggers, and the consequences of the behavior, to determine potential variables to manipulate in order to change the behavior. RFCBT incorporates the functional-analytic and contextual principles and techniques of behavioral activation (BA; Martell et al., 2001) but explicitly and exclusively focuses on rumination (for further details, see Watkins, 2009; Watkins et al., 2007;). RFCBT adopts the view that rumination is a form of avoidance and uses functional analysis to facilitate more helpful approach behaviors. RFBCT also uses functional analysis to help patients realize that their rumination about negative self-experience can be helpful or unhelpful and to coach them in how to shift to a more helpful style of thinking. In addition, patients use directed imagery to recreate previous mental states when a more helpful thinking style was active, such as memories of being completely absorbed in an activity (e.g., "flow" or "peak" experiences) and experiences of increased compassion, which act directly counter to rumination (for more information on therapeutic interventions related to imagery, see Clark and colleagues, Chapter 7). RFCBT significantly reduced rumination and depression in a multiple baseline case series of patients with residual depression (Watkins et al., 2007) and significantly outperformed treatment-as-usual (continuation antidepressants) in reducing rumination and depression in a phase II randomized controlled trial (Watkins et al., 2011). Moreover, over the six months of the trial, RFCBT significantly reduced relapse relative to treatment-as-usual.

In parallel to these treatment developments, there is an emergent line of research examining whether increasing the specificity of autobiographical memory retrieval can itself be therapeutic. Because overgeneral autobiographical memory retrieval has been implicated in increased vulnerability to depression, and because generic mental representations influence emotional reactivity, it is a plausible hypothesis that increasing the specificity of memory recall may reduce depression and rumination. Novel treatment approaches that target the specificity of autobiographical memories provide a proof-of-principle test of the hypothesis that generic processing contributes to the maintenance of rumination and depression. Two forms of memory training have recently been evaluated: Competitive Memory Training (COMET; Ekkers et al., 2011) and Memory Specificity Training (MEST; Raes et al., 2009).

In COMET, patients repeatedly practice generating specific counter-ruminative memories to situations in which rumination may occur, typically memories of times when the individual let go of concerns or was indifferent to difficult events. The recall of these specific memories is made as vivid as possible by utilizing posture, facial expression, and self-verbalizations to enhance imagery of these events. The COMET approach has parallels with both concreteness training, by encouraging patients to repeatedly practice an alternative response to warning signs for rumination, and with RFCBT, by involving a focus on generating experiential states that are counter to rumination. In a pilot randomized controlled trial, ninety-five older patients with major depression (aged sixty-five years or older) were randomized to seven weeks of COMET plus treatment-as-usual (TAU) versus TAU only. COMET plus TAU showed a significant improvement in depression and rumination compared with TAU alone. This provides initial evidence of this approach but leaves unresolved the mechanism of the effect – without an active treatment control, we do not know whether these effects are due to nonspecific treatment effects or which element of COMET was efficacious.

Memory Specificity Training (MEST; Raes et al., 2009) involves four one-hour-long group sessions in which patients are educated about depression and memory specificity, and then practice recalling positive and neutral specific memories that include contextual and sensory-perceptual details, before moving on to recall of specific memories to negative cues. In a case series of ten patients with depression, Raes et al. (2009) found that the training improved specificity on the autobiographical memory test and reduced rumination and symptoms of depression. However, this was an uncontrolled design, and a randomized controlled trial of MEST is required.

Together, these studies provide evidence that training patients with depression to become more concrete and more specific is therapeutic, whether this training is focused on how events are represented (concreteness training) or on the recall of memories to cues (MEST). A key next step is to examine whether these interventions are all acting on common elements (e.g., Does concreteness training improve specificity of memory retrieval? Does MEST improve problem solving?) and identify the active mediators of these interventions.

Nonetheless, these results are consistent with the hypothesis that increasing specificity may be an important mechanism in effective psychological interventions for depression (Watkins, 2009). Increasing specificity and concreteness is an element within traditional CBT for depression, a major focus within RFCBT, and the primary target of concreteness training and MEST. Moreover, as noted earlier, overgeneralization is an important cognitive bias in depression, and these interventions may reduce this bias. There is also evidence implicating increased concreteness and specificity within effective treatment: concrete methods (e.g., asking for specific examples) predict subsequent symptom reduction when assessed early in CBT, whereas abstract methods (e.g., discussion of meaning) do not (DeRubeis & Feeley, 1990; Feeley et al, 1999). Furthermore, improvement in situational analysis, which involves specific and detailed descriptions of problems and their context, in the first six weeks of CBT predicted reduced depression at the end of treatment (Manber et al., 2003).

Common theoretical constructs between rumination and overgeneral memory: discrepancy and hierarchy

The evidence reviewed above suggests that manipulating rumination can influence overgeneral memory but also that manipulating specificity of autobiographical memory can influence rumination. The unifying factor across this bidirectional causal relationship appears to be the adoption of more abstract processing, which drives both increased overgeneral autobiographical memory and the negative consequences of rumination.

I propose that this common role of abstraction in both memory retrieval and rumination emerges from common theoretical properties implicated in models of both rumination and overgeneral memory, namely, iterative processing across multiple levels of information organized in a hierarchy. Control theory accounts of rumination hypothesize that rumination is triggered and maintained by unresolved goal discrepancies (Martin & Tesser, 1996; Watkins, 2008). Rumination is proposed to continue in an iterative fashion until this goal discrepancy is resolved, through either attaining or abandoning the goal. Similarly, the generative search involved in voluntary autobiographical memory retrieval is hypothesized to involve the matching of information retrieved against search criteria. This search continues iteratively until the search criteria are satisfied, that is, there is no discrepancy between information generated and search criteria. Consistent with this account, there is evidence that overgeneral memory recall is more likely to occur when participants are asked to retrieve specific memories to positive cue words after a self-discrepancy induction (rating positive trait words for the extent that the participant currently possessed this quality versus the extent that the participant ideally wants to possess this quality; Raes et al., 2012; Schoofs et al., 2012).

Furthermore, the voluntary recall of overgeneral autobiographical memory is located within a hierarchical model of generative memory search (Williams et al., 2007), in which lifetime period information leads down to generic information, which in turn leads to specific (sensory-perceptual) information. Likewise, recent theoretical accounts of rumination have located it within a hierarchical model of goal and action identification (Watkins, 2008; 2011). Within these accounts, goals and actions are organized hierarchically: abstract levels in the hierarchy represent the ends and meaning of a goal or action (e.g., "why" a goal or action is sought or performed), whereas more subordinate concrete levels represent the detail and means of "how" the superordinate goal or action is enacted (e.g., programs and sequences of actions). Within this hierarchical organization, pursuit toward abstract goals occurs by specifying reference values at the next lower level of abstraction, all the way down to the concrete representations required to specify the actual behaviors needed to progress toward the goal. For example, one classification of levels within control theory approaches (Carver & Scheier, 1990) proposes that the reference values at the most abstract levels may represent a global sense of idealized self (i.e., a decontextualized, superordinate meaning capturing the essence of the self), which in turn sets the broad principles that organize goals and behavioral standards across multiple situations (e.g., to be an honest person), whereas the reference values at the more concrete levels represent the specific actions and behavioral programs and sequences necessary to implement the principles in a particular situation (e.g., telling the truth to a friend, i.e., more contextualized, specific details of how to do the action).

Control theory accounts further propose that a particular level in the hierarchy may be functionally and operationally prepotent and superordinate at any moment in time, reflecting whether the individual is focusing attention and awareness on a more abstract or concrete level, and thereby representing reference values (goals) and perceptual signals (from the environment) in a more abstract or concrete manner (i.e., this corresponds to the adoption of a concrete or abstract processing mode).

Furthermore, this theoretical model can account for the prior experimental findings that processing difficult and stressful situations at the abstract level may be problematic. Depending on context, a level of control that is too abstract or too concrete or that fails to link abstract levels to concrete levels is hypothesized to be detrimental (Carver & Scheier, 1998). Processing at an abstract level can be problematic because it can (1) make the relevant concern more personally important, resulting in greater emotional distress when the goal is not achieved and making it harder to abandon the unresolved goal, and (2) provide less specification of alternatives and concrete steps to proceed, impairing problem solving.

Thus, both overgeneral memory retrieval and rumination share the tendency, perhaps functionally reinforced, to preferentially adopt a more abstract level of processing when moving through their respective hierarchies of information. This can be conceptualized as both depressive rumination and overgeneral memory retrieval adopting abstract construals focused on decontextualized mental representations that convey the essential gist and meaning of events, goals, and actions. It is important to recognize that this observed relationship between overgeneral memory retrieval and rumination is focused on voluntary memory retrieval, such as studied with the Autobiographical Memory Test. Although there is growing research into involuntary autobiographical memories (for further information, see Moulds and Krans, Chapter 8; Berntsen, Chapter 9), the relationship between rumination and involuntary autobiographical memory is largely unexamined, with the exception of Watson et al. (2013), who found rumination correlated with reduced specificity of both voluntary and involuntary memories in depressed patients. Determining the causal relationship between rumination and involuntary autobiographical memory is a priority for future research.

Conclusion

In sum, the evidence reviewed in this chapter suggests that rumination causally influences the retrieval of overgeneral autobiographical memories and overgeneral thinking, but also that more abstract and generic processing, including the retrieval of categoric memories, causally influences the consequences and frequency of rumination. Moreover, interventions that target abstract processing, including those that increase specificity of autobiographical memory, reduce rumination and depression. There is thus robust evidence indicating a bidirectional relationship between rumination and overgeneral autobiographical memory, with each mutually reinforcing the other. Moreover, it is proposed that this mutual reinforcement occurs as a function of increased abstraction of representations being shared across depressive rumination and overgeneral autobiographical memory, reflecting iterative processing through hierarchical models being common to theoretical accounts of both phenomena.

REFERENCES

Barnard, P. J., Watkins, E. R., & Ramponi, C. (2006). Reducing specificity of autobiographical memory in non-clinical participants: the role of rumination and schematic models. *Cognition and Emotion, 20*, 328–350.

Beck, A. T. (1976). *Cognitive Therapy and the Emotional Disorders*. London: Penguin Books.

Brittlebank, A. D., Scott, J., Williams, J. M. G., & Ferrier, I. N. (1993). Autobiographical memory in depression: state or trait marker? *British Journal of Psychiatry, 162*, 118–121.

Carver, C. S. (1998). Generalization, adverse events, and development of depressive symptoms. *Journal of Personality, 66*, 607–619.

Carver, C. S., & Ganellen, R. J. (1983). Depression and components of self-punitiveness: high standards, self-criticism, and overgeneralization. *Journal of Abnormal Psychology, 92*, 330–337.

Carver, C. S., & Scheier, M. F. (1990). Origins and functions of positive and negative affect: a control-process view. *Psychological Review, 97*, 19–35.

 (1998). *On the Self-Regulation of Behavior*. New York: Cambridge University Press.

Carver, C. S., La Voie, L., Kuhl, J., & Ganellen, R. J. (1988). Cognitive concomitants of depression: a further examination of the roles of generalization, high standards, and self-criticism. *Journal of Social and Clinical Psychology, 7*, 350–365.

Caselli, G., Ferretti, C., Leoni, M., Rebecchi, D., Rovetto, F., & Spada, M. M. (2010). Rumination as a predictor of drinking behaviour in alcohol abusers: a prospective study. *Addiction, 105*, 1041–1048.

Conway, M. A., & Pleydell-Pearce, C. W. (2000). The construction of autobiographical memories in the self-memory system. *Psychological Review, 107*, 261–288.

Dalgleish, T., Spinks, H., Yiend, J., & Kuyken, W. (2001). Autobiographical memory style in seasonal affective disorder and its relationship to future symptom remission. *Journal of Abnormal Psychology, 110*, 335–340.

DeRubeis, R. J., & Feeley, M. (1990). Determinants of change in cognitive therapy for depression. *Cognitive Therapy and Research, 14*, 469–482.

Dykman, B. M. (1996). Negative self-evaluations among dysphoric college students: a difference in degree or kind? *Cognitive Therapy and Research, 20*, 445–464.

Edelman, R. E., Ahrens, A. H., & Haaga, D. A. F. (1994). Inferences about the self, attributions, and overgeneralization as predictors of recovery from dysphoria. *Cognitive Therapy and Research, 18*, 551–566.

Ehlers, A., Mayou, R. A., & Bryant, B. (1998). Psychological predictors of chronic posttraumatic stress disorder after motor vehicle accidents. *Journal of Abnormal Psychology, 107*, 508–519.

Ehring, T., & Watkins, E. R. (2008). Repetitive negative thinking as a transdiagnostic process. *International Journal of Cognitive Therapy, 1*, 192–2005.

Ekkers, W., Korrelboom, K., Huijbreachts, I., Smits, N., Cuijpers, P. & van der Gaag, M. (2011). Competitive Memory Training for treating depression and rumination in depressed older adults: a randomized controlled trial. *Behaviour Research and Therapy*, *49*, 588–596.

Feeley, M., DeRubeis, R. J., & Gelfand, L. A. (1999). The temporal relation of adherence and alliance to symptom change in cognitive therapy for depression. *Journal of Consulting and Clinical Psychology*, *67*, 578–582.

Ganellen, R. J. (1988). Specificity of attributions and overgeneralization in depression and anxiety. *Journal of Abnormal Psychology*, *97*, 83–86.

Harvey, A. G., Watkins, E., Mansell, W., & Shafran, R. (2004). *Cognitive Behavioural Processes across Psychological Disorders*. Oxford: Oxford University Press.

Holm-Denoma, J. M., & Hankin, B. L. (2010). Physical appearance competence as a mediator of the rumination and bulimic symptom link in female adolescents. *Journal of Child and Adolescent Clinical Psychology*, *39*, 537–544.

Kao, C. M., Dritschel, B. H., & Astell, A. (2006). The effects of rumination and distraction on over-general autobiographical memory retrieval during social problem solving. *British Journal of Clinical Psychology*, *45*, 267–272.

Kuyken, W., & Brewin, C. R. (1995). Autobiographical memory functioning in depression and reports of early abuse. *Journal of Abnormal Psychology*, *104*, 585–591.

Lyubomirsky, S., & Nolen-Hoeksema, S. (1995). Effects of self-focused rumination on negative thinking and interpersonal problem-solving. *Journal of Personality and Social Psychology*, *69*, 176–190.

Mackinger, H. F., Kunz-Dorfer, A., Schneider, B., & Leibetseder, M. M. (2000). Episodisches Gedächtnis als Vulnerabilitätsmarker: eine empirische Untersuchung zur Prognose prämenstrueller Dysphorie [Episodic memory as a vulnerability marker: an empirical study on the prediction of premenstrual dysphoria]. *Zeitschrift für Klinische Psychologie, Psychiatrie und Psychotherapie*, *48*, 45–56.

Manber, R., Arnow, B., Blasey, C., Vivian, D., McCullough, J. P., Blalock, J. A., Klein, D. N., Markowitz, J. C., Riso, L. P., Rothbaum, B., Rush, A. J., Thase, M. E., & Keller, M. B. (2003). Patient's therapeutic skill acquisition and response to psychotherapy, alone or in combination with medication. *Psychological Medicine*, *33*, 693–702.

Martell, C. R., Addis, M. E., & Jacobson, N. S. (2001). *Depression in Context: Strategies for Guided Action*. New York: Norton.

Martin, L. L., & Tesser, A. (1996). Some ruminative thoughts. In R. S. Wyer (ed.), *Ruminative Thoughts: Advances in Social Cognition* (vol. 9, pp. 1–47). Hillsdale, NJ: Lawrence Erlbaum Associates.

McLaughlin, K. A., & Nolen-Hoeksema, S. (2011). Rumination as a transdiagnostic factor in depression and anxiety. *Behaviour Research and Therapy*, *49*, 186–193.

Moberly, N. J., & Watkins, E. R. (2006). Processing mode influences the relationship between trait rumination and emotional vulnerability. *Behaviour Therapy*, *37*, 281–291.

Mor, N., & Winquist, J. (2002). Self-focused attention and negative affect: a meta-analysis. *Psychological Bulletin, 128*, 638–662.

Nolen-Hoeksema, S. (1991). Responses to depression and their effects on the duration of depressive episodes. *Journal of Abnormal Psychology, 100*, 569–582.

(2000). The role of rumination in depressive disorders and mixed anxiety/depressive symptoms. *Journal of Abnormal Psychology, 109*, 504–511.

Nolen-Hoeksema, S., & Watkins, E. R. (2011). A heuristic for developing transdiagnostic models of psychopathology: explaining multifinality and divergent trajectories. *Perspectives on Psychological Science, 6*, 589–609.

Nolen-Hoeksema, S., Stice, E., Wade, E., & Bohon, C. (2007). Reciprocal relations between rumination and bulimic, substance abuse, and depressive symptoms in female adolescents. *Journal of Abnormal Psychology, 116*, 198–207.

Nolen-Hoeksema, S., Wisco, B. E., & Lyubomirsky, S. (2008). Rethinking rumination. *Perspectives on Psychological Science, 3*, 400–424.

Park, R. J., Goodyer, I. M., & Teasdale, J. D. (2004). Effects of induced rumination and distraction on mood and overgeneral autobiographical memory in adolescent Major Depressive Disorder and controls. *Journal of Child and Adolescent Psychology and Psychiatry, 45*, 996–1006.

Raes, F., Hermans, D., Williams, J. M. G., & Eelen, P. (2006). Reduced autobiographical memory specificity and affect regulation. *Cognition and Emotion, 20*, 402–429.

Raes, F., Watkins, E. R., Williams, J. M. G., & Hermans, D. (2008). Non-ruminative processing reduces overgeneral autobiographical memory retrieval in students. *Behaviour Research and Therapy, 46*, 748–756.

Raes, F., Williams, J. M. G., & Hermans, D. (2009). Reducing cognitive vulnerability to depression: a preliminary investigation of memory specificity training (MEST) in inpatients with depressive symptomatology. *Journal of Behavior Therapy and Experimental Psychiatry, 40*, 24–38.

Raes, F., Schoofs, H., Griffith, J. W., & Hermans, D. (2012). Rumination relates to reduced autobiographical memory specificity in formerly depressed patients following a self-discrepancy challenge: the case of autobiographical memory specificity reactivity. *Journal of Behavior Therapy and Experimental Psychiatry, 43*, 1002–1007.

Rimes, K. A., & Watkins, E. (2005). The effects of self-focused rumination on global negative self-judgements in depression. *Behaviour Research and Therapy, 43*, 1673–1681.

Schoofs, H., Hermans, D., & Raes, F. (2012). Effect of self-discrepancy on specificity of autobiographical memory retrieval. *Memory, 20*, 63–72.

Skitch, S. A., & Abela, J. R. Z. (2008). Rumination in response to stress as a common vulnerability factor to depression and substance misuse in adolescence. *Journal of Abnormal Child Psychology, 36*, 1029–1045.

Smets, J., Griffith, J. W., Wessel, I., Walschaerts, D., & Raes, F. (2013). Depressive symptoms moderate the effects of a self-discrepancy induction on overgeneral autobiographical memory. *Memory, 21*(6), 751–761.

Spasojević, J., & Alloy, L. B. (2001). Rumination as a common mechanism relating depressive risk factors to depression. *Emotion, 1*, 25–37.
Watkins, E. (2004). Adaptive and maladaptive ruminative self-focus during emotional processing. *Behaviour Research and Therapy, 42*, 1037–1052.
Watkins, E., & Baracaia, S. (2002). Rumination and social problem-solving in depression. *Behaviour Research and Therapy, 40*, 1179–1189.
Watkins, E., & Brown, R. G. (2002). Rumination and executive function in depression: an experimental study. *Journal of Neurology, Neurosurgery and Psychiatry, 72*, 400–402.
Watkins, E., & Moulds, M. (2005). Distinct modes of ruminative self-focus: impact of abstract versus concrete rumination on problem solving in depression. *Emotion, 5*, 319–328.
Watkins, E., & Teasdale, J. D. (2001). Rumination and overgeneral memory in depression: effects of self-focus and analytic thinking. *Journal of Abnormal Psychology, 110*, 353–357.
  (2004). Adaptive and maladaptive self-focus in depression. *Journal of Affective Disorders, 82*, 1–8.
Watkins, E., Teasdale, J.D., & Williams, R.M. (2000). Decentering and distraction reduce overgeneral autobiographical memory in depression. *Psychological Medicine, 30*, 911–920.
Watkins, E., Scott, J., Wingrove, J., Rimes, K., Bathurst, N., Steiner, H., et al. (2007). Rumination-focused cognitive behaviour therapy for residual depression: a case series. *Behaviour Research and Therapy, 45*, 2144–2154.
Watkins, E. R. (2008). Constructive and unconstructive repetitive thought. *Psychological Bulletin, 134*, 163–206.
  (2009). Depressive rumination: investigating mechanisms to improve cognitive-behavioral treatments. *Cognitive Behaviour Therapy, 38*, 8–14.
  (2011). Dysregulation in level of goal and action identification across psychological disorders. *Clinical Psychology Review, 31*, 260–278.
Watkins, E. R., & Moberly, N. J. (in preparation). Processing mode causally influences overgeneralization following failure.
Watkins, E R., Moberly, N. J., & Moulds, M. L. (2008). Processing mode causally influences emotional reactivity: distinct effects of abstract versus concrete construal on emotional response. *Emotion, 8*, 364–378.
Watkins, E. R., Baeyens, C. B., & Read, R. (2009). Concreteness training reduces dysphoria: proof-of-principle for repeated cognitive bias modification in depression. *Journal of Abnormal Psychology, 118*, 55–64.
Watkins, E. R., Mullan, E., Wingrove, J., Rimes, K., Steiner, H., Bathurst, N., Eastman, R., Scott, J. (2011). Rumination-focused cognitive-behavioral therapy for residual depression: phase II randomized controlled trial. *British Journal of Psychiatry, 199*, 317–322.
Watkins, E. R., Taylor, R. S., Byng, R., Baeyens, C., Read, R., Pearson, K., & Watson, L. (2012). Guided self-help concreteness training as an intervention for major depression in primary care: a phase II randomized controlled trial. *Psychological Medicine, 42*, 1359–1371.

Watson, L. A., Berntsen, D, Kuyken, W., & Watkins, E. R. (2013). Involuntary and voluntary autobiographical memory specificity as a function of depression. *Journal of Behaviour Therapy and Experimental Psychiatry, 44*, 7–13.

Wenzlaff, R. M,. & Grozier, S. A. (1988). Depression and the magnification of failure. *Journal of Abnormal Psychology, 97*, 90–93.

Williams, J. M. G., & Broadbent, K. (1986). Autobiographical memory in suicide attempters. *Journal of Abnormal Psychology, 95*, 144–149.

Williams, J. M. G, Barnhofer, T., Crane, C., Hermans, D., Raes, F., Watkins, E., & Dalgleish, T. (2007). Autobiographical memory specificity and emotional disorder. *Psychological Bulletin, 133*, 122–148.

11 Overgeneral memory in borderline personality disorder

Kris Van den Broeck, Laurence Claes, Guido Pieters, Dirk Hermans, and Filip Raes

Introduction

First described by Williams and Broadbent (1986), overgeneral memory (OGM) is a robust finding in depressed, previously depressed, and traumatized patients (for an overview, see Moore & Zoellner, 2007; Williams et al., 2007). OGM refers to the difficulties these clinical groups experience in retrieving specific information from their autobiographical memory, typically assessed using the Autobiographical Memory Test (AMT; Williams & Broadbent, 1986). In this task, respondents are asked to recall specific memories in response to cue words (e.g., "anxious"). Instead of recalling, as instructed, detailed information on "personally experienced events that happened only once and did not last longer than one day," the aforementioned patients tend to retrieve categories of events rather than specific recollections (e.g., "Whenever I visit my mother-in-law," rather than "When my mother-in-law turned 60 and invited us over for coffee and cake"). OGM is also associated with poor problem-solving abilities (e.g., Goddard et al., 1996), higher levels of rumination (e.g., Raes et al., 2005; Watkins, Chapter 10), and an avoidant coping style (e.g., Hermans et al., 2005; Muenks, 2010).

Initially, OGM was considered as a symptom of emotional disorders, for example, following the premature abortion of guided search processes (Norman & Bobrow, 1979; Reiser et al., 1985). However, more recent frameworks, such as the self-memory system (SMS; Conway, 2005; Conway & Pleydell-Pearce, 2000; Conway et al., 2004) and the CaR-FA-X model (Williams et al., 2007) suggest that OGM also may play a more causal role in the onset and/or maintenance of a depressive state or posttraumatic symptoms. According to these models, specific retrieval of painful memories may reactivate related emotions, which may in turn be threatening for the stability of one's self-concept. Therefore, in order to avoid reliving painful memories, patients are thought to have learned, by means of negative reinforcement and generalization, to stay at a more general level. This is known as functional avoidance (FA). Although FA may prevent emotional turmoil on the short term, it is believed to lead to the enduring existence of traumatic intrusions on the longer term.

The SMS more closely describes the mechanisms that may be underlying FA, suggesting the likelihood of retrieving OGMs may differ from one person to another and depending on the AMT cues that are used. In 2004, Conway et al. defined the Working Self (WS), which has two, potentially conflicting tasks. First, and foremost, the WS should construct and maintain an accurate, integrated, and stable sense of self over time ("self-coherence"). It therefore makes information that supports current self-concepts highly available. Second, the WS should monitor progress in goal-directed activities ("adaptive correspondence"). Problems may arise when discrepancies between one's actual condition and one's desired state (goal) are strongly emphasized. A businessman who has always dreamed of being successful and rich probably finds it very difficult when he finds himself being dejected due to a missed promotion. To prevent destabilization of one's self-concept (and potentially a fullblown depression), resources are then shifted away from adaptive correspondence to self-coherence. In case of guided search processes, this action will result in the inability to retrieve event-specific knowledge. The SMS thus suggests that it would be more difficult (or unlikely) to recall specific information in response to cues that tap into domains that are highly discrepant from one's actual self. Data from Crane et al. (2007) support this idea.

The CaR-FA-X model identifies two additional mechanisms that alone or in combination with FA may be responsible for OGM and associated complaints: capture and rumination (CaR), and impaired executive resources (X). Executive resources are necessary to adequately fulfill a search process but have been shown to be impaired in depressed (e.g., Hertel & Hardin, 1990) and traumatized patients (e.g., Moradi et al., 2000). CaR then, refers to problems that may arise during the first orienting stages of a search process. Ruminators or people who have highly elaborated networks concerning the self may get entangled ("captured") in their thoughts and self-descriptions, which then impedes a more thorough search for specific memories.

In this chapter we focus on the findings on OGM in patients suffering from borderline personality disorder (BPD). DSM-IV criteria of BPD are listed in Table 11.1 (American Psychiatric Association [APA], 1994), showing that BPD is characterized by disturbed relatedness, affective, and behavioral dysregulation (Sanislow et al., 2002). BPD is a severe mental illness, associated with high morbidity (e.g., Paris & Zweig-Frank, 2001) and frequent use of mental health resources (e.g., Bender et al., 2001; Zanarini et al., 2001). In addition, comorbid Axis I

Table 11.1 *DSM-IV (APA, 1994) criteria for borderline personality disorder (BPD)*

BPD is manifested by a pervasive pattern of instability of interpersonal relationships, self-image, and affects, and marked impulsivity beginning by early adulthood and present in a variety of contexts, as indicated by five (or more) of the following:
1. Frantic efforts to avoid real or imagined abandonment. Note: Do not include suicidal or self-mutilating behavior covered in (5).
2. A pattern of unstable and intense interpersonal relationships characterized by alternating between extremes of idealization and devaluation.
3. Identity disturbance: markedly and persistently unstable self-image or sense of self.
4. Impulsivity in at least two areas that are potentially self-damaging (e.g., spending, sex, substance abuse, reckless driving, binge eating). Note: Do not include suicidal or self-mutilating behavior covered in (5).
5. Recurrent suicidal behavior, gestures, or threats, or self-mutilating behavior.
6. Affective instability due to a marked reactivity of mood (e.g., intense episodic dysphoria, irritability, or anxiety usually lasting a few hours and only rarely more than a few days).
7. Chronic feelings of emptiness.
8. Inappropriate, intense anger or difficulty controlling anger (e.g., frequent displays of temper, constant anger, recurrent physical fights).
9. Transient, stress-related paranoid ideation or severe dissociative symptoms.

(e.g., Grant et al., 2008; Zanarini et al. 2004a) and Axis II (e.g., Grant et al., 2008; Zanarini et al., 2004b) disorders are very common among BPD patients. General prevalence is rather high – prevalence rates are estimated at 0.4 to 5.9% in the general population, and about 15% to 25% in residential psychiatric health care (Torgersen et al., 2001; Grant et al., 2008; Gunderson, 2009) – with no differences between males and females (Leichsenring et al., 2011).

Patients diagnosed with BPD often have comorbid posttraumatic stress disorder (PTSD; APA, 1994; up to 31.6% of BPD patients meet criteria for PTSD during the last 12 months, according to Grant et al., 2008) and major depressive disorder (MDD; APA, 1994; up to 19.3% of BPD patients meet criteria for MDD during the last 12 months), and they report mood-state independent rumination (e.g., Smith et al., 2006) and disturbed executive resources (Maurex, 2009). Furthermore, many BPD patients suffer from an unstable sense of self ("identity disturbance"; DSM-IV, APA, 1994) and regularly experience difficulties in solving problems (e.g., Kremers et al., 2006b; Maurex et al., 2010). Therefore, and given the assumed role of OGM as an emotion regulation strategy during psychopathology, we would expect that BPD patients, too, would show problems retrieving specific memories. In any case, it could be useful to investigate OGM in BPD patients, given the current ideas and findings on the role of autobiographical memory in the construction of one's self-concept (e.g., Conway & Pleydell-Pearce, 2000; Jørgensen et al., 2012) and its involvement in problem solving (e.g., Sutherland & Bryant, 2008).

In this chapter we discuss in detail the findings on OGM in patients with BPD. Additionally, we investigate to what extent these findings are consistent with the prevailing theoretical models on autobiographical memory organization described above. Finally, directions for further research are outlined.

Studies on OGM in relation to BPD

Reviewing the literature, we found twelve publications describing eight different samples[1] directly examining OGM in relation to BPD. In eight studies, consisting of seven different samples, control groups were included, consisting of either healthy individuals (Jones et al., 1999; Jørgensen et al., 2012; Kremers et al., 2004; 2006b; Maurex et al., 2010; Reid & Startup, 2010; Renneberg et al., 2005) or clinical populations (Arntz et al., 2002; Jørgensen et al., 2012; Kremers et al., 2004; Renneberg et al., 2005). Some studies also investigated the relationships between OGM and borderline-related symptoms such as dissociation (Jones et al., 1999; Kremers et al., 2004; 2006a; Renneberg et al., 2005), self-harm (Maurex et al., 2010; Renneberg et al., 2005; Startup et al., 2001), problem-solving abilities (Kremers et al., 2006b; Maurex et al., 2010), traumatic intrusions (Maurex et al., 2010; Kremers et al., 2004; 2006a), and rumination (Van den Broeck et al., 2012) in BPD patients.

Table 11.2 presents an overview of the studies of interest, describing the studied samples and the type of Autobiographical Memory Test (AMT) that was used.

OGM in BPD patients

OGM in relation to diagnostic status, severity of psychopathology, and BPD-related symptoms

This section consecutively summarizes findings on whether or not OGM is associated with (1) diagnostic status of BPD, MDD, PTSD, or other anxiety disorders; (2) severity of BPD, depression, or anxiety; and

---

[1] Jones et al. (1999) and Startup et al. (2001) reported on one sample. Also, Kremers et al. (2004; 2006a; 2006b) and Spinhoven et al. (2007) reported on one sample.

Table 11.2 Sample and Autobiographical Memory Test (AMT) characteristics of the studies on overgeneral memory (OGM) in relation to borderline personality disorder (BPD) (symptoms)

			AMT characteristics					
	Participants	Controls	Number and valence of cues	Kind of cues	Cue presentation	Time limit	Scoring system	Variable of interest
Jones et al. (1999)	23 BPD outpatients (5 males)	23 healthy controls, matched for age, gender, and years of education	6+/6−/6°	Nouns and adjectives	Verbally	30 seconds	S/G/O	#G
Startup et al. (2001)	Same as those of Jones et al. (1999)	No control group	6+/6−/6°	Nouns and adjectives	Verbally	30 seconds	S/G/O	#G
Arntz et al. (2002)	9 outpatients with BPD as first diagnosis (3 males)	9 patients with MDD as first diagnosis; 11 patients with primarily an AD; 10 patients suffering primarily from a PD other than BPD	Dutch translation of original AMT of Williams & Broadbent (1986): 5+/5−	Adjectives (traits)	Not reported	60 seconds	S/NS	#S
Kremers et al. (2004)	83 BPD outpatients (6 males), of which 47 also suffered from MDD and 24 had PTSD	30 healthy controls (0 males) without childhood sexual or physical abuse nor Axis I pathology; 26 MDD outpatients (no bipolar or psychotic disorder, no substance abuse)	AMT version of McNally et al., (1995): "a specific moment at witch you exhibited the trait presented"; 5+/5−	Adjectives (traits)	Visually + Verbally	60 seconds	S/C/E/No comply or missed/O	%S

225

Table 11.2 (cont.)

	Participants	Controls	Number and valence of cues	Kind of cues	Cue presentation	Time limit	Scoring system	Variable of interest
Renneberg et al. (2005)	30 BPD inpatients (0 males), of which 19 also suffered from MDD, and 11 had PTSD	30 healthy controls (0 males; BDI < 12; max 1 BPD criterion of SCID), matched for age and years of education to BPD group; 27 MDD inpatients (no Axis II cluster B diagnosis)	5+/5−/5°	Adjectives	Visually	60 seconds	S/C	#S/#C, but also latency to S, valence of memory content, and age of memory
Kremers et al. (2006a)	At T1: Id Kremers et al. (2004); at T3, 55 participants (5 males) remained, of which 37 suffered initally from MDD, and 18 did not	No control group	AMT version of McNally et al. (1995); see Kremers et al. (2004); 5+/5−	Adjectives (traits)	Visually + Verbally	60 seconds	S/C/E/No comply or missed/O	%S
Kremers et al. (2006b)	78 BPD patients from the Kremers et al. (2004) study, of which 44 also had MDD (3 males), and 34 (3 males) had a history of parasuicidal acts	30 healthy controls from the Kremers et al. (2004) study	AMT version of McNally et al. (1995); see Kremers et al. (2004); 5+/5−	Adjectives (traits)	Visually + Verbally	60 seconds	S/C/E/No comply or missed/O	%S
Spinhoven et al. (2007)	82 BPD patients from the Kremers et al. (2004) study	No control group	AMT version of McNally et al. (1995); see Kremers et al. (2004); 5+/5−	Adjectives (traits)	Visually + Verbally	60 seconds	S/C/E/No comply or missed/O	%S

Table 11.2 (*cont.*)

		AMT characteristics					
	Participants	Controls	Number and valence of cues	Kind of cues	Cue presentation	Time limit	Scoring system	Variable of interest
Maurex et al. (2010)	47 BPD outpatients (0 males), with at least two suicide attempts of which at least one during the past 6 months	30 healthy controls (no BPD according to SCID, no trauma exposure), matched for educational level with the BPD patients	12+/12−/12°	Adjectives (only?)	Verbally	30 seconds	S/C/E/SA/O	#S/#C/#E/ #SA/#O
Reid and Startup (2010)	31 BPD outpatients (7 males), of which 22 also had MDD (5 males), who were all engaged in at least three episodes of self-harming behavior during the last 12 months	29 healthy controls (6 males), matched for age and gender with the BPD patients, and without BPD and MDD	6+/6−	Nouns and adjectives	Verbally	60 seconds	S/C/E/O	%S/%C/% E/%O
Jørgensen et al. (2012)	17BPD inpatients (all female), and without comorbid OCD diagnosis; 16 of them met the identity disturbance criterion as measured by the SCID	23 psychology students ("nonclinical controls"; all female); 14 OCD inpatients (7 males), 3 of whom had a comorbid no-BPD Axis II diagnosis as measured by the SCID	No AMT, but modified version of the Life Story Event Task (Rubin et al., 2009) was used					

Table 11.2 (cont.)

AMT characteristics

Participants	Controls	Number and valence of cues	Kind of cues	Cue presentation	Time limit	Scoring system	Variable of interest
Van den Broeck et al. (2012)	34 BPD inpatients (7 males), 11 of whom were considered currently depressed (4 MDD, 1 depressive disorder NOS, 8 adjustment disorder)	No control group	9+/9–	Adjectives	Written version	No time limit	S/C/E/NM-SA/SE/O Participant-rated/ corrected by researcher	pS/pC

#C, number of general categorical memories; #E, number of general extended memories; #G, number of general memories; #O, number of omissions; #S, number of specific memories; #SA, number of semantic associates; %C, percentage of general categorical memories; %E, percentage of general extended memories; %O, percentage of omissions; %S, percentage of specific memories; AD, anxiety disorder; BPD, borderline personality disorder; C, general categorical memories; E, general extended memories; G, general memories; MDD, major depressive disorder; NM-SA, no memory/semantic associate; NOS, not otherwise specified; NS, nonspecific; O, omissions; OCD, obsessive compulsive disorder; pC, proportion of general categorical memories; PD, personality disorder; pS, proportion of specific memories; PTSD, posttraumatic stress disorder; S, specific memories; SA, semantic associates; SCID, Structured Clinical Interview for DSM-IV disorders; SE, same event.

(3) symptoms often associated with BPD, such as dissociation, self-harm, deficient problem-solving skills, and rumination.

In three studies, BPD patients were found to produce more overgeneral (Jones et al., 1999; Maurex et al., 2010) and fewer specific memories than healthy controls (Maurex et al., 2010; Reid & Startup, 2010). In other studies, in contrast, BPD patients were found to produce just as many categorical (Reid & Startup, 2010) or specific (Renneberg et al., 2005) memories as healthy and depressed controls. Also, Arntz et al. (2002) found that a diagnosis of BPD was unrelated to the number of specific memories retrieved, $r = 0.004$. One study by Jørgensen et al. (2012) found a trend for lower proportions of specific memories in BPD patients as compared with patients with obsessive-compulsive disorder and healthy controls. Thus, when comorbid disorders during BPD are not controlled for, evidence for OGM in BPD is divided: some data support the hypothesis of OGM being present in BPD patients (Jones et al., 1999; Maurex et al., 2010), whereas others refute it (Arntz et al., 2002; Jørgensen et al., 2012; Renneberg et al., 2005) or are inconclusive (Reid & Startup, 2010).

Arntz et al. (2002) discovered that MDD (and personality disorder other than BPD), rather than BPD or any form of anxiety disorder, predicted AMT outcome with regard to specificity. The data of Kremers et al. (2004) also suggested that OGM was more related to MDD than to BPD. They found that only the currently depressed BPD patients retrieved fewer specific memories than controls, as did their control group of MDD patients. When studying the role of cue discrepancy, Spinhoven et al. (2007) and Van den Broeck et al. (2012) found that highly discrepant cues led to reduced memory specificity, especially in currently depressed BPD patients. These findings suggest that, in addition to cue discrepancy and in line with the results of Arntz et al. (2002) and Kremers et al. (2004), a comorbid diagnosis of MDD is more important in predicting OGM than the diagnosis of BPD. However, other studies (Maurex et al., 2010; Reid & Startup, 2010; Renneberg et al., 2005) found no differences between (currently/previously) depressed BPD patients and non/never depressed BPD patients in memory specificity, yet Renneberg et al. (2005) found that MDD patients retrieved more categorical memories than BPD patients (with and without MDD). Somewhat surprisingly, Reid and Startup (2010) found that difficulties retrieving specific memories especially emerged in their nondepressed BPD sample.

Memory specificity was also found to be unrelated to a comorbid diagnosis of PTSD in BPD patients (Kremers et al., 2004; Renneberg et al., 2005). Maurex et al. (2010) found that memory specificity was negatively associated with lifetime exposure to violence; however, Kremers et al. (2004) were not able to replicate such an association between trauma exposure and OGM in BPD patients (for more information on the relationship between trauma and overgeneral memory, see McNally and Robinaugh, Chapter 12). According to Arntz et al. (2002), neither trauma exposure nor the presence of an anxiety disorder is related to reduced memory specificity (in a sample that at least in part consisted of patients suffering from BPD).

With regard to the association between OGM and the severity of psychopathology reported, the data indicate a more coherent picture. Memory specificity seems to be unrelated to BPD severity (Kremers et al., 2006a; Maurex et al., 2010). Also, no relation was found between anxiety severity and OGM in BPD patients (Jones et al., 1999; Maurex et al., 2010). Depression severity was mostly found to be unrelated to reduced memory specificity in BPD patients (Jones et al., 1999; Kremers et al., 2004; 2006a; Maurex et al., 2010; Renneberg et al., 2005), except in the study by Van den Broeck et al. (2012), who observed a negative association between the proportion of specific memories retrieved and scores on the Beck Depression Inventory (BDI).

OGM, considered an emotion regulation strategy since the beginning of theorizing, has also been studied in relation to other symptoms that have been thought to have similar functions and that regularly occur in BPD patients, for example, dissociation and parasuicidal acts. In addition, because of the robust associations in depressed samples between OGM on the one hand and problem-solving abilities and rumination on the other, analogous relationships were hypothesized in BPD patients, whom are known to have poor problem-solving capabilities (e.g., Kremers et al., 2006b; Maurex et al., 2010) and high levels of rumination (e.g., Smith et al., 2006). In general, with regard to these borderline-related symptoms, few associations have been found, and none of them has been replicated by other studies. Jones et al. (1999) found that more dissociation was reported when respondents retrieved more general memories, but memory specificity was not found to be associated with scores on the Dissociative Experiences Scale (DES) in BPD patients (Kremers et al., 2004; 2006a; Renneberg et al., 2005). In the BPD sample of Jones et al. (1999), Startup et al. (2001) discovered that the more general memories were retrieved, the fewer parasuicidal acts were reported during the four months prior to testing; however, neither Renneberg et al. (2005) nor Maurex et al. (2010) was able to replicate these findings. The latter, however, found that reduced memory specificity was associated with poor problem-solving abilities in BPD patients, thereby contradicting earlier findings of Kremers et al. (2006b). These authors found that problem-solving abilities did not correlate significantly different with memory specificity in (depressed and nondepressed) BPD patients than in controls. Furthermore, only Van den Broeck et al. (2012) have so far found a negative association between memory specificity and rumination, but the correlation disappeared when depression severity was controlled for. No associations were found between memory specificity and trait anger (Jones et al., 1999), the prevalence of intrusions (Kremers et al., 2004; Maurex et al., 2010), or avoidance regarding intrusions (Kremers et al., 2004; 2006a; Maurex et al., 2010).

In sum, it can be concluded that neither PTSD nor severity of other symptoms of psychopathology (depression, anxiety, or BPD) relate to OGM in BPD patients. With respect to BPD-associated symptoms, the low number of available studies does not allow us to draw clear conclusions. Results regarding the role of MDD suggest that memory specificity in BPD is at least in part associated with MDD (Arntz et al., 2002; Kremers et al., 2004; Spinhoven et al., 2007; Van den Broeck et al., 2012), although there are contradictory findings (Maurex et al., 2010; Reid & Startup, 2010; Renneberg et al., 2005). Finally, given the current studies, a relationship between memory specificity and a diagnosis of BPD cannot be ruled out, either. Data of Jones et al. (1999), Maurex et al. (2010), and Reid and Startup (2010) suggest that OGM and a diagnosis of BPD are associated, whereas data of Arntz et al. (2002), Kremers et al. (2004), and Renneberg et al. (2005) found no association.

OGM in relation to socio-demographics and AMT characteristics in BPD patients

This section first overviews findings on whether or not OGM is associated with socio-demographic variables, such as sex, marital status, age, and education (in terms of years or level of education). We then describe the associations between memory specificity on the one hand and cue valence, retrieval latency, and the extent to which cues are meaningful for the respondent ("cue discrepancy") on the other hand.

OGM has not been found to be associated with gender (Arntz et al., 2002; Kremers et al., 2004) or marital status (Arntz et al., 2002). Age was sometimes found to be negatively correlated with memory specificity (Arntz et al., 2002; Maurex et al., 2010; and Spinhoven et al., 2007, when cue discrepancy was taken into account), but not always (Kremers et al., 2004; Renneberg et al., 2005; Spinhoven et al., 2007). Education (in terms of years or level of education) was found to correlate positively with memory specificity (Arntz et al., 2002; Maurex et al., 2010) or negatively with OGM (Spinhoven et al., 2007). This is in line with previous findings in traumatized (e.g., Schönfeld & Ehlers, 2006), depressed, anxious, and healthy participants (e.g., Wessel et al., 2001). Nevertheless, after controlling for educational level, group differences generally remain (Williams et al., 2007), suggesting that education explains only part of the variance.

Kremers et al. (2004) found no main effect of cue valence on memory specificity in BPD patients. However, according to Jones et al. (1999), BPD patients retrieved more generic memories following negative cues than after positive or neutral cues. Renneberg et al. (2005) found that healthy controls, depressed controls, and BPD patients retrieved more specific memories following negative cues than after neutral or positive cues. Kremers et al. (2006a) found the opposite in a BPD sample that had followed long-term psychotherapy. Regardless of BPD, samples of depressed and traumatized patients also show mixed evidence with regard to whether memory specificity varies with the valence of the cue (Williams et al., 2007). Meta-analyses by van Vreeswijk and de Wilde (2004) and by Williams et al. (2007) suggest that OGM generally emerges following both positive and negative cues.

Renneberg et al. (2005) were the only researchers to investigate latency when retrieving specific memories. In general, BPD patients do not differ in retrieval latency for specific memories from depressed or healthy controls, although they tend to retrieve memories faster than MDD patients. Specific memories following negative cues were found to be retrieved the fastest.

As described above, according to the SMS, cues that tap into domains that are highly discrepant from one's actual self would be more likely to evoke OGMs. Spinhoven et al. (2007) discovered that BPD patients retrieved fewer specific memories in response to cues that were thematically related to a participant's relevant set of dysfunctional attitudes.[2] Van den Broeck et al. (2012) computed an index expressing the degree to which the AMT as a whole was discrepant toward a respondent's actual self-concept. This index was negatively and highly correlated with memory specificity in their depressed BPD patients, $r = -0.89$, $p < 0.01$ (but not in the nondepressed BPD subsample). These findings are in line with what has been found previously in depressed patients (Barnhofer et al., 2007; Crane et al., 2007; Spinhoven et al., 2007), suggesting that memory specificity in (depressed) BPD patients depends, at least in part, on the meaning the cues have for the respondents.

---

[2] Dysfunctional attitudes, such as "If I fail partly, it is as bad as being a complete failure" (item 14 from the Dysfunctional Attitude Scale [DAS; Weissman & Beck, 1978]), are thought to be indicatory for maladaptive schemas that may trigger self-referent thinking.

In sum, we can conclude that results regarding the association between memory specificity and cue valence are varied. Regarding cue discrepancy, findings are limited, but consistent: the more a cue taps into a domain that is highly discrepant toward one's self-concept, the more likely it is that the cue will evoke general memories.

Methodological issues

The present findings consistently suggest that OGM in BPD is reliably associated with educational level and that there is no relation between memory specificity and illness severity, or PTSD in this group of patients. However, the studies presented above are inconclusive on whether or not OGM is directly associated with a diagnosis of BPD and/or MDD in BPD. Several reasons prevent us from drawing unambiguous conclusions in this regard.

First, contrasting results regarding a possible association between OGM and diagnosis of BPD may result from methodological and sample differences between the studies. Table 11.2 shows that studies differed in samples (outpatients, inpatients, and different exclusion criteria, e.g., participants with substance abuse were sometimes excluded and in other studies included, or special demands, e.g., a certain number of suicide attempts) and control groups (clinical groups, healthy control, no control group). In fact, the hypothesis that BPD patients show OGM seems to hold in BPD outpatients when compared with healthy controls (Jones et al., 1999; Maurex et al., 2010; Reid & Startup, 2010) but not in BPD inpatients (Jørgensen et al., 2012; Renneberg et al., 2005) or when compared with other clinical samples (Arntz et al., 2002; Jørgensen et al., 2012). Furthermore, with the exception of Jørgensen et al. (2012), all the studies presented above used the Autobiographical Memory Test (AMT). These tests varied in number of stimuli (10 to 36), kind of stimuli (nouns, adjectives, or both, or traits), stimulus presentation (verbally, visually, or both), response time (30 or 60 seconds), response requirements (verbal or written), and scoring procedure (tests were mostly scored by researchers only, but Van den Broeck et al. [2012] built on the ratings of participants). Most authors were interested in the number or percentage of general (Jones et al., 1999; Startup et al., 2001), general categorical (Maurex et al., 2010; Reid & Startup, 2010; Renneberg et al., 2005), or specific memories (Arntz et al., 2002; Kremers et al., 2004; 2006a; 2006b; Maurex et al., 2010; Reid & Startup, 2010; Renneberg et al., 2005; Spinhoven et al., 2007); however, Van den Broeck et al. (2012) used the proportion (i.e., the percentage corrected for the presence of omissions) of specific memories.

Griffith et al. (2012) described in more detail how these variables may influence AMT outcome and complicate comparability. Jørgensen et al. (2012) used a completely different methodology to collect memories by asking respondents "to write down three memories that are most central to one's life story."[3] No explicit instruction to recall *specific* memories was included. Therefore, comparability of the specificity scores obtained from this procedure with those obtained from the traditionally used AMT may be questioned.

Second, over the past twenty-five years, OGM has mainly been studied in relation to MDD and trauma. Axis II disorders were often not diagnosed nor were they explicitly excluded. It is only reasonable to expect that many samples definitely would have included BPD patients, given that lifetime prevalence of BPD in patients diagnosed with MDD or PTSD is estimated at 11.5% and 24.3%, respectively (Grant et al., 2008). Moreover, some authors (e.g., Williams & Broadbent, 1986) included only patients who had reported suicidal gestures just before test admission. It is of relevance to note that surprisingly few publications are available that specifically focused on BPD patients alone.

Third, except for Kremers et al. (2004) and Maurex et al. (2010), none of the studied samples exceeded thirty-five BPD patients. According to DSM-IV (APA, 1994), a BPD diagnosis requires the presence of at least five out of nine distinguished criteria, leading to a wide variety of BPD phenotypes. Theoretically, 256 different BPD phenotypes are possible. Studying a limited sample size of thirty BPD patients, as is often the case in the studies of interest, may not cover the heterogeneity and complexity of BPD diagnoses. Therefore, inconsistent findings may be an artifact of sample selection, or, alternatively, when samples consist of many different BPD phenotypes, unique associations, for instance, between OGM and suicidal gestures, may not be revealed.

Finally, potentially important factors are often neglected in the studies that have been conducted until now. For example, none of the studies controlled for medication/substance use, and only some studies took education or trauma (exposure) into account. Nevertheless, Kremers et al. (2006a) suggested that the complexity or the severity of the trauma may codetermine OGM. Furthermore, Van den Broeck et al. (2012) argued that depressive status in BPD patients could be considered in terms of affective instability following traumatic experiences, thereby differing from MDD in non-BPD patients.

[3] Jørgensen et al. (2012) used a modified version of the Life Story Event Task (Rubin et al., 2009). Two independent raters agreed in 87% of the cases in judging the specificity of the memory.

Overall, up to now, conclusions on the association between OGM and BPD are confounded by differences in samples and instruments and by the heterogeneity of the BPD diagnosis, which is not reflected in the small sample sizes that have been studied so far. The robustness with which OGM has been found in traumatized or depressed patients strongly contrasts with the minority of available publications that specifically focused on OGM in BPD, although it is possible that BPD patients make up part of the traumatized and depressed samples in which OGM has been identified. Finally, current studies may have neglected meaningful variables that may contribute to OGM in general or to BPD in particular, such as medication or substance (ab)use, affective instability, or characteristics of trauma exposure.

Conclusions and directions for future studies

According to the CaR-FA-X model (Williams et al., 2007), OGM results from ruminative and self-focused processes (CaR), functional avoidance (FA), limited executive resources (X), or an interplay between these variables. Because these processes have been repeatedly demonstrated in depressed and traumatized patients, the applicability of the framework is justified in these clinical groups (Williams et al., 2007).

In BPD patients, visual (Maurex et al., 2010) and verbal (Reid & Startup, 2010) working memory and education, which may also to some extent reflect executive functioning (X; Reid & Startup, 2010), have been found to be associated with memory specificity (Arntz et al., 2002; Maurex et al., 2010; Spinhoven et al., 2007). Rumination (CaR), on the other hand, has not been found to be associated with OGM in BPD patients, at least not after controlling for depression severity (Van den Broeck et al., 2012). Furthermore, avoidance of intrusions (Kremers et al., 2004; 2006a; Maurex et al., 2010) and dissociation, which can be considered as the ultimate avoidance strategy (FA; Kremers et al., 2004; 2006a; Renneberg et al., 2005), have systematically been shown to be unrelated to memory specificity in BPD patients – although Jones et al. (1999) found that dissociation scores were positively associated with more general memories. These findings question the applicability of the CaR-FA-X model and its predecessors for explaining potential OGM in BPD patients.

Although many BPD patients report dissociative episodes, BPD patients are often clinically described as easily getting overwhelmed by their emotions. Linehan (1993) additionally mentions relatively low thresholds for emotional reaction and highly intense feelings in BPD patients, meaning that just minor stressors (or memories) can make them seriously upset. Non-BPD subjects, who can tolerate more stress before an emotional reaction is evoked, might have the opportunity to apply other strategies on stressors before threshold values are exceeded. They might, for instance, increase the psychological distance toward emotional memories by not exploring all the details of an event (or by not recalling all the details of a memory; OGM). OGM could thus be considered as a (unconscious, passive, preemptive) mechanism by which one alters a memory, in a way that one's threshold will be less likely to be exceeded by it.

Linehan (1993) further assumes that stress reduction is slower in BPD patients compared with people without BPD ("slow return to baseline"). It is hypothesized that by the time the emotional reaction to a stressor has faded, a new experience starts another series of intense feelings, preventing adequate emotion regulation. In fact, BPD patients risk moving further away from the baseline instead of approaching it. At extreme levels, the only way to return to baseline quickly may seem to be to perform extreme acts. Indeed, the clinical presentation of BPD suggests that BPD patients apply more stringent methods of emotion regulation such as self-injurious behaviors or dissociation in an attempt to control difficult emotions. However, findings on cue discrepancy suggest that OGM is used in BPD patients when specific prompts are used (Spinhoven et al., 2007; Van den Broeck et al., 2012).

This idea closely relates to the inflexibility concept proposed by Debeer et al. (2012), stating that healthy respondents would be more flexible in manipulating the specificity of their own memories during retrieval in response to situational demands when compared with clinical populations. This is considered an adequate reaction during daily life: one will be able to retrieve specific solutions out of memory in response to problems one is confronted with, and one would recall at a more general level when it is inappropriate to get overwhelmed by emotions and the memory threatens to do so. Depressed and traumatized patients, then, are thought to be inflexibly overgeneral, whereas BPD patients may be inflexibly specific, both leading to deficient emotion regulation and processes maintaining the disorder. The overgeneral memory style of depressed patients, for instance, prevents them from correcting their experiences and schemas about their selves, the world, and others by not incorporating contradicting specific information. In contrast, the specific style of BPD patients may impede the construction of a solid self-concept and trustworthy and predictable descriptions of others. According to the self-memory system (Conway, 2005), information is hierarchically stored. Information selectively derived from event-specific knowledge at the lower levels is integrated into higher order (thematic or time) categories, conceived as being part of one's conceptual self (Conway et al., 2004). The SMS thus suggests that the creation of self- (and other?) descriptions that are coherent over time and across experiences requires the ability to somehow reflectively zoom out, thereby selectively neglecting event-specific knowledge (the concept of narrative identity as conceptualized by, e.g., McAdams & Pals, in Shiner, 2009, may also be of relevance here). Being inflexibly specific, BPD patients may be failing to chunk event-specific knowledge into higher order categories.

Further research is necessary to test the value of cognitive flexibility as a mediator between one's personal reactivity (thresholds) and final affect. If so, studies should also investigate to what degree and how (in)flexibility can be changed during therapy. Kremers et al. (2006a, p. 490) state that "the defensive function of an overgeneral memory style might not be adequate when traumatic events as complex and severe as often is the case in patients with BPD are involved," suggesting that flexibility may turn into inflexibility following severe trauma. Can it be turned around?

Nevertheless, it should be noted that the available studies are rather limited in number, making it difficult to truly investigate the applicability of the CaR-FA-X model in BPD patients. Future studies should therefore study the associations between OGM and working memory, rumination, and avoidance measures in BPD patients.

In addition, the current findings do not sufficiently exclude the possibility that OGM in BPD is mainly associated with comorbid MDD[4] or exposure to trauma. Therefore, future studies should carefully record respondents' history and severity of MDD and trauma, as well as other potentially influential factors such as medication use and substance abuse. Furthermore, given the heterogeneity of the BPD diagnosis, future studies should also include large samples of BPD patients in order to study whether or not OGM in BPD is associated with one or more specific BPD criteria and to assure whether the current findings are not due to selection effects.

As outlined above, the clinical burden of BPD is large, for patients as well as for society. All would therefore benefit from a clear understanding of information processes in these patients, being both a target for therapy as well as the medium by which therapy works. Studying autobiographical memory in BPD is particularly relevant, because of its role in the formation of one's sense of self, which is by definition (APA, 1994) unstable in BPD patients. As for now, the current

---

[4] However, depression in BPD may differ from depression in MDD (see, e.g., Van den Broeck et al., 2012).

theories on autobiographical memory organization seem to apply insufficiently to BPD, although the idea of cognitive flexibility may open up interesting perspectives. We formulated a number of issues that should be taken into account when conducting future research, in order to control for methodological concerns and the complexity of the BPD diagnosis.

REFERENCES

American Psychiatric Association (APA) (1994). *Diagnostic and Statistical Manual of Mental Disorders* (4th ed.). Washington, DC: American Psychiatric Association.

Arntz, A., Meeren, M., & Wessel, I. (2002). No evidence for overgeneral memories in borderline personality disorder. *Behaviour Research and Therapy*, *40*, 1063–1068.

Barnhofer, T., Crane, C., Spinhoven, P., & Williams, J. M. G. (2007). Failures to retrieve specific memories in previously depressed individuals: random errors or content-related. *Behaviour Research and Therapy*, *45*, 1859–1869.

Bender, D. S., Dolan, R. T., Skodol, A. E., Sanislow, C. A., Dyck, I. R., McGlashan, T. H., ..., Gunderson, J. G. (2001). Treatment utilization by patients with personality disorders. *American Journal of Psychiatry*, *158*, 295–302.

Conway, M. A. (2005). Memory and the self. *Journal of Memory and Language*, *53*, 594–628.

Conway, M. A., & Pleydell-Pearce, C. W. (2000). The construction of autobiographical memories in the self-memory system. *Psychological Review*, *107*, 261–288.

Conway, M. A., Singer, J. A., & Tagini, A. (2004). The self and autobiographical memory: correspondence and coherence. *Social Cognition*, *22*, 491–529.

Crane, C., Barnhofer, T., & Williams, J. M. G. (2007). Cue self-relevance affects autobiographical memory specificity in individuals with a history of major depression. *Memory*, *15*, 312–323.

Debeer, E., Raes, F., Williams, J. M. G., & Hermans, D. (2012). Flexible use of overgeneral autobiographical memory as an avoidant coping strategy in nonclinical individuals. Paper presented at the International Meeting of the FWO Scientific Research Network "Temperamental and cognitive vulnerability to the dysregulation of affect and behaviour," Leuven, Belgium.

Goddard, L., Dritschel, B., & Burton, A. (1996). Role of autobiographical memory in social problem solving and depression. *Journal of Abnormal Psychology*, *105*, 609–616.

Grant, B. F., Chou, S. P., Goldstein, R. B., Huang, M. P. H. B., Stinson, F. S., Saha, T. D., et al. (2008). Prevalence, correlates, disability, and comorbidity of DSM-IV borderline personality disorder: results from the Wave 2 National Epidemiologic Survey on Alcohol and Related Conditions. *Journal of Clinical Psychiatry*, *69*, 533–545.

Griffith, J. W., Sumner, J. A., Raes, F., Barnhofer, T., Debeer, E., & Hermans, D. (2012). Current psychometric and methodological issues in the measurement of overgeneral autobiographical memory. *Journal of Behavior Therapy and Experimental Psychiatry, 42,* S21–S31.

Gunderson, J. G. (2009). Borderline personality disorder: ontogeny of a diagnosis. *American Journal of Psychiatry, 166,* 530–539.

Hermans, D. Defranc, A., Raes, F., Williams, J. M. G., & Eelen, P. (2005). Reduced autobiographical memory specificity as an avoidant coping style. *British Journal of Clinical Psychology, 44,* 583–589.

Hertel, P. T., & Hardin, T. S. (1990). Remembering with and without awareness in a depressed mood: evidence of deficits in initiative. *Journal of Experimental Psychology: General, 119,* 45–59.

Jones, B. Heard, H., Startup, M., Swales, M., Williams, J. M. G., & Jones, R. S. P. (1999). Autobiographical memory and dissociation in borderline personality disorder. *Psychological Medicine, 29,* 1397–1404.

Jørgensen, C. R., Berntsen, D., Bech, M., Kjølbye, M., Bennedsen, B. E., & Ramsgaard, S. B. (2012). Identity-related autobiographical memories and cultural life scripts in patients with borderline personality disorder. *Consciousness and Cognition, 21,* 788–798.

Kremers, I. P., Spinhoven, Ph., & Van der Does, A. J. W. (2004). Autobiographical memory in depressed and non-depressed patients with borderline personality disorder. *British Journal of Clinical Psychology, 43,* 17–29.

Kremers, I. P., Spinhoven, Ph., Van der Does, A. J. W., & Van Dyck, R. (2006a). Autobiographical memory in depressed and nondepressed patients with borderline personality disorder after long-term psychotherapy. *Cognition and Emotion, 20,* 448–465.

(2006b). Social problem solving, autobiographical memory and future specificity in outpatients with borderline personality disorder. *Clinical Psychology and Psychotherapy, 13,* 131–137.

Leichsenring, F., Leibing, E. Kruse, J., New, A. S., & Leweke, F. (2011). Seminar: borderline personality disorder. *The Lancet, 377,* 74–84.

Linehan, M. (1993). *Cognitive-Behavioral Treatment of Borderline Personality Disorder.* New York: Guilford Press.

Maurex, L. (2009). Neuropsychological functions in women with borderline personality disorder and a history of suicide attempts. Ph.D. thesis, Karolinska Institutet.

Maurex, L., Lekander, M., Nilsonne, Å., Andersson, E. E., Åsberg, M., & Öhman, A. (2010). Social problem solving, autobiographical memory, trauma, and depression in women with borderline personality disorder and a history of suicide attempts. *British Journal of Clinical Psychology, 49,* 327–342.

McNally, R. J., Lasko, N. B., Macklin, M. L., & Pitman, R. K. (1995). Autobiographical memory disturbance in combat-related posttraumatic stress disorder. *Behaviour Research and Therapy, 33,* 619–630.

Moore, S. A., & Zoellner, L. A. (2007). Overgeneral autobiographical memory and traumatic events: an evaluative review. *Psychological Bulletin, 133,* 419–437.

Moradi, A. R., Taghavi, R., Neshat-Doost, H. T., Yule, W., & Dalgleish, T. (2000). Memory bias for emotional information in children and adolescents with posttraumatic stress disorder: a preliminary study. *Journal of Anxiety Disorders*, *14*, 521–534.

Muenks, K. (2010). Overgeneral memory as an emotion regulation strategy. Senior honors thesis, Ohio State University.

Norman, D. A., & Bobrow, D. G. (1979). Description: an intermediate stage in memory retrieval. *Cognitive Psychology*, *11*, 107–123.

Paris, J., & Zweig-Frank, H. (2001). A 27-year follow-up of patients with borderline personality disorder. *Comprehensive Psychiatry*, *42*, 482–487.

Raes, F. Hermans, D., Williams, J. M. G., Demyttenaere, K., Sabbe, B. Pieters, G., & Eelen, P. (2005). Reduced specificity of autobiographical memory: a mediator between rumination and ineffective social problem-solving in major depression? *Journal of Affective Disorders*, *87*, 331–335.

Reid, T., & Startup, M. (2010). Autobiographical memory specificity in borderline personality disorder: associations with co-morbid depression and intellectual ability. *British Journal of Clinical Psychology*, *49*, 413–420.

Reiser, B. J., Black, J. B., & Abelson, R. P. (1985). Knowledge structures in the organization and retrieval of autobiographical memories. *Cognitive Psychology*, *17*, 89–137.

Renneberg, B., Theobald, E., Nobs, M., & Weisbrod, M. (2005). Autobiographical memory in borderline personality disorder and depression. *Cognitive Therapy and Research*, *29*, 343–358.

Rubin, D. C., Berntsen, D., & Hutson, M. (2009). The normative and the personal life: individual differences in life scripts and life story events among USA and Danish undergraduates. *Memory*, *17*, 54–68.

Sanislow, C. A., Grilo, C. M., Morey, L. C., Bender, D. S., Skodol, A. E. Gunderson, J. G., et al. (2002). Confirmatory factor analysis of DSM-IV criteria for borderline personality disorder: findings from the collaborative longitudinal personality disorders study. *American Journal of Psychiatry*, *159*, 284–290.

Schönfeld, S., & Ehlers, A. (2006). Overgeneral memory extends to pictorial retrieval cues and correlates with cognitive features in posttraumatic stress disorder. *Emotion*, *6*, 611–621.

Shiner, R. L. (2009). The development of personality disorders: perspectives from normal personality development in childhood and adolescence. *Development and Psychopathology*, *21*, 715–734.

Smith, J. M., Grandin, L. D., Alloy, L. B., & Abramson, L. Y. (2006). Cognitive vulnerability to depression and axis II personality dysfunction. *Cognitive Therapy and Research*, *30*, 609–621.

Spinhoven, P., Bockting, C. L. H., Kremers, I. P., Schene, A. H., & Williams, J. M. G. (2007). The endorsement of dysfunctional attitudes is associated with an impaired retrieval of specific autobiographical memories in response to matching cues. *Memory*, *15*, 324–338.

Startup, M., Heard, H., Swales, M., Jones, B., Williams, J. M. G., & Jones, R. S. P. (2001). Autobiographical memory and parasuicide in borderline personality disorder. *British Journal of Clinical Psychology, 40*, 113–120.

Sutherland, K., & Bryant, R. A. (2008). Social problem solving and autobiographical memory in posttraumatic stress disorder. *Behaviour Research and Therapy, 46*, 154–161.

Torgersen, S., Kringlen, E., & Cramer, V. (2001). The prevalence of personality disorders in a community sample. *Archives of General Psychiatry, 58*, 590–596.

Van den Broeck, K., Claes, L., Pieters, G., & Raes, F. (2012). Memory specificity in borderline personality disorder: associations with depression and self-discrepancy. *Journal of Behavior Therapy and Experimental Psychiatry, 43*, S51–S59.

van Vreeswijk, M. F., & De Wilde, E. J. (2004). Autobiographical memory specificity, psychopathology, depressed mood and the use of the Autobiographical Memory Test: a meta-analysis. *Behaviour Research and Therapy, 42*, 731–743.

Weissman, A. N., & Beck, A. T. (1978). Development and validation of the dysfunctional attitude scale: a preliminary investigation. In: *Proceedings of the American Educational Research Association*. Toronto, Ontario, Canada.

Wessel, I., Meeren, M., Peeters, F., Arntz, A., & Merckelbach, H. (2001). Correlates of autobiographical memory specificity: the role of depression, anxiety and childhood trauma. *Behavioural Research and Therapy, 39*, 409–421.

Williams, J. M. G., & Broadbent, K. (1986). Autobiographical memory in suicide attempters. *Journal of Abnormal Psychology, 95*, 144–149.

Williams, J. M. G., Barnhofer, T., Crane, C., Hermans, D., Raes, F., Watkins, Ed, & Dalgleish, T. (2007). Autobiographical memory specificity and emotional disorder. *Psychological Bulletin, 133*, 122–148.

Zanarini, M. C., Frankenburg, F. R., Khera, G. S., & Bleichmar, J. (2001). Treatment histories of borderline inpatients. *Comprehensive Psychiatry, 42*, 144–150.

Zanarini, M. C., Frankenburg, F. R., Hennen, J., Reich, D. B., & Silk, K. R. (2004a). Axis I comorbidity in patients with borderline personality disorder: 6-year follow-up and prediction of time to remission. *American Journal of Psychiatry, 161*, 2108–2114.

Zanarini, M. C., Frankenburg, F. R., Vujanovic, A. A., Hennen, J. Reich, D. B., Silk, K. R. (2004b). Axis II comorbidity of borderline personality disorder: description of 6-year course and prediction to time-to-remission. *Acta Psychiatrica Scandinavica, 110*, 416–420.

12 Difficulties remembering the past and envisioning the future in people with trauma histories or complicated grief

Richard J. McNally and Donald J. Robinaugh

In this chapter, we review studies by our research group, concentrating on autobiographical memory abnormalities in people who have experienced stressful events such as warfare, childhood sexual abuse, and the loss of a loved one. Among these abnormalities are overgeneral memory problems, difficulty envisioning one's future, and the psychological consequences of having major stressful experiences central to one's sense of self. We also summarize studies on how current emotional disturbance may alter one's recollection of stressors in war veterans and in personnel who experienced a shooting rampage at an elementary school. Finally, we discuss memory functioning in people reporting multiple personalities, abduction by space aliens, and repressed and recovered memories of sexual abuse.

Posttraumatic stress disorder (PTSD) is a disorder of memory (Bryant, Chapter 2; Rubin, Chapter 3; McNally, 2003; Rubin et al., 2008). People with PTSD have encoded a representation of an extremely disturbing experience that provides the source for vivid, haunting, involuntary recollections of their trauma. Memory activation manifests itself in flashbacks – sensory images *of* the trauma – and intrusive thoughts *about* the trauma (e.g., Hackmann et al., 2004; McNally, 2006). It also manifests itself in nightmares and psychophysiological activation in response to reminders of the event (Orr et al., 2004). The other symptoms of PTSD, such as avoidance of reminders and hypervigilance, arise from this central disturbance in memory.

The centrality of memory to PTSD is evident in another important way (McNally, 2009). Several core symptoms of PTSD possess *intentionality*, or "aboutness" (Brentano, 1889/1984). That is, intrusive thoughts, nightmares, and avoidance behavior are not merely *caused* by the trauma; they are also *about* the trauma. For example, one cannot have intrusive thoughts without having them be about something. In PTSD, that something is the trauma. The referential character of these symptoms underscores the logical necessity of Criterion A (exposure to trauma) to the diagnosis of PTSD. The traumatic memory unifies the otherwise disparate symptoms into a syndromic whole (Breslau et al., 2002; Young, 1995, p. 7).

In view of the prominent cognitive features of PTSD, our research group began applying the methods of experimental cognitive psychology to elucidate information-processing abnormalities in Vietnam veterans with PTSD (e.g., McNally et al., 1987; Trandel & McNally, 1987). We found that the intrusive ease of activating encoded representations of trauma was especially evident on the emotional Stroop task (e.g., Williams et al., 1996a). That is, despite instructions to ignore the meanings of the words and to name the colors in which the words appeared, PTSD patients experienced great difficulty doing this when the words concerned the Vietnam War (e.g., "firefight"). Relative to healthy veterans, those with PTSD took longer to name the colors of words related to trauma than to name the colors of neutral, positive, and other negative words (Kaspi et al., 1995; McNally et al., 1990; 1993; 1996; Metzger et al., 1997). We found similar results with rape victims with and without PTSD (Cassiday et al., 1992).

As we were embarking on this research program, Williams and colleagues reported that people who had recently attempted suicide (Williams & Broadbent, 1986) or who suffered from depression (Williams & Dritschel, 1988) experience difficulties retrieving specific episodic autobiographical memories in response to cue words, relative to healthy control subjects (Watkins, Chapter 10). Instead, they often recalled categoric memories concerning a type of event (e.g., flying on airplanes) or extended memories spanning far more time than a single day (e.g., the summer following college graduation). Hence, although instructed to recall specific episodes on this Autobiographical Memory Test (AMT), depressed and suicidal patients recalled overgeneral memories that did not reference a specific event.

Overgeneral memory in PTSD

Inspired by the work of Williams and colleagues, we tested whether patients with PTSD would exhibit difficulties retrieving specific autobiographical memories (McNally et al., 1994). Our intuition was that PTSD patients, troubled by intrusive thoughts, would experience diminished cognitive capacity, thus finding it difficult to sustain the effortful memory retrieval essential for performing well on the AMT. We recruited three groups of Vietnam veterans. One group comprised patients with a primary diagnosis of PTSD; the psychiatric contrast group comprised patients with disorders other than PTSD (e.g., panic disorder, major depression, social phobia); and the healthy contrast group was free of mental illness. To test whether priming of war memories would affect performance, we randomly assigned subjects to view either a trauma videotape consisting of photographs of a combat event accompanied by battle sounds or a neutral videotape consisting of photographs of furniture accompanied by relaxing classical music. We suspected that PTSD patients would experience especially marked difficulty retrieving specific memories after viewing a videotape likely to activate intrusive thoughts about the war. The cue words had positive (e.g., "happiness"), negative (e.g., "panic"), or neutral (e.g., "appearance") emotional valence.

Relative to healthy veterans, those with PTSD retrieved more overgeneral memories. Veterans with other psychiatric disorders fell midway between these two groups. Relative to PTSD patients who viewed the neutral prime, PTSD patients who viewed the combat prime exhibited an increase in overgeneral memories in response to neutral and positive cue words. PTSD patients tended to retrieve fewer overgeneral memories in response to negative than to other words, regardless of the prime condition. These findings suggest that exposure to trauma reminders may consume cognitive capacity required for delving deep into one's autobiographical memory database to retrieve specific memories in response to nonnegative cues.

Wondering whether problems with intrusive cognition may drive overgeneral memory, we tested patients with obsessive-compulsive disorder (OCD), investigating whether they were more overgeneral than were healthy contrast subjects (Wilhelm et al., 1997). The groups did not differ on the AMT. Yet when we divided the OCD group into those with and without current major depressive disorder (MDD), we found that OCD patients with depression exhibited the memory deficit, whereas those without depression did not. OCD alone was unrelated to overgeneral memory. Other researchers have likewise found that patients with anxiety disorders, other than PTSD or acute stress disorder (ASD; Harvey et al., 1998), do not exhibit difficulties retrieving specific autobiographical memories (Wenzel et al., 2002; 2004; Wessel et al., 2001). Even patients with specific phobia caused by trauma do not exhibit overgeneral memory (Kleim & Ehlers, 2008).

Returning to PTSD, our research team modified the AMT to test conjectures about pathological self-representation in PTSD (McNally et al., 1995). In addition to having terrifying memories of the trauma, people with the disorder often suffer from shame and guilt. Accordingly, self-representations may be especially negative in people with PTSD relative to combat veterans with no mental disorder.

To investigate these issues, we recruited Vietnam veterans with and without PTSD and administered a modified AMT. In this version of the

AMT, we presented subjects with word cues denoting positive (e.g., "kind") and negative (e.g., "hostile") traits and asked them to retrieve a specific memory when they exhibited the trait. If PTSD is associated with maladaptive self-representation, then subjects with the disorder ought to experience difficulty retrieving specific memories when they exhibited positive traits and experience little difficulty retrieving specific memories when they exhibited negative traits.

The results partly confirmed our hypotheses. Relative to healthy combat veterans, those with PTSD retrieved fewer specific memories in response to the positive trait words than did the healthy combat veterans, and when those with PTSD did retrieve a specific memory, it took longer for them to do so. However, contrary to our other hypothesis, the groups did not differ in terms of the percentage of specific memories retrieved in response to negative trait words or in the time to retrieve them. Taken together, these data suggested that the self-representation of veterans with PTSD concerns diminished positivity, not heightened negativity.

As I (RJM) was testing subjects in this study, I noticed that some of those with PTSD, but none of the healthy ones, were immediately identifiable as Vietnam veterans in terms of their appearance. These men wore combat fatigues, baseball caps proclaiming their status as a Vietnam veteran, and jacket patches signifying various military units. In addition to his jacket patch, one subject arrived at the lab carrying a loaded handgun. These "regalia vets" seemed truly stuck in the past. One might wonder why someone would wear reminders of their traumatic experiences in everyday life. After all, people with spider phobia, for example, surely never wear shirts depicting tarantulas. Their former role as warriors seemed profoundly central to their identity today, even though the war had ended decades earlier. Frozen in the past, these subjects seemed especially prone to disturbance in autobiographical memory.

In fact, a posthoc analysis revealed that the regalia vets were largely driving the overgeneral memory effect in the PTSD group. Although the other PTSD subjects exhibited this effect, too, the regalia subjects did so far more dramatically. They also exhibited another anomaly. Unlike the other PTSD and healthy subjects, they tended to recall relatively few recent memories in response to cue words and relatively more memories from the Vietnam era. The regalia findings suggested a connection between the centrality of the trauma to their personal identity, memory problems, and psychopathology. Consistent with our findings, Sutherland and Bryant (2005) reported that trauma survivors with PTSD more often mention traumatic memories as self-defining than do survivors without PTSD.

Some years later, we directly explored the relations among identity, memory, and psychopathology by administering Berntsen and Rubin's (2006) Centrality of Event Scale (CES) to women who reported having experienced sexual abuse as children (Robinaugh & McNally, 2011). The CES assesses the extent to which people consider a target experience as central to their identity and life story (Boals and colleagues, Chapter 4). In our study, subjects completed the CES in reference to childhood sexual abuse (CSA; Alley and colleagues, Chapter 5), defined as sexual contact (e.g., fondling) occurring prior to the age of seventeen with a perpetrator at least five years older than the victim. Consistent with work by Berntsen and Rubin (2006), we found a strong positive association between event centrality and PTSD symptom severity. The more the subject regarded the abuse as central to her life story, the worse were her PTSD symptoms. Moreover, this relationship remained significant after we controlled statistically for the effects of age, intelligence, dissociation, depression symptom severity, and self-esteem.

Although early research indicated that CES items are loaded onto a single "event centrality" factor (Berntsen & Rubin, 2006), Berntsen and Rubin designed it to measure three distinct constructs: (1) the extent to which the event is central to one's identity, (2) a turning point in one's life story, and (3) a reference point structuring the organization of autobiographical memory. Accordingly, we conducted a principal component analysis to assess for the presence of these underlying factors and their association with PTSD symptom severity.

Our results suggest that the CES comprises three factors. The first factor reflects both the centrality to identity and the extent to which the event functions as a reference point for organizing one's autobiographical memories. The second factor reflects whether the person views the event as a turning point in her life. Both of these factors were positively associated with PTSD symptom severity.

The third factor surprised us. It reflected the extent to which the subjects viewed their future through the lens of the traumatic event (e.g., "When I reflect upon my future, I often think back to this event"). Interestingly, this factor exhibited the strongest association with PTSD symptom severity. These findings suggest that holding a traumatic event as a reference point by which to understand one's future may be more pathogenic than appraising the event as a key to one's past or present identities.

The literature on overgeneral memory has grown tremendously. Researchers have discovered that overgeneral retrieval has important clinical implications (for a review, see Williams et al., 2007). It is associated with slow recovery from depression (e.g., Brittlebank et al., 1993), impaired problem-solving skills (e.g., Evans et al., 1992), and difficulty envisioning one's future (Williams et al., 1996b).

Other researchers have further examined overgeneral memory in people with trauma histories (e.g., Kuyken & Brewin, 1995). In a cross-cultural study, Iranian combat veterans of the Iran–Iraq war with PTSD retrieved fewer specific memories than did healthy combat veterans, who, in turn, retrieved fewer specific memories than did control subjects without combat exposure (Moradi et al., 2012). This study notwithstanding, most studies show that PTSD per se, not exposure to trauma, best predicts overgeneral memory effects (Moore & Zoellner, 2007).

Harvey et al. (1998) studied overgeneral memory in survivors of motor vehicle accidents who had ASD, a syndrome arising within one month following exposure to trauma. ASD is a kind of acute PTSD accompanied by dissociation symptoms such as derealization and depersonalization. They found that subjects with ASD had greater difficulty retrieving specific memories in response to positive cue words than did subjects without ASD. Neither group exhibited difficulty retrieving specific memories to negative cue words. It is notable that difficulty in recalling specific memories predicted PTSD symptoms six months later.

Studies showing that the overgeneral retrieval style predicts subsequent PTSD (e.g., Kleim & Ehlers, 2008) suggest that overgeneral memory may be a risk factor for PTSD and not merely a consequence of developing PTSD. However, one cannot tell whether this style results from trauma or whether it precedes it and constitutes a risk factor for PTSD among victims of trauma. Addressing this issue, Bryant et al. (2007) administered the AMT to sixty trainee firefighters who were free of PTSD and had yet to encounter the traumatic events common to their occupation. They reassessed forty-six of them four years later; all had encountered traumatic events, and 15% had developed PTSD. Bryant et al. found that difficulty retrieving specific memories to positive cues at baseline predicted severity of PTSD symptoms four years later, implying that an overgeneral retrieval style functions as risk factor for PTSD among those exposed to trauma.

Researchers have also examined factors that may mediate the relation between the overgeneral retrieval style and emotional disorder. One such factor may be problem-solving ability. People who cannot readily recall detailed memories about how they overcame problems in the past are likely to encounter obstacles to solving them in the present. Studying civilian trauma survivors, Sutherland and Bryant (2008) administered the AMT and a modified means–ends problem-solving test in counterbalanced order to subjects with and without PTSD. The problem-solving task involved vignettes relevant to the aftermath of a trauma, such as a man whose injuries following an accident resulted in his job loss, imperiling his ability to support his family. Yet the man did achieve financial security. The subject's task was to describe plausible steps that the man could have taken to solve his problem. The results revealed that subjects with PTSD retrieved fewer specific memories irrespective of cue word valence than did the healthy trauma survivors. Moreover, subjects with PTSD performed less well on the problem-solving task than did the healthy subjects. Higher memory specificity was associated with higher scores on measures of problem solving (e.g., good choice of means, likely effectiveness of the steps taken to solve the problem).

Another factor that may mediate the association between overgeneral memory and psychopathology is the ability to imagine specific future events. In our early work on PTSD (McNally et al., 1994), we speculated that a relative inability to retrieve specific memories from the past might be associated with an inability to imagine specific events in the future. Recently, Brown et al. (2013) found evidence to support this possibility. In their study, American combat veterans of the Afghanistan and Iraq wars who developed PTSD retrieved fewer specific memories than did healthy combat veterans of these wars. Relative to healthy combat veterans, those with PTSD also experienced difficulty envisioning specific future events.

Overgeneral memory and memories of childhood sexual abuse

In addition to our work with combat veterans, we also conducted a program of research testing hypotheses arising from claims concerning alleged repressed and recovered memories of CSA. Drawing on cognitive psychology paradigms, including the AMT, our experiments targeted mechanisms that might enable a person to inhibit memories of CSA or inadvertently develop false memories of CSA (for a review, see McNally, 2012c). One hypothesis current at the time we began this research program was that difficulty recalling memories from one's childhood may itself signal a history of CSA, albeit a history dissociated from awareness (e.g., Loewenstein, 1991). Accordingly, subjects who believe that they harbored repressed memories of CSA might experience marked difficulty retrieving specific memories, especially from their childhoods.

To examine this possibility, we recruited four groups of subjects (McNally et al., 2006). The *repressed memory* group comprised subjects who suspected that they harbored memories of abuse that they could not recall. They inferred their presumed history of CSA from diverse indicators (e.g., nightmares, depressed mood, and sexual problems). Note that our use of the term "repressed memory" merely underscores the phenomenology of these subjects; we had no evidence that these subjects had encoded memories of abuse that they were unable to recall. The *recovered memory* group comprised subjects who recalled their memories of abuse after a long period when they said the memories had never come to mind. Note that not having thought about one's CSA in many years does not necessarily imply that one has been *incapable* of recalling the memory during the extended period when it apparently never came to mind. That is, a recovered memory is not necessarily a previously repressed one. The *continuous memory* group included subjects who said that they had never forgotten their abuse, and the *control* group reported no history of sexual abuse. Each group comprised both men and women.

In this study, we administered an altered version of the AMT. As with the standard AMT, we provided subjects with negative and positive cue words and asked them to retrieve a specific event. However, for half of these trials, we instructed subjects to recall a specific event occurring before the age of thirteen ("childhood"). For the remaining words, we asked them to retrieve a memory after the age of thirteen ("postchildhood").

The results revealed no significant differences among the groups in the specificity of memories from adulthood. However, the repressed memory group retrieved significantly fewer specific memories from childhood than did the control group and the recovered memory group. Yet the repressed memory group did not differ from the continuous memory group.

Although these findings are partly consistent with the notion that massive repression of a terrible childhood produced widespread deficits for retrieving specific memories from childhood, there is another explanation as well. An inference about repression may arise because of a diminished ability to retrieve specific memories. In other words, rather than repression causing difficulty with memory, difficulty with memory may lead the individual to infer repression. It is possible that highly distressed individuals hit on the theory that they harbor repressed memories of CSA because it provides an explanation for their otherwise inexplicable distress. Moreover, this explanation provides someone to blame for the distress.

Although memory phenomenology, not psychopathology, was the key to group assignment in this study, we did assess PTSD and depression in our subjects. Much to our surprise, we found not a shred of evidence suggesting that subjects with PTSD (or depression) more often retrieved overgeneral memories relative to subjects free of these disorders. Only nonverbal cognitive ability predicted the specificity of childhood memories ($r = 0.33$, $p < 0.01$); questionnaires measuring anxiety, dissociation, verbal cognitive ability, absorption, and depression were not significantly related to the specificity of childhood memories.

Our failure to replicate the overgeneral memory effect in our CSA cases with PTSD or depression raises questions about how best to measure the phenomenon, including among people free of psychopathology. Indeed, if this style is a risk factor for depression or PTSD, we should be able to detect it among subjects at risk for these disorders. However, in studies examining overgeneral memory in nonclinical subjects, researchers have reported very low rates of overgeneral memory (Raes et al., 2007). This finding is consistent with at least two explanations. First, nonclinical subjects simply may not exhibit overgeneral memory when completing the AMT at the same rates as do clinical subjects. Second, these subjects may have overgeneral memory, but the AMT may be insufficiently sensitive to detect it.

Based on this latter possibility, Raes et al. (2007) designed the Sentence Completion for Events from the Past Test (SCEPT), an alternative assessment of overgeneral memory in which subjects complete sentence stems (e.g., "In the past...") with autobiographical information. However, unlike the AMT, the SCEPT does not contain any instructions to recall specific events. Accordingly, the SCEPT assesses the general or default tendency to respond with specific memories rather than the ability to do so when instructed.

To examine whether SCEPT specificity would be associated with symptoms of psychopathology, we administered the SCEPT to a nonclinical sample composed predominately of university students (Robinaugh et al., 2013). In addition, we administered a Sentence Completion for Events from the Future Test (SCEFT) to assess the tendency to complete sentence stems with specific future events. The results showed that subjects exhibited a high rate of responses that were either categoric memories or semantic information on both the SCEPT and the SCEFT (37% and 65% of responses, respectively). However, after controlling for multiple comparisons, we detected no significant associations between SCEPT and SCEFT specificity and measures of depression symptom severity, PTSD symptom severity, or repetitive negative thought.

These findings raise the possibility that it is the *ability* to recall or imagine specific events (as measured by the AMT) rather than the *tendency* to recall or imagine specific events (as measured by the SCEPT and SCEFT), that is associated with symptoms of psychopathology.

Alternatively, the association between the tendency to be overgeneral and symptoms of psychopathology may exist but may be context dependent. Indeed, researchers have found that associations between overgeneral memory and psychopathology emerged only in specific contexts such as following a rumination induction (e.g., Debeer et al., 2011).

The null findings from this study and from our CSA study suggest that we need further work to clarify the relation between overgeneral memory and psychopathology and the contexts in which the association emerges.

Relevant to the controversy concerning recovery of previously repressed (or dissociated) memories of trauma is the claim that dissociative identity disorder (DID) arises from horrific childhood physical and sexual abuse that victims are unable to recall (e.g., Young et al., 1991). That is, trauma supposedly fractures the minds of victims, producing multiple personalities that harbor memories too horrific for the host personality to contemplate consciously. This theory arose during the epidemic of multiple personality disorder that erupted following the publication of the bestseller *Sybil* (Schreiber, 1973) and the television movie based on the book. Ironically, recent historical scholarship indicates that the woman known as Sybil admitted fabricating the trauma histories that surfaced during the countless hypnotic memory recovery sessions conducted by her psychiatrist. Moreover, scholars have found no evidence that Sybil's mother was psychotic or abusive (Borch-Jacobsen, 2009, pp. 64–99; Nathan, 2011; Rieber, 2006, pp. 205–287).

The trauma theory of DID rests on two assumptions related to autobiographical memory. First, it presupposes that the mind protects itself from traumatic memories by rendering them inaccessible until it becomes psychologically safe for victims to recover the memories (Brown et al., 1998, p. 647). In fact, the notion that dissociation renders victims amnesic for their trauma provided the justification for so-called recovered memory therapy. However, there is no convincing evidence that trauma produces amnesia for the central features of the traumatic experience (McNally, 2003, pp. 186–228; 2007), as PTSD so dramatically illustrates. That is, the stress hormones released during terror render the experience especially memorable.

Although there is no convincing evidence that victims of trauma can become incapable of recalling terrifying events, some victims of sexual abuse report not thinking about their abuse for many years, only to encounter reminders in adulthood that prompt recollection. Yet these victims often failed to understand their molestation and failed to experience the terror integral to canonical traumatic events (e.g., combat, rape; Clancy & McNally, 2005/2006). However, many report PTSD symptoms after recalling their abuse and viewing it through the eyes of an adult. Hence, they forgot their abuse because they did not encode it as a terrifying trauma. There is no evidence that the memory was inaccessible (i.e., repressed or dissociated) during the period when it never came to mind. Accordingly, one can recover (recall) a memory of CSA without it having been previously repressed and hence inaccessible and without it having been encoded as traumatic (McNally, 2012c).

The second assumption of the trauma theory of DID is that memories of trauma harbored by certain "alters" or personalities are inaccessible to the host personality. That is, there is interidentity amnesia among the personalities. Using a concealed information task, Huntjens et al. (2012) tested this assumption of interidentity amnesia in patients with DID. We recruited three groups of women: patients diagnosed with DID, amateur actors trained to simulate DID, and another group consisting of non-actors. We administered an autobiographical questionnaire to all subjects, asking about the names of their best friends, their favorite foods, favorite sports, and so forth. The DID patients completed the questionnaire twice, once as the trauma identity who reported memories of CSA, and again as an identity reportedly amnesic for memories of abuse. For example, a DID trauma identity might have written down the words *Janet, pizza,* and *swimming* in response to questions about the name of her best friend, favorite food, and favorite sport, whereas the amnesic identity might have written down the answers *Mary, steak,* and *tennis.* We had subjects rate the personal emotional relevance of words drawn from these questionnaires, plus many other irrelevant words, and the DID patients did so in their amnesic identity, thus enabling selection of words from the trauma identity's questionnaire that the amnesic identity rated as personally irrelevant.

The concealed information task itself occurred two weeks after subjects had completed the questionnaires. Subjects viewed a series of words in uppercase letters on a computer screen, and had to decide as quickly as possible whether they recognized the word as a member of a target set of three words (e.g., *SUSAN, CHOCOLATE, BOWLING*) that they had previously memorized or whether the word was a nontarget word. The computer recorded the reaction times of subjects as they performed the recognition/classification procedure. Among the large set of nontarget words were the three words having autobiographical significance for a DID patient's trauma identity (e.g., *JANET, PIZZA,* and *SWIMMING*) and the three words having autobiographical significance for the patient's amnesic identity (e.g., *MARY, STEAK,* and *TENNIS*).

The results confirmed that subjects were fast to classify irrelevant words and slow to classify nontarget words that possessed autobiographical significance (e.g., their best friend's names). The slowed reaction times signified recognition of the word's personal relevance. That is, they had to inhibit the impulse to respond "yes" to the question of recognition. Accordingly, in the DID group, the amnesic identities performed this task, and their reaction times to respond "no" to words having considerable autobiographical significance was very slow (e.g., *MARY, STEAK,* and *TENNIS*), signifying their recognition of the personal importance of these items. Crucially, these patients were just as slow to respond to the corresponding items of their trauma identity of which they were allegedly amnesic (e.g., *JANET, PIZZA,* and *SWIMMING*). These data are inconsistent with the notion of interidentity amnesia. Indeed, if the amnesic identity were truly unable to access the autobiographical material of the trauma identity, then the reaction times to classify these items would not have been just as slow for classifying the autobiographical items of the amnesic identity. Hence, these data indicate that the second assumption of the trauma theory of DID, as well as the first one, is empirically untenable.

Distorted and false autobiographical memories

The reconstructive character of recollection implies that autobiographical memory is subject to distortion. Memory does not operate like a videotape, faithfully recording our experience for subsequent recall (Loftus & Loftus, 1980; Schacter, 1999). Our research group has studied distortion in autobiographical recollection in people exposed to trauma. In one study, we found that the severity of PTSD symptoms affects how victims recall their traumatic experiences (Schwarz et al., 1993). Six months after a shooting rampage at an elementary school in suburban Chicago, we asked school personnel to complete a questionnaire assessing their memories of the traumatic experience. Eighteen months after the event, we asked the subjects to complete the questionnaire again. Strikingly, each subject remembered his or her traumatic experience at eighteen months differently from at six months. Severity of PTSD symptoms at eighteen months predicted subjects' recalling the event as worse than they recalled it at six months. School personnel whose symptoms remained severe remembered the experience as more traumatic than they had before, whereas those whose symptoms had improved by eighteen months tended to remember the event as less traumatic than they had earlier.

A subsequent study on memory inconsistency involved Dutch infantry troops who had served in the Iraq War (Engelhard et al., 2008). Soldiers completed questionnaires, including measures of neuroticism and extroversion, six weeks prior to deployment. Approximately five months after returning from Iraq, they completed questionnaires concerning exposure to traumatic and nontraumatic stressors and symptoms of PTSD, and they completed them again fifteen months postdeployment. For each item on the stressor measures, soldiers indicated whether they had experienced it and rated how much of a negative impact it had on them (1 = no impact, 2 = little negative, 3 = moderately negative, 4 = extremely negative). Among the 133 soldiers for whom we had data at both postdeployment assessments, twenty-one had scores indicative of PTSD, whereas 112 soldiers were free of PTSD. The results revealed that subjects in the PTSD group endorsed having experienced more traumatic stressors in Iraq at fifteen months than they did at five months. Moreover, higher scores on PTSD symptom severity and neuroticism and lower scores on extroversion (and fewer previous deployments) predicted the tendency to report more stressors at fifteen months than at five months.

In neither study could we tell whether subjects remembered events at fifteen months that they had forgotten to endorse at five months or whether they developed false memories of trauma at fifteen months. The confusing fog of war may have led some soldiers to incorporate stressful events occurring to others into their own autobiographical databases. That is, at fifteen months postdeployment, they may have misremembered the source of a memory record, assuming incorrectly that an episode that had happened to someone else had actually happened to them. From the safe perspective of later postdeployment life, they may have also endorsed some items as more dangerous than they originally did.

Not only can people misremember details during autobiographical recollection, occasionally attributing others' memories to themselves, but they can also develop full-blown "memories" of traumatic experiences that never occurred, such as victimization by satanic cults (McNally, 2003, pp. 229–259).

Our research group has studied people whose detailed, vivid autobiographical memories were surely false (McNally, 2012a). We have studied memory in "reincarnated" individuals who have recovered "memories" from their previous lives (Meyersburg & McNally, 2011; Meyersburg et al., 2009). However, these past-lifers seldom recover memories of trauma from the lives of their previous "incarnations." In contrast, people who recover "memories" of having experienced abduction by space aliens describe these encounters as highly traumatic, even though many of them eventually regard the experience as spiritually transformative (Clancy, 2005; McNally & Clancy, 2005), suggestive of posttraumatic growth (Boals and colleagues, Chapter 4).

Interested in the formation of false autobiographical memories, we investigated why sincere, nonpsychotic individuals come to believe they have been victims of extraterrestial kidnapping (Clancy et al., 2002; McNally et al., 2004). In brief, we found that the typical space alien abductee scores high on measures of absorption and magical ideation, is familiar with the cultural narrative of alien abduction, and has undergone hypnotic memory recovery sessions after having had episodes of isolated sleep paralysis accompanied by hypnopompic ("as one awakens") hallucinations of intruders ("space aliens") in their bedrooms. It is during these recovered-memory sessions that abductees "recall" their otherwise inaccessible memories of undergoing sexual probing on board spaceships and so forth.

In one of our studies, we tested whether space alien abductees exhibit the psychophysiological signature of PTSD when listening to audiotaped scripts of their terrifying encounters with space aliens (McNally et al., 2004). After interviewing ten abductees, we asked them to provide written accounts of their two most terrifying encounters with aliens. Additionally, we also asked them to describe their most stressful experience unrelated to abduction (e.g., an accident), their most positive experience (e.g., birth of a child), and a neutral experience (e.g., washing the dishes the previous night). For each autobiographical episode, we had them read a list of physiological reactions (e.g., sweating, pounding heart) that they recalled having during the events described in the narratives. We converted these accounts into 30-second audiotaped narratives written in the second person, present tense.

Our comparison group consisted of twelve individuals who denied a personal history of space alien abduction. We "yoked" each of these subjects to an abductee so that they heard the audiotaped neutral, positive, stressful, and abduction scripts of a stranger. Contrast analyses revealed that relative to comparison subjects, the abductees exhibited greater reactivity to trauma scripts (abduction and stressful) than to nontrauma scripts (positive and neutral). That is, the abductees responded indistinguishably to abduction and trauma scripts, and much more than to positive and neutral scripts, whereas the control subjects responded minimally to all scripts. This pattern occurred for all three psychophysiological measures: heart rate, skin conductance, and electromyographic activity in the left lateral frontalis muscle, signifying facial muscle tension. Strikingly, their reactivity to the abduction scripts was at least as great as the reactivity of Vietnam veterans with chronic PTSD who listened to scripts of their war-related traumatic events (Keane et al., 1998). As terrifying as they described their alien encounters to have been, the abductees did not suffer from

PTSD, although three of them had once had subclinical PTSD emerging after they had recovered their memories, and one still had some symptoms. Current psychiatric diagnoses were rare among the ten abductees. There was one diagnosis each of panic disorder, specific phobia (insects), bipolar disorder (NOS; not otherwise specified), and anxiety disorder due to alcohol dependence (McNally, 2012a). Finally, all but one subject reported that they were glad that they had been abducted, as terrifying as the experiences had been. Knowing that aliens are "out there" deepened their spiritual view of the universe.

Complicated grief

Most recently, we have extended our work to examine autobiographical memory in bereaved adults with complicated grief (CG). CG is a bereavement-specific syndrome characterized by separation distress, yearning, intrusive memories related to the deceased, and a sense of hopelessness about the future (Prigerson et al., 2009; Shear et al., 2011). CG is distinguishable from depression and is notable for the marked impairment it produces (Bryant, 2012). Relative to bereaved adults without CG, those with CG exhibit difficulty recalling specific autobiographical memories (Maccallum & Bryant, 2010a), and severity of CG symptoms correlates negatively with memory specificity (Boelen et al., 2010). Moreover, patients with CG exhibit deficits in problem solving even after researchers have controlled for levels of PTSD and depression (Maccallum & Bryant, 2010b). However, Golden et al. (2007) found that when recalling events from the life of the deceased, bereaved adults with CG were no less specific than were bereaved control subjects. Taken together, these findings suggest that overgeneral memory in people with CG may vary depending on whether the recollected memories concern their lost loved ones.

To further test this possibility, we administered two versions of the AMT: one in which subjects recalled autobiographical memories that include the deceased (AMT-With) and one in which subjects recalled memories that did not include the deceased (AMT-Without; Robinaugh & McNally, 2013). Consistent with Golden et al. (2007), we found that bereaved adults with CG exhibited reduced memory specificity when recalling events that did not include the deceased but were no less specific than were bereaved control subjects when recalling events that did include the deceased.

In addition, we assessed a potential mechanism that might contribute to difficulty retrieving autobiographical memories without the deceased.

Given the highly accessible memories related to the deceased in those with CG, we reasoned that the first memory retrieved in response to a memory cue on the AMT would often be a memory that includes the deceased. Consequently, when completing the AMT-Without, bereaved adults with CG would be likely to first retrieve a memory that does not fit the search criteria. Accordingly, they would have to inhibit this memory of the deceased so that they could continue to search for a memory not involving the deceased. If so, individuals with CG who have a greater ability to inhibit this prepotent response should be more specific when recalling events in the AMT-Without.

To test this hypothesis, we assessed working memory capacity (WMC), a construct closely associated with the ability to inhibit interfering information (Barrett et al., 2004; Engle, 2002). We found that a significant interaction between WMC and CG symptom severity predicted memory specificity on the AMT-Without. For subjects with low CG symptom severity, there was no effect of WMC. These subjects exhibited high specificity regardless of WMC. In contrast, for those with high CG symptom severity, there was an effect of WMC. Subjects high in CG symptom severity and high in WMC exhibited high specificity. In contrast, those with low WMC (i.e., those subjects who should have a difficult time inhibiting interfering information such as a prepotent memory with the deceased) exhibited low rates of specificity. These findings are consistent with the possibility that memory competition is one mechanism that may contribute to reduced specificity.

Finally, in this study we also examined the ability to imagine future events in CG. Maccallum and Bryant (2011) found that patients with CG have difficulty imagining specific future events. Investigating this further, we administered two versions of the future event task: one in which subjects imagined future events that include the deceased (i.e., events that could have occurred if the deceased had not passed away) and one in which subjects imagined events that do not include the deceased (i.e., events that could realistically occur in the future). Paralleling our findings on memory, we found that bereaved adults with CG were less specific than were bereaved control subjects when imagining future events without the deceased but were no less specific when imagining future events that included the deceased. Strikingly, bereaved adults with CG were more specific when imagining a counterfactual future that included the deceased than when imagining future events that did not include the deceased. The ease of imagining a future with the deceased coupled with difficulty imagining the future without the deceased may provide a cognitive basis for the core symptom of yearning.

Conclusions

Although research on overgeneral memory originated in the depression field, we, and others, have extended this work into the areas of PTSD and CG. These two syndromes present an apparent paradox. Central to both is retrieval of highly specific emotional memories of trauma and loss, respectively. Yet AMT studies indicate that people with PTSD and CG often retrieve overgeneral memories in response to cue words. Our original intuition was that intrusive cognition about trauma preempts cognitive capacity, rendering it difficult for patients to retrieve specific memories unrelated to trauma in response to cue words. Hence, the ease of retrieval of trauma memories, whether arising from direct or generative search, interferes with accessing other memories. To be sure, people with PTSD often aim to avoid thoughts and emotions associated with trauma. Yet to attempt to avoid does not entail that one will be successful doing so.

Our research on CG confirms and extends our research on PTSD. That is, CG sufferers seem to experience difficulty retrieving specific memories only when those memories do not include the deceased. Moreover, working memory capacity moderates this process. Individuals with high CG and low WMC exhibited the lowest specificity. This finding supports our initial intuition that highly accessible thoughts preempt cognitive capacity and contribute to difficulty retrieving other less accessible memories.

Consistent with research on cognitive neuroscience showing the mechanisms that mediate autobiographical recollection also mediate envisioning one's future (Schacter, 2012), people with CG can easily envision a counterfactual future with their dead spouses, yet experience problems envisioning a future without their loved ones. Recent findings in combat veterans suggest that those with PTSD exhibit similar difficulty imagining specific future events (Brown et al., 2013).

Finally, people with PTSD or CG commonly suffer from major depressive disorder (MDD), making it difficult to determine whether the former syndromes alone result in overgeneral memory. However, this issue arises chiefly because of our categorical diagnostic system. Yet if we conceptualize these disorders as a causal network of functionally interconnected symptoms (Borsboom et al., 2011; McNally 2012b), not as an expression of a latent, underlying diagnostic variable, then the problem of comorbidity vanishes (Cramer et al., 2010). That is, rather than framing the question as one of determining whether overgeneral memory is a function of PTSD, CG, or MDD, we would address which symptoms result in this memory problem (e.g., intrusive thought, rumination) or result from this memory problem (e.g., a sense of hopeless or foreshortened future). Given the transdiagnostic nature of overgeneral memory and the substantial overlap in cognitive symptoms between MDD, CG, and PTSD, there is good reason to believe that memory bias or impairment may play a prominent role in the development or maintenance of these symptom networks.

REFERENCES

Barrett, L. F., Tugade, M. M., & Engle, R. W. (2004). Individual differences in working memory capacity and dual-process theories of mind. *Psychological Bulletin, 130*, 553–573.

Berntsen, D., & Rubin, D. C. (2006). The Centrality of Event Scale: a measure of integrating a trauma into one's identity and its relation to posttraumatic stress disorder symptoms. *Behaviour Research and Therapy, 44*, 219–231.

Boelen, P. A., Huntjens, R. J. C., van Deursen, D. S., & van den Hout, M. A. (2010). Autobiographical memory specificity and symptoms of complicated grief, depression, and posttraumatic stress disorder following loss. *Journal of Behavior Therapy and Experimental Psychiatry, 41*, 331–337.

Borch-Jacobsen, M. (2009). *Making Minds and Madness: From Hysteria to Depression.* Cambridge: Cambridge University Press.

Borsboom, D., Cramer, A. O. J., Schmittmann, V. D., Epskamp, S., & Waldorp, L. J. (2011). The small world of psychopathology. *PLoS ONE, 6*(11), e27407, 1–11.

Brentano, F. (1984). On the origin of our knowledge of right and wrong. In C. Calhoun & R. C. Solomon (eds.), *What is an Emotion?* (pp. 205–214). New York: Oxford University Press. (Originally published in 1889.)

Breslau, N., Chase, G. A., & Anthony, J. C. (2002). The uniqueness of the *DSM* definition of post-traumatic stress disorder: implications for research. *Psychological Medicine, 32*, 573–576.

Brittlebank, A. D., Scott, J., Williams, J. M. G., & Ferrier, I. N. (1993). Autobiographical memory in depression: state or trait marker? *British Journal of Psychiatry, 162*, 118–121.

Brown, A. D., Root, J. C., Romano, T. A., Chang, L. J., Bryant, R. A., & Hirst, W. (2013). Overgeneralized autobiographical memory and future thinking in combat veterans with posttraumatic stress disorder. *Journal of Behavior Therapy and Experimental Psychiatry, 44*, 129–134.

Brown, D., Scheflin, A. W., & Hammond, D. C. (1998). *Memory, Trauma Treatment, and the Law.* New York: Norton.

Bryant, R. A. (2012). Grief as a psychiatric disorder. *British Journal of Psychiatry, 201*, 9–10.

Bryant, R. A., Sutherland, K., & Guthrie, R. M. (2007). Impaired specific autobiographical memory as a risk factor for posttraumatic stress after trauma. *Journal of Abnormal Psychology, 116*, 837–841.

Cassiday, K. L., McNally, R. J., & Zeitlin, S. B. (1992). Cognitive processing of trauma cues in rape victims with post-traumatic stress disorder. *Cognitive Therapy and Research, 16*, 283–295.

Clancy, S. A. (2005). *Abducted: How People Come to Believe They Were Kidnapped by Aliens.* Cambridge, MA: Harvard University Press.

Clancy, S. A., & McNally, R. J. (2005/2006). Who needs repression? Normal memory processes can explain "forgetting" of childhood sexual abuse. *Scientific Review of Mental Health Practice, 4*, 66–73.

Clancy, S. A., McNally, R. J., Schacter, D. L., Lenzenweger, M. F., & Pitman, R. K. (2002). Memory distortion in people reporting abduction by aliens. *Journal of Abnormal Psychology, 111*, 455–461.

Cramer, A. O. J., Waldorp, L. J., van der Maas, H. L. J., & Borsboom, D. (2010). Comorbidity: a network perspective. *Behavioral and Brain Sciences, 33*, 137–193.

Debeer, E., Raes, F., Williams, J. M. G., & Hermans, D.(2011). Context-dependent activation of reduced autobiographical memory specificity as an avoidant coping style. *Emotion, 11*, 1500–1506.

Engelhard, I. M., van den Hout, M. A., & McNally, R. J. (2008). Memory consistency for traumatic events in Dutch soldiers deployed to Iraq. *Memory, 16*, 3–9.

Engle, R. W. (2002). Working memory capacity as executive attention. *Current Directions in Psychological Science, 11*, 19–23.

Evans, J., Williams, J. M. G., O'Loughlin, S., & Howells, K. (1992). Autobiographical memory and problem-solving strategies of parasuicide patients. *Psychological Medicine, 22*, 399–405.

Golden, A. M., Dalgleish, T., & Mackintosh, B. (2007). Levels of specificity of autobiographical memories and of biographical memories of the deceased in bereaved individuals with and without complicated grief. *Journal of Abnormal Psychology, 116*, 786–795.

Hackmann, A., Ehlers, A., Speckens, A., & Clark, D. M. (2004). Characteristics and content of intrusive memories in PTSD and their changes with treatment. *Journal of Traumatic Stress, 17*, 231–240.

Harvey, A. G., Bryant, R. A., & Dang, S. T (1998). Autobiographical memory in acute stress disorder. *Journal of Consulting and Clinical Psychology, 66*, 500–506.

Huntjens, R. J. C., Verschuere, B., & McNally, R. J. (2012). Inter-identity autobiographical amnesia in patients with dissociative identity disorder. *PLoS ONE, 7*(7), e40580.

Kaspi, S. P., McNally, R. J., & Amir, N. (1995). Cognitive processing of emotional information in post-traumatic stress disorder. *Cognitive Therapy and Research, 19*, 433–444.

Keane, T. M., Kolb, L. C., Kaloupek, D. G., Orr, S. P., Blanchard, E. B., Thomas, R. G., Hsieh, F. Y., & Lavori, P. W. (1998). Utility of psychophysiological measurement in the diagnosis of posttraumatic stress disorder: results from a Department of Veterans Affairs Cooperative Study. *Journal of Consulting and Clinical Psychology, 66*, 914–923.

Kleim, B., & Ehlers, A. (2008). Reduced autobiographical memory specificity predicts depression and posttraumatic stress disorder after recent trauma. *Journal of Consulting and Clinical Psychology, 76*, 231–242.

Kuyken, W., & Brewin, C. R. (1995). Autobiographical memory functioning in depression and reports of early abuse. *Journal of Abnormal Psychology, 104,* 585–591.

Loewenstein, R. J. (1991). An office mental status examination for complex chronic dissociative symptoms and multiple personality disorder. *Psychiatric Clinics of North America, 14,* 567–604.

Loftus, E. F., & Loftus, G. R. (1980). On the permanence of stored information in the human brain. *American Psychologist, 35,* 409–420.

Maccallum, F., & Bryant, R. A. (2010a). Impaired autobiographical memory in complicated grief. *Behaviour Research and Therapy, 48,* 328–334.

(2010b). Social problem solving in complicated grief. *British Journal of Clinical Psychology, 49,* 577–590.

(2011). Imagining the future in complicated grief. *Depression and Anxiety, 28,* 658–665.

McNally, R. J. (2003). *Remembering Trauma*. Cambridge, MA: The Belknap Press of Harvard University Press.

(2006). Cognitive abnormalities in post-traumatic stress disorder. *Trends in Cognitive Sciences, 10,* 271–277.

(2007). Dispelling confusion about traumatic dissociative amnesia. *Mayo Clinic Proceedings, 82,* 1083–1087.

(2009). Can we fix PTSD in DSM-V? *Depression and Anxiety, 26,* 597–600.

(2012a). Explaining "memories" of space alien abduction and past lives: an experimental psychopathology approach. *Journal of Experimental Psychopathology, 3,* 2–16.

(2012b). The ontology of posttraumatic stress disorder: natural kind, social construction, or causal system? *Clinical Psychology: Science and Practice, 19,* 220–228.

(2012c). Searching for repressed memory. In R. F. Belli (ed.), *True and False Recovered Memories: Toward a Reconciliation of the Debate* (pp. 121–147). Vol. 58: Nebraska Symposium on Motivation. New York: Springer.

McNally, R. J., & Clancy, S. A. (2005). Sleep paralysis, sexual abuse and space alien abduction. *Transcultural Psychiatry, 42,* 113–122.

McNally, R. J., Luedke, D. L., Besyner, J. K., Peterson, R. A., Bohm, K., & Lips, O. J. (1987). Sensitivity to stress-relevant stimuli in posttraumatic stress disorder. *Journal of Anxiety Disorders, 1,* 105–116.

McNally, R. J., Kaspi, S. P., Riemann, B. C., & Zeitlin, S.B. (1990). Selective processing of threat cues in posttraumatic stress disorder. *Journal of Abnormal Psychology, 99,* 398–402.

McNally, R. J., English, G. E., & Lipke, H. J. (1993). Assessment of intrusive cognition in PTSD: use of the modified Stroop paradigm. *Journal of Traumatic Stress, 6,* 33–41.

McNally, R. J., Litz, B. T., Prassas, A., Shin. L. M., & Weathers, F. W. (1994). Emotion priming of autobiographical memory in post-traumatic stress disorder. *Cognition and Emotion, 8,* 351–367.

McNally, R. J., Lasko, N. B., Macklin, M. L., & Pitman, R. K. (1995). Autobiographical memory disturbance in combat-related posttraumatic stress disorder. *Behaviour Research and Therapy, 33,* 619–630.

McNally, R. J., Amir, N., & Lipke, H. J. (1996). Subliminal processing of threat cues in posttraumatic stress disorder? *Journal of Anxiety Disorders, 10,* 115–128.

McNally, R. J., Lasko, N. B., Clancy, S. A., Macklin, M. L., Pitman, R. K., & Orr, S. P. (2004). Psychophysiological responding during script-driven imagery in people reporting abduction by space aliens. *Psychological Science, 15,* 493–497.

McNally, R. J., Clancy, S. A., Barrett, H. M., Parker, H. A., Ristuccia, C. S., & Perlman, C. A. (2006). Autobiographical memory specificity in adults reporting repressed, recovered, or continuous memories of childhood sexual abuse. *Cognition and Emotion, 20,* 527–535.

Metzger, L. J., Orr, S. P., Lasko, N. B., McNally, R. J., & Pitman, R. K. (1997). Seeking the source of emotional Stroop interference effects in PTSD: a study of P3s to traumatic words. *Integrative Physiological and Behavioral Science, 32,* 43–51.

Meyersburg, C. A., & McNally, R. J. (2011). Reduced death distress and increased meaning in life among individuals reporting past life memory. *Personality and Individual Differences, 50,* 1218–1221.

Meyersburg, C. A., Bogdan, R., Gallo, D. A., & McNally, R. J. (2009). False memory propensity in people reporting recovered memories of past lives. *Journal of Abnormal Psychology, 118,* 399–404.

Moore, S. A., & Zoellner, L. A. (2007). Overgeneral autobiographical memory and traumatic events: an evaluative review. *Psychological Bulletin, 133,* 419–437.

Moradi, A. R., Abdi, A., Fathi-Ashtiani, A., Dalgleish, T., & Jobson, L. (2012). Overgeneral autobiographical memory recollection in Iranian combat veterans with posttraumatic stress disorder. *Behaviour Research and Therapy, 50,* 435–441.

Nathan, D. (2011). *Sybil Exposed: The Extraordinary Story behind the Famous Multiple Personality Case.* New York: Free Press.

Orr, S. P., McNally, R. J., Rosen, G. M., & Shalev, A. Y. (2004). Psychophysiological reactivity: implications for conceptualizing PTSD. In G. M. Rosen (ed.), *Posttraumatic Stress Disorder: Issues and Controversies* (pp. 101–126). Chichester, UK: Wiley.

Prigerson, H. G., Horowitz, M. J., Jacobs, S. C., Parkes, C. M., Aslan, M., Goodkin, K., Raphael, B., Marwit, S. J., Wortman, C., Neimeyer, R. A., Bonanno, G., Block, S. D., Kissane, D., Boelen, P., Maercker, A., Litz, B. T., Johnson, J. G., First, M. B., & Maciejewski, P. K. (2009). Prolonged grief disorder: psychometric validation of criteria proposed for *DSM-V* and *ICD-11*. *PLoS Medicine, 6,* e1000121.

Raes, F., Hermans, D., Williams, J. M., & Eelen, P. (2007). A sentence completion procedure as an alternative to the Autobiographical Memory Test for assessing overgeneral memory in non-clinical populations. *Memory, 15,* 495–507.

Rieber, R. W. (2006). *The Bifurcation of the Self: The History and Theory of Dissociation and Its Disorders*. New York: Springer.

Robinaugh, D. J., & McNally, R. J. (2011). Trauma centrality and PTSD symptom severity in adult survivors of childhood sexual abuse. *Journal of Traumatic Stress*, 24, 483–486.

(2013). Remembering the past and envisioning the future in bereaved adults with and without complicated grief. *Clinical Psychological Science*, 1, 290–300.

Robinaugh, D. J., Lubin, R., Babic, L., & McNally, R. J. (2013). Are habitual overgeneral recollection and prospection maladaptive? *Journal of Behavior Therapy and Experimental Psychiatry*, 44, 227–230.

Rubin, D. C., Berntsen, D., & Bohni, M. K. (2008). A memory-based model of posttraumatic stress disorder: evaluating basic assumptions underlying the PTSD diagnosis. *Psychological Review*, 115, 985–1011.

Schacter, D. L. (1999). The seven sins of memory: insights from psychology and cognitive neuroscience. *American Psychologist*, 54, 182–203.

(2012). Adaptive constructive processes and the future of memory. *American Psychologist*, 67, 603–613.

Schreiber, F. (1973). *Sybil*. New York: Warner Books.

Schwarz, E. D., Kowalski, J. M., & McNally, R. J. (1993). Malignant memories: posttraumatic changes in memory in adults after a school shooting. *Journal of Traumatic Stress*, 6, 95–103.

Shear, M. K., Simon, N., Wall, M., Zisook, S., Neimeyer, R., Duan, N., Reynolds, C., Lebowitz, B., Sung, S., Ghesquiere, A., Gorscak, B., Clayton, P., Ito, M., Nakajima, S., Konishi, T., Melhem, N., Meert, K., Schiff, M., O'Connor, M.-F., First, M., Sareen, J., Bolton, J., Skritskayra, N., Mancini, A. D., & Keshaviah, A. (2011). Complicated grief and related bereavement issues for DSM-5. *Depression and Anxiety*, 28, 103–117.

Sutherland, K., & Bryant, R. A. (2005). Self-defining memories in post-traumatic stress disorder. *British Journal of Clinical Psychology*, 44, 591–598.

(2008). Social problem solving and autobiographical memory in posttraumatic stress disorder. *Behaviour Research and Therapy*, 46, 154–161.

Trandel, D. V., & McNally, R. J. (1987). Perception of threat cues in posttraumatic stress disorder: semantic processing without awareness? *Behaviour Research and Therapy*, 25, 469–476.

Wenzel, A., Jackson, L. C., & Holt, C. S. (2002). Social phobia and the recall of autobiographical memories. *Depression and Anxiety*, 15, 186–189.

Wenzel, A., Werner, M. M., & Cochran, C. K., & Holt, C. S. (2004). A differential pattern of autobiographical memory retrieval in social phobia and nonanxious individuals. *Behavioural and Cognitive Psychotherapy*, 32, 1–13.

Wessel, I., Meeren, M., Peeters, F., Arntz, A., & Merckelbach, H. (2001). Correlates of autobiographical memory specificity: the role of depression, anxiety and childhood trauma. *Behaviour Research and Therapy*, 39, 409–421.

Wilhelm, S., McNally, R. J., Baer, L., & Florin, I. (1997). Autobiographical memory in obsessive-compulsive disorder. *British Journal of Clinical Psychology*, 36, 21–31.

Williams, J. M. G., & Broadbent, K. (1986). Autobiographical memory in suicide attempters. *Journal of Abnormal Psychology*, *95*, 144–149.

Williams, J. M. G., & Dritschel, B. H. (1988). Emotional disturbance and the specificity of autobiographical memory. *Cognition and Emotion*, *2*, 221–234.

Williams, J. M. G., Mathews, A., & MacLeod, C. (1996a). The emotional Stroop task and psychopathology. *Psychological Bulletin*, *120*, 3–24.

Williams, J. M. G., Ellis, N. C., Tyers, C., Healy, H., Rose, G., & MacLeod, A. K. (1996b). The specificity of autobiographical memory and imageability of the future. *Memory and Cognition*, *24*, 116–125.

Williams, J. M. G., Barnhofer, T., Crane, C., Hermans, D., Raes, F., Watkins, E., & Dalgleish, T. (2007). Autobiographical memory specificity and emotional disorder. *Psychological Bulletin*, *133*, 122–148.

Young, A. (1995). *The Harmony of Illusions: Inventing Posttraumatic Stress Disorder*. Princeton, NJ: Princeton University Press.

Young, W. C., Sachs, R. G., Braun, B. G., & Watkins, R. T. (1991). Patients reporting ritual abuse in childhood: a clinical syndrome. Report of 37 cases. *Child Abuse and Neglect*, *15*, 181–189.

Part IV

Autobiographical memory, identity, and psychological well-being

13 A model of psychopathological distortions of autobiographical memory narratives: an emotion narrative view

Tilmann Habermas

This chapter introduces a comprehensive descriptive model of which aspects of autobiographical memory narratives may be distorted in diverse clinical disorders, by defense and coping efforts, and how they may change in the course of psychotherapy. The different features will be systematically related to each other by the concepts of narrative perspective and emotion. Narrative perspective helps organize the narrative features, and emotion is assumed to be the motivating force behind the distortions. To indicate the organizing power of the model, various constructs that capture distortions of autobiographical memories will be located within the model, thus creating an integrative framework. Selected disorders and selected findings on the process of coping and psychotherapy will also be interpreted in terms of the model. The general approach to clinical dysfunctions of autobiographical memory is a narrative one, which is inspired by basic tenets of psychoanalysis.

Autobiographical memories and narratives

Memories are first of all subjective experiences of recollection, sometimes accompanied by images or other sensory aspects. An episodic quality is important, as stressed by Tulving (2002), who highlights a sense of reliving as an essential element of episodicity. However, more partial, fragmented elements may also count as memories, such as when a sense of familiarity arises and one could say, "This reminds me of something." But one would speak of a memory only if this feeling of familiarity actually led to some kind of rough contextualization in terms of place and time. And most of the time a recollection would involve not just a stationary sensory input but a temporally structured, sequential series of events.

In everyday life, we normally come to know about someone else's memory when he or she tells us about it. As autobiographical memories concern events, these communications will normally take the form of a narrative, because this is the text format for communicating temporally ordered information, usually events. Psychological research, in contrast, most often poses specific questions to be answered by the remembering person. In the most reduced form, questions require yes-or-no answers, such as when asking whether something is recognized. Other formats ask for scalar introspective judgments of memories by offering rating scales (see Rubin, Chapter 3). The formats closest to everyday sharing of memories are verbal memory reports. Most studies use verbal memory reports to judge very specific aspects of memories, for example, whether they regard a specific day (Williams et al., 2007) or how veridical or detailed they are (Levine et al., 2002). However, if one takes vividness of a memory report as a criterion for autobiographical remembering, as is suggested by the metaphor of reliving (Tulving, 2002), vividness is associated with neither memory specificity nor detailedness but whether the report takes the form of a narrative text, and not that of a chronicle that summarizes events, a static description, or a logical argumentation (Habermas & Diel, 2013). Therefore, narrative is the most natural, canonical means to communicate autobiographical memories.

When research participants are asked for memory reports, they most often produce some kind of rudimentary narrative. In everyday life, when we experience an event that arouses our emotions, we tend to talk about it to others, that is, to narrate the event, often quite extensively (Rimé, 2009). In psychotherapy, especially in insight-oriented psychotherapies, patients tend to tell stories of the near or distant past about events that move them. When we as therapists speak to patients about their problems, we tend to ask them for narratives of problematic experiences, to be able to work on these narrated memories, possibly to interpret and reinterpret them. Thus narrative is the format in which patients and therapists communicate about memories.

Homologous structures of narrative and emotion

Personally important autobiographical memories tend to be narrated, and, vice versa, what tends to be narrated is usually to some degree emotional. First, I outline the functions of narrative to replicate event sequences and to evaluate them, and then I show how narrative and emotion are closely linked and how they have comparable process structures.

Narratives have two major functions: communication of events and their evaluation. Narratives imitate the sequence of events by telling them in a basically linear fashion. Labov and Waletzky (1967) have condensed this central characteristic in defining narrative clauses as those main clauses the order of which cannot be changed without changing their meaning. Narrative clauses are typically introduced by "and then..., and then...." Besides re-presenting event chains, narratives are expected to

Table 13.1: *Homologous process structures of narratives and emotion*

Narrative structure (Labov, 1997)	Emotion process (Frijda, 1986)
Abstract	–
Evaluation	–
Orientation	(State of normality)
Complication	Event
Evaluation (juncture emotion)	*Appraisal*
	Emotion (mimic, physiological, feeling) = action tendency
Attempts to solve	Attempts to normalize situation
Result	Result
Evaluation (outcome emotion)	*Emotion*
Coda	–
Evaluation	–

offer an evaluation of the events. Broadly conceived, evaluation comprises all subjective views of the events, including, for example, emotions and cognitions. Internal evaluations stem from the participants of the event at the time of the event and are thus part of the narrated event sequence, whereas external evaluations stem from nonparticipant perspectives. These may include the evaluation of the narrator looking back on him- or herself as protagonist. Whereas events follow a plot, evaluation is basically bound to perspectives: evaluations are always made by someone. Evaluations therefore always refer to someone's subjective perspective.

Emotion is a specific kind of evaluation. Emotions are spontaneous, prereflective evaluative reactions to events. Therefore, they are an integral part of narrated events. This is reflected in a basic homology of the process structure of narrative and emotion. Whether events are worth being told depends on whether listeners find them interesting. Therefore, event reportability (Labov, 1997) or tellability (Chafe, 1994) depends on how new, exceptional, or unexpected an event is. Similarly, emotions are elicited by events that are appraised as being of high personal relevance to the individual and that correspond to an event prototype (Frijda, 1986) or a relationship prototype (Lazarus, 2006) that typically requires a specific emotion.

Everyday narratives follow a normative structure (Table 13.1, left column). The reportable event is often announced initially in the abstract to ask the interlocutors' permission to continue narrating the whole story. The orientation contains information about the context of the event to follow, the "who" and "where" and "when" of the time when things were still normal. Then the complication contains the event that is deemed reportable, the essence of what happened, the reason for telling the story. It is something unexpected that violates canonical expectations (Bruner, 1990). Both the abstract and the complication are usually evaluated. What follows are attempts to solve the complication, which may take several steps, all of which may be evaluated. The final result is again evaluated, usually as successful or not successful. This motivated Hogan (2003) to expect that the outcome is evaluated only by happiness about success or by sorrow about failure, but never by other emotions. These other emotions, Hogan argues, can evaluate only the complication section. He termed happiness and sorrow "outcome emotions" and all the other emotions "juncture emotions" (for contradicting evidence, cf. Habermas et al., 2009). The coda serves to lead listeners from the time of narrated events back to the present.

The emotion process as conceived by Frijda (1986) and many others basically parallels the structure of narratives (Table 13.1, right column), except for the introductory and concluding parts of narratives (abstract and coda) that connect present with past are missing. The evaluation is split in a cognitive appraisal of the situation and an ensuing emotional reaction, which provides an action readiness that motivates attempts to solve the complication.

Narrative and emotion are thus intricately parallel processes. Narrative, however, adds a second temporal level to the event sequence by transporting it from the past of experiencing the events to the present situation in which it is remembered and narrated. Because of the temporal distance, narrators and listeners can evaluate events retrospectively, externally. These evaluations may differ from the internal evaluations made at the time of the events.

A unified model of clinically relevant narrative levels

This basic architecture of narratives will now be further specified so as to allow a systematic description of the impact of clinical disorders on autobiographical memory and narrative and to relate them to emotions. The model chooses a narrative language both because of its vicinity to emotion and because covert remembering would be most fully explicated and communicated in narrative form.

The following five levels of narrative (see Table 13.2) were selected both to do justice to major structural features of narratives and to allow describing major clinical abnormalities of remembering. A first version of the model was elaborated using narratological concepts in a bottom-up

Table 13.2: *Five levels of narrative*

Narrative level	Variations in perspectives
1. Temporal event sequences: narrative clauses	—
2. Intentional structure	
Narrative structure	
Motivated agency	Personal
	Temporal
3. Direct evaluations	Personal
Reported speech (direct or indirect, internal monologue)	Temporal
Mental clauses (perception, emotion, cognition, volition)	Local
Global evaluations	
4. Reflective evaluations	Personal
Local explanations and interpretations	
Autobiographical arguments	
5. Listener orientation	—
Consistency	
Completeness	

fashion to analyze three autobiographical narratives that intuitively represented three degrees of defensive distortion (Habermas, 2006). Here I do not describe different narrative styles, but only present analytical narrative levels and relate them, in the following section, to known distortions of remembering.

A central phenomenon that structures most narrative levels is that of perspectivity. Both emotions and narratives are inherently structured by perspectives. Some levels can differ by personal perspective (the "who"), some by temporal perspective (the "when"), and some by local perspective (the "where"). The first level begins with the most elementary, objective level of sequential events, which is followed by a second narrative level of events that are qualified as actions. The third and fourth levels comprise what Labov (1997) termed "evaluations": the third level includes more immediate evaluations that are often internal to the level of narrated events, and the fourth level comprises more distanced, usually external evaluations in the form of arguments. While the first four levels can be defined in formal linguistic ways, the fifth level is defined more semantically and pragmatically in terms of fit of content and comprehensibility.

Level 1: narrativity

Memories can be communicated in different formats. They may be reported in a summarized fashion, which is termed a "chronicle." The most complete way to communicate events is to narrate them by using narrative clauses that imitate the sequence of events. The use of narrative clauses renders the report vivid and draws the listener into the story (Nelson et al., 2008). By offering information in the temporal sequence of events, the listener is put in the position of the protagonist who experiences events in temporal sequence. Therefore, listeners tend to react to narrated events as if they themselves were witnessing or experiencing them. If the events have the potential to elicit emotion, listeners will react emotionally. The same is true for (autobiographical) narrators, in the sense that the more they narrate, the more they also put themselves in the shoes of their past selves, and the more they will relive past emotions due to the sequential reliving of the event sequence. Narrating thus involves confrontation with past events and invokes emotions.

Level 2: agency

Stories are structured not only by the temporal succession of events, but more specifically by their emplotment. This requires an intentional structuring of the story, which is implied by the global structure introduced above. Complication sections of narratives violate canonical expectations and pose a threat to major personal concerns. The threat sets into motion intentions to normalize the state of affairs, to solve the problems. The pursuit of this goal by the protagonists provides direction and meaning to the story (Herman, 2013; Trabasso et al., 1992) and creates suspense in the listener. Good stories require negative events caused or intended by external forces or chance that the protagonist confronts with a plan of action structured by the intention to normalize the complication. Different kinds of prototypical plots define narrative genres. Hogan (2011), for example, suggests there are some major universal plot structures such as sacrifice, heroism, and romantic love.

Narratives differ not only in the genre they use and in their specific plots, but also, more generally, in the degree to which a story actually depicts the pursuit of purposeful actions. For a story to be interesting, it needs a plot driven by intentional actors. Complications are events that happen to the protagonist. Stories vary in the degree to which protagonists actively pursue a solution to the problem, or even in the degree to which protagonists act, and not just react. Some stories present protagonists as mere victims of circumstance and higher powers (*Verlaufskurve*; Schütze, 1983). Victim stories and hero stories define a continuum of protagonist agency. Actions form the basic fabric of the intentional structure of stories.

Autobiographical narrators, who claim identity with the main protagonist, are expected to narrate the protagonist as an intentional actor who tries to give purpose and direction to his or her life. Narrators who portray their past selves as not agentic not only tell stories that are probably less interesting, but also convey the impression of being helpless individuals who do not take responsibility for their past. Listeners expect narrators to at least retrospectively assume some responsibility for what they did in the past to conform to what it means to be a person in the intersubjective sphere: someone who answers questions about past behavior and who takes responsibility, if possible, for the personal past (MacIntyre, 1981).

The principal linguistic form for expressing agency is using the protagonist as the syntactic subject with an active verb, as in the statement "I opened the door." Many more different linguistic forms are available for expressing a downgrading of agency. These comprise, among others, the use of passive forms or impersonal syntactic subjects, posing the protagonist as recipient of an action by a more powerful other, and expressions of a restricted ability to act (cf. de Silveira & Habermas, 2011).

The intentional structure of the story's plot is organized both temporally and by the personal perspectives of the protagonists. Conflicting intentions create the tension and complication necessary to drive a plot. The protagonists' intentions develop as the plot unfolds. In narratives, personal intentional perspectives are primarily those of the protagonists. However, as just mentioned, narrators may complement motives retrospectively, by adding a motive of which they originally may not have been aware.

Level 3: direct evaluations

Actions form the intentional fabric of narratives and also a ground level of subjectivity. The next, more conscious, and somewhat more reflective level of subjectivity is also more explicitly evaluative. Here I group several narrative means that transport protagonists' mental processes and acts that may or may not be communicated by them. The kind of evaluation closest to the level of action is reported speech. Formally, speech content may be mentioned without using specific syntactic means, such as in "He admitted his misdeeds to the prosecutor." Special syntactic constructions allow reporting subjectivity better by staying closer to the words actually used by the speaker. These are direct speech with a verbum dicendi and a verbatim quote of the words spoken ("He finally said, 'Yes, I made them up'") and, slightly more remote from the act, indirect speech, in which a verbum dicendi in the main clause is combined with a subordinate clause containing the propositional content of the utterance, such as in "He admitted that he had fabricated data." A special form is the representation of thoughts in direct speech, internal monologue.

The next, most extensive class of means for expressing subjectivity comprises mental clauses (Halliday, 2004). These are divided into perceptual, emotive, cognitive, and desiderative, or volitional clauses. Usually, mental acts are expressed by mental verbs such as "see," "fear," "think," or "decide." As they are intentional in the sense of always having an object, this object may be expressed as the syntactic object ("I saw him coming") or in a subordinate phrase typically introduced by "that" or "whether" (termed "projection" by Halliday, 2004). However, in everyday speech emotions are frequently named without their object (in psychological terms, their eliciting situation, as in "I was panicking"), so that they may be expressed by adjectives ("He looked so anxious"), nouns ("I was full of fear"), and metaphors. Sometimes emotions are also narrated by describing expressive acts such as crying.

A third class of evaluative devices referring to a first-person perspective comprises what I term "global evaluations." In these the speaker expresses a global judgment of positive or negative valence ("That was really bad"), a judgment of normality or exceptionality ("That was nothing special," "It was just unbelievable"), or a judgment of importance.

All three direct evaluations can vary in personal perspective. Reported speech tends to have a past temporal perspective; global evaluation a present temporal perspective; and mental clauses may have any temporal perspective. Perceptual mental clauses may also vary in locational perspective.

Level 4: reflective evaluations

Evaluations may also be more reflective and argumentative, establishing logical relations between statements by explaining and interpreting both events and direct evaluations. A special class of reflective evaluations are (auto-)biographical arguments. They serve to frame past events in a biographical perspective by relating them to distant other events, to biographical consequences, and to the individual's personal development (cf. Habermas, 2011). Arguments are mostly used from the narrator's perspective but may also be attributed to other individuals.

Level 5: listener orientation

This level cannot be defined formally but is of semantic and pragmatic nature. It concerns whether the narrative corresponds to common sense, which is used by the listener to understand the narrative. Common sense is the shared stock of knowledge and beliefs about human motivation and the world, and therefore is a point of reference that depends on both narrator and listener.

What I term here "consistency" is sometimes also termed "coherence," for example, in the attachment literature (Main et al., 1985). Its main characteristic is the absence of contradictions, or, put positively, the fitting together of various parts. Internal consistency is violated by contradictions between different statements in the narrative. Consistency may also be violated by contradictions between parts of the narrative and common sense. In this case the actions of a protagonist may not make sense because they violate common-sense assumptions about valid motives in a given situation. Also in most cases of internal contradictions it is necessary to refer to common sense. Often, statements do not contradict each other outrightly but their implications do, which need to be inferred with the help of common sense.

Another aspect judged by reference to common sense is whether the narrative contains all pieces of information necessary to understand the course of events, and only relevant information. This regards mainly the contextual information provided in the orienting section regarding time, place, participants, and special circumstances necessary to understand the significance of the complication. But the completeness of information also regards the sections containing the complication and the attempts to solve it. The actions, reactions, and outcomes must be recounted in a motivated and causally convincing manner. Completeness of information is, of course, a relative term, as information provided in a narrative is always selective, as is the punctuation of the flow of events by choosing a starting and an end point.

Grice's (1975) maxims of cooperation define how communication has to adapt to the listeners' needs in order for communication to be successful. The requirement of consistency corresponds to the maxim of clarity, while the requirement of completeness follows from the maxims of quantity and relevance.

Dramatizing use of several levels of narrative induces transportation into the story world

A specific, dramatic style of narrating (Chafe, 1994) is constituted by a high degree of narrativity, mental clauses from the past first-person perspective, with a preference for the perceptual and sometimes also the emotional mode, direct speech, historical present tense, a shift of the point of reference of temporal ("now") and local ("here") deictic expressions from the narrator to the protagonist constitute. It is typically combined with a subjective narrative point of view, defined as the limitation of narrated information to that information accessible to the main protagonist. All these means serve to draw listener and narrator into the exclusive perspective of the past protagonist, to immerge the listener in the story world.

Autobiographical memory narratives in psychological disorders

Narratives are complex phenomena, and the five levels do not describe them exhaustively. Generally speaking, psychopathological processes do not show in a specific type of narrative. Rather, there are many different ways in which psychopathology shows in narratives. I propose that these ways are best conceived as deviations from an ideal type of what listeners would consider a good story. Listeners prefer stories to be engaging and emotional, memorable and original; in other words, entertaining (Baron & Bluck, 2011).

To demonstrate that the typical psychopathological characteristics of autobiographical remembering can be described in terms of the five narrative levels, I will describe established constructs and phenomena in terms of deviations from an assumed ideal narrative (see Table 13.3). I will propose how characteristics of psychological disorders are reflected in narrative terms as deviations from the ideal form on theoretical grounds and based on evidence. The phenomena differ in terms of their theoretical status. Some are genuinely cognitive, emotional, or linguistic phenomena; others, I will argue, are narrative phenomena proper.

Depression

A stable finding is that when asked for specific autobiographical memories that come to mind in response to cue words, depressed individuals more often than healthy controls do not oblige, offering no response or only general memories, that is, repeated ("When we used to go to the ice cream parlor") or temporally extended events ("Vacation in Italy"). These *overgeneral memories* also predict risk for first time depression and relapse in the chronically depressed (Sumner, 2012; Williams et al., 2007). The way overgeneral memories are operationalized, they are a quality of memory reports, not a genuine memory phenomenon. The term "overgeneral memory" does not exactly translate into narrative terms because it typically requires that an event lasting no longer than a day is nominated. However, there is a large overlap with level 1; that is,

Table 13.3: *Characteristic narrative distortions in some psychological disorders*

Narrative levels	Depression	PTSD	Panic disorder	Personality disorders
1. Narrative clauses	Less	More	More	
2. Intentional structure				
a. Narrative structure	Less			
b. Motivated agency		Less	Less	Less
3. Direct evaluations				
a. Reported speech		Dramatic	Dramatic	
b. Mental clauses		Dramatic	Dramatic	
c. Global evaluations				
4. Reflective evaluations				
a. Local interpretations	More			
b. Autobiographical arguments	More	Less	Less	
5. Listener orientation				
a. Consistency				Less
b. Complenetess				Less
Special dramatic devices		More	More	

PTSD, posttraumatic stress disorder.

specific memories are narrated because that is the normative way to speak about specific events (Habermas & Diel, 2013).

Williams and colleagues (2007) hypothesized that overgeneral memories result from ruminative thinking (see Watkins, Chapter 10), from a lack of goal-directed activity, and from generalized avoidance of specific memories that tend to have more emotions associated with them, especially negative emotions. As narrating an event evokes the course of the event and tends to transport narrator and listener back into the situation more so than does merely thinking of or nominating a specific event (Nelson et al., 2008), I hypothesize that avoidance of negative memories might show even more clearly in the avoidance of actually narrating the event rather than in the avoidance of merely naming a specific event.

Brooding or *ruminating* is a pattern of thinking that is symptomatic for depression. It has a degree of involuntariness in that it captures the attention of the depressed individual. It has a cyclical, repetitive quality in that it gravitates around the ever same subject, that is, the self. Finally, it has an abstract, theoretical quality in that it appears to be geared toward finding reasons for past and present inadequacies. Rumination is essentially a cognitive phenomenon, a quality of thinking, which may be reflected in the way it is narrated (see Watkins, Chapter 10). Rumination is usually measured by self-report, or some aspect of rumination may be experimentally induced. To better understand what the essential aspects of rumination are, it would be necessary to study it with a think-aloud method (Sumner, 2012). Although speaking ruminating thoughts aloud might change these to some degree by forcing them to be organized more explicitly and linearly, ruminating about past events should still be reflected in memory reports by a relative absence of narrative (level 1) and a preponderance of argumentative evaluation (level 4). Narrative should be absent because narrative by definition requires linear temporal progression, whereas argumentative evaluation, explaining, and interpreting require stepping back from a specific sequence of events to abstract and generalize from it.

In the absence of narrative analyses of the answers to cue words by depressed patients, we consider the results of a study of life narratives of patients with major depression (Habermas et al., 2008). We did not code for amount of narrative clauses (level 1), but we did find more deviations from a linear order in depressed patients than in controls. However, explanations in general (level 4a) and specifically autobiographical arguments (level 4b) were *not* more frequent. In addition, depressed narrators were more stuck in the past, as indicated by the distribution of the temporal perspective of direct evaluations (level 3), which were more in the past than in the present, and by a preponderance of the more immediate perceptual and emotional versus the more distanced cognitive and volitional mental clauses.

This latter finding of being more in the past and closer to what happened in the past contradicts the overgenerality of autobiographical memories found in depression with the cueing method. However, the difference may lie in the method: if asked only for a series of memory nominations, depressed individuals less often recall specific past events; if, however, they are motivated to remember seven specific memories and then are invited to narrate these embedded in entire life narratives for half an hour, depressed patients apparently do remember, and also remember perceptual and emotional details. Nevertheless, they still are less flexible in distancing themselves from the past and evaluating it from a present point of view.

Confirmed in narratives is an additional finding that had been studied earlier only in questionnaires, namely, a depressive explanatory style (Habermas et al., 2008; see similarly Adler et al., 2006). Thus, agency in depression is exaggerated for negative and underdeveloped for positive outcomes.

Posttraumatic stress disorder

The polarity of avoidance and an intense reliving of the past that defines posttraumatic stress disorder (PTSD) may also produce an avoidance of narrating past events, or, alternatively, when individuals with PTSD are pushed or drawn to indeed confront the past, narratives may reflect this involuntary reliving. The avoidant side of PTSD is reflected in the tendency to produce overgeneral memories when confronted with cue words (see McNally and Robinaugh, Chapter 12). The reliving side is picked up by a long tradition that characterizes trauma narratives as internally fragmented and not integrated into the life story due to the lack of organization of memories (see Ehlers, Chapter 6). The most outspoken recent representatives of this current are van der Kolk and Fisler (1995), who cite Pierre Janet (1919) as an early proponent of the fragmented nature of traumatic narratives, as shown in his treatment of the patient Irène. They suggest that narrative fragmentation was a product of psychic dissociation. Janet had postulated that traumatic memories were encoded at the sensori-motor or affective levels, but not in a way that renders narration of the event possible. Van der Kolk and Fisler (1995) point to patient reports of remembering mainly the sensory aspects of the event, such as images, smells, sound, bodily sensations, or intensive affective states, which, patients claimed, made the memory appear as an exact replication of past sensations. Van der Kolk and Fisler (1995) imply that this contributes to a lack of narrative organization.

Pierre Janet was one of the first to conceive memory in narrative terms (1928). Speaking of the traumatized patient Irène, who denied the death of her mother and tended to reenact in a dissociated state of mind the scenes before her death, Janet (1919, p. 274) states that she "has not at all constructed the memory narrative..., and she is even less able to attach the narrative of her mother's death to her own life story." To cure traumatic memories "they need to be put in a specific place in our life story" (p. 277). I believe that Janet used these formulations to express that his patient had no narrative of her mother's death that she was able to tell and that the event was not solidly integrated temporally into the life story and thereby lacked the quality of being in the past. Janet's statement was a statement not about the quality of trauma narratives but about their absence (because the trauma was not remembered) and about his patient's tendency to reenact scenes from before the traumatic event.

Neither the claim that trauma memories were fragmented and the claim that they were not integrated into the life story have not been borne out in systematic research (see Rubin, Chapter 3; Berntsen, Chapter 9; and McNally and Robinaugh, Chapter 12), especially if instead of subjective ratings objective qualities of narratives were used to measure narrative fragmentation (Bedard-Gilligan & Zoellner, 2012; O'Kearny & Perrot, 2006). Also in one of our studies of fourteen mistreated (sexually and nonsexually), traumatized women and controls, trauma narratives, compared with distress narratives of the control group, were not more fragmented in terms of speech fluency (Römisch et al., 2014). However, another characteristic of trauma narratives emerged when compared with distress narratives in nontraumatized controls: trauma narratives were more immerged in past events. This showed in increased overall length, a more frequent use of the dramatic devices of historic present and shifting of the origo of deictic words to the past protagonist. In addition, even though nonsignificantly, traumatic narratives tended to use more perceptual relative to cognitive mental clauses, and to use more mental clauses from the past than from other temporal perspectives. David Rubin (2011) also found more perceptual words in trauma narratives of traumatized students than in distress narratives of nontraumatized students.

In terms of the five levels of formal analysis of narratives, this means that trauma narratives are *not* inconsistent and probably also not more incomplete (level 5) than comparable narratives in nontraumatized individuals, nor do they differ in the proportion of direct evaluations (level 3; Römisch et al., 2014). However, trauma narratives do use more devices for dramatic narration, which is a preference of the past protagonist perspective in mental clauses, and also use additional devices for inducing the experiential perspective of the past protagonist. There is no evidence regarding the other elements of dramatic speech (a high degree of narrativity (level 1) and a subjective point of view) while direct speech (level 3a) did not differ (Römisch et al., 2014) Given the nature of a traumatic experience, trauma narratives most probably are low in agency (level 2), at least as far as the event itself is concerned. Finally, the amount of argumentative evaluations might at least initially be low, although the centrality of traumatic events to identity (Rubin, Chapter 3; Boals and colleagues, Chapter 4) might suggest otherwise.

The dramatizing nature of trauma narratives is certainly not an indicator of fragmentation, of missing coherence. Dramatized narratives can be very coherent and consistent, not the least because they are limited to one person's perspective, that of the past protagonist. They correspond to what Laub and Auerhahn (1993) termed "overwhelming narratives," in which narrators seem to be transported back into the event and to relive what they originally experienced. They contrasted this narrative with "witnessed narrative," in which a variety of perspectives is added, foremost the narrator's present perspective, but also the perspectives of other people in the past, the present, and possibly also in the hypothetical mode.

Römisch and colleauges (2014) suggest that the "psychotherapists' folklore" (McNally, 2003) that trauma narratives are fragmented results from the effects of dramatized narratives on listeners. Dramatized narratives draw the listener into the past scene, into the subjective perspective of the protagonist. This leads to a heightened empathetic emotional response (Habermas & Diel, 2010; Polya et al., 2005), thus to an intense emotional experience in the listener. Listening to dramatized trauma narratives threatens the listener to be exposed to affective experiences similar to the original traumatic experience of the narrator. This creates in the listener an intense urge to avoid listening to the trauma narrative. The refusal of potential listeners precludes interpersonal confirmation of an exceptional and therefore not very credible experience and contributes to the continuation of the traumatic effect of the event (Laub & Auerhahn, 1989). Against expectations, in our study of listeners' emotional reactions to sad narratives, dramatic narration did not decrease the plausibility of narratives. However, dramatic narratives of traumatic experiences may tax listeners to such a degree that they feel overwhelmed by the intensity of affect and the extreme violence of the event, so that they gain the impression that the narrative is fragmented because it has no closure and remains to be intellectually and emotionally processed.

Anxiety disorders

PTSD involves an extreme form of fear. Other psychological disorders involving fear are panic disorder, generalized anxiety disorder, and various phobias. Clinical psychologist Lisa Capps and linguist Elinor Ochs (1995) dedicated an entire monograph to analyzing the panic narratives of a woman afflicted with agoraphobia, talking both with the researcher and with family members. The authors found that the narratives of panic attacks had three main characteristics. They had very short orienting sections, such that the complicating eliciting situation appeared as surprising and therefore uncontrollable. Second, the protagonist was narrated in a nonagentic way, using some of the means mentioned above (level 2) that limit agency and depict the protagonist as helpless. Third, panic episodes were narrated in a dramatizing way, using the historical present, shifting the origo of deictic terms to the past protagonist, and using direct speech. Especially conspicuous was the use of internal dialog, which draws the listener into the experiential perspective of the protagonist.

Thus, there is a formal similarity between this agoraphobic woman's narrations of panic attacks and trauma narratives, which is a dramatizing way of narrating. Although some aspects of dramatic speech have been analyzed only in one or the other case, both share the core elements of shifting the origo of deictic expressions and historical present tense. The narratives differ in that trauma narratives refer to experiences that would have been terrorizing to anybody, whereas panic attacks are by definition elicited by situations that others do not find exceedingly threatening. Therefore, it could be that the use of internal monologue was typical only for narratives of panic attacks, as they focus on the subjective reaction and not the situational threat.

However, internal monologue has been described by Labov and Waletzky (1967) as a type of direct evaluation that is typically placed before the high point to increase suspense. Labov (1997) based his analysis on narratives of near-death experiences, in other words, on fear narratives. An internal monologue actually seems to be typical for any kind of fear narrative when compared with narratives of other emotions (Habermas et al., 2009) and when comparing well-told to not so well-told fear stories (Ulatowska et al., 2004). Other possible commonalities of (good) fear stories are the sparse naming of emotional reactions compared with narratives of other emotions in normal individuals (Habermas et al., 2009) and in individuals with and without PTSD (Römisch et al., 2014).

These shared characteristics of fear stories do not deny that trauma narratives differ from other fear or distress narratives in terms of the degree of narrative immersion, as indicated by length of narrative, dramatizing narration, and focus on the past perceptual perspective of the protagonist (Römisch et al., 2014). However, it could be that trauma narratives only exceed in linguistic qualities typical of what otherwise is judged as good fear narratives (Ulatowska et al., 2004). Variations in length of narrative support this hypothesis: trauma narratives were longer than fear narratives of a control group (Römisch et al., 2014), and the narratives judged as better stories were longer (Ulatowska et al., 2004). In both cases it seems safe to assume that the trauma stories and the good stories were also more emotional.

These results imply that trauma and panic narratives do not differ categorically, but differ only gradually from other narratives of threatening experiences. This conclusion would nicely concur with what memory researchers have concluded about the nature of traumatic memories (Rubin et al., 2008). While I argued above that memory overgenerality is first of all a linguistic phenomenon, the specific characteristics of trauma and panic narratives may result both from the emotional intensity of corresponding memories and from peculiarities of the communicative situation of narrating experiences of extreme anxiety.

Now why might narrating extremely scary experiences require a dramatizing style? Communicating emotional experiences generally serves three functions: cathartic release, understanding the event by organizing it narratively, and sharing the experience and emotion with others. Sharing aims at eliciting empathetic emotions in listeners who are willing to put themselves emotionally in the shoes of the narrator and the protagonist. Dramatic narration is the best way to achieve this aim (Chafe, 1994; Habermas & Diel, 2010). But then should not all narratives of very strong emotions revert to dramatized narration? To a certain degree this is probably true. However, it appears that fear is especially suited to be narrated in a dramatic fashion. Systematic comparison of narratives of events that provoked fear, anger, sadness, pride, and happiness suggests that fear narratives more than others have the dramatic structure of spiraling tension leading up to a high point, supported by internal monologue (Habermas et al., 2009). Sad everyday stories, in contrast, may indeed dramatize the situation leading to the loss in order to elicit compassion (Habermas & Diel, 2010), but they then also need to underscore the greatness and irrecuperability of the loss. Sad narratives therefore tend to focus less on action, containing fewer narrative clauses (level 1) and less reported speech (level 3a), and focus more on describing an unchanging state, often lacking a narrative resolution to a loss. Stories of angering everyday events, in contrast, aim at eliciting sympathetic indignation. Therefore, they need to depict the size of the damage experienced, narrate the wrongdoer's causal authorship and moral responsibility, and, at the same time, show that the narrator had done everything morally required. Therefore, anger narratives contain much indirect speech to show the superiority of the narrator's reasons over the reasons provided by the angering agent (Habermas et al., 2009).

Personality disorders

Thus far clinical variations in autobiographical memory narratives could be described mainly in terms of narrativity (level 1) and perspectives chosen for direct evaluations (level 3). In addition, agency (level 2) was reduced in trauma and panic narratives. Now I turn from disorders defined primarily by aberrations of emotions to the more encompassing personality disorders. Narrative studies are even more sparse in this field. However, one of the dominant theories of personality disorders, or, in other theoretical terms, a borderline personality organization (not to be equated with the more specific borderline personality disorder), is conceptualized by Kernberg (1984) as resulting from the use of splitting as the dominant defense mechanism, resulting in identity diffusion. This conception has been adapted by the DSM-5 (American Psychiatric Association, 2013) as an alternative way to conceptualize personality disorders in general. Kernberg describes that the splitting of one's emotions, action tendencies, and corresponding views of self and other into positive and negative ones has the effect that the nondominant tendency and view is not constantly repressed, but basically alters with the contrasting view. But these alternating views do not communicate with each other, are not consciously apprehended as contradictory, so that no higher level integration or comment can be made. Since entire aspects of others and self are split off, identity is only partially accessible and therefore diffuse.

Splitting shows in narratives in terms of unacknowledged contradictions, which tend to irritate or confuse the listener. Contradictions may also show between what is said and what is done or implied in the interaction with the listener. Splitting shows in partial, incomplete descriptions of story protagonists and the self, so that the listener has difficulty grasping the characters of the protagonists of the autobiographical narratives. In addition, listeners find it difficult to imagine empathically how the narrator of a life story has become the person he or she is today (Kernberg, 1984).

In terms of the five levels of narrative, these characteristics are located at level 5 (listener orientation), because they make it hard for the listener to empathize due to contradictions and missing parts. In addition, agency (level 2) may be diminished by leaving out motives not fitting the dominant evaluative tone or, in the case of narcissistic personality disorder, may be exaggerated.

Two studies were dedicated to autobiographical memory narratives in a specific kind of personality disorder, namely, borderline personality disorder (BPD; for a more general review of research on BPD and autobiographical memory, see Van den Broeck and colleagues, Chapter 11). Jørgensen and colleagues (2012) compared the global narrative structures (level 2a) of the three most important memories provided by patients with a diagnosis of BPD, by patients with a diagnosis of obsessive compulsive disorder, and by nonclinical controls. Compared with the other groups, almost half of the BPD patients' narratives were disordered and confused or had essential parts left out, whereas the obsessive compulsive group's narratives were more orderly and complete; 40% stopped at the high point or complication without offering a resolution. Roughly a quarter of both clinical groups' narratives were impoverished, that is, they were short and not narrated. In addition, the BPD group tended to talk about a lower proportion of specific events. This basically confirms Kernberg's description of narratives in personality disorders, although not specifically in terms of splitting of evaluatively contrasting parts, but merely in terms of narrative incoherence (level 5) and, in addition, a tendency not to narrate at all (level 1).

A second study compared narratives of selected episodes from the life story (high point, low point, turning point) from patients with BPD and from a nonclinical control group (Adler et al., 2012). Narratives were content-coded for agency, and a composite score of narrative coherence was calculated from whether the narratives were well oriented, whether they had a logical flow, whether there were emotional evaluations, and whether they were connected to other parts of life. This composite coherence score thus drew on several narrative levels, mainly levels 2, 3, and 4. The narratives of the personality disorder group were both less agentic and less coherent than those of the control group. Furthermore, agency predicted depression after six and twelve months, and both agency and coherence predicted quality of primary relationships after six months. Although the coherence score used here cannot be taken as a measure of contradictoriness or incompleteness of narratives (level 5), these two characteristics may have contributed to the low coherence values. In addition, the specific BPD group also seems to be low in agency. However, there may be other specific personality disorders in which this may not be the case, especially in narcissistic personality disorder.

Autobiographical memory narratives in the course of insight-oriented psychotherapy

What are the possible implications of characteristic distortions in autobiographical memory narratives for psychotherapy? Theories of change in insight-oriented psychotherapies generally assume that defended-against impulses and action tendencies become conscious and understood in a process of successive symbolization, that is, of being perceived in terms of sensations or images, which then can be put into words and finally be reflected on and integrated into existing views of self and others and into the life story. Wilma Bucci (1997) developed a measure of the vividness of language used in psychotherapy, which reflects the middle phase of symbolizing impulses, whereas the later phase is marked by more reflective evaluations. More specifically geared toward the recounting of past episodes is Stiles's theory of the assimilation of problematic experiences (e.g., Stiles, 2005; Stiles, Honos-Webb, & Lani, 1999), which suggests a process that starts with the nonacknowledgment of a problematic experience, going through phases of initial, but diffuse awareness, to a phase in which problematic experiences can be fully and explicitly narrated, interpreted, and integrated.

Earlier we presented example narratives to show how they change in the process of successful coping and psychotherapy from a rudimentary story that leaves out relevant information, evaluations, and reflections to more elaborate narratives in which the work of understanding and evaluating is clearly visible to finally more condensed, but clearly understandable narratives (Habermas, 2012; Habermas & Berger, 2011). In light of the different kinds of narrative distortions typical for different psychological disorders, this linear model needs to be differentiated, because the initial psychopathological distortions differ between disorders. The specific disorders discussed in this chapter rather suggest, as a starting point of defense against too intense negative emotions aroused by past experiences, a double position, between which individuals may, depending on the specific psychopathology, switch to varying degrees. Instead of a total exclusion of past experiences there may alternatively be a mode of being overpowered by emotions elicited by past events. However, this is not merely a result of failing defensive mechanisms, but may also constitute an attempt to engender empathetic listeners to share the experience and thereby help establish an intersubjective reality that therefore may be more bearable.

To substantiate this idea (cf. Laub & Auerhahn, 1989) let me finally point to two example cases that contain rich illustrative material. Sverre Varvin and William Stiles (1999) present the case of a traumatized refugee in Norway with the intention of illustrating Stiles's model of assimilation of problematic experiences. However, their case, which is illustrated with many verbatim excerpts from therapy sessions, also illustrates the essential role of the listener. The therapist helps the patient to finally narrate her horrifying memories by offering his unbending interest and empathy. In a highly original study, Beran Beran and Unoka (2005) analyzed formal aspects of verbal interaction in the sessions of a two-year psychodynamic psychotherapy of a woman with strong dissociative tendencies, resulting in the assumption of various personalities. They demonstrate how the therapist succeeded in introducing additional, more external perspectives to the patient's very exclusive perspective confined to a specific past situation. The patient gradually integrated these external perspectives into her narratives, which in the long term led her to give up multiple partial identities to adopt a more encompassing, integrative self. Thus a willing, empathetic listener may help narrators to confront and immerge in frightening past experiences, to tolerate the pain, and to possibly start integrating other temporal and personal perspectives into the experience so as to start constructing a full narrative.

REFERENCES

Adler, J. M., Kissel, E. C., & McAdams, D. P. (2006). Emerging from the CAVE: attributional style and the narrative study of identity in midlife adults. *Cognitive Therapy and Research, 30*, 39-51.

Adler, J. M., Chin, E. D., Kolisetty, A. P., & Oltmanns, T. F. (2012). The distinguishing characteristics of narrative identity in adults with features of borderline personality disorder: an empirical investigation. *Journal of Personality Disorders, 26*, 498-512.

American Psychiatric Association (2013). *Diagnostic and Statistical Manual of Mental Disorders* (5th ed.). Washington, DC: American Psychiatric Association.

Baron, J. M., & Bluck, S. (2011). That was a good story! Preliminary construction of the Perceived Story Quality index. *Discourse Processes, 48*, 93-118.

Bedard-Gilligan, M., & Zoellner, L. A. (2012). Dissociation and memory fragmentation in post-traumatic stress disorder: an evaluation of the dissociative encoding hypothesis. *Memory, 20*, 277-299.

Beran, E., & Unoka, Z. (2005). Construction of self-narrative in psychotherapeutic setting: an analysis of the mutual determination of narrative perspective taken by patient and therapist. In T. Becker & U. M. Quasthoff (eds.), *Narrative Interaction* (pp. 151-169). Amsterdam: John Benjamins.

Bruner, J. (1990). *Acts of Meaning*. Cambridge, MA: Harvard University Press.

Bucci, W. (1997). *Psychoanalysis and Cognitive Science: A Multiple Code Theory*. New York: Guilford Press.

Capps, L., & Ochs, E. (1995). *Constructing Panic: The Discourse of Agoraphobia*. Cambridge, MA: Harvard University Press.

Chafe, W. (1994). *Discourse, Consciousness, and Time: The Flow and Displacement of Conscious Experience in Speaking and Writing*. Chicago, IL: University Press.

De Silveira, C., & Habermas, T. (2011). Narrative means to manage responsibility in life narratives across adolescence. *Journal of Genetic Psychology, 172*, 1-20.

Frijda, N. H. (1986). *The Emotions*. Cambridge: Cambridge University Press.

Grice, H. P. (1975). Logic and conversation. In P. Cole & J. L. Morgan (eds.), *Speech Acts* (pp. 41-58). New York: Academic Press.

Habermas, T. (2006). Who speaks? Who looks? Who feels? Point of view in autobiographical narratives. *International Journal of Psychoanalysis, 87*, 497-518.

(2011). Autobiographical reasoning: mechanisms and functions. In T. Habermas (ed.), *The Development of Autobiographical Reasoning in Adolescence and Beyond* (pp. 1-17). New Directions in Child and Adolescent Development, 131. San Francisco, CA: Jossey-Bass.

(2012). Identity, emotion, and the social matrix of autobiographical memory: a psychoanalytic narrative view. In D. Berntsen & D. C. Rubin (eds.), *Understanding Autobiographical Memory: Theories and Approaches* (pp. 33-53). Cambridge: Cambridge University Press.

Habermas, T., & Berger, N. (2011). Retelling everyday emotional events: condensation, distancing, and closure. *Cognition and Emotion*, 25, 206–219.
Habermas, T., & Diel, V. (2010). The emotional impact of loss narratives: event severity and narrative perspectives. *Emotion*, 10, 312–323.
  (2013). The episodicity of verbal reports of personally significant autobiographical memories: vividness correlates with narrative text quality more than with detailedness or memory specificity. *Frontiers in Behavioral Neuroscience*, 7, 110.
Habermas, T., Ott, L. M., Schubert, M., Schneider, B., & Pate, A. (2008). Stuck in the past: negative bias, explanatory style, temporal order, and evaluative perspectives in life narratives of clinically depressed individuals. *Depression and Anxiety*, 25, E121–E132.
Habermas, T., Meier, M., & Mukhtar, B. (2009). Are specific emotions narrated differently? *Emotion*, 9, 751–762.
Halliday, M. A. K. (2004). *An Introduction to Functional Grammar* (3rd, rev. ed.). London: Arnold.
Herman, D. (2013). *Storytelling and the Sciences of Mind*. Boston: MIT Press.
Hogan, P. C. (2003). *The Mind and Its Stories: Narrative Universals and Human Emotion*. Cambridge: Cambridge University Press.
Hogan, P- C. (2011). *Affective Narratology*. Lincoln, NB: University of Nebraska Press.
Janet. P. (1919). *Les médications psychologiques*, vol. 2. Paris: Alcan.
  (1928). *L'évolution de la mémoire et de la notion du temps*. Paris: Alcan.
Jørgensen, C. R., Berntsen, D., Bech, M., Kjølbye, M., Bennedsen, B. E., & Ramsgaard, S. (2012). Identity-reated autobiographical memories and cultural life scripts in patients with borderline personality disorder. *Consciousness and Cognition*, 21, 788–798.
Kernberg, O. F. (1984). *Severe Personality Disorders*. New York: Aronson.
Labov, W. (1997). Some further steps in narrative analysis. *Journal of Narrative and Life History*, 7, 395–415.
Labov, W., & Waletzky, J. (1967). Narrative analysis: oral versions of personal experience. In I. Helm (ed.), *Essays on the Verbal and Visual Arts: Proceedings of the 1966 Annual Spring Meeting of the American Ethnological Society* (pp. 12–44). Seattle: University of Washington Press.
Laub, D., & Auerhahn, N. (1989). Failed empathy: a central theme in the survivor's Holocaust experience. *Psychoanalytic Psychology*, 6, 377–400.
  (1993). Knowing and not knowing massive psychic trauma: forms of traumatic memory. *International Journal of Psychoanalysis*, 74, 287–299.
Lazarus, R. S. (2006). Emotions and interpersonal relationships: towards a person-centered conceptualization of emotions and coping. *Journal of Personality*, 74, 9–46.
Levine, B., Svoboda, E., Hay, J. F., Winocur, W., & Moscovitch, M. (2002). Aging and autobiographical memory: dissociating episodic from semantic memory. *Psychology and Aging*, 17, 677–689.
MacIntyre, A. (1981). *After Virtue*. London: Bloomsbury.

Main, M., Kaplan, N., & Cassidy, J. (1985). Security in infancy, childhood, and adulthood: a move to the level of representation. *Monographs of the Society for Research in Child Development*, *50*(1/2), 66–104.

McNally, R.J. (2003). *Remembering Trauma*. Cambridge, MA: Harvard University press.

Nelson, K. L., Moskovitz, D. J., & Steiner, H. (2008). Narration and vividness as measures of event-specificity in autobiographical memory. *Discourse Processes*, *45*, 195–209.

O'Kearney, R., & Perrott, K. (2006). Trauma narratives in posttraumatic stress disorder: a review. *Journal of Traumatic Stress*, *19*, 81–93.

Polya, L., Laszlo, J., & Forgas, J. P. (2005). Making sense of life stories: the role of narrative perspective in perceiving hidden information about social identity. *European Journal of Social Psychology*, *35*, 785–796.

Rimé, B. (2009). Emotion elicits the social sharing of emotion: theory and empirical review. *Emotion Review*, *1*, 60–85.

Römisch, S., Leban, E., Habermas, T., & Döll, S. (2014). Evaluation, involvement, and fragmentation in narratives of distressing, angering, and happy events from traumatized and non-traumatized women. *Psychological Trauma: Theory, Research, Practice and Policy*, *6*, 465–472.

Rubin, D. C. (2011). The coherence of memories for trauma: evidence from posttraumatic stress disorder. *Consciousness and Cognition*, *20*, 857–865.

Rubin, D. C., Berntsen, D., & Bohni, M. K. (2008). A memory-based model of posttraumatic stress disorder: evaluating basic assumptions underlying the PTSD diagnosis. *Psychological Review*, *115*, 985–1011.

Schütze, F. (1983). Biographieforschung und narratives Interview [Biographical studies and narrative interview]. *Neue Praxis*, *13*, 283–293

Stiles, W. B. (2005). Extending the Assimilation of Problematic Experiences Scale. *Counselling Psychology Quarterly*, *18*, 85-93.

Stiles, W. B., Honos-Webb, L., & Lani, J. A. (1999). Some functions of narrative in the assimilation of problematic experience. *Journal of Clinical Psychology*, *55*, 1213–1226.

Sumner, J. A. (2012). The mechanisms underlying overgeneral autobiographical memory: an evaluative review of evidence for the CaR-FA-X model. *Clinical Psychology Review*, *32*, 34–48.

Trabasso, T., Stein, N. L., Rodkin, P. C., Munger, M. P., & Baughn, C. R. (1992). Knowledge of goals and plans in the on-line narration of events. *Cognitive Development*, *7*, 133–170.

Tulving, E. (2002). Episodic memory: from mind to brain. *Annual Review of Psychology*, *53*, 1–25.

Ulatowska, H. K., Olness, G. S., Samson, A. M., Keebler, M. W., & Goins, K. E. (2004). On the nature of personal narratives of high quality. *Advances in Speech-Language Pathology*, *6*, 3–14.

Van der Kolk, B., & Fisler, R. (1995). Dissociation and the fragmentary nature of traumatic memories: overview and exploratory study. *Journal of Traumatic Stress*, *8*, 505–525.

Varvin, S., & Stiles, W. (1999). Emergence of severe traumatic experiences: an assimilation analysis of psychoanalytic therapy with a political refugee. *Psychotherapy Research, 9,* 381–404.

Williams, J. M. G., Barnhofer, T., Crane, C., Hermans, D., Raes, F., Watkins, E., & Dalgleish, T. (2007). Autobiographical memory specificity and emotional disorder. *Psychological Bulletin, 133,* 122–148.

14 Self-images and autobiographical memory in memory impairment

Clare J. Rathbone and Chris J. A. Moulin

> The self is not an intrinsic feature of the brain and it is possible to become derailed through psychosis ... or as a result of brain damage. The degradation of personality is a neurological commonplace.
> (Broks, 2003, p. 42)

In July 2010, the Alzheimer's Society (UK) launched an advertising campaign with a picture of an empty, outmoded double bed with the tagline: "I wake up with someone new every day." For Alzheimer's Awareness Week, 2011, the same society launched a campaign entitled "Remember the Person," where a portrait of someone appeared alongside descriptions such as "Phillip, 80/Father and Grandfather/Tailor/Ex–pole vault champion of Grenada/Lives with dementia/Loves sport." In these two contrasting campaigns, there are two conflicting ideas. There is the notion that selfhood is lost with memory impairment, captured in the description of the carer of someone with dementia waking up with someone new every day, and there is the idea that the memory impairment masks the ongoing identity of the person suffering with it: "Remember the person." This confusion can be placed further in context. A recent survey of the general public in the United States found that 83% of respondents endorsed the statement "People suffering from amnesia typically cannot recall their own name or identity" (Simons & Chabris, 2011). Expert opinion, in the same study, was unanimous in its disagreement with this statement.

The debate about whether selfhood is impaired in memory dysfunction is nothing new. This chapter reviews recent studies aiming to address the relationship between self and memory in clinical populations. In particular, we address the question: what is retained of selfhood when autobiographical memory is impaired? We begin with some background on the link between autobiographical memory and the self.

Autobiographical memory and the self

Autobiographical memory is closely linked to our goals, our emotions, and our sense of self and identity. The idea that autobiographical

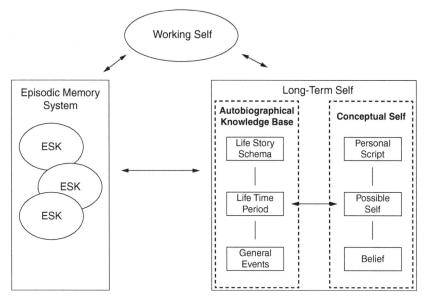

Figure 14.1 The self-memory system (based on Conway et al., 2004, p. 498). ESK, event-specific knowledge.

memories are the basis for our sense of self extends back to philosophers such as Locke, who claimed that the self exists entirely as a result of the process of memory (Locke, 1694/1975). Modern psychological accounts conceptualize the self as a complex, cognitive structure that plays an executive role in mental processing, enabling an individual to be consciously aware of knowledge about themselves and events from their lives. A recent cognitive model of the relationship between self and memory is the self-memory system (SMS) (Conway, 2005; Conway & Pleydell-Pearce, 2000), which views episodic memories and semantic, conceptual information about the long-term self (such as where one went to school) as separate systems that both operate bidirectionally with the working self (see Figure 14.1). The working self is a control mechanism, employing the transient goals of the self to govern autobiographical retrieval. The working self is, in turn, constrained by the memories and knowledge within the autobiographical knowledge base (Conway, 2005).

Subsets of autobiographical knowledge and episodic memories can be viewed as supporting particular self-images, such as being a mother or an honest person. The conceptual self (a subcomponent of semantic autobiographical memory) contains beliefs about past, present, and future selves (e.g., "I hope to become a professor and I once was an undergraduate"). These beliefs about the self are often termed self-images. The self is not a unitary structure, but instead reflects multidimensional constructs and processes (e.g., Greenwald, 1980). Many envisage the self as a combination of sets of self-schemata or self-images, including cognitive representations developed from specific autobiographical events, as well as general representations such as "I am a mother" (Markus, 1977). Indeed, we are thought to possess multiple self-constructs, such that the "self" may be viewed as consisting of many separate constructs or self-images (e.g., Conway, 2005; Conway et al., 2004). These self-images can be based on many factors, including traits, hobbies, physical appearance, relationships, and social roles (e.g., "I am thoughtful; I am a fan of the television show 'The Wire'; I am a homeowner"). Arguably, a conscious awareness of possessing a set of these self-images might help to give rise to a sense of self. Our interest is in how memories might support and organize self-images.

Organization of memories across the lifespan

One well-established finding in autobiographical memory research is that the distribution of memories is not equal across the lifespan. The lifespan retrieval curve consists of three components: the period of childhood amnesia (from birth to approximately five years of age), the period of the reminiscence bump (from 10 to 30 years), and the period of recency (from the present declining back to the period of the reminiscence bump). Of particular interest to those studying the relationship between the self and memory is the reminiscence bump, since this is the period of life from which, in a free recall task, people produce the most memories (Rubin et al., 1986).

One explanation for the high accessibility of memories from the reminiscence bump period is their enduring relation to the self. Many memories from the period of the reminiscence bump are of "self-defining" experiences (Singer & Salovey, 1993), as this period of life reflects a time of great change and development in the self (Erikson, 1950; Fitzgerald, 1988). The reminiscence bump thus corresponds with a time that is critical for the formation and maintenance of a stable self (e.g., Rubin et al., 1998).

If we consider our autobiographical memories to be shaped around a chapter-based life story structure (e.g., Thomsen, 2009), we may envisage particular chapters as associated with emerging aspects of identity (e.g., "when I went to university and became independent"; "when I had my first baby and became a mother"). A key question, then, is whether the start of new identities (e.g., new chapters in the life story) are

Table 14.1 *Self-images and associated memories*

Self image	Memories cued
I am an extrovert.	Carol singing in dark neighborhood and being the star and liking it.
I am a European.	Going alone on an overnight train from Kyiv to Lviv in Ukraine.

associated with heightened accessibility of autobiographical memories associated with that identity. To address this question, we developed the I Am Memory (IAM) Task (Rathbone, Moulin & Conway, 2008), a tool for examining the distribution of self-cued autobiographical memories.

The IAM Task

The IAM Task taps into memories that are central to the way people define their identity. One criticism previously posed by researchers in the field of autobiographical memory has been that some tasks may not promote access to memories that are particularly important for the individual (Jansari & Parkin, 1996). For example, a neutral cue-word such as "car" might prompt retrieval of uneventful and insignificant car journeys. If one of the key roles of autobiographical memory is, as we argue, to support the self, then it seems prudent to develop tasks that specifically index memories that are significant to the self.

The IAM Task asks participants to generate a series of "I am" statements, reflecting the self-images that they feel are most important in defining their sense of identity. This element of the task is based on the Twenty Statements Test (TST), an empirical measure of the self developed by Kuhn and McPartland (1954). Next, each self-image is re-presented to the participant as an autobiographical memory cue. Examples of our participants' self-images and associated memories are shown in Table 14.1.

Finally, both the autobiographical memories and the self-images are dated by the participant (memories by age at event recalled and self-images by age at which they became a defining part of the participant's identity).

It is thus possible to examine the temporal distance between a particular self-image (e.g., "I am an extrovert") and the set of memories with which it is associated. Across a series of studies (Rathbone et al., 2008; 2009; 2011) we have produced a robust pattern: the memories people retrieve in association with aspects of their identity are temporally

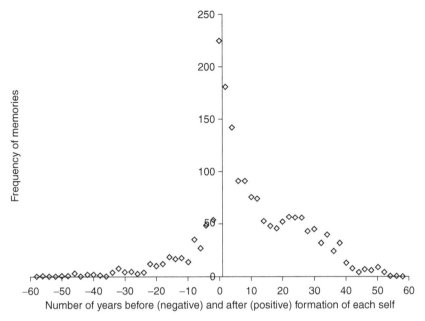

Figure 14.2 Distribution of memories around age of self-emergence (based on Rathbone et al., 2008).

clustered around the time that identity emerges, with the highest frequency of memories coming from the year that each self-image is formed (see Figure 14.2 for a sample with a mean age of fifty-four years in Study 2 of Rathbone et al., 2008). Thus, a person for whom being a parent is an important self-image is highly likely to recall a set of memories from around the time his or her first child was born. Thus, memories cluster temporally around times of self-image formation, in a process that we argue reflects the use of memories to support information about the self (e.g., Figure 14.2, in which year 0 is year of self-image formation; negative years show memories from before self-image formation, and positive years show memories after self-image formation).

We examined whether this pattern would hold for different types of self-images. There is a clear distinction between abstract, personality trait-based self-images (such as being cheerful, a worrier, or hard-working) and more concrete, role-based self-images (such as being a sister, a Muslim, or a student). We examined the memory distributions for both abstract and concrete self-images and found a similar pattern for both. This was important, given that abstract identities (e.g., "I am cheerful") tie in more closely with Singer's concept of self-defining memory (Singer & Blagov, 2001), concerning the formation of personality traits and other more abstract self-concepts, whereas concrete identities can be linked to specific life events such as marriage ("I am a husband") and starting a job ("I am a nurse"). We suggest that each self-image serves an organizational function within autobiographical memory and that activation of a particular self-image leads to the activation of a network of memories for specific events associated with that aspect of the self. These results suggest that autobiographical memories cluster around times of self-image formation, rather than simply being generated in higher numbers for certain lifetime periods such as adolescence. Further research has demonstrated a similar clustering pattern for imagined future events around future self-images, in the form of "I will be" statements (Rathbone et al., 2011).

The self in memory impairment

Thus far we have given an overview of the self-memory system, and how the self possibly operates as an organizational structure in autobiographical memory. Various research programs into self and memory have offered paradigms that can be of use in measuring the relationship between self and memory in clinical disorders. An obvious question is, given that there is a proposed bidirectional relationship between self and memory, what happens when memory fails? Is there a parallel defect in access to self-concepts?

A particularly influential paper on this topic by Addis and Tippett (2004) showed that memory impairments in Alzheimer's disease were associated with changes in the self-concept. Addis and Tippet measured self and personality through existing questionnaire measures and looked at how such measures in dementia were related to the retrieval of autobiographical memories. They found correlations between autobiographical memory and their self and personality measures, such that people with lower levels of autobiographical recall, for instance, had weaker measures of identity quality as measured on the Tennessee Self-Concept Scale.

Broadly speaking, there are two ways in which clinical groups have elucidated the link between self and memory. On the one hand are studies with neuropsychological populations and cases of memory impairment (through disease or injury) that allow us to examine which components of autobiographical memory are necessary for self-knowledge (see Klein et al., 2002a). On the other hand, research with neuropsychiatric groups that demonstrate *alterations* in memory (e.g., overgeneral memory in depression; Williams et al., 2007; flashbacks in

PTSD; Hackmann et al., 2004) enable an examination of the impact that changes in memory have on the self. To obtain the deepest level of understanding, it seems prudent to examine what research from both types of clinical groups can tell us about the self-memory relationship. In studies with neurological cases (e.g., amnesia) the memory deficit is the core feature. As such, these cases can provide vital information on how self-processes might be supported in cases of memory loss. In research based on neuropsychiatric groups, such as autism and schizophrenia, alterations in memory are one aspect of a range of cognitive abilities that might be affected. Thus, these groups enable us to explore other processes that might play a role in supporting self and identity.

Our view is that, regardless of whether memory deficits exist as a result of a neuropsychiatric or neurological condition, the self acts as a powerful organizational process in memory (no matter how few memories are accessible or how semantic they might be in nature). This organizational function acts primarily to lend a sense of personal coherence and continuity. In cases where memories are inaccessible or less episodic and specific in nature (as we describe in detail in the following sections) it is thought that some core conceptual information about the self persists and shapes autobiographical retrieval in ways that are meaningful to the individual. In the following section we describe some recent research that has investigated self and memory in amnesia, epilepsy, schizophrenia, and autism.

Amnesia

We first met PJM, a thirty-eight-year-old female, in 2007. PJM had developed focal retrograde amnesia as a result of a bicycle accident, and this had left her unable to recall episodic details for many of the events in her life, including the birth of her second child and a recent house move. Focal retrograde amnesia (FRA) is an organic form of memory loss, restricted to the period of time prior to trauma. FRA is particularly relevant to the study of differences between semantic and episodic memory, as many case studies have revealed a dissociation between these memory systems (Cermak & O'Connor, 1983; Conway & Fthenaki, 2003; Nadel & Moscovitch, 1997; Tulving et al., 1988). A review by Wheeler and McMillan (2001) showed that the majority of people with FRA demonstrate differential impact on episodic and semantic memory function. In particular, the authors describe several cases in which autobiographical episodic details were impaired but autobiographical semantic knowledge was preserved. For example, they cite the case of a woman who knew her house had been burgled on two occasions but could not recall any episodic details associated with the events (Evans et al., 1996). Our interest was how PJM's deficits in episodic autobiographical memory would impact on her sense of self.

Previous work with neuropsychological cases conducted by Klein and colleagues (e.g., Klein et al., 2002a; 2002b) has suggested that information about the self may be preserved, even in cases of very dense amnesia. For example, Klein et al. (1996) reported case study WJ, who experienced a concussion that caused her to lose access to episodic memories covering a seven-month period pretrauma. During her amnesia, and following her full recovery, WJ was asked to describe her personality during her first term at university (the time that was inaccessible by memory). In spite of substantial changes in episodic memory performance, WJ's descriptions of herself were very stable over time. This finding may be viewed as evidence that the self can be known without autobiographical retrieval of specific events, but it is also possible that WJ drew on memories of herself before the amnesic period and used these memories to report a stable self (Klein et al., 2002a). However, other cases have shown that accurate self-knowledge can be generated even when amnesia covers all autobiographical memories. Patient KC's amnesia prevented him from recalling a single event from his life, but he was able to accurately rate traits for self-descriptiveness over two separate occasions, and these ratings were consistent with those his mother generated to rate his personality (Tulving, 1993). In essence, KC possessed accurate knowledge about his conceptual self, in spite of an inability to recall any specific instances to support his beliefs (Tulving, 1993).

A growing body of work with patients therefore points toward a complex relationship between memory and self in amnesia. Through anecdotal reports, tests of conceptual knowledge, and assessment of personality variables, it appears that knowledge of the self remains intact in spite of severe episodic amnesia. Our work with PJM aimed to elucidate the relative contributions of episodic and semantic autobiographical memory in supporting a coherent sense of self. One aspect missing from the foregoing literature was the extent to which patients could generate memories to self-relevant cues, and how such memories are organized temporally.

PJM's neuropsychological test scores showed above-average intelligence (IQ = 116) and normal executive function with an isolated memory deficit. Her scores on the Autobiographical Memory Interview (AMI; Kopelman et al., 1989) revealed a borderline rating for semantic autobiographical memory and a "probably abnormal" rating for episodic autobiographical memory. In a twenty-item Crovitz word cue task (e.g., Crovitz & Schiffman, 1974) PJM generated semantic "facts" rather than

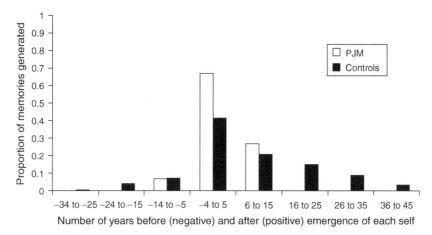

Figure 14.3 Distributions of PJM's and controls' memories around age of self-emergence (based on Rathbone et al., 2009).

specific episodic events. For example, to the cue "Restaurant" she responded: "Restaurant, yes, I remember lots of restaurants, but there's no one memory I can think of" and for "Letter": "I used to write to Kirstin after I moved." In addition, PJM's memories were rated as significantly less emotional and less vivid than age- and gender-matched controls – phenomenological features that are typical hallmarks of rich, episodic recollections. In the IAM Task, PJM also tended toward generation of semantic facts rather than episodic events. Thus, for the cue "I am the survivor of an accident," PJM recalled: "I remember being in the hospital, and I remember things like changing my room, but I have no definite events that I can describe." For this and her other "I am" statements ("I am a mum," "I am active," and "I am academic"), PJM was aware of her inability to recall specific details. In her own words: "I have those *facts* I can tell you, not 'memories'" (her asterisks). However, when we plotted PJM's IAM Task memories around ages of identity formation, her memories showed a distribution similar to controls' (see Figure 14.3).

We were also interested in the way PJM defined her identity more broadly. To enable us to assess this, PJM completed the standard Twenty-Statements Test (TST; Kuhn & McPartland, 1954), which asks participants to complete twenty statements that begin with "I am." PJM responded with twelve statements, reflecting both role-based concrete identities (e.g., being a mother, a geologist, and a caver) and trait-like abstract identities (e.g., a worrier, a lovely person). Although she was unable to generate a full set of twenty statements, PJM's self-images are similar to the range of statements given by participants across studies from our laboratory using this task. PJM marked the first four selves in the list as the most important for defining her identity, which also matches our findings with student populations and indicates again that PJM's sense of self is not disordered and is similar to that of controls. Our data suggest that PJM's memory impairments do not impair her ability to describe aspects of her sense of self and to subjectively experience this sense of self coherently and with temporal continuity. PJM's deficits, however, clearly reflect a very different pattern of memory loss compared with the global cognitive impairments associated with Alzheimer's disease (cf. Addis & Tippett, 2004) that might indeed pose more of a threat to the integrity of the self (for a recent review of the relationship between the self, episodic, and semantic memory, see Prebble et al., 2013).

Our interpretation of these data is that semantic autobiographical memory supports the self in a way similar to episodic autobiographical memory. In cases where episodic memories are inaccessible (either through organic amnesia or, as we discuss later in this chapter, as a result of memory deficits associated with disorders such as epilepsy or autism), semantic facts about one's life may serve to organize and structure knowledge about the self to give rise to a coherent sense of identity.

Transient epileptic amnesia

Focal retrograde amnesia (as suffered by PJM) is somewhat atypical of memory impairment. In dementia and other more common memory deficits, the onset of memory difficulties is slow and gradual, and the problems are rather more diffuse. In dementia, there is not a focal loss of episodic memory, but more global cognitive changes. There will also be changes in awareness and personality that may be related to the disease itself.

Transient epileptic amnesia (TEA) is a more subtle deficit of memory (for an overview, see Butler and Zeman, 2008). It is characterized by a subjective complaint of autobiographical memory loss, while clinical tests of episodic memory are normal. Typically, patients will have "lost" periods or events in their lives, which can be anywhere in the lifespan. These deficits are somewhat more nebulous and subtle than the amnesia seen in head injury or dementia. The idea is that low-level epileptiform changes affect memory consolidation and retrieval across the lifespan.

We were interested in how life events and self-images were organized in TEA (Illman et al., 2011). Patient EB, a seventy-three-year-old man with TEA, characterized his problems as twenty years of "memory attacks," which involved periods of repetitive questioning and forgetfulness. These attacks were successfully treated with epileptic medication. However, EB complained of a loss of salient autobiographical information from his retired life, such as being unable to provide details of what his wife described as highly memorable holidays in New Zealand and Fiji. He also complained that his memories in general lacked the vividness they once had. On a series of experimental tasks, we were able to show that EB's autobiographical memory functioned essentially the same as controls', except that whereas controls have a series of self-images that are connected to episodic memories that are rich and vivid when they are reexperienced, EB had a series of memories that were less rich and were – again – more like a set of semantic facts about his life – even though he also produced the same self-centered organizational pattern in his memories.

Schizophrenia

Accounts of disturbance to sense of self have long been described in patients with schizophrenia (e.g., Freedman, 1974). However, there is still a degree of uncertainty about which aspects of the self are most affected by schizophrenia and the extent to which changes in the self might be related to changes in autobiographical memory. Baddeley et al. (1996) described apparent incongruencies between knowledge of self and autobiographical memories in several schizophrenic patients whose beliefs about themselves clashed dramatically with the autobiographical knowledge they possessed. For example, one patient believed himself to be a famous rock guitarist, while also knowing he could not play the guitar, and another man who thought he was a Russian grand chess master knew he could not play chess well nor speak Russian.

Previous research has revealed an established episodic memory deficit in schizophrenia (e.g., Cuervo-Lombard et al., 2007; Danion et al., 2005; Riutort et al., 2003). However, only one study to date has explored the relationship between autobiographical memory and the self in schizophrenia. Bennouna-Greene et al. (2012) used the TST (Kuhn & McPartland, 1954) and the IAM Task in a sample of twenty-five schizophrenic patients and twenty-five controls. Participants first completed the TST, generating twenty "I am" statements (e.g., self-images). In line with Rhee et al. (1995), these statements were later coded by the experimenter using a set of categories and subcategories. Each self-image was classified as either abstract (referring to a general response such as a personality trait or an emotional state) or specific (qualified by specific details, e.g., "I am fond of eating herrings"; "I am a sister"). For each participant, the proportion of abstract responses (reflecting "identity quality"; Rhee et al., 1995) and the number of categories and subcategories sampled ("identity complexity") were calculated.

Following standard IAM Task procedures, each participant then selected the four statements that they considered central to defining their identity. These self-images were then each used as cues for six memories (e.g., twenty-four memories in total). As described earlier in this chapter, the IAM Task allows an examination of the distribution of dated memories around age of self-image emergence (e.g., *temporal organization*). Additionally, Bennouna-Greene et al. extended their investigation to assess *thematic organization* of memories, in terms of how thematically linked each memory was to the self-image that cued it. This was measured by both the participant and the experimenter. The participant's score was generated as a rating between 1 (very weak) and 5 (very strong) to express their interpretation of the strength of the thematic link between each memory and its related self-statement. In contrast, the experimenter used a two-point scale in which a strong link between the theme of a memory and the "I am" statement that cued it was scored as 1, whereas an absent or vague link was scored as 0.

Results revealed few differences between the self-images of schizophrenic participants and controls (e.g., there were no differences in identity quality or complexity, and both groups generated mainly trait-based, positive statements in the TST); however, differences emerged regarding the recollective experience ratings for the autobiographical memories and the thematic link between each self-image and its associated memories. In line with previous findings, the memories of the control group were more specific and a higher percentage was assigned a Remember response, compared with the schizophrenic group. Although this had previously been established in this population, this study was the first to show that this deficit extends to memories directly linked to long-term and important (as judged by the participant) self-images that give rise to the conceptual self (e.g., Conway, 2005).

Results also indicated that, while no significant differences were found between patients and controls regarding the thematic link scores rated by the participants, there was a significant difference between the thematic ratings conducted by the (blind to group) experimenter, with the thematic link score between schizophrenic patients' memories and self-images being significantly lower. In spite of this difference in thematic organization, the temporal organization of schizophrenic participants' memories showed a pattern similar to that of controls. Thus, the clustering pattern of memories around age of self-image emergence was the same for both schizophrenic participants and controls. This is in line with recent research by Morise et al. (2011) that showed similar performance between schizophrenic participants and controls regarding temporal and conceptual organization in sets of interrelated autobiographical memories. There is thus a coherent temporal organization of self-supporting memories in control participants and indication that this temporal organization is preserved, at least in this sample, in schizophrenia. In contrast, the thematic organization between autobiographical memories and their related self-statements appears to be selectively affected in schizophrenia.

Previous work has shown differences in the conceptual organization of memories in schizophrenic populations, for example, results from Berna et al. (2011) suggested an impairment of self-event connection (e.g., the ability to give meaning to past events such as self-defining memories; Singer and Salovey, 1993). The ability to form conceptual links between memories and the self is likely to rely on a range of cognitive functions. Several executive functions including selective attention, working memory, and mental flexibility have been shown to be impaired in schizophrenia (Johnson-Selfridge & Zalewski, 2001). It is likely that these impairments might account for changes in memory performance, as previous research has established that executive deficits are related to episodic deficits in both healthy (Piolino et al., 2010) and neurologically affected (Piolino et al., 2007) populations.

Autism

The final clinical group we review is autism, a neurodevelopmental disorder characterized by deficits in social reciprocal interaction, verbal and nonverbal communication, and repetitive patterns of behavior (American Psychiatric Association, 1994; World Health Organization, 1993). Autism is also characterized by atypical autobiographical memory: recall of fewer autobiographical memories and generation of memories that contain less episodic detail, compared with controls (e.g., Bruck et al., 2007; Goddard et al., 2007). For a review of autobiographical memory in autism, see Watson and Dritschel, Chapter 16. Particularly relevant to the self-memory relationship are the results of a recent study by Crane and Goddard (2008), which, similar to the research reviewed earlier regarding amnesia, highlights the dissociation between personal factual knowledge (e.g., semantic autobiographical memory) and episodic memories. In their study, personal facts and episodic memories were assessed in a group of adults with autism and a control group, using an episodic memory narrative task, an autobiographical memory interview (CAMI; Bekerian et al., 2001), and an autobiographical fluency task (Dritschel et al., 1992). Results from the fluency and episodic memory narrative tasks showed a personal episodic memory deficit in the autism spectrum disorder (ASD) group, while personal semantic memory showed no differences. This suggests a dissociation between diminished episodic memories and preserved personal factual knowledge in ASD.

The question of whether episodic deficits have an impact on the self is a theme that runs through this chapter. On the one hand, one might consider that selective episodic deficits when remembering the self in the past (as demonstrated in autism, epilepsy, schizophrenia, and some forms of amnesia) might have implications for the way one views oneself in the present, and thus potentially affect identity. However, as we have pointed out, recent evidence has also suggested that identity is not necessarily reliant on episodic processes (e.g., Klein et al., 2002b; Rathbone et al., 2009; Tulving, 1993; Wilson & Wearing, 1995). We will return to the more general question of how episodic and semantic memory processes might support the self later in this chapter. Regarding autism, it is important to note that a growing body of evidence suggests that people with autism demonstrate differences in conceptions of identity and self-related processes compared with matched controls. For example, Lee and Hobson (1998) used the self-understanding interview (Damon & Hart, 1988) and found that autistic participants had difficulties viewing themselves as part of a wider social group. Additionally, several studies have shown that ASD individuals show a reduced self-reference effect (SRE) (Hare et al., 2007; Lombardo et al., 2007; Millward et al., 2000). The SRE refers to the robust finding that most people are better at retrieving information from memory that was encoded with reference to the self (Rogers et al., 1977). It seems that people with ASD do not show this effect, perhaps due to differences in the way self-related information is organized and processed. Thus, while the question remains whether episodic memory is a necessary component of the self, the evidence suggests that both episodic memory ability and self-related processing are altered in autism. To date, however, there has been little research examining how these two processes might be related in autism. The study we shall now review in some detail sought to develop understanding of the link between self and memory in autism, by adopting the Remember/Know paradigm (Gardiner & Java, 1993) and coding of self-images generated in the Twenty Statements Test (Kuhn & McPartland, 1954; Rhee et al., 1995).

Tanweer et al. (2010) tested eleven individuals with ASD (mean age 34.1) and fifteen comparison participants (mean age 32.7). The task used was based on an established measure of autonoetic consciousness developed for studying changes in aging: the TEMPau Task (Piolino et al., 2003). Participants were asked to provide autobiographical memories from three lifetime periods: 0–17 years of age (period A), the last five years excluding the last twelve months (period B), and recent life, which comprised the last twelve months of one's life (period C). Within each time period, memories were cued using a number of themes (for details on themes and memory generation instructions, see Piolino et al., 2003; Tanweer et al., 2010).

Following memory generation, each event was scored using a four-point episodic scale (see Piolino et al., 2003), ranging from 4 (a specific event situated in time and space) to 0 (failure to recall any event or generation of only basic information about the theme). As in the schizophrenia study described earlier (Bennouna-Greene et al., 2012), participants were asked to give a Remember/Know/Guess judgment for each memory. In addition, following Piolino et al. (2003), for Remember judgments participants were also asked to provide justification by stating details about the event (e.g., thoughts, feelings, or contextual details related to the event). This was calculated as a Justified Remember (JR) score, which was also assessed by an independent rater.

Finally, participants completed the Twenty Statements Test (TST; Kuhn & McPartland 1954) to provide a measure of identity. This enabled ratings of identity complexity (number of different categories and subcategories sampled), identity quality (number of abstract self-images generated), and identity strength (number of self-images generated) to be calculated for each participant (e.g., Addis & Tippett, 2004; Rhee et al., 1995). Self-images were also coded to reflect the proportion of autonomous statements given by each participant. Following previous studies using the TST (Markus & Kitayama, 1991; Rhee et al., 1995), all statements were coded as either autonomous or social. Autonomous identities are characterized as being stable over time and context, representing internalized feelings, beliefs, or abilities (e.g., "I am helpful"), while social identities include reference to other people, specific locations, or social context (e.g., "I am from Oxford").

The results of Tanweer et al. (2010) showed that adults with ASD recalled fewer memories overall compared with controls. Critically, they also recalled fewer episodic memories, showing that the memories recalled lacked specific details (e.g., Crane and Goddard, 2008). These results suggest that autobiographical memory in ASD might be characterized by overgenerality, defined as the tendency to recall repeated and/or extended events rather than specific events (Williams et al., 2007). ASD participants tended to rate their memories as known rather than remembered, and thus they corroborate previous research showing that ASD is characterized by a lack of recollective experience (e.g., Bowler et al., 2007; Crane & Goddard, 2008; Goddard et al., 2007).

Analysis of the data on self-images also showed differences between the ASD participants and controls, with the ASD group generating more abstract (e.g., "I am studious"), fewer specific, fewer social, and more autonomous identities than the control participants. One way of looking at these results is that the ASD participants expressed their identities using significantly more abstract trait-linked self-images. However, another way of viewing these data is via the dichotomy of social versus autonomous self-images. The ASD group provided many more trait-linked statements about themselves as isolated individuals (e.g., "I am hard-working," "I am cheerful"), whereas in the comparison group the balance tipped the other way, with fewer trait-linked statements and more that were associated with social categories (e.g., "I am a wife," "I am a student rep"). This prevalence of more autonomous, self-focused statements in the ASD group is unsurprising, given that autism is often associated with deficiencies in social interaction (e.g., Lee & Hobson, 1998). There was also a significant difference in the identity complexity measure, with ASD participants producing self-images that spanned a smaller range of categories and subcategories than the control participants.

There are perhaps parallels between the lower level of self-complexity and the overgeneral (e.g., less specific and complex) memories in the ASD group. Recollective experience is characterized by a richness of specific details, thus the paucity of episodic memories combined with the generation of less specific and less complex sets of self-images might reflect a more general underlying process. At a general level, we suggest that the differences in both memory and identity in ASD are perhaps best characterized by a broad lack of specificity. It is possible that this lack of specificity is related to reductions in executive function and cognitive flexibility (e.g., Williams et al., 2007).

The importance of personal continuity

A strong theme thus far has been that where episodic memory fails, self-knowledge – semantic facts about one's own life – come to the fore. As is often the case in neuropsychology, much can be learned from groups of patients with the opposite deficit. One such population is semantic dementia patients, who have relatively intact episodic memory but a significant impairment of semantic memory. Piolino and colleagues (Duval et al., 2012) adapted the "I am" and "I will be" tasks for use in a group of semantic dementia patients. The patients were less able than controls to generate a set of structural self-representations, which was shown in having fewer semantized representations of personal events, whereas episodic accounts of personal events were no different from controls. Strength of self, measured by the amount of information yielded in the "I am" stage was equal between the semantic dementia patients and controls.

Klein et al. (2002a) have proposed that there is something "special" about self-knowledge, citing cases showing its dissociation from both episodic retrieval and nonautobiographical semantic memory. More recently, Klein et al. (2008) have suggested that episodic and semantic self-knowledge should be thought of as functionally independent – thus, they are capable of operating individually though may be most efficient working in conjunction. Indeed, it is likely that for healthy functioning it is important to maintain a stable, coherent sense of self that persists through time by whatever means available (e.g., Conway, 2005). This suggests that there is a driving force to achieve personal continuity and this can be supported by either episodic or semantic systems.

It is therefore likely that the clusters of memories/future images that support knowledge of past, present, and future self-images aid a sense of personal continuity. Although it is philosophically contentious whether or not the self actually exists as a continuous entity (e.g., Dennett, 1991), as psychologists we recognize the importance of the *perception* of personal continuity. Indeed, research has suggested that a failure to experience a sense of personal continuity has negative effects on psychological well-being. For example, Lampinen et al. (2004) found clear associations between diachronic disunification (e.g., a lack of personal continuity over time) and pathological dissociation. Recent research has suggested that nostalgia might function to preserve psychological well-being by improving a sense of personal continuity (e.g., Sedikides et al., 2008). Sedikides et al. suggested that nostalgia may enable such continuity by strengthening links between past and present selves.

It is possible that clusters of salient self-related memories, such as those generated in the IAM Task, play a similar role by rooting the individual in a meaningful past. Such memories might support personal continuity by facilitating the development of a personal narrative or life script (Habermas & Bluck, 2000; McAdams, 2003). Berntsen and Rubin's life script hypothesis (2002; 2004) proposed that autobiographical memory is organized by culturally shared *life scripts*. A life script is defined as a form of semantic knowledge, outlining the typical, culturally expected events that occur at given times in the lifespan. Across a range of studies, Berntsen and Rubin found that people do not show reminiscence bumps for sad and traumatic memories, but only for positive, important life events. In particular, people's life narratives often focused on normative "happy" events, such as marriage and childbirth (Berntsen

& Rubin, 2002). In support of the life script hypothesis, our 2011 study showed that participants' future self-images almost exclusively focused on typical normative events, such as marriage, child-rearing, and career progression. These results support an emerging body of research (e.g., Berntsen & Bohn, 2010; Bohn & Berntsen, 2011) showing that the normative life script is used when imagining the future as well as remembering the past.

Conclusions

This chapter has reviewed research on autobiographical memory and the self in a small number of clinical groups. We direct the reader to other chapters in this book for excellent reviews of related research. For example, Boals and colleagues (Chapter 4) discuss event centrality in autobiographical memory narratives following trauma; McNally and Robinaugh (Chapter 12) provide an extensive review of research on autobiographical memory in cases of complicated grief and trauma histories; and Brown and colleagues (Chapter 15) discuss self-identity and autobiographical memory in PTSD.

We introduced the idea that there are strong theoretical reasons why selfhood and memory are interlinked. We can clearly measure the effect of self structures as a form of narrative, in the organization of memories across the lifespan. And yet where memory systems break down, we have seen that there is still the organization and retrieval of information pertinent to the self. If you ask someone with dementia or schizophrenia to produce some self-relevant information in the form of an "I am" statement, he or she will be able to do this – even if it does not share the same phenomenology or richness of healthy participants. We would like to emphasize the clinical importance of this finding – people can generate "I am" statements and a population of memories to support them even in the face of impoverished memory or otherwise disorganized cognition. We think that the "I am" procedure will therefore have clinical utility: you can ask someone with memory impairment to describe him- or herself, and a meaningful response will be generated.

Undoubtedly, however, the organization of self-knowledge temporally and in response to self-generated cues does not capture the nebulous and dynamic nature of the self. We would like to finish therefore by briefly setting out a few issues that will dominate our future research program and that we hope will be incorporated into others' too. We suggest that there are a number of dimensions on which the self can be measured that echo the proposed structure and characteristics of the memory system. One that we have explored here is the relationship between conceptual and event based self-knowledge – that is, the difference between semantic and episodic memories anchored to self-images. The difference between semantic and episodic memory is one way in which we carve up the human memory system.

New directions

Here we suggest other ways in which we might conceptualize the self. First, we might want to return to Conway's concept of the working self, which clearly maps onto Baddeley's working memory (Baddeley, 1990). The working self therefore should be seen as dynamic, concerned with simultaneous storage and manipulation of material, just as in the working memory model. The majority of studies of self and memory consider long-term concepts of selfhood and remote autobiographical memories, but perhaps to see the working self at work, we need to consider behaviors and the extent to which people draw on self-knowledge and autobiographical memory in certain situations. For instance, the mechanisms of (and indeed the existence of) working memory become clear when one is faced with tasks that require doing two things at the same time: for example, processing a sentence for meaning while memorizing its last word. Perhaps an analogy in the self would pertain to the ability to update and maintain self-identity when confronted with change or when in different social situations. In the context of unawareness of memory deficit (anosognosia), which is found in Alzheimer's disease, for instance, Mograbi et al. (2009) have described the "petrified" self – in the sense that selfhood is preserved in Alzheimer's disease but does not change, that is, is "set in stone." This leads to a failure to update self-representations. Of course, the studies we reviewed here look at retrospective retrieval of facts and concepts rather than the ability to form new ones, and it is perfectly possible that all of the cases reviewed here will fail to produce any enduring aspects of personality. This ability to generate new aspects of self is a clear research priority and maps directly onto the differences between anterograde (inability to form new memories) and retrograde (inability to retrieve already existing memories) amnesia. If people with Alzheimer's disease can generate a set of accurate self-descriptions and yet have a petrified self unable to deal with the changes involved in dementia progression, it may well be that both poster campaigns described at the start of this chapter are accurate depictions of memory impairment.

Our final comment concerns the predominantly correlational nature of much of the existing research on self and memory, particularly that (including our own) which is based on the bidirectional self-memory system proposed by Conway and Pleydell-Pearce (2000). Research to date has shown that the self is intimately related to memory, but we currently know little about the causational processes that underlie this relationship. Many research areas begin with cross-sectional investigations that lay the groundwork for the design of experimental studies. Indeed, other areas of clinical autobiographical memory research have followed this progression (see Clark and colleagues, Chapter 7; Moulds and Krans, Chapter 8; and Brown and colleagues, Chapter 15). Future experimental studies in the field of self and memory could examine the relative strengths of the path from self to autobiographical memory and the path from autobiographical memory to the self. For example, does experimentally manipulating autobiographical memory valence impact on valence of the current self, and is this effect equally strong when examining memory valence following an experimental manipulation of self-valence? These questions have important implications for clinical groups because a deeper understanding of these processes will indicate where therapeutic interventions may be most effective (for example, focusing on rescripting memories or starting with the self-image). Work in our laboratories is beginning to address these questions using experimental paradigms with healthy populations.

Acknowledgments

This work was supported by a Future Research Leader award from the Economic and Social Research Council (ES/K000918/1) held by C. J. Rathbone.

REFERENCES

Addis, D. R., & Tippett, L. J. (2004). Memory of myself: autobiographical memory and identity in Alzheimer's disease. *Memory*, *12*(1), 56–74.

Alzheimer's Society (2010). Retrieved November 12, 2012, from http://www.coloribus.com/adsarchive/prints/alzheimers-society-someone-new-13819555/.

American Psychiatric Association (1994). *Diagnostic and Statistical Manual of Mental Disorders* (4th ed.). Washington, DC: American Psychiatric Association.

Baddeley, A. D. (1990) *Human Memory: Theory and Practice*. London: Lawrence Erlbaum Associates.

Baddeley, A. D., Thornton, A., Chua, S. E., & McKenna, P. (1996). Schizophrenic delusions and the construction of autobiographical memory. In D. C. Rubin (ed.), *Remembering Our Past: Studies in Autobiographical Memory* (pp. 384–428). Cambridge: Cambridge University Press.

Bekerian, D., Dhillon, D., & O'Neill, M. H. (2001). The children's autobiographical memory inventory, poster presentation. Valencia: Third International Conference on Memory.

Bennouna-Greene, M., Berna, F. Conway, M. A., Rathbone, C. J., Vidailhet, P., & Danion J. (2012). Self images and related autobiographical memories in schizophrenia. *Consciousness and Cognition*, 21(1), 247–257.

Berna, F., Bennouna-Greene, M., Potheegadoo, J., Verry, P., Conway, M. A., & Danion, J. M. (2011). Impaired ability to give a meaning to personally significant events in patients with schizophrenia. *Consciousness and Cognition*, 20(3), 703–711.

Berntsen, D., & Bohn, A. (2010). Remembering and forecasting: the relation between autobiographical memory and episodic future thinking. *Memory and Cognition*, 38(3), 265–278.

Berntsen, D., & Rubin, D. C. (2002). Emotionally charged autobiographical memories across the life span: the recall of happy, sad, traumatic, and involuntary memories. *Psychology and Aging*, 17(4), 636–652.

(2004). Cultural life scripts structure recall from autobiographical memory. *Memory & Cognition*, 32(3), 427–442.

Bohn, A., & Berntsen, D. (2011). The reminiscence bump reconsidered: children's prospective life stories show a bump in young adulthood. *Psychological Science*, 22, 197–202.

Bowler, D. M., Gardiner, J. M., & Gaigg, S. B. (2007). Factors affecting conscious awareness in the recollective experience of adults with asperger's syndrome. *Consciousness and Cognition*, 16, 124–143.

Broks, P. (2003). *Into the Silent Land: Travels in Neuropsychology*. London: Atlantic Books.

Bruck, M., London, K., Landa, B., & Goodman, J. (2007). Autobiographical memory and suggestibility in children with autism. *Development and Psychopathology*, 17, 73–95.

Butler, C. R., & Zeman, A. Z. (2008). Recent insights into the impairment of memory in epilepsy: transient epileptic amnesia, accelerated long-term forgetting and remote memory impairment. *Brain*, 131, 2243–2263.

Cermak, L. S., & O'Connor, M. (1983). The anterograde and retrograde retrieval ability of a patient with amnesia due to encephalitis. *Neuropsychologia*, 21(3), 213–234.

Conway, M. A. (2005). Memory and the self. *Journal of Memory and Language*, 53(4), 594–628.

Conway, M. A., & Fthenaki, A. (2003). Disruption of inhibitory control of memory following lesions to the frontal and temporal lobes. *Cortex*, 39(4–5), 667–686.

Conway, M. A., & Pleydell-Pearce, C. W. (2000). The construction of autobiographical memories in the self-memory system. *Psychological Review*, 107(2), 261–288.

Conway, M. A., Singer, J. A., & Tagini, A. (2004). The self and autobiographical memory: correspondence and coherence. *Social Cognition*, 22(5), 491–529.

Crane, L., & Goddard, L. (2008). Episodic and semantic autobiographical memory in adults with autism spectrum disorders. *Journal of Autism and Developmental Disorders, 38*(3), 498–506.

Crovitz, H. F., & Schiffman, H. (1974). Frequency of episodic memories as a function of their age. *Bulletin of the Psychonomic Society, 4*(NB5), 517–518.

Cuervo-Lombard, C., Jovenin, N., Hédelin, G., Rizzo-Peter, L., Conway, M. A., & Danion, J. M. (2007). Autobiographical memory of adolescence and early adulthood events: An investigation in schizophrenia. *Journal of the International Neuropsychological Society: JINS, 13*(2), 335–343.

Damon, W., & Hart, D. S. (1988). *Self-Understanding in Childhood and Adolescence*. New York: Cambridge University.

Danion, J. M., Cuervo, C., Piolino, P., Huron, C., Riutort, M., Peretti, C. S., et al. (2005). Conscious recollection in autobiographical memory: an investigation in schizophrenia. *Consciousness and Cognition, 14*(3), 535–547.

Dennett, D. C. (1991). *The Reality of Selves*. London: Penguin.

Dritschel, B. H., Williams, J. M., Baddeley, A. D., & Nimmo-Smith, I. (1992). Autobiographical fluency: a method for the study of personal memory. *Memory and Cognition, 20*(2), 133–140.

Duval, C., Desgranges, B., de La Sayette, V., Belliard, S., Eustache, F., & Piolino, P. (2012). What happens to personal identity when semantic knowledge degrades? A study of the self and autobiographical memory in semantic dementia. *Neuropsychologia, 50*(2), 254–265.

Erikson, E. H. (1950). *Childhood and Society*. New York: W. W. Norton.

Evans, J. J., Breen, E. K., Antoun, N., & Hodges, J. R. (1996). Focal retrograde amnesia for autobiographical events following cerebral vasculitis: a connectionist account. *Neurocase, 2*(1), 1–11.

Fitzgerald, J. M. (1988). Vivid memories and the reminiscence phenomenon: the role of a self narrative. *Human Development, 31*(5), 261–273.

Freedman, B. J. (1974). The subjective experience of perceptual and cognitive disturbances in schizophrenia: a review of autobiographical accounts. *Archives of General Psychiatry, 30*(3), 333–340.

Gardiner, J. M., & Java, R. I. (1993). Recognition memory and awareness: an experiential approach. *European Journal of Cognitive Psychology, 5*, 337–346.

Goddard, L., Howlin, P., Dritschel, B., & Patel, T. (2007). Autobiographical memory and social problem-solving in Asperger syndrome. *Journal of Autism and Developmental Disorders, 37*(2), 291–300.

Greenwald, A. G. (1980). The totalitarian ego: fabrication and revision of personal history. *American Psychologist, 35*(7), 603–618.

Habermas, T., & Bluck, S. (2000). Getting a life: the emergence of the life story in adolescence. *Psychological Bulletin, 126*(5), 748–769.

Hackmann, A., Ehlers, A., Speckens, A., & Clark, D. M. (2004). Characteristics and content of intrusive memories in PTSD and their changes with treatment. *Journal of Traumatic Stress, 17*, 231–240.

Hare, D. J., Mellor, C., & Azmi, S. (2007). Episodic memory in adults with autistic spectrum disorders: recall for self- versus other-experienced events. *Research in Developmental Disabilities, 28*(3), 317–329.

Illman, N. A., Rathbone, C. J., Kemp, S., & Moulin, C. J. A. (2011). Autobiographical memory and the self in a case of transient epileptic amnesia. *Epilepsy and Behavior*, *21*(1), 36–41.
Jansari, A., & Parkin, A.J. (1996). Things that go bump in your life: explaining the reminiscence bump in autobiographical memory. *Psychology and Aging*, *11*(1), 85–91.
Johnson-Selfridge, M., & Zalewski, C. (2001). Moderator variables of executive functioning in schizophrenia: meta-analytic findings. *Schizophrenia Bulletin*, *27*(2), 305–316.
Klein, S. B., Loftus, J., & Kihlstrom, J. F. (1996). Self-knowledge of an amnesic patient: toward a neuropsychology of personality and social psychology. *Journal of Experimental Psychology-General*, *125*(3), 250–260.
Klein, S. B., Rozendal, K., & Cosmides, L. (2002a). A social-cognitive neuroscience analysis of the self. *Social Cognition*, *20*(2), 105–135.
Klein, S. B., Cosmides, L., Costabile, K. A., & Mei, L. (2002b). Is there something special about the self? A neuropsychological case study. *Journal of Research in Personality*, *36*(5), 490–506.
Klein, S. B., Robertson, T. E., Gangi, C. E., & Loftus, J. (2008). The functional independence of trait self-knowledge: commentary on Sakaki (2007). *Memory*, *16*(5), 556–565.
Kopelman, M. D., Wilson, B. A., & Baddeley, A. D. (1989). The autobiographical memory interview: a new assessment of autobiographical and personal semantic memory in amnesic patients. *Journal of Clinical and Experimental Neuropsychology*, *11*(5), 724–744.
Kuhn, M. H., & McPartland, T. S. (1954). An empirical investigation of self-attitudes. *American Sociological Review*, *19*(1), 68–76.
Lampinen, J. M., Odegard, T. N., & Leding, J. K. (2004). Diachronic disunity. In D. R. Beike, J. M. Lampinen & D. A. Behrend (eds.), *The Self and Memory* (pp. 227–253). New York: Psychology Press.
Lee, A., & Hobson R.(1998). On developing self concepts: controlled study of children and adolescence with autism. *Journal of Child Psychology and Psychiatry*, *39*(8), 1131–1144.
Locke, J. (1694/1975). An Essay Concerning Human Understanding. In J. Perry (ed.), *Personal Identity*. Berkeley: University of California Press.
Lombardo, M. V., Barnes, J. L, Wheelwright, S. J., & Baron-Cohen, S. (2007). Self-referential cognition and empathy in autism. *Public Library of Science*, *2*(9), 883.
Markus, H. (1977). Self-schemata and processing information about self. *Journal of Personality and Social Psychology*, *35*(2), 63–78.
Markus, H. R., & Kitayama, S. (1991). Culture and the self: implications for cognition, emotion, and motivation. *Psychological Review*, *98*, 224–253.
McAdams, D. P. (2003). *Identity and the Life Story*. Mahwah, NJ: Lawrence Erlbaum Associates.
Millward, C., Powell, S., Messer, D., & Jordan, R. (2000). Recall for self and other in autism: children's memory for events experienced by themselves and their peers. *Journal of Autism and Developmental Disorders*, *30*, 15–28.

Mograbi, D. C., Brown, R. G., & Morris, R. G. (2009). Anosognosia in Alzheimer's disease: the petrified self. *Consciousness and Cognition*, *18*(4), 989–1003.

Morise, C., Berna, F., & Danion, J. M. (2011). The organisation of autobiographical memory in patients with schizophrenia. *Schizophrenia Research*, *128*(1–3), 156–160.

Nadel, L., & Moscovitch, M. (1997). Memory consolidation, retrograde amnesia and the hippocampal complex. *Current Opinion in Neurobiology*, *7*(2), 217–227.

Piolino, P., Desgranges, B., Belliard, S., Matuszewski, V., Lalevée, C., de la Sayette, V., & Eustache, F. (2003). Autobiographical memory and autonoetic consciousness: triple dissociation in neurodegenerative diseases. *Brain*, *126*, 2203–2219.

Piolino, P., Desgranges, B., Manning, L., North, P., Jokic, C., & Eustache, F. (2007). Autobiographical memory, the sense of recollection and executive functions after severe traumatic brain injury. *Cortex*, *43*(2), 176–195.

Piolino, P., Coste, C., Martinelli, P., Macé, A., Quinette, P., Guillery-Girard, B., et al. (2010). Reduced specificity of autobiographical memory and aging: do the executive and feature binding functions of working memory have a role? *Neuropsychologia*, *48*(2), 429–440.

Prebble, S. C., Addis, D. R., & Tippett, L. J. (2013). Autobiographical memory and sense of self. *Psychological Bulletin*, *139*, 815–840.

Rathbone, C. J., Moulin, C. J. A., & Conway, M. A. (2008). Self-centred memories: the reminiscence bump and the self. *Memory and Cognition*, *36*(8), 1403–1414.

(2009). Autobiographical memory and amnesia: using conceptual knowledge to ground the self. *Neurocase*, *15*(5), 405–418.

Rathbone, C. J., Conway, M. A., & Moulin, C. J. A. (2011). Remembering and imagining: the role of the self. *Consciousness and Cognition*, *20*(4), 1175–1182.

Rhee, E., Uleman, J. S., Roman, R. J., & Lee, H. K. (1995). Spontaneous self-descriptions and ethnic identities in individualistic and collectivistic cultures. *Journal of Personality and Social Psychology*, *69*(1), 142–152.

Riutort, M., Cuervo, C., Danion, J. M., Peretti, C. S., & Salamé, P. (2003). Reduced levels of specific autobiographical memories in schizophrenia. *Psychiatry Research*, *117*(1), 35–45.

Rogers, T. B., Kuiper, N. A., & Kirker, W. S. (1977). Self-reference and the encoding of personal information. *Journal of Personality and Social Psychology*, *35*, 677–688.

Rubin, D. C., Wetzler, S. E., & Nebes, R. D. (1986). Autobiographical memory across the adult lifespan. In D. C. Rubin (ed.), *Autobiographical Memory* (pp. 202–221). Cambridge: Cambridge University Press.

Rubin, D. C., Rahhal, T. A., & Poon, L. W. (1998). Things learned in early adulthood are remembered best. *Memory and Cognition*, *26*(1), 3–19.

Sedikides, C., Wildschut, T., Gaertner, L., Routledge, C., & Arndt, J. (2008). Nostalgia as enabler of self-continuity. In F. Sani (ed.), *Individual and Collective Self-Continuity: Psychological Perspectives* (pp. 227–242). Mahwah, NJ: Lawrence Erlbaum Associates.

Simons, D. J., & Chabris, C. F. (2011). What people believe about how memory works: a representative survey of the U.S. population. *PloS ONE, 6*(8), e22757.
Singer, J. A., & Blagov, P. S. (2001). *Classification System and Scoring Manual for Self-Defining Memories*. New London, CT: Department of Psychology, Connecticut College.
Singer, J. A., & Salovey, P. (1993). *The Remembered Self: Emotion and Memory in Personality*. New York: Free Press.
Tanweer, T., Rathbone, C. J., & Souchay, C. (2010). Autobiographical memory, autonoetic consciousness and identity in Asperger syndrome. *Neuropsychologia, 48*(4), 900–908.
Thomsen, D. K. (2009). There is more to life stories than memories. *Memory, 17*(4), 445–457.
Tulving, E. (1993). Self-knowledge of an amnesic individual is represented abstractly. In T. K. Srull & R. S. Wyer (eds.), *Advances in Social Cognition*, vol. 5. Hillsdale, NJ: Erlbaum.
Tulving, E., Schacter, D. L., McLachlan, D. R., & Moscovitch, M. (1988). Priming of semantic autobiographical knowledge: a case-study of retrograde-amnesia. *Brain and Cognition, 8*(1), 3–20.
Wheeler, M. A., & McMillan, C. T. (2001). Focal retrograde amnesia and the episodic-semantic distinction. *Cognitive, Affective, and Behavioral Neuroscience, 1*(1), 22–36.
Williams, M. J. G., Barnhofer, T., Crane, C., Hermans, D., Raes, F., Watkins, E., & Dalgleish, T. (2007). Autobiographical memory specificity and emotional disorder. *Psychological Bulletin, 133*(1), 122–148.
Wilson, B. A., & Wearing, D. (1995). Prisoner of consciousness: a state of just awakening following herpes simplex encephalitis. In R. Campbell & M. A. Conway (eds.), *Broken Memories: Case Studies in Memory Impairment* (pp. 14–30). Oxford: Blackwell.
World Health Organization (WHO) (1993). *The ICD-10 Classification of Mental and Behavioural Disorders: Diagnostic Criteria for Research*. Geneva: WHO.

15 Experimentally examining the role of self-identity in posttraumatic stress disorder

Adam D. Brown, Nicole A. Kouri, Amy Joscelyne, Charles R. Marmar, and Richard A. Bryant

> It got to the point where I got so angry with the insurgents out there that I used that anger to my advantage. And um I started to enjoy patrols. I wanted to be out there. I wanted to find the enemy. I wanted to kill the enemy. *I don't think I'm ever gonna be the same person again, no I don't, don't think I, I am.*
> (Stitt, 2012, emphasis added)

Posttraumatic stress disorder (PTSD) has long been believed to be associated with lasting changes in self-identity. In fact, there is a robust body of theoretical work and clinical observations suggesting that changes in self-identity that take place in the wake of a traumatic event represent a core factor in the pathogenesis of the disorder (e.g., Berntsen & Rubin, 2006; Conway & Pleydell-Pearce, 2000; Ehlers & Clark, 2000; Foa & Riggs, 1993; Horowitz, 1997; Janoff-Bulman, 1992). In contrast to how much has been written on the subject, however, experimental studies examining the impact of trauma on self-identity have received far less attention. The reasons for this are unclear. It may have emerged out of assumptions that autobiographical memory and the self are a unitary construct (Ryle, 1949). Alternatively, the lack of self-identity research in PTSD may have resulted from perceived methodological challenges to operationalizing something as complex and dynamic as self-identity and developing paradigms that can test its different functions and characteristics in a carefully controlled manner. That being said, growing evidence from cognitive neuroscience, neuropsychology, and behavioral studies has started to shed light on the ways in which these constructs overlap and diverge (for a review, see Prebble et al., 2013). Although such work is offering important insights into the basic processes involved in memory and self-identity, its translation to clinical populations, and in particular individuals with PTSD, may help to advance the next generation of trauma theories and therapeutic interventions.

This chapter surveys the extant findings from experimental studies conducted in relation to self-identity and PTSD, much of which is rooted in autobiographical memory research. We also discuss burgeoning experimental studies in clinical and nonclinical samples examining how different aspects of self-identity impact vulnerability to PTSD. The organization of the chapter is as follows: first we briefly discuss current theories that posit self-identity as a core mechanism involved in PTSD. Then we review the self-memory system of Conway and Pleydell-Pearce (2000), which provides a framework for conceptualizing and empirically testing the interdependence of self-identity and autobiographical memory. Next, we will review research pertaining to overgeneralized autobiographical memory (OGM), a phenomenon that has been implicated in PTSD in addition to other psychological disorders (Williams et al., 2007), and how OGM relates to self-identity. We then examine how a person's perception of his or her self in relation to a traumatic event influences PTSD symptomatology. More specifically, we will explore the concepts of trauma centrality, self-defining memories, mental death, and self-efficacy.

Self-identity in models of PTSD

Numerous theorists suggest that there is the potential for a traumatic memory to lead to structural change(s) in the personality of an individual (Dalgleish & Power 2004; van der Hart et al., 2005), which is consistent with narratives of trauma survivors; "I'm not like before. I've changed. My personality changed," describes one torture victim (Grady, 2011). This is consistent with theories showing that these types of negative appraisals about posttraumatic changes in self-identity represent a key factor in symptom maintenance and promote maladaptive behavioral patterns increasing the severity of symptoms (e.g., Ehlers & Clark, 2000; Foa & Rothbaum, 1998).

Moreover, traumatic events, like other personally significant events, may serve as turning points in a person's life, redirecting its course (Pillemer, 1998). This in turn may be associated with maladaptive views of the self and the world (Berntsen & Rubin, 2007; Brewin, 2003; Dunmore et al. 2001; Ehlers et al., 2000; Herman, 1992; Janoff-Bulman, 1992; Rubin et al., 2008). As an anchoring event, the trauma validates the current (negatively appraised) psyche and attributes internal and stable characteristics of the self to the trauma (Abramson & Seligman, 1978). This "attributional style" is associated with depression (Peterson & Seligman, 1984) and may help to explain why PTSD and depression are highly comorbid (Greening et al., 2002).

In addition, traumatic memories can lead to the oversimplification of one's life story (Berntsen & Rubin, 2006, p. 221). Sergeant Matthew Pennington explains,

You can deny PTSD and you know I knew I had it but I never understood the fact that there's no cure to it. I was always looking for where's this cure that's gonna get me back to where I was. I had a great life. I want it back. (Pennington, 2012)

Within this man's mental life exists a dichotomy between his pretrauma self and the posttrauma, PTSD patient that he now considers himself to be. According to Brewin (2011), the complexity of a trauma-related disorder is positively related to the severity of the fragmentation of the patient's self-identity. Furthermore, the discontinuity of identity may be associated with a tendency toward unintentional, intrusive recollection versus recall of specific autobiographical memories (e.g., Ehlers & Clark, 2000, for alternative explanations, see Rubin et al., 2008).

The self-memory system

Shifts in self-identity due to a traumatic experience are prevalent in theoretical models of PTSD (Berntsen & Rubin, 2006; Conway & Pleydell-Pearce, 2000; Ehlers & Clark, 2000; Foa & Riggs, 1993; Horowitz, 1997; Janoff-Bulman, 1992), yet compared with closely related processes, such as autobiographical memory, the basic mechanisms underlying the relationship between self-identity and the pathogenesis of PTSD are less known. Given the fact that PTSD is considered in part to be a disorder of memory (van der Kolk, 2007) and that an understanding of the self relates closely to the way in which a person constructs his or her life stories (e.g., Berntsen & Rubin, 2004; Fitzgerald, 1988; McAdams, 2001; Pillemer, 1998), autobiographical memory is one pathway that may connect the two variables in question – self-identity and PTSD. Moreover, certain cognitive models of autobiographical memory may serve as useful frameworks for scientifically investigating how self-identity, memory, and trauma may interact with one another. In particular, we draw on the self-memory system (SMS; Conway & Pleydell-Pearce, 2000) – a theory that emphasizes the bidirectional functions of autobiographical memory and self-identity and in which autobiographical memory is contextualized in terms of the self and its goals (e.g., Rathbone and Moulin, Chapter 14).

According to the SMS, autobiographical memories are organized hierarchically at different levels of abstraction. These range from lifetime periods to general events to episodic details. The construction of any autobiographical memory incorporates elements from these three categories and contains important information about the self. Lifetime periods are considered "knowledge about one's global personal history like 'my career as a scientist'" (Hauer, 2008, p. 9; Conway & Pleydell-Pearce, 2000).

General events are more specific in both theme and time period, for example, "When I graduated from college and backpacked around Europe with my best friend from boarding school." Last, at the bottom of the autobiographical knowledge base, is episodic specific knowledge, which includes the distinct sights, sounds, and tastes that someone recalls about the event (e.g., "Looking at a field of sunflowers in Marche, Italy"). According to the SMS model, although episodic details of personal events form the basis of autobiographical memories, their long-term retention and impact on self-identity depends primarily on how these details are integrated into one's conceptual self.

Another facet of the SMS (Conway & Pleydell-Pearce, 2000) is the working self. The working self is posited to provide executive control over the hierarchically organized levels of memory in order to integrate them in a way that is consistent with the current goals and views of the self. Thus, the working self is believed to be actively involved in the encoding, construction, and retrieval of autobiographical memories. Therefore, how and which autobiographical memories are remembered is shaped by the current needs of the working self. According to Conway (2005; Conway & Pleydell-Pearce, 2000), the interaction between the working self and the autobiographical knowledge base leads to stable representations of the conceptual self. Importantly, this model highlights the extent to which self-identity and autobiographical memory are reciprocal. That is, autobiographical memories may serve as the building blocks for self-identity, but the accessibility, content, and characteristics of these autobiographical memories are shaped considerably by self-identity.

One area of research in which the SMS model has been applied is overgeneral memory. Although findings directly related to self-identity have received less focus than the memories themselves, such findings have helped to identify critical mechanisms underlying PTSD (Moore & Zoellner, 2007) and more recently to guide treatments (Neshat-Doost et al., 2013).

Overgeneral memory

One phenomenon seen in patients with PTSD is *overgeneral memory* (OGM), the systematic recall of repeated events and/or events lasting longer than one day in response to cue words versus (in accordance with the directions of the task) recalling memories of specific autobiographical events lasting no longer than one day (Williams et al., 2007). Research has shown that OGM is evident in psychological disorders such as depression, PTSD, and acute stress disorder (Moore & Zoellner, 2007;

Williams et al., 2007; for a recent review, see Watkins, Chapter 10) but is less often associated with exposure to trauma in and of itself. The phenomenon of greater overgenerality in PTSD has been documented across multiple trauma-exposed populations, including Vietnam veterans (see McNally and Robinaugh, Chapter 12), cancer survivors (Kangas et al., 2005), and injured individuals with acute stress disorder (Harvey et al., 1998). Research has shown that overgenerality is associated with the onset, maintenance, and recovery from PTSD. A prospective study of firefighters identified overgenerality as a risk factor for PTSD; firefighters exhibiting greater overgenerality before trauma exposure were found to be at greater risk for developing PTSD following trauma exposure (Bryant et al., 2007; for similar findings in depression, see Hermans et al., 2008). Overgenerality in PTSD has also been linked with deficits in social problem solving, suggesting a role in symptom maintenance (Sutherland & Bryant, 2008). Furthermore, a decline in overgeneralized memories may be a marker of recovery. For example, the remission of PTSD symptoms following cognitive behavioral therapy appears to correspond with a reduction in overgeneral memories (Sutherland & Bryant, 2007).

Despite the possible link between overgeneralized autobiographical memory and changes in self-identity, few studies have investigated this possible connection. However, McNally and his colleagues (1995; for a review, see McNally and Robinaugh, Chapter 12) conducted a study of autobiographical memory disturbances in Vietnam veterans with and without PTSD. During the study, the researchers observed that out of the nineteen male Vietnam combat veterans previously diagnosed with PTSD, seven of them were wearing military regalia during the study. When comparing the specificity of episodic memories between the nineteen PTSD subjects and thirteen control subjects, specificity differed only in terms of a positivity bias; PTSD subjects exhibited no difference in specificity of memories prompted by positive and negative cue words, whereas controls showed a positive bias – they tended to recall more specific memories in response to positive cue words than negative cue words. Additionally, PTSD subjects showed less specificity in response to positive cue words than their control counterparts but no difference in response to negative cue words (McNally et al., 1995). In contrast, the PTSD subjects that wore battle regalia displayed an overall increase in OGM compared with PTSD subjects that did not wear Vietnam War regalia and control subjects. Additionally, PTSD subjects who wore war regalia took longer to retrieve memories than both control subjects and PTSD subjects that wore civilian clothing (McNally et al., 1995).

McNally et al. (1995) suggested that wearing vestiges of a war fought more than twenty years ago represented a self-referential psychological fixation with one's past self. Indeed, despite the tendency toward overgeneralized memories and latency in retrieving them, the preponderance of memories for regalia-wearing PTSD subjects was of war times. In contrast, both control subjects and PTSD subjects who did not wear Vietnam War regalia displayed the recency effect, whereby individuals tend to remember events that took place within the past month (McNally et al., 1995). Considering that PTSD subjects wearing war regalia were more likely to remember fewer episodes from the past month and more episodes from more than ten years ago in response to both positive and negative cues, the researchers (McNally et al., 1995) proposed that focusing on the past is not entirely an aversive process. What then about the past or remembrance of it enervates the self? This is discussed later on in the chapter.

Brown et al. (2013) also found that compared with combat veterans without PTSD, those diagnosed with PTSD tended to show less specificity in both autobiographical remembering and future imagining. Participants were asked to retrieve a past or imagine a future episode in response to neutral cue words, both of which rely on mental time travel (MTT). MTT is the ability to reexperience or preexperience episodes from life (Tulving, 1985). Brain imaging has shown overlap in neural activation when remembering the past and imagining the future (Addis et al., 2007). Not only did PTSD participants display a lack of specificity in content, the information they did share when recalling and/or simulating events was more combat focused. Brown et al. (2013) argued that the tendency to remember combat-related content might lead to anticipatory behavior focused on the potential for future trauma. Hyperarousal toward indiscriminate current threats is characteristic of PTSD (Ehlers & Clark, 2000). This hyperawareness is believed to be facilitated by overgeneralized negative appraisals of the future self, such as "Bad things will always happen to me" (Ehlers & Clark, 2000, p. 321), and the world (e.g., "The world is no longer safe"). Perhaps OGM and negative appraisals about the future promote a PTSD patient's sense of current threat, which subsequently leads them to turn to maladaptive behaviors such as avoidance. Furthermore, evidence suggests that deficits in episodic specificity lead to poor social problem solving in patients with depression, PTSD, and complicated grief (Evans et al., 1992; Maccallum & Bryant, 2010; Sutherland & Bryant, 2008).

Taken together, studies consistently show that individuals with PTSD tend to have difficulty recalling specific autobiographical memories. The findings from McNally and colleagues (1995) suggest that this may be due, in part, to the extent to which an individual with PTSD remains fixated on the traumatic event and sees it as a critical part of his or her identity, long after the event occurred. This phenomenon may also be driven by broader cognitive difficulties, such as reduced executive processes and rumination, all of which would likely affect both autobiographical memory and perceptions of the self.

These findings seem to apply to the construction of autobiographical future events as well. As Brown and colleagues (2013) demonstrated, OGM is observed in PTSD for past and future events. Subjects were also more likely to imagine trauma-related scenarios in response to neutral cue words, which may be consistent with the SMS model. That is, negative appraisals about one's self in the present may have been projected back to the past and into the future.

Trauma centrality

One explanation for OGM in PTSD is the lack of integration of the trauma into one's self-narrative (Ehlers & Clark, 2000; however, for a comprehensive account of possible mechanisms underlying OGM in PTSD, see the CaR-FA-X model, Williams et al., 2007). In other words, the memory of the traumatic experience exists outside the autobiographical knowledge base, without any contextual or temporal organization. However, building on theoretical models and findings from basic memory research, Berntsen and Rubin (2006) have proposed that PTSD occurs because traumatic memories are highly accessible as a result of the central role they play in one's self-identity. This would suggest that traumatic events that precipitate PTSD, like other momentous events, are remembered in great detail (Berntsen & Rubin, 2006). Berntsen and Rubin (2006) developed the Centrality of Event Scale (CES), which measures the salience of an event in one's life story. They propose that the disruption that proceeds from a traumatic event necessitates its importance to the self and by extension its high accessibility (Berntsen & Rubin, 2007). In turn, the traumatic event becomes an internal reference point for nontraumatic experiences and future goals. The latter echoes the finding of Brown et al. (2013) that PTSD patients tend to envision trauma-related future simulations. Berntsen & Rubin (2006) found that among a large sample of undergraduate students, the CES correlated to PTSD symptom severity and depression. The implication is that "trauma centrality" increases the accessibility of trauma-related autobiographical memories, which in turn, increase the symptom severity of PTSD (see Boals and colleagues, Chapter 4).

Similar data have been collected for both veterans with PTSD (Brown et al., 2010) and adult survivors of childhood sexual abuse (Robinaugh & McNally, 2011; for an overview, see McNally and Robinaugh, Chapter 12). In the former study, Brown and his colleagues (2010) found that among Operation Enduring Freedom/Operation Iraqi Freedom combat veterans, the CES predicted PTSD symptom severity, even after controlling for depression. Similarly, Robinaugh and McNally (2011) found that the CES scores correlated with PTSD symptom severity, depression severity, and self-esteem in a group of women who reported histories of childhood sexual abuse. Moreover, Robinaugh & McNally (2011) found that the CES comprised three factors: (1) the integration of the trauma into one's self-identity and life story, (2) the extent to which one's life story pivots on the traumatic event (i.e., the event represents one life chapter ending and a new one beginning), and (3) whether the trauma is regarded as a determinant for future life events. Interestingly, Robinaugh & McNally (2011) also found that beliefs about how the trauma impacts one's future were the strongest predictor of symptom severity.

Despite the consistent results, Robinaugh & McNally (2011) do allude to the need for future research, such as a definitive consensus of what it means to integrate a trauma with one's autobiographical memory. Brewin (2011) similarly argued that any contradictions proposed in reference to high OGM and trauma centrality are the result of a failure to distinguish between conceptual knowledge and episodic memory.

Self-defining memories

Returning to the SMS of Conway (2004; Conway & Pleydell-Pearce, 2000), conceptual knowledge and episodic memory are separate albeit not mutually exclusive. Conceptual knowledge facilitates the selective retrieval of autobiographical memories. Sutherland and Bryant (2005) hypothesized that, as a disorder characterized by heightened awareness of suspected threats, PTSD will lead a person to selectively recall memories that are related to harmful experiences. To this end, Sutherland and Bryant (2005) assessed the self-defining memories of subjects with PTSD, trauma-exposed subjects without PTSD, and non-trauma-exposed controls. Self-defining memories were defined as "affectively intense, repetitive, vivid, and comprise enduring concerns about oneself" (Singer & Salovey, 1993; as cited in Sutherland & Bryant, 2005, p. 593). In accordance with Conway and Pleydell-Pearce (2000), Sutherland and Bryant (2005) hypothesized that subjects with PTSD versus control subjects would retrieve more negative, trauma-related memories that pertained to trauma-focused priorities and concerns. This is exactly what the researchers found. Compared with both the trauma-exposed non-PTSD participants and control participants, trauma-exposed PTSD participants reported more negative self-defining memories (Sutherland & Bryant, 2005).

Additionally, between the two trauma-exposed groups, those diagnosed with PTSD retrieved fewer positive memories. Moreover, subjects with PTSD recalled fewer self-defining memories from childhood than both trauma-exposed non-PTSD subjects and control subjects. This suggests that for this patient cohort self-defining memories were by and large situated in and around the traumatic experience. That being said, Sutherland and Bryant (2005) explained that the traumatic experiences for all participants took place during what autobiographical researchers consider to be the reminiscence bump, the period from ten to thirty years old during which individuals retrieve the most memories (Neisser & Libby, 2000). Thus, the traumatic experiences may have been given preferential treatment independent of their content. Last, the extent to which a trauma-exposed participant focused on goals and/or expectations relating to the traumatic experience was directly proportional to the number of self-defining, negative, and trauma-related memories retrieved by the participant. An example of a trauma-focused goal is expressed in the following: "I want to be safe again. I want to have no pain" (Sutherland & Bryant, 2005, p. 596).

In another study, Sutherland and Bryant (2008) found that when compared with civilian trauma survivors without PTSD, those civilian trauma survivors with PTSD retrieved more trauma-related memories in response to positive cue words. Furthermore, those PTSD subjects exhibiting a self-discrepant image between the actual and ideal self were more likely to retrieve trauma-related memories in response to positive cue words. In contrast, trauma-focused memories prompted by negative cues were not associated with discrepancy of self. Thus, taken together, the findings from Sutherland and Bryant (2005; 2008) suggest that PTSD is in part characterized by negative self-defining memories.

Self-appraisals and PTSD

In another approach to examine how PTSD may affect self-identity, Brown et al. (2011) compared temporal self and social appraisals among combat veterans with and without PTSD. Subjects were asked to evaluate their own predeployment, present, and future functioning and that of a hypothetical peer. Consistent with findings from nonclinical populations (Wilson & Ross, 2001), combat veterans without PTSD displayed a perceived improvement with the self over time. That is, they rated their current functioning more favorably than their predeployment functioning. Moreover, they anticipated their functioning to be even better in the future. In contrast, Brown et al. (2011) found that those subjects with PTSD appraised their current and future selves less favorably than their past selves and did not anticipate improving over the next decade. Additionally, although both participant groups conjectured that their hypothetical counterparts would improve with time, those subjects with PTSD rated other combat veterans more favorably than those subjects without PTSD. These results would suggest that not only do persons with PTSD consider themselves different with regard to their own life trajectories, but they also perceive others to be generally "better" than themselves.

Sergeant Pennington expands on this point:

The physical injury that took me about 9 months total and I was healed up. Physically, I had residual pain and things like that. PTSD on the other hand is uh. I've lost friends. Why? Because I don't I call them. Why don't I call them? Because I feel like I have nothing to talk about. And then that will stop me from just picking up a phone and saying hello, you know? I got really withdrawn from my wife and I just wouldn't talk to her at all. And I figured the more I opened my mouth the worse I would make myself look or things of that nature. And you know you just really withdraw because it becomes the only defensive method you have to basically keep yourself from losing everything even more. (Pennington, 2012)

Mental death

The sense of loss alluded to in the above quotation is pervasive among trauma survivors. In its most extreme form, this loss is known as *mental death*, "the loss of the victim's pre-trauma identity" (Ebert & Dyck, 2004, p. 617). Identity in this context is defined as "the perception of sameness and continuity of the self – and the self in relation to others – based on the relative constancy of one's assumptions, beliefs, values, attitudes and behavior" (Drever & Froehlich, 1975; as cited in Ebert & Dyck, 2004, p. 621). To date, theories (e.g., Ebert & Dyck, 2004) and clinical studies (Ehlers et al., 1998) suggest that mental death (or defeat) is an important mechanism in the course of PTSD, but it has yet to be examined experimentally. The reality of mental death is acutely expressed by the Iraqi torture victim, R.: "I was destroyed.... I was tortured and raped more than once.... It feels as if something is missing. I don't mingle at all with people" (Grady, 2011). The loss of one's identity is accompanied by feelings of shame and guilt (Ebert & Dyck, 2004). R. explains, "I am ashamed.... It's as if I am now an emotionally damaged child" (Grady,

2011). Only the therapists know the exact nature of his torture. He refuses to tell his wife everything that happened to him while in captivity, "This is personal," he says. "I'm a father, I have two daughters. I don't dare to talk about it" (Grady, 2011).

The sergeant previously cited in this chapter is haunted by an incident that happened to him while overseas: "Well this one day I was about to light these people and just take 'em right out and then they held a baby out the window and slammed on their brakes?. How do you deal with that? And she [his wife] would say 'I don't know' and I'd say yeah me neither. The day sucks" (Pennington, 2012). He was prevented from shooting the people when his gun jammed (Dao, 2012). Who is to say if Sergeant Pennington would have taken the shot had his gun been working properly? A female Coast Guard diagnosed with PTSD felt a sense of guilt because she did not entertain her superior's sexual advances after which the commander preyed on other female crew members. This victim felt responsible for the other women who were sexually assaulted (Schlemmer, 2012). After the experience, the woman's personality appeared to have changed; she described herself as having become "rebellious and defensive in relationships, snapping at family and friends, and not trusting anyone" (Schlemmer, 2012). Feelings of shame and guilt can alienate the person from seeking beneficial social support (Ebert & Dyck, 2004).

Bearing on this topic, Robinaugh and McNally (2010) found that shame predicted both PTSD and depression. When levels of shame were high there was a positive relationship between guilt and PTSD symptoms. In contrast, low levels of shame were associated with a negative relationship between guilt and PTSD symptoms. This incongruent relationship suggests that guilt is an adaptive emotion when not associated with shame (Robinaugh & McNally, 2010). The results also showed that a higher score on the CES for a shame or guilt memory correlated with greater levels of PTSD and depression symptoms (Robinaugh & McNally, 2010), once again suggesting the importance of the self in PTSD.

Self-efficacy

Mental death (Ebert & Dyck, 2004) and, in its less extreme forms, mental defeat (Ehlers & Clark, 2000) and mental exhaustion (Wenzel et al., 2000), all highlight the role played by self-efficacy in self-identity and PTSD symptomatology. Self-efficacy involves perceiving the self to be an agent of and in control of one's own thoughts, emotions, and behaviors (Bandura, 1993). Therefore, to some extent, it is separate from one's actual abilities. To be self-efficacious one must believe that he or she possesses those abilities. Therefore, researchers have examined the extent to which a wide range of outcomes is affected by perceived changes in self-efficacy (see Litt et al., 1993; Bandura et al., 1985). In relation to mechanisms that bear on PTSD, Brown et al. (2012a) looked at the effects of perceived self-efficacy on memories of negative experiences, by inducing conditions of high or low coping self-efficacy (HSE and LSE, respectively) in participants prior to them viewing a video of the aftermath of a serious car accident. The induction involved participants receiving false feedback after completing questionnaires they had filled out in their "Introduction to Psychology" course. The participant was told that he or she fell either in the top 1% of "copers" or in the lower fiftieth to thirtieth percentile of "copers" and was then asked to complete measures of perceived self-efficacy and current mood. As predicted, although the groups did not differ on ratings of self-efficacy prior to the induction, they did so after they were given the false feedback. Furthermore, the induction did not lead to group differences in either positive or negative mood states during the study.

After participants viewed the film they were then asked to recall different aspects of the scene. Although HSE and LSE subjects did not differ in memory accuracy of peripheral details, those participants in the LSE group remembered central traumatic elements more accurately twenty-four hours after viewing the film. Brown et al. (2012a) argued that this is consistent with evidence showing that individuals with low self-efficacy show heightened sensitivity to current and potential threat in their environment. Additionally, the HSE cohort reported fewer negative intrusions and distress after watching the film. This supports emerging research that has shown across a wide range of traumatic events, including war, natural disasters, terrorism, and interpersonal violence, that individuals reporting higher levels of self-efficacy also display more resilience to negative outcomes associated with trauma (Benight & Bandura, 2004).

Using the same paradigm for self-efficacy induction explained previously, Brown et al. (2012b) found that participants with enhanced self-efficacy reported more specific past and future events with greater episodic specificity and used more positive words and self-efficacious statements. Additionally, HSE subjects were more successful on social problem-solving tasks.

This study suggests that one aspect of the working self (Conway & Pleydell-Pearce, 2000) that mediates an individual's perception of the past and future is self-efficacy. This is critical in that trauma can weaken an individual's level of self-efficacy. For example, undergoing totalitarian control has been shown to damage a person's sense of autonomy, which in turn predicts the onset of PTSD (Dunmore et al., 1997; Ehlers et al., 1998; 2000). The trauma in and of itself may directly deprive the person of his or her resourcefulness, but on top of this, PTSD and its sequelae may enervate a person's sense of agency to an even greater degree, which in turn leads to maladaptive coping techniques and poorer mental health outcomes, including more severe presentations of PTSD (Ebert & Dyck, 2004). Active coping requires mental planning, a form of self-protection that aims to reduce physical and/or psychological harm, during and after a traumatic experience (Ebert & Dyck, 2004). King et al. (1999) found that those American prisoners of war who displayed active coping techniques during the Vietnam War had better prognoses posttrauma.

Conclusion

This chapter aimed to elucidate the ways in which self-identity is associated with vulnerability or resistance to PTSD. Although self-identity is a core feature of many theories of PTSD and is intimately connected to autobiographical memory, experimental studies on self-identity in PTSD is a burgeoning area of inquiry ripe for future research. Importantly, we suggest that the experimental approaches seek to delineate how aspects of self-identity, separate from and in conjunction with autobiographical memory, contribute to mental health trajectories in the wake of trauma. Several areas may be particularly important: first, the self is not temporally limited to the present. Although the relation between self-identity and memory has been the focus of theory and research, very little has been studied in relation to the way in which individuals with PTSD construct and imagine themselves in the future. For example, Markus and Nurius (1986) proposed the concept of *possible selves* as "individuals' ideas of what they might become, what they would like to become, and what they are afraid of becoming" (p. 954). Thus, the future self in this model is a cognitive schema that directly impacts a wide range of cognitive, affective, and behavioral processes. Helping patients to construct and imagine healthier versions of themselves may promote adaptive behaviors in order to obtain such goals, but this has yet to be examined.

Second, although analog studies increasing self-efficacy appear to be associated with better coping, these findings need to be tested in clinical samples. Along these lines, paradigms that manipulate the degree to which a person experiences "perceived permanent change" and "trauma centrality" will elucidate important mechanisms associated with PTSD.

As illustrated in an interview in the *New York Times*, a psychologist working for the Center for Victims of Torture in Amman admits, "I don't think you can be totally healed.... You're just different. You try to adjust to your life" (Grady, 2011). Although this change may have been caused by trauma, it remains unknown to what extent memory continues to exert its influence on one's self-identity. Furthermore, this quotation implies that, in some cases, recovery from PTSD may be contingent not on the retrieval of one's past self-identity and autobiographical memory, but on establishing a sense of agency to (re)construct an efficacious and resilient self.

Future research should also examine the role that culture plays in the construction of self-identity (e.g., Jobson & Kearney, 2008). For example, burgeoning research has proposed that trauma-focused goals, self-defining memories, self-cognitions, mental defeat, alienation, permanent change, and mental planning differ between independent and interdependent cultures (see Jobson & Kearney, 2009). Additionally, future research should assess the effect(s) a person's role in the trauma has on self-identity, such as the impact of perpetrating violence versus being the victim of one. For instance, although killing and use of excessive force is a strong predictor of PTSD (Komarovskaya et al., 2011; Maquen et al., 2010), and anecdotally patients often say that they were "changed" after participating in violent, unethical, immoral acts of duty, how these changes impact cognition and behavior remain unknown.

Additionally, the emphasis on the self will also help to shed light on the link between trauma exposure and mental health outcomes. For example, diagnostic classification systems such as the *Diagnostic and Statistical Manual of Mental Disorders* (DSM) emphasize the role of the type of stressor in order to meet criteria for diagnosis (e.g., Criteria A). However, in line with cognitive theories and frameworks (e.g., Rubin et al., 2008; see also McNally and Robinaugh, Chapter 12), a critical mechanism underlying PTSD is not the event per se but how the event is remembered. We suggest that similar thinking may be applied to self-identity as well. That is, understanding the negative impact of a traumatic event on a person's mental health requires insight into how that person views the event in the context of his or her self-identity.

In summary, the groundbreaking study of McNally et al. (1995) on autobiographical memory in PTSD appeared more than fifteen years ago and continues to inform how we characterize traumatic memory. With a firm understanding about the past, we believe that the next fifteen years would similarly benefit from looking into the self.

REFERENCES

Abramson, L. Y., & Seligman, M. E. P. (1978). Learned helplessness in humans: critique and reformulation. *Journal of Abnormal Psychology, 87,* 49–74.

Addis, D. R., Wong, A. T., & Schacter, D. L. (2007). Remembering the past and imagining the future: common and distinct neural substrates during event construction and elaboration. *Neuropsychologia, 45,* 1363–1377.

Bandura, A. (1993). Perceived self-efficacy in cognitive development and functioning. *Educational Psychologist, 28,* 117–148.

Bandura, A., Taylor, C. B., Williams, S. L., Mefford I. N., & Barchas, J. D. (1985). Catecholamine secretion as a function of perceived coping self-efficacy. *Journal of Consulting and Clinical Psychology, 53,* 406–414.

Benight, C. C., & Bandura, A. (2004). Social cognitive theory of post-traumatic recovery: the role of perceived self-efficacy. *Behaviour Research and Therapy, 4,* 1129–1148.

Berntsen, D., & Rubin, D. C. (2004). Cultural life scripts structure recall from autobiographical memory. *Memory and Cognition, 32,* 427–442.

(2006). The centrality of event scale: a measure of integrating a trauma into one's identity and its relation to post-traumatic stress disorder symptoms. *Behaviour Research and Therapy, 44,* 219–231.

(2007). When a trauma becomes a key to identity: enhanced integration of trauma memories predicts posttraumatic stress disorder symptoms. *Applied Cognitive Psychology, 21,* 417–431.

Brewin C. R. (2003). *Posttraumatic Stress Disorder: Malady or Myth?* New Haven, CT: Yale University Press.

(2011). The nature and significance of memory disturbance in posttraumatic stress disorder. *Annual Review of Clinical Psychology, 7,* 203–227.

Brown, A. D., Antonius, D., Kramer, M., Root, J. C., & Hirst, W. (2010). Trauma centrality and PTSD in veterans returning from Iraq and Afghanistan. *Journal of Traumatic Stress, 23*(4), 496–499.

Brown, A. D., Buckner, J. P., & Hirst, W. (2011). Time, before, and after time: temporal self and social appraisals in posttraumatic stress disorder. *Journal of Behavior Therapy and Experimental Psychiatry, 42,* 344–348.

Brown, A. D., Joscelyne, A., Dorfman, M. L., Marmar, C. R., & Bryant, R. A. (2012a). The impact of perceived self-efficacy on memory for aversive experiences. *Memory, 20*(4), 374–383.

Brown, A. D., Dorfman, M. L., Marmar, C. R., & Bryant, R. A. (2012b). The impact of perceived self-efficacy on mental time travel and social problem solving. *Consciousness and Cognition, 21,* 299–306.

Brown, A. D., Root, J. C., Romano, T. A., Chang, L. J., Bryant, R. A., & Hirst, W. (2013). Overgeneralized autobiographical memory and future thinking in combat veterans with posttraumatic stress disorder. *Journal of Behavior Therapy and Experimental Psychiatry, 44,* 129–134.

Bryant, R. A., Sutherland, K. G., & Guthrie, R. M. (2007). Impaired specific autobiographical memory as a risk factor for posttraumatic stress after trauma. *Journal of Abnormal Psychology, 116,* 837–841.

Conway, M. A. (2005). Memory and the self. *Journal of Memory and Language*, 53, 594–628.
Conway, M. A., & Pleydell-Pearce, C. W. (2000). The construction of autobiographical memories in the self-memory system. *Psychological Review*, *107*(2), 261–288.
Dalgleish T., & Power, M. J. (2004). The I of the storm: relations between self and conscious emotion experience: comment on Lambie and Marcel (2002). *Psychological Review*, *111*, 812–819.
Dao, J. (2012, January 1). Acting out war's inner wounds. *New York Times*. Retrieved from http://www.nytimes.com/2012/01/02/us/acting-helps-soldier-cope-with-post-traumatic-stress-disorder.html.
Drever, J., & Froehlich, W. D. (1975). *Woerterbuch zur Psychologie*. Munich, DE: Dtv.
Dunmore E., Clark, D. M., & Ehlers A. (1997). Cognitive factors in persistent versus recovered post-traumatic stress disorder after physical or sexual assault: a pilot study. *Behavioural and Cognitive Psychotherapy*, *25*, 147–159.
(2001). A prospective investigation of the role of cognitive factors in persistent posttraumatic stress disorder (PTSD) after physical or sexual assault. *Behaviour Research and Therapy*, *39*, 1063–1084.
Ebert. A., & Dyck, M. J. (2004). The experience of mental death: the core feature of complex posttraumatic stress disorder. *Clinical Psychology Review*, *24*, 617–635.
Ehlers, A., & Clark, D. M. (2000). A cognitive model of posttraumatic stress disorder. *Behaviour Research and Therapy*, *38*, 319–345.
Ehlers, A., Clark., D. M., Dunmore, E., Jaycox, L., Meadows, E., & Foa, E. B. (1998). Predicting response to exposure treatment in PTSD: the role of mental defeat and alienation. *Journal of Traumatic Stress*, *11*(3), 457–471.
Ehlers, A., Maercker, A., & Boos, A. (2000). Post-traumatic stress disorder following political imprisonment: the role of mental defeat, alienation, and perceived permanent change. *Journal of Abnormal Psychology*, *109*, 45–55.
Evans, J., Williams, J. M. G., O'Loughlin, S., & Howells, K. (1992), Autobiographical memory and problem-solving strategies of parasuicide patients. *Psychological Medicine*, *22*, 399–405.
Fitzgerald, J. M. (1988). Vivid memories and the reminiscence phenomenon: the role of a self narrative. *Human Development*, *31*, 261–273.
Foa, E. B., & Riggs, D. S. (1993). Post-traumatic stress disorder in rape victims. In J. Oldham, M. B. Riba, & A. Tasman (eds.), *American Psychiatric Press Review of Psychiatry* (vol. 12, pp. 273–303). Washington, DC: American Psychiatric Press.
Foa, E. B., & Rothbaum B. O. (1998). *Treating the Trauma of Rape: Cognitive Behavioral Therapy for PTSD*. New York: Guilford Press.
Grady, D. (2011, May 2). Tugging at threads to unspool stories of torture. *New York Times*. Retrieved from http://www.nytimes.com/2011/05/03/health/03torture.html?pagewanted=all.
Greening, L., Stoppelbein, L., & Docter, R. (2002). The mediating effects of attributional style and event-specific attributions on postdisaster adjustment. *Cognitive Therapy and Research*, *26*, 261–274.

Harvey, A. G., Bryant, R. A., & Dang, S. T. (1998). Autobiographical memory in acute stress disorder. *Journal of Consulting and Clinical Psychology, 66*, 500–506.

Hauer, B. (2008). Autobiographical memory retrieval: overgeneral memory and intrusions. Retrieved from http://arno.unimaas.nl/show.cgi?fid=9707.

Herman, J. L. (1992). Complex PTSD: a syndrome in survivors of prolonged and repeated trauma. *Journal of Traumatic Stress, 5*, 377–391.

Hermans, D., de Decker, A., de Peuter, S., Raes, F., Elen, P., & Williams, J. M. (2008). Autobiographical memory specificity and affect regulation: coping with a negative life-event. *Depression and Anxiety, 25*, 787–792.

Horowitz, M. J. (1997). *Stress Response Syndromes: PTSD, Grief and Adjustment Disorders*. Northvale, NJ: Jason Aroson.

Janoff-Bulman, R. (1992). *Shattered Assumptions: Toward a New Psychology of Trauma*. New York: The Free Press.

Jobson, L., & O'Kearney, R. T. (2008). Cultural differences in personal identity in post-traumatic stress disorder. *British Journal of Clinical Psychology, 47*, 95–109.

(2009). Impact of cultural differences in self on cognitive appraisals in posttraumatic stress disorder. *Behavioural and Cognitive Psychotherapy, 37*, 249–266.

Kangas, M., Henry, J. L., & Bryant, R. A. (2005). A prospective study of autobiographical memory and posttraumatic stress disorder following cancer. *Journal of Consulting and Clinical Psychology, 73*, 293–299.

Kelly, G. A. (1955). *The Psychology of Personal Constructs*, vol. 1. New York: W. W. Norton.

King, D. W., King, L. A., Foy, D. W., Keane, T. M., & Fairbank, J. A. (1999). Posttraumatic stress disorder in a national sample of female and male Vietnam veterans: risk factors, war-zone stressors, and resiliency-recovery variables. *Journal of Abnormal Psychology, 108*, 164–170.

Komarovskaya, I., Maquen S., McCaslin, S. E., Metzler, T. J., Madan, A., Brown, A. D., Galatzer-Levy, I. R., Henn-Haase, C., & Marmar, C. R. (2011). The impact of killing and injuring others on mental health symptoms among police officers. *Journal of Psychiatric Research, 45*, 1332–1336.

Litt, M. D., Nye, C., & Shafer, D. (1993). Coping with oral surgery by self-efficacy enhancement and perceptions of control. *Journal of Dental Research, 72*, 1237–1243.

Maccallum, F., & Bryant, R. A. (2010). Impaired social problem solving in complicated grief. *British Journal of Clinical Psychology, 49*, 577–590.

Maquen S., Lucenko, B. A., Reger, M. A., Gahm, G. A., Litz, B. T., Seal, K. H., Knight, S. J., & Marmar, C. R. (2010). The impact of reported direct and indirect killing on mental health symptoms in Iraq war veterans. *Journal of Traumatic Stress, 23*, 86–90.

Marcus, H., & Nurius, P. (1986). Possible selves. *American Psychologist, 41*, 954–969.

McAdams, D. P. (2001). The psychology of life stories. *Review of General Psychology, 5*, 100–122.

McNally, R. J., Lasko, N. B., Macklin, M. L., & Pitman, R. K. (1995). Autobiographical memory disturbance in combat-related posttraumatic stress disorder. *Behaviour Research and Therapy*, *33*, 619–630.

Moore, S. A. & Zoellner, L. A. (2007). Overgeneral autobiographical memory and traumatic events: an evaluative review. *Psychological Bulletin*, *133*, 419–437.

Neisser, U., & Libby, L. K. (2000). Remembering life experiences. In E. Tulving & F. I. M. Craik (eds.), *The Oxford Handbook of Memory* (pp. 315–332). London: Oxford University Press.

Neshat-Doost, H. T., Dalgleish, T., Yule, W., Kalantari, M., Ahmadi, S. J., Dyregov, A., & Jobson, L. (2013). Enhancing autobiographical memory specificity through cognitive training: an intervention for depression translated from basic science. *Clinical Psychological Science*, *1*, 84–92.

Pennington, M. (2012, January 2). The hard road back: multiple wounds [video file]. Retrieved from http://www.nytimes.com/interactive/us/the-hard-road-back.html??ref=us#/matthew-pennington.

Peterson, C., & Seligman, M. E. (1984). Causal explanations as a risk factor for depression: theory and evidence. *Psychological Review*, *91*, 347–374.

Pillemer, D. B. (1998). *Momentous Events, Vivid Memories*. Cambridge, Harvard University Press.

Prebble, S. C., Addis, D. R., & Tippett, L. J. (2013). Autobiographical memory and sense of self. *Psychological Bulletin*, *139*(4), 815–840.

Robinaugh, D. J., & McNally, R. J. (2010). Autobiographical memory for shame or guilt provoking events: association with psychological symptoms. *Behaviour Research and Therapy*, *48*, 646–652.

Robinaugh, D. J., & McNally, R. J. (2011). Trauma centrality and PTSD symptom severity in adult survivors of childhood sexual abuse. *Journal of Traumatic Stress*, *24*(4), 483–486.

Rubin, D. C., Berntsen, D., & Joahnsen, M. K. (2008). A memory based model of posttraumatic stress disorder: evaluating basic assumptions underlying the PTSD diagnosis. *Psychological Review*, *115*, 985–1011.

Ryle, G. (1949). *The Concept of Mind*. London: Hutchinson.

Schlemmer, Ashley (2012, November 25). Just one of the guys [web blog comment]. Retrieved from http://veteransptsdproject.com/blog/guest-posts/just-one-of-the-guys-by-ashley-schlemmer/.

Singer, J. A., & Salovey, P. (1993). *The Remembered Self: Emotion and Memory in Personality*. New York: The Free Press.

Stitt, T. (2012, April 29). The hard road back: a companion for the journey [video file]. Retrieved from http://www.nytimes.com/interactive/us/the-hard-road-back.html??ref=us#/tori-stitt.

Sutherland, K., & Bryant, R. A. (2005). Self-defining memories in post-traumatic stress disorder. *British Journal of Clinical Psychology*, *44*, 591–598.

(2007). Autobiographical memory in posttraumatic stress disorder before and after treatment. *Behaviour Research and Therapy*, *45*, 2915–2923.

(2008). Autobiographical memory and the self-memory system in posttraumatic stress disorder. *Journal of Anxiety Disorders*, *22*, 555–560.

van der Hart, O., Nijenhuis, E. R. S., & Steele K. (2005). Dissociation: an insufficiently recognized major feature of complex posttraumatic stress disorder. *Journal of Traumatic. Stress, 18*, 413–423.

van der Kolk, B. A. (2007). The history of trauma in psychiatry. In M. J. Friedman, T. M. Keane, & P. A. Resick (eds.), *Handbook of PTSD: Science in Practice* (pp. 19–36). New York: Guilford Press.

Tulving, E. (1985). Memory and consciousness. *Canadian Psychologist, 26*, 1–12.

Wenzel, T., Griengl, H., Stompe, T., Mirzai, S., & Kieffer, W. (2000). Psychological disorders in survivors of torture: exhaustion, impairment and depression. *Psychopathology, 33*, 292–296.

Williams, J. M., Barnhofer, T., Crane, C., Hermans, D., Raes, F., Watkins, E., & Dalgleish, T. (2007). Autobiographical memory specificity and emotional disorder. *Psychological Bulletin, 133*, 122–148.

Wilson, A. E., & Ross, M. (2001). From chump to champ: people's appraisals of their earlier and present selves. *Journal of Personality and Social Psychology, 80*, 572–584.

16 The role of self during autobiographical remembering and psychopathology: evidence from philosophical, behavioral, neural, and cultural investigations

Lynn A. Watson and Barbara Dritschel

The self has been a point of academic discussion for centuries and remains a topic of discussion across religion, philosophy, and psychology. The aim of the present chapter is to review discussions on the self from its roots in philosophy up until the present day across a broad range of contexts. The chapter reviews the historical roots of the self-concept from behavioral, cognitive, neural, and cultural perspectives, examining how the self-concept impacts our memory for past events and our psychological well-being. The chapter covers basic research into self-referential processing and examines the basis of self-identity within the brain. The following sections then review autobiographical memory models of self-regulation and how such models account for emotional experience during both healthy and disordered cognition. Current research outlining two key disruptions in self-referential processing and autobiographical memory retrieval during psychopathology are then examined, namely, high levels of self-relevance and self-discrepancy. A new model of the depressive self developed from neuroimaging studies (Lemogne et al., 2012) is then presented as a potential account of autobiographical memory retrieval during psychopathology. Finally, research into how cultural identity influences autobiographical memory retrieval and psychopathology is presented. The chapter ends with a review of our current understanding of self-identity, autobiographical memory, and psychopathology across behavioral, cognitive, neural, and cultural levels.

Throughout the chapter we take a broad view of psychological well-being and psychopathology, reviewing research on healthy individuals; individuals reporting subclinical symptoms of psychopathology, for example, dysphoria; individuals who have received some form of formal diagnosis, for example, major depression or borderline personality disorder; and individuals who have formerly received a clinical diagnosis. In this sense we consider memory functioning in relation to the experience of psychopathology across a continuum, from healthy (minimal or no symptoms) to disordered cognition (high levels of reported symptoms and severe impact on life function). We consider this approach important if we are to fully understand how autobiographical memory is altered as a function of psychological disorders.

What is self? A historical review

Psychological theories of the self have their origins in philosophy. In relation to the self, Descartes (1596–1650) asserted that: "I think, and my thoughts cannot be separated from me, therefore I exist," or "*Cogito ergo sum*" (Cottingham et al., 1984). This statement represents a definition of the self in its simplest form, referring specifically to our conscious awareness of the immediate present. This initial definition of the minimal self influenced the writings of John Locke (1632–1704), who is cited as establishing the modern concept of self (Chappell, 1994). Locke stressed that real-life experience, extended memory, and the existence of other selves were also important. Using several thought experiments Locke showed that personal identity exists only to the extent that the self has conscious awareness of its past thoughts and actions (Lowe, 1995). This definition provides an early example of the view that memory for our personal past plays a key role in self-identity.

In contrast to the views of Locke, David Hume's (1711–1776) bundle theory of self categorically stated that no unitary self exists; instead, human perception consists of a series of ideas and impressions (Hume, 1739). Although opposing the existence of self in memory, Hume's discussion of self was important for several reasons. First, his view made no reference to a self existing outside the life of the individual, separating it from similar concepts, such as "the soul," used by religions of the time. This allowed the concept of self to be investigated empirically. In addition, Hume introduced the concept of a multifaceted self, allowing for the possibility of multiple identities existing within one individual (see Markus & Cross, 1990).

At that time, the self and many other concepts within psychology were still placed within the realms of religious or moral philosophy. Investigations of the self continued within the philosophical realm until Williams James (1842–1910) brought together literature in psychology, philosophy, and physiology to form an arena for scientific investigation (see James, 1890). Although he did not conduct any empirical research, James provided a framework for the study of self within psychology by describing the elementary components of the self. His position is similar to that of Locke. He proposed that the self provides unity to our thoughts and underlies our stream of consciousness across past, present, and future.

What is striking is the extent to which the concept of self has remained relatively stable across the centuries; therefore, this definition of self is used as a working definition of the self within the present chapter. The core self consists of conscious awareness of the thought of an individual mind as distinguished from other minds. This thought can be unified across time by a stream of consciousness through past, present, and future events. The identity of the self is also developed and consolidated across time through our memory for previous events, today known as autobiographical memory. Unlike the unified stream of consciousness, the self in memory is adaptive and can be modified by the environment in which it is contained. Strong parallels can be identified between these early writings and more recent theoretical models of self and memory; see the self-memory system, described later in the chapter (Conway & Plydell-Pearce, 2000).

The role of memory in developing the self has been a focus of research in psychology; self-identity is created by accessing information in memory. One route of access and structure is through self-schemas. Schemata (Bobrow & Norman, 1975) refer to cognitive structures that represent knowledge about a concept or type of stimulus, including its attributes and the relations among those attributes. Information about the self would be stored in a self-schema, and evidence for their existence came from work on the self-reference paradigm. In the self-reference paradigm (Rogers et al., 1977) participants were asked to rate a set of personality adjectives within four different encoding conditions: structure (is the word presented in big letters?), phonemic (this word rhymes with XXXX?), semantic (this word means the same as XXXX?) and self-referent (this word describes you?). Participants showed greatest recall of words presented within the self-reference condition when compared with the other conditions. This effect is known as the self-reference effect and has been replicated many times under a variety of conditions (see Symons & Johnson, 1997). Symons and Johnson (1997) concluded that processing of information about the self is highly efficient, suggesting that information about the self forms a well-organized and elaborate schema within memory.

Researchers then began to examine the self-concept at a neural level in order to identify potential regions or networks within the brain that preferentially process self-referential information. Using the self-reference paradigm, Craik et al. (1999) identified increased frontal activations associated with self-reference. Subsequently, a number of other studies have identified similar activations within the medial prefrontal cortex (MPFC) and posterior and anterior cingulate cortices associated with self-referential processing (see Northoff et al., 2006). A number of studies have similarly identified the involvement of cortical midline structures such as the dorsal and ventral medial prefrontal cortex (DMPFC, VMPFC) during the retrieval of autobiographical memories (e.g., Addis et al., 2009; Fink et al., 1996).

The consensus from these studies is that the concept of self and the processing of self-related information is central to the encoding and retrieving of information stored in episodic and autobiographical memory and that neural activations associated with this type of processing occur in cortical midline brain structures (Gilboa, 2004; Northoff et al., 2006). These findings demonstrate that the self is a powerful concept involved in the regulation and evaluation of personal identity and facilitates the processing of self-related information during decision making and memory retrieval.

The self within autobiographical memory

Current theoretical models discussing the self in relation to autobiographical memory reflect this reciprocal relationship between self-identity and memory (Conway & Pleydell-Pearce, 2000) Well-being depends on having a well-integrated model of self that arises by having coherence between one's current perception of the self and how one would like to see the self. The self-memory system (SMS) model developed by Conway and Pleydell-Pearce (2000) explicitly suggests that models of self drive autobiographical memory retrieval. According to this model, the self and more specifically the goals of the self function as control processes that modulate the formation of autobiographical memories. The SMS is conceptualized as being composed of the autobiographical memory knowledge base and the "working self," which operates numerous working memory control processes to maintain consistent and integrated representations of the self across time (Conway & Pleydell-Pearce, 2000).

A central process of the SMS is the construction of autobiographical memories. Generative retrieval involves a conscious strategy often used to retrieve specific autobiographical memories that serve to maintain self-identity. The initial stage in generative retrieval involves developing search criteria by specifying and elaborating on the mnemonic cues used in the memory search. At this stage criteria are also developed for establishing when activated representations correspond to retrieval specifications. The working self plays a central role in developing these criteria. The search process proceeds hierarchically. For instance, if a person wants to retrieve a happy memory, generative retrieval would first activate general event representations (e.g., "I am happy going out with friends on Saturday nights"). The activation of general event knowledge then facilitates the activation of event-specific knowledge (e.g., "Last Saturday night I went out for a birthday dinner"). Once these pathways through the knowledge base are activated, this knowledge becomes available to central executive control processes and to the retrieval model that reiteratively evaluates whether the goal of specific retrieval has been met. A second type of memory retrieval discussed as part of the SMS is known as direct retrieval (Conway& Pleydell-Pearce, 2000), or retrieval during which memories come to mind spontaneously, without the need for a strategic memory search. Somewhat similar distinctions between strategic and automatic memory retrieval processes are also present in other models of autobiographical memory; in such models, these retrieval processes are labeled voluntary and involuntary retrieval, respectively (Berntsen & Hall, 2004; Rubin et al., 2011). For an extended discussion of more automatic memory retrieval processes, see Berntsen (2009); see also Moulds and Krans, Chapter 8; Berntsen, Chapter 9.

Our memory for and reactions to self-related information, including our autobiographical memories, are stronger than for other types of information (Symons & Johnson, 1997). One potential explanation for this is that one of the roles of the self is to evaluate information and memories in terms of relevance to our current circumstances and working self-goals (Conway & Pleydell-Pearce, 2000). Therefore, information we perceive as personally relevant is often highly emotional in content (Berntsen et al., 2011).

Studies have shown that individuals remember positive information more frequently than negative information when this information is self-related. No such valence effects are identified when information is encoded in reference to someone else or when processed for general meaning (Denny & Hunt, 1992; Watson et al., 2008). Similar positivity biases are also evident in autobiographical memory; a review by Walker et al. (2003a) found that, in general, peoples' perceptions of past recollections were positively biased. Reviewing a number of studies that examined retrieval of positive, negative, and neutral events, they found that while 50% of the events people retrieved were associated with positive mood, only half that number (25%) were associated with negative mood, supporting the view that individuals more frequently retrieve positive memories. Furthermore, Rasmussen and Berntsen (2009) found that when participants were retrospectively asked to rate memory characteristics of important positive and negative autobiographical memories, participants were faster to retrieve positive memories and these memories came with stronger physical and emotional reactions and higher levels of reliving. More nuanced investigations have shown that this bias is not always present to the same degree (see studies of dysphoria, Walker et al., 2003b; and central and peripheral details, Berntsen, 2002); however, the bias remains robust within autobiographical memory research. Models of self-regulation suggest that the motivation to actively construct and maintain a positive view of the self might facilitate access to positive information and/or inhibit access to negative information when processed in a self-referential context (Baumeister, 1998). Furthermore, when this association between self-identity and positive information is altered, individuals report higher levels of psychopathology (Bradley & Mathews, 1983; Watson et al., 2008).

In the SMS model of autobiographical memory, Conway and Pleydell-Pearce (2000) employ motivational theory and self-discrepancy to explain the occurrence of emotions during autobiographical memory retrieval (Carver & Scheier, 1990). They suggest that emotions arise due to goal-monitoring processes within the SMS that aim to reduce discrepancy between actual (current self), ideal (the self one hopes to be), and ought self-representations (the self that society tells one he or she should be). Positive emotions reflect an acceptable rate of discrepancy reduction, whereas negative emotions reflect an increasing failure to reduce discrepancy between self-representations. In this way emotions are hypothesized to occur when changes in working self-goals have been attained, blocked, or threatened.

Based on this model, the self-positivity bias would indicate attainment or maintenance of an acceptable rate of progress toward working self-goals leading to maintenance of a positive self-concept. In contrast, when reductions in the self-positivity bias are identified during psychopathology, this would indicate a need to change some aspect of the self-memory system such as current working goals or current self-representations. Based on the assumptions of the SMS model, the function of emotions is then to regulate and maintain equilibrium within the self-memory system. Furthermore, the negative emotions present during higher levels of psychopathology would indicate disequilibrium within the self-memory model. However, increases in self-discrepancy may not be the only mechanism that influences psychological well-being. Evidence from clinical studies suggests that psychological well-being can be compromised not only by high levels of self-discrepancy but also by increased self-relevance and that both of these situations are associated with deficits in emotion regulation and increased levels of psychopathology.

Self-discrepancy and psychopathology

There is well-established evidence from the social cognition literature that a core feature of depression is a perceived discrepancy between actual self and ideal self (Higgins et al., 1986). The idea that discrepancy between actual and ideal selves can influence autobiographical memory retrieval is a core feature of the SMS model (Conway & Pleydell-Pearce, 2000). When a retrieval cue triggers a discrepancy, emotional deregulation may be initiated, particularly if ruminative brooding or depressive mood is present. During psychopathology when tension arises from emotional deregulation, activations of more abstract conceptual representations of the self occur. A priority for the SMS becomes maintenance of self-coherence, and, consequently, resources are directed away from retrieval of specific memories in order to avoid the retrieval of, and the emotions associated with, self-discrepant autobiographical memories. According to the SMS model, due to the interplay between self-identities and self-discrepant information during psychopathology the retrieval of categorical, nonspecific autobiographical memories is more likely to occur. The retrieval of fewer specific autobiographical memories and higher numbers of categorical memories has been implicated in the onset and maintenance of psychological disorders (Williams et al., 2007).

The relationship between self-discrepancy and autobiographical memory was first considered by Crane et al. (2007). In their study, formerly depressed individuals judged how relevant cue words on the autobiographical memory test were to their ideal, ought, and feared self-representations. They found that in formerly depressed individuals, higher numbers of cue words matching ideal, ought, and feared self-concepts were associated with reduced autobiographical memory specificity. This work inspired other research looking at the discrepancy between ideal and actual models of self and how such discrepancies can disrupt well-being through the retrieval of categoric memories.

A subsequent investigation by Van den Broeck et al. (2012) utilizing borderline patients further investigated the importance of depressed mood and trait rumination in producing a relationship between cue self-discrepancy and autobiographical memory retrieval (see also Van den Broeck and colleagues, Chapter 11). All participants constructed multiple self-guides of actual, ideal, ought, and feared selves by rating words on these dimensions. Discrepancy indices were computed by subtracting ratings of actual self from ratings of ideal, ought, and feared selves. An independent sample of raters then judged how close in meaning the words were to the autobiographical memory cues. From these ratings two measures were constructed, one assessing relevancy and the other assessing discrepancy. When compared with the remaining sample, the results of the borderline patients with comorbid depression showed that self-discrepancy but not self-relevancy was associated with reduced autobiographical memory specificity. Van den Broeck et al. (2012) extended the findings of Crane et al. (2007) by showing that discrepancy as opposed to relevancy was associated with reductions in memory specificity. The reductions in memory specificity were not found to be associated with rumination. One limitation of the study is that self-guides were generated before the autobiographical memory test was completed, perhaps priming certain schemas. Further, in both studies, there was no manipulation of the actual content of the retrieval cues.

In contrast, Schoofs et al. (2012) manipulated the self-discrepancy of the words employed to cue memory retrieval. An independent group of clinicians judged whether particular positive cue words would be likely to evoke discrepant responses. Words that would elicit the highest discrepancy and still be matched for frequency, imageability, and concreteness were selected. In the first study a large sample of adolescents retrieved significantly fewer specific memories to highly discrepant cues. In a second study the authors also obtained ratings of cue importance for the individual. Ratings of depressed mood and trait rumination were also obtained. The results of the second study replicated those of the first; once again the highly discrepant cues elicited fewer specific autobiographical memories. However, in contrast to Crane et al., who found self-relevancy to be related to autobiographical memory retrieval, self-relevance of the word cue was not found to be an important factor. Another inconsistency with previous work (e.g., Crane et al., 2007; Van den Broeck et al., 2012) is that these effects were found to be independent of depressed mood. Similarly, no association was found between trait rumination and cue self-discrepancy during autobiographical memory retrieval.

Several factors could account for the different findings across studies. One explanation for the lack of relationship with depressed mood in the study by Schoofs et al. may be that this study utilized adolescent participants. A more fragile and less-developed self-concept exists in this group; therefore, these participants may be more susceptible to the effects of self-discrepancy than young adults. Furthermore, in this study, cue discrepancy was directly manipulated during the autobiographical memory test, whereas this was not the case in the studies conducted by Crane et al. or Van den Broeck et al. It is also important to note that there are several limitations associated with this work. First, only positive cues were used, prohibiting an examination of the effects of the feared self.

Also, the cues were generated not by the adolescents but by a separate group of adults; therefore, the self-relevance of these cues may not directly tap into the self-representations of the adolescent group.

Another study, by Wessel et al. (2014), examined how the relationship between cue self-discrepancy and autobiographical memory retrieval was related to different processes in the CaR-FA-X model contributing to overgeneral autobiographical memory retrieval, namely, rumination and functional avoidance (Williams et al., 2007). The study also examined how autobiographical memory retrieval patterns elicited by self-discrepancy cues compared with affective cues related to self-report measures were associated with scores on measures of functional avoidance and two components of rumination, brooding and reflection. In this study of formerly depressed patients and controls, self-discrepancy measures were computed for actual, ideal, and feared selves by having participants rate word cues on these dimensions. Higher scores on an index of functional avoidance were related to memory performance on the affective cues but not the self-discrepancy cues. In contrast to previous findings, the self-discrepancy index between actual and ideal selves was associated with greater specificity in formerly depressed individuals scoring high on reflective rumination but not controls. The relationship between the brooding component of rumination and actual-ideal self-discrepancy was not associated with reduced memory specificity. This study suggests that individuals who engage in functional avoidance are more sensitive to cues reflecting affect as opposed to self-discrepancy and that the relationship between rumination, self-discrepancy, and autobiographical memory retrieval is contingent on the type of rumination that is undertaken.

Other research has examined self-discrepancy from a different perspective by investigating how it induces cognitive reactivity and subsequently impacts on the retrieval of autobiographical memory. Cognitive reactivity refers to how processing particular types of information associated with psychopathology induces emotional deregulation. In a study of formerly depressed patients (Raes et al., 2012), one group of participants made judgments about levels of ideal versus actual positive traits, while a second control group did not make these judgments. The instruction to compare ideal positive traits versus actual positive traits generated a state of cognitive reactivity. In the group experiencing cognitive reactivity, individuals who were high on trait rumination retrieved fewer specific autobiographical memories, whereas no such interaction was identified in the control group. A subsequent study by Smets et al. (2013) used the same discrepancy procedure to induce cognitive reactivity with a group of adolescents who were also assessed on trait rumination and depressive symptoms. Autobiographical memory specificity was measured before and after the self-discrepancy manipulation. In this study, depressive symptoms were associated with greater overgeneral recall following the self-discrepancy manipulation but not before it. However, in contrast to the formerly depressed patients in the Raes et al. study, the self-discrepancy manipulation produced no relationship between rumination symptoms and overgeneral memory assessed either before or after the discrepancy manipulation. These studies indicate that contrasting models of self induce a powerful cognitive reactivity that leads to overgeneral memory; however, there seems to be a lack of consistency as to whether this reactivity is associated with trait rumination or depressive symptomatology, and future work is needed to examine this issue further.

In summary, the research findings suggest that discrepancy between actual and ideal self-representations in retrieval cues leads to reductions in autobiographical memory specificity in individuals reporting high levels of depressive symptoms (Raes et al., 2012; Schoofs et al., 2012; Van den Broeck et al., 2012). However, self-discrepancy can also lead to increased specificity when higher levels of reflective rumination are employed (Wessel et al., 2014). The results highlight that cues reflecting self-discrepancy may be more sensitive in identifying differences in the ability to retrieve autobiographical memories. Furthermore, the way this discrepancy is appraised may also be important; engaging in reflective rumination as opposed to brooding may determine whether the impact of discrepancy on autobiographical memory retrieval is either facilitative or debilitative.

Self-relevance and psychopathology

One of the most robust findings related to depression is that depressed individuals show a bias toward self-negative information (e.g., Bradley & Mathews, 1983). In fact a growing body of research suggests that individuals reporting high levels of psychopathology have a tendency to focus on or report emotionally negative events as highly self-referent or important for their personal identities. A series of studies by Segal and colleagues (e.g., Segal, 1988) utilized a modified version of the Stroop naming task that involved a self-referential component. Their studies showed that interference on the Stroop color naming task was greatest for depressed compared with nondepressed individuals when both prime and target words were highly self-referent. Furthermore, Segal et al. (1995) found that Stroop latencies were particularly long when self-referent negative information was primed with a similar self-referent negative stimulus. Dozois and Dobson (2001) also found that relative to nonpsychiatric controls, depressed individuals endorsed more negative attributes as self-referential, recalled higher numbers of self-negative stimuli, and showed greater interconnectedness between self-negative information within their own self-representation. When compared with nonpsychiatric and anxious controls, both depressed and mixed depressed/anxious groups also showed a complementary bias in self-positive information; participants endorsed fewer and recalled lower numbers of positive attributes and had less interconnectedness between self-positive information. These findings support the view that at the level of general cognition, high levels of psychopathology are associated with increased attention toward and increased retrieval of highly self-referential material and that this effect is particularly pronounced when the self-referential task involves a focus on negative emotional material.

Extensive literature on self-focus and rumination has also shown that depressed individuals dedicate higher levels of self-focused attention to negative self-related information and depressive symptoms (Mor & Winquist, 2002) and that this negative analytical thinking about the self impacts on autobiographical memory retrieval (see Watkins, Chapter 10). Studies by Watkins (2004) and Watkins and Teasdale (2001) found that increased levels of abstract ruminative thinking are associated with lower levels of memory specificity in dysphoric and depressed individuals when asked to retrieve autobiographical memories in response to emotional cue words. Studies have also identified that analytical ruminative style is implicated in the onset and maintenance of psychological disorders such as depression (Watkins, 2008) and that therapies aimed at reducing analytical self-focus lead to reductions in rumination and improvements in symptoms of depression (Watkins et al., 2012). High levels of self-relevance have also been associated with high levels of clinical symptoms in naturally occurring autobiographical memories. Diary studies looking at involuntary and voluntary memories in clinical populations have found that relative to healthy controls, individuals with posttraumatic stress disorder (PTSD; Rubin et al., 2011; see also Rubin, Chapter 3) and depression (Watson et al., 2012) rate both types of memories as far more central to their personal identities and life stories. Similar relationships between event centrality for negative events and psychopathology have also been identified in retrospective autobiographical memory studies (Berntsen et al., 2011; Boals & Schuettler, 2011; see Boals and colleagues, Chapter 4), supporting the view that high levels of self-reference are associated with high levels of psychopathology during strategic and spontaneous autobiographical memory retrieval.

These findings suggest that identifying emotional, particularly negative information as highly self-relevant or important for personal identity is associated with higher levels of psychopathology. Diary studies of naturally occurring autobiographical memories and research into ruminative thinking also suggest that focusing on highly self-referential emotional material during daily life has implications for psychological well-being. Where the SMS employs motivational goal theories to account for the experience of emotion and psychological well-being (Conway & Pleydell-Pearce, 2000), these findings suggest that even a simple, potentially automatic, association between self-concept and negative emotions may be enough to drive changes in levels of psychopathology without the need for controlled conflict-monitoring processes associated with high levels of psychopathology during strategic memory retrieval.

The role of self-discrepancy and self-relevance in psychopathology: implications for memory retrieval

There is clear evidence that self-discrepancy between ideal and actual self-representations and high levels of self-focus or self-relevance result in disruptions during autobiographical memory retrieval and problems with psychological well-being. One important question then becomes: do findings extending from these two components of self-regulation represent similar or diverging disruptions in cognitive processing during psychopathology? Within the field of autobiographical memory, research into both of these areas is relatively recent; however, a review of a number of neuroimaging studies investigating self-referential processing during psychopathology may help clarify these issues further.

As outlined above the medial prefrontal cortex (MPFC) and other cortical midline brain structures are involved in the processing of self-referential material (Northoff et al., 2006). To further investigate the role of self-identity in depression, Lemogne et al. (2012) reviewed four studies that employed fMRI to investigate self-referential processing during major depressive disorder. All studies identified differential neural activations in areas of the MPFC in individuals reporting major depressive disorder relative to controls. Two studies that employed an event-related design requiring participants to switch from self-referential to non-self-referential tasks for each stimulus identified that depressed individuals reported lower activations in ventral regions of the MPFC than controls under conditions of self-reference (Grimm et al., 2009; Johnson et al., 2009). In the study by Johnson et al. (2009), reduced activation of the MPFC in depressed relative to control participants during self-reference was mainly due to a smaller deactivation of this area in the non-self-referent condition for controls relative to depressed participants. Johnson et al. (2009) then conducted a second study during which participants were asked to attend to self-referent and non-self-referent stimuli under conditions of analytical and experiential self-focus and distraction. In this second study, activations in the MPFC were less for depressed than control participants in the analytical self-focus condition, again due to the fact that the MPFC in the control participants was deactivated to a lesser extent in the distraction condition relative to depressed participants. No group differences were identified in the experiential self-focus condition. These findings suggest that both groups show relatively high activations of the MPFC during self-referential tasks. However, during distraction tasks, while MPFC activations are reduced in healthy individuals, MPFC activations remain higher in depressed participants.

In the two studies employing a block design during which trial stimuli were presented in blocks (i.e., one block of ten stimuli where participants made a self-referential evaluation followed by one block of ten stimuli where participants made a semantic judgment) activations in the MPFC showed a different pattern. Both studies found increased activations in dorsal regions of the MPFC in depressed participants relative to controls (Lemogne et al., 2009; Yoshimura et al., 2010). Furthermore, relative to controls, depressed individuals showed increased activations and functional connectivity between ventral and dorsal regions of the MPFC, including the supragenual anterior cingulate cortex (ACC) and the dorsolateral prefrontal cortex (DLPFC) (Lemogne et al., 2009).

Although initially these results seem contradictory, the authors outline a theoretical model of the depressive self based on how differences in mode of task/stimuli presentation across the studies leads to differences in MPFC activations and neural connectivity identified in depressed participants. This model outlines two potential neural pathways by which self-referential processing can be disrupted during depression. First, the authors suggest that differential activations in the ventral MPFC during depression, under conditions of event-related design (in which self and non-self-related stimuli are presented side by side), may reflect the relatively automatic process of tagging incoming information as self-referent. Furthermore, the lower levels of deactivation in this region during the distraction task in the study conducted by Johnson et al. (2009) may reflect increased self-focused attention being maintained during non-self-referential tasks during depression. These findings parallel findings in autobiographical memory literature that individuals reporting high levels of psychopathology show a natural and relatively automatic tendency to identify negative information as highly relevant. Furthermore, this relatively automatic process may also be associated with high levels of spontaneous forms of self-focus, such as rumination as seen in depressed participants.

The second set of findings revealed that under block design conditions (where self-referential judgments were made repeatedly) depressed individuals showed increased activations in the dorsal MPFC relative to controls and that compared with controls, depressed individuals displayed increased activations and functional connectivity between regions in the MPFC, including the ACC and the DLPFC. The DLPFC is thought to be involved in cognitive control (Brass et al., 2005) and the supragenual ACC is implemented in conflict monitoring (Kerns et al., 2004). Based on the increased connectivity between these regions in the depressed participants during self-referential tasks, the authors suggest that these regions are involved in strategic cognitive processes involving self-focus. They suggest that increased activations in the regions involving cognitive control and conflict monitoring during depression and the increased connectivity between these regions and regions in the MPFC reflect increased use of the self-monitoring system when discrepancy occurs between actual and ideal self-representations during self-referential evaluations. One limitation of these studies is that rather than measuring self-discrepancy directly, the authors infer use of conflict monitoring systems within self-reference based on the neural activations identified. Despite this limitation, the authors present a potentially useful account of how high levels of self-focus and self-relevance and increased self-discrepancy between self-representations may result in disturbances in cognitive processing during depression.

Within this model Lemogne et al. (2012) suggest that high levels of self-focus during depression are pervasive and are reflected in automatic cognitive processes, whereas the use of conflict monitoring during self-referential judgments involves greater use of cognitive control processes and therefore may occur to a greater extent during self-referential tasks involving strategic or top-down processes. The distinction between automatic and strategic cognitive processes is also evident in models of autobiographical memory retrieval such that involuntary memory retrieval is thought to be based on automatic cognitive processes, whereas voluntary retrieval involves more strategic processing (Berntsen, 2010; Conway & Pleydell-Pearce, 2000; Williams et al., 2007). Based on the model outlined by Lemogne et al. (2012), one may predict that while rumination and high levels of self-focus may influence both involuntary and voluntary autobiographical memory retrieval, discrepancies between actual and ideal self-representations may lead to greater disruptions in voluntary than involuntary memory retrieval when cognitive control is required; however, this hypothesis is yet to be tested. What the research outlined above suggests is that both self-relevance and self-discrepancy may lead to disruptions in autobiographical memory retrieval during psychopathology. The important task for us now as researchers is to determine whether these two pathways differentially affect cognitive impairments of the self during psychopathology.

Self-identity, culture, and psychopathology

Our identity reflects not just ourselves as individuals but also the culture in which we grow up. In line with this, cultural identity has been found to influence autobiographical memory retrieval. Individuals from Western cultures retrieve more specific memories, while individuals from Eastern cultures retrieve more general categoric memories. Han et al. (1998) found that in free narrative interviews American as opposed to Chinese children describe more specific past events, focus more on themselves as opposed to others, and produce more detailed narratives. Wang (2001) obtained similar findings investigating the qualities of early autobiographical memories reported by Chinese and European American college students. The Americans' earliest memories were more specific, self-focused, lengthier, and emotionally elaborate than those of their Chinese counterparts. In addition, the Americans' memories were also characterized as reflecting more autonomy and self-determination. In this study participants also generated self-descriptions. The greater focus on self in these descriptions positively correlated with the greater self-focus of the autobiographical memories. Wang (2001) concluded that models of self differ across cultures and therefore influence the autobiographical memory retrieval process.

According to Markus and Kitayama (2003), Western cultures have a more individualistic model of self, while Eastern cultures have a more collectivistic view. Western cultures are characterized as emphasizing an independent-oriented self whereby the self is viewed as an autonomous being that is separate from other individuals (Wang, 2001). This view of self arises from a culture emphasizing self-expression, individual uniqueness, and personal efficiency. In contrast, Eastern cultures emphasize an interdependent self whereby the self has important social roles, duties, and responsibilities and is viewed as part of existing relationships. This view of self arises from a culture emphasizing group solidarity, interpersonal connectedness, and personal humility. Thus one account for why there may be differences in specific and categoric retrieval as a function of culture may be due to the functionality of the memory (Wang, 2001). Distinctive, specific autobiographical memories (e.g., one's wedding day) help to create an individualistic representation of the self and a unique self-identity. Specific memories are also retrieved in Eastern cultures, but when retrieved they are more likely to reflect less self-autonomy than specific memories recalled by individuals from Western cultures (Wang, 2001). Conversely, categoric memory retrieval or retrieval of collections of events is more likely to occur in a cultural context where reduced self-differentiation is expected. Categoric memories are argued to facilitate integration into social networks (Wang, 2001). Knowledge about social conventions and rules comes from memories that represent scripts for social behavior (e.g., "going to school during the week"). The form of these script memories is often categoric. The origins of these functions may arise in childhood. There are differences in narrative style that arise as a function of culture (Wang, 2001). In American culture parent–child interactions tend to be highly elaborative and focus on discussions of individual feelings, choices, and opinions. In contrast in Chinese culture, parent–child interactions are more often characterized by factual descriptions and discussion of social responsibilities and behavioral expectations.

With respect to depression a cross-cultural study by Dritschel et al. (2011) illustrated how depression can disrupt this relationship between culture and self-representation. In this study, clinically depressed and nondepressed participants were recruited from both Taiwan and Britain. Participants were asked to retrieve specific autobiographical memories to emotionally valenced cue words. In line with previous studies the Taiwanese nondepressed participants retrieved fewer specific and more categoric memories than their British counterparts. With respect to the depressed samples this relationship was altered; culture did not differentiate autobiographical memory retrieval style as the depressed participants were universally overgeneral in their memory retrieval style.

This finding of cultural differences in specificity being overridden by depression was replicated with groups experiencing a history of trauma. Humphries and Jobson (2012) examined undergraduate British and Chinese students, with respect to their ability to retrieve specific autobiographical memories. The key finding that was irrespective of culture, individuals who experienced high levels of trauma were less specific in their autobiographical memory retrieval than individuals with low exposure to trauma. The conclusion from both studies was that mechanisms responsible for overgeneral retrieval in both depressed and traumatized populations are likely to override the effects of identity. A review of overgeneral memory in psychopathology suggests that the mechanisms leading to overgeneral memory consist of rumination, functional avoidance, and impaired executive functioning and are described in the CaR-FA-X model of Williams et al. (2007) (see Watkins, Chapter 10; Van den Broeck and colleagues, Chapter 11). A causal test of these mechanisms with respect to culture has not been conducted. However, this research reveals that when these mechanisms are in play, emotional deregulation occurs that disrupts the impact of cultural identity on autobiographical memory retrieval.

One further study from the PTSD literature illustrates how alterations in self influence the relationship between autobiographical memory retrieval and adjustment from PTSD using two different cultural groups. Jobson (2011) examined self-concept expressed in memories utilizing two dimensions of autonomous orientation: (1) the tendency to express autonomy and (2) self-determination. These dimensions were first described by Wang (2001). Culture creates schematic expectations about the level of autonomous orientation that should be expressed in memories. Reminiscing styles in collectivistic cultures focus on relationships, social interaction, and significant others while minimizing the role of autonomy and self-determination (Mullen & Yi, 1995; Wang & Fivush, 2005). In contrast, there is evidence that adults and children from individualistic cultures engage in a different reminiscent style that is more self-revealing and self-focused and expresses more autonomy and self-determination. In the study by Jobson (2011), the level of autonomous orientation of everyday and trauma memories were compared across individuals from individualistic and collectivistic cultures. In participants from the individualistic culture those with PTSD reported lower levels of autonomous orientation than trauma survivors without PTSD. Conversely, in the collectivistic culture group, trauma survivors with PTSD reported higher levels of autonomous orientation than trauma survivors without PTSD.

These findings were linked with appraisal; Ehlers and Clark (2000) report that a reciprocal relationship exists between appraisal and the nature of the trauma memory (see also Ehlers, Chapter 6). Trauma survivors with PTSD from both cultural groups reported greater appraisals of alienation. This appraisal of alienation functions to maintain post-traumatic stress symptoms but arises differently. In a collectivistic culture, alienation maintains PTSD because it results in the self becoming more disengaged from society. In contrast, in an individualistic culture the sense of self is lost, which causes greater alienation as the self is less differentiated in society. As Berntsen and Rubin (2007) highlight, trauma memories reflect schematic deviation that becomes the central cognitive reference.

Overall, these findings suggest that while the effects of cultural identity on the retrieval of specific autobiographical memories are overridden during psychopathology, some features of cultural identity such as autonomous orientation and alienation evident in traumatic and everyday remembering do contribute to psychological adjustment following trauma.

Conclusions

Research and thinking on the concept of self has a long and broad historical tradition, engaging the minds of religious scholars, philosophers, cognitive and clinical psychologists and neuroscientists alike. What is interesting is that despite this long and diverse research history our understanding of the self-concept has remained surprisingly stable. As proposed by early philosophers, consciousness forms an integral part of the self; our sense of self is influenced by our ability to remember past events; and we have multiple representations of self. What modern psychological research has helped to clarify is how psychopathology can influence these basic principles. Of relevance within the context of clinical perspectives on autobiographical memory is the repeated finding that changes in our self-representation are often associated with emotional dysregulation, increased levels of psychopathology, and reductions in psychological well-being.

Current models of the self in autobiographical memory (Conway & Pleydell-Pearce, 2000) suggest that discrepancies between actual and ideal self-representations are often associated with increased emotional dysregulation and higher levels of psychopathology. However, more recent research into self-focus (Watkins, 2008) and event centrality (Berntsen et al., 2011) together with evidence from neuroimaging studies (Lemogne et al., 2012) suggests that high levels of spontaneous self-focus and the automatic tagging of negative emotions or events as self-relevant may represent another pathway by which the relationship between self-identity and autobiographical memory is disrupted during psychopathology. What is novel about this model of the depressive self is that it suggests potential pathways by which the relationship between self-identity and emotional experience can be altered during both automatic and strategic cognitive processing. This component of the model may be particularly relevant to the study of clinical perspectives of autobiographical memory retrieval in which automatic or involuntary memory and strategic or voluntary memory retrieval processes are known to lead to the retrieval of memories with both similar and divergent memory characteristics during depression (Watson et al., 2012; 2013).

The research reviewed suggests that the relationship between self-identity and psychopathology is influenced not just at the level of the individual but also with regard to our cultural identity, which is shaped by the type of culture in which we grow up. This research suggests that outside the laboratory setting, we are surrounded by more information that we might use to help guide our self-identity judgments and memory retrieval, such as our culture, the views of our peers/family, our current situation, and our location. This additional information can be used in many ways to help shape our identity, thus acting as part of our emotion regulation system. In individualistic cultures traumatic experiences during PTSD are associated with lower levels of autonomous orientation, whereas the opposite is true for individuals reporting PTSD in collectivistic cultures (Jobson, 2011). Ultimately, regardless of culture these memory characteristics during PTSD were associated with increased alienation from cultural identity, causing individuals to feel excluded or detached from other individuals within their own society, again highlighting how disruptions to our identity at the level of both the individual and the culture have implications for our psychological well-being.

Overall, the studies reviewed here suggest a growing complexity in our understanding of how self-identity operates within autobiographical memory retrieval at the level of both the individual and the culture. Goals for future research may be unpacking the roles of self-relevance and self-discrepancy during psychopathology, considering the impact of cultural identity on psychopathology, and investigating the extent to which these features of self-identity can be implemented within psychological treatments. One implication is that training to have a more compassionate view of self may be just as important as specificity training in improving autobiographical memory retrieval. Training in self-compassion refers to learning how to be kind to instead of critical of ourselves when thinking about less desirable qualities and suboptimal achievements of the self (Neff et al., 2007). Indeed, Neff et al. (2007) have demonstrated that increased levels of self-compassion are associated with greater well-being. Thus, training the self presents an exciting new area for research in autobiographical memory.

REFERENCES

Addis, D. R., Pan, L., Vu, M. A., Laiser, N., & Schacter, D. L. (2009). Constructive episodic simulation of the future and the past: distinct subsystems of a core brain network mediate imagining and remembering. *Neuropsychologia, 47*, 2222–2238.

Baumeister, R. F. (1998). The self. In D. T. Gilbert, S. T. Fiske & G. Lindzey (eds.), *Handbook of Social Psychology* (4th ed.) (vol. 1, pp. 680–740). New York: McGraw-Hill.

Berntsen, D. (2002). Tunnel memories for autobiographical events: central details are remembered more frequently from shocking than from happy experiences. *Memory & Cognition, 30*, 1010–1020.

(2009). *Involuntary Autobiographical Memories: An Introduction to the Unbidden Past*. Cambridge University Press.

(2010). The unbidden past involuntary autobiographical memories as a basic mode of remembering. *Current Directions in Psychological Science, 19*(3), 138–142.

Berntsen, D., and Hall, N. M. (2004). The episodic nature of involuntary autobiographical memories. *Memory and Cognition, 32,* 789–803.

Berntsen, D., & Rubin, D. C. (2007). When a trauma becomes a key to identity: enhanced integration of trauma memories predicts posttraumatic stress disorder symptoms. *Applied Cognitive Psychology, 21,* 417–431.

Berntsen, D., Rubin, D. C., & Siegler, I. C. (2011). Two versions of life: emotionally negative and positive life events have different roles in the organization of life story and identity. *Emotion, 11,* 1190.

Boals, A., & Schuettler, D. (2011). A double-edged sword: event centrality, PTSD and posttraumatic growth. *Applied Cognitive Psychology, 25,* 817–822.

Bobrow, D. G., & Norman, D. A. (1975). Some principal memory schemata. In D. G. Bobrow., & A. Collins. (eds), *Representation and Understanding.* London: Academic Press.

Bradley, B., & Mathews, A. (1983). Negative self-schemata in clinical depression. *British Journal of Clinical Psychology, 22,* 173–181.

Brass, M., Derrfuss, J., Forstmann, B., & von Cramon, D.Y. (2005). The role of the inferior frontal junction area in cognitive control. *Trends in Cognitive Sciences, 9,* 314–316.

Carver, C. S., & Scheier, M. F. (1990). Origins and functions of positive and negative affect: a control-process view. *Psychological Review, 97,* 19.

Chappell, V. (1994). *The Cambridge Companion to Locke.* Cambridge: Cambridge University Press.

Conway, M. A., & Pleydell-Pearce, C. W. (2000). The construction of autobiographical memories in the self-memory system. *Psychological Review, 107,* 261–288.

Cottingham, J., Stoothoff, R., & Murdoch, D. (eds.) (1984). *The Philosophical Writing of Descartes.* Cambrige: Cambridge University Press.

Craik, F. I. M., Moroz, T. M., Moscovitch, M., Stuss, D., Winocur, G., Tulving, E., & Kapur, S. (1999). In search of self: a positron emission tomography study. *Psychological Science, 10,* 26–34.

Crane, C., Barnhofer, T., & Williams, J. M. G. (2007). Cue self-relevance affects autobiographical memory specificity in individuals with a history of major depression. *Memory, 15,* 312–323.

Denny, E. B., & Hunt, R. R. (1992). Affective valence and memory in depression: dissociation of recall and fragment completion. *Journal of Abnormal Psychology, 101,* 575.

Dozois, D. J., & Dobson, K. S. (2001). Information processing and cognitive organization in unipolar depression: specificity and comorbidity issues. *Journal of Abnormal Psychology, 110,* 236.

Dritschel, B., Kao, C. M., Astell, A., Neufeind, J., & Lai, T. J. (2011). How are depression and autobiographical memory retrieval related to culture? *Journal of Abnormal Psychology, 120,* 969–974.

Ehlers, A., & Clark, D. M. (2000). A cognitive model of posttraumatic stress disorder. *Behaviour Research and Therapy*, *38*, 319–345.
Fink, G. R., Markowitsch, H. J., Reinkemeier, M., Bruckbauer, T., Kessler, J., & Heiss, W. D. (1996). Cerebral representation of one's own past: neural networks involved in autobiographical memory. *Journal of Neuroscience*, *16*, 4275–4282.
Gilboa, A. (2004). Autobiographical and episodic memory – one and the same? Evidence from prefrontal activation in neuroimaging studies. *Neuropsychologia*, *42*, 1336–1349.
Grimm, S., Ernst, J., Boesiger, P., Schuepbach, D., Hell, D., Boeker, H., & Northoff, G. (2009). Increased self-focus in major depressive disorder is related to neural abnormalities in subcortical-cortical midline structures. *Human Brain Mapping*, *30*, 2617–2627.
Han, J. J., Leichtman, M. D., & Wang, Q. (1998). Autobiographical memory in Korean, Chinese, and American children. *Developmental Psychology*, *34*, 701–713.
Higgins, E. T., Bond, R. N., Klein, R., & Strauman, T. (1986). Self-discrepancies and emotional vulnerability: how magnitude, accessibility, and type of discrepancy influence affect. *Journal of Personality and Social Psychology*, *51*, 5.
Hume, D. (1739). *A Treatise of Human Nature*. Book 1, Part 4, Section 6.
Humphries, C., & Jobson, L. (2012). Short report: influence of culture and trauma history on autobiographical memory specificity. *Memory*, *20*, 915–922.
James, W. (1890). *Principles of Psychology*. London: Macmillan.
Jobson, L. (2011). Cultural differences in levels of autonomous orientation in autobiographical remembering in posttraumatic stress disorder. *Applied Cognitive Psychology*, *25*, 175–182.
Johnson, M. K., Nolen-Hoeksema, S., Mitchell, K. J., & Levin, Y. (2009). Medial cortex activity, self-reflection and depression. *Social Cognitive and Affective Neuroscience*, *4*, 313–327.
Kerns, J. G., Cohen, J. D., MacDonald, A.W. III, Cho, R. Y., Stenger, V. A., & Carter, C. S. (2004). Anterior cingulate conflict monitoring and adjustments in control. *Science*, *303*, 1023–1026.
Lemogne, C., le Bastard, G., Mayberg, H., Volle, E., Bergouignan, L., Lehéricy, S., Allilaire, J. F., & Fossati, P. (2009). In search of the depressive self: extended medial prefrontal network during self-referential processing in major depression. *Social Cognitive and Affective Neuroscience*, *4*, 305–312.
Lemogne, C., Delaveau, P., Freton, M., Guionnet, S., & Fossati, P. (2012). Medial prefrontal cortex and the self in major depression. *Journal of Affective Disorders*, *136*, e1–e11.
Lowe, E. (1995). *Locke on Human Understanding*. London: Routledge Publishing.
Markus, H., & Cross, S. (1990). The interpersonal self. In Pervin, L. A. (ed.), *Handbook of Personality: Theory and Research* (pp. 576–608). New York: Guilford Press.
Markus, H. R., & Kitayama, S. (2003). Culture, self, and the reality of the social. *Psychological Inquiry*, *14*, 277–283.

Mor, N., & Winquist, J. (2002). Self-focused attention and negative affect: a meta-analysis. *Psychological Bulletin, 128,* 638.

Mullen, M. K., & Yi, S. (1995). The cultural context of talk about the past: implications for the development of autobiographical memory. *Cognitive Development, 10,* 407–419.

Neff, K., Kirkpatrick, K., & Rude, S. (2007). Self compassion and adaptive psychological. functioning. *Journal of Research in Personality, 41,* 139–154.

Northoff, G., Heinzel, A., de Greck, M., Bermpohl, F., Dobrowolny, H., & Panksepp, J. (2006). Self-referential processing in our brain: a meta-analysis of imaging studies on the self. *Neuroimage, 31,* 440–457.

Raes, F., Schoofs, H., Griffith, J. W., & Hermans, D. (2012). Rumination relates to reduced autobiographical memory specificity in formerly depressed patients following a self-discrepancy challenge: the case of autobiographical memory specificity reactivity. *Journal of Behavior Therapy and Experimental Psychiatry, 43,* 1002–1007.

Rasmussen, A. S., & Berntsen, D. (2009). Emotional valence and the functions. *Memory & Cognition, 37,* 477–492.

Rogers, T. B., Kuiper, N. A., & Kircher, W. S. (1977). Self-reference and the encoding of personal information. *Journal of Personality and Social Psychology, 35,* 677–688.

Rubin, D. C., Dennis, M. F., & Beckham, J. C. (2011). Autobiographical memory for stressful events: the role of autobiographical memory in posttraumatic stress disorder. *Consciousness and Cognition, 20,* 840–856.

Schoofs, H., Hermans, D., & Raes, F. (2012). Effect of self-discrepancy on specificity of autobiographical memory retrieval. *Memory, 20,* 63–72.

Segal, Z. V. (1988). Appraisal of the self-schema construct in cognitive models of depression. *Psychological Bulletin, 103,* 147–162.

Segal, Z. V., Gemar, M., Truchon, C., & Horowitz, L. M. (1995). A priming methodology for studying self-representation in major depressive disorder. *Journal of Abnormal Psychology, 104,* 205–213.

Smets, J., Griffith, J. W., Wessel, I., Walscherts, D. & Raes, F. (2013) Depressive symptoms moderate the effects of a self-discrepancy induction on overgeneral autobiographical memory. *Memory, 21,* 751–761.

Symons, C. S., & Johnson, B. T. (1997). The self-reference effect in memory: a meta-analysis. *Psychological Bulletin, 121,* 371–394.

Van den Broeck, K., Claes, L., Pieters, G., & Raes, F. (2012). Memory specificity in borderline personality disorder: associations with depression and self-discrepancy. *Journal of Behavior Therapy and Experimental Psychiatry, 43,* S51–S59.

Walker, W. R., Skowronski, J. J., & Thompson, C. P. (2003a). Life is pleasant – and memory helps to keep it that way! *Review of General Psychology, 7,* 203.

Walker, W. R., Skowronski, J., Gibbons, J., Vogl, R., & Thompson, C. (2003b). On the emotions that accompany autobiographical memories: dysphoria disrupts the fading affect bias. *Cognition and Emotion, 17,* 703–723.

Wang, Q. (2001). Culture effects on adults' earliest childhood recollection and self-description: implications for the relation between memory and the self. *Journal of Personality and Social Psychology, 81,* 220–233.

Wang, Q., & Fivush, R. (2005). Mother–child conversations of emotionally salient events: exploring the functions of emotional reminiscing in European-American and Chinese families. *Social Development, 14*, 473–495.

Watkins, E. (2004). Adaptive and maladaptive ruminative self-focus during emotional processing. *Behaviour Research and Therapy, 42*, 1037–1052.

Watkins, E., & Teasdale, J. D. (2001). Rumination and overgeneral memory in depression: effects of self-focus and analytic thinking. *Journal of Abnormal Psychology, 110*, 353.

Watkins, E. R. (2008). Constructive and unconstructive repetitive thought. *Psychological Bulletin, 134*, 163.

Watkins, E. R., Taylor, R. S., Byng, R., Baeyens, C., Read, R., Pearson, K., & Watson., L. A. (2012). Guided self-help concreteness training as an intervention for major depression in primary care: a phase II randomized controlled trial. *Psychological Medicine, 42*, 1359.

Watson, L. A., Dritschel, B., Jentzsch, I., & Obonsawin, M. C. (2008). Changes in the relationship between self-reference and emotional valence as a function of dysphoria. *British Journal of Psychology, 99*, 143–152.

Watson, L. A., Berntsen, D., Kuyken, W., & Watkins, E. R. (2012). The characteristics of involuntary and voluntary autobiographical memories in depressed and never depressed individuals. *Consciousness and Cognition, 21*, 1382–1392.

Watson, L. A., Berntsen, D., Kuyken, W., & Watkins, E. R. (2013). Involuntary and voluntary autobiographical memory specificity as a function of depression. *Journal of Behavior Therapy and Experimental Psychiatry, 44*, 7–13.

Wessel, I., Postma, I. R., Huntjens, R. J., Crane, C., Smets, J., Zeeman, G. G., & Barnhofer, T. (2014). Differential correlates of autobiographical memory specificity to affective and self-discrepant cues. *Memory, 22*, 655–668.

Williams, J. M. G., Barnhofer, T., Crane, C., Herman, D., Raes, F., Watkins, E., & Dalgleish, T. (2007). Autobiographical memory specificity and emotional disorder. *Psychological Bulletin, 133*, 122–148.

Yoshimura, S., Okamoto, Y., Onoda, K., Matsunaga, M., Ueda, K., & Suzuki, S. I. (2010). Rostral anterior cingulate cortex activity mediates the relationship between the depressive symptoms and the medial prefrontal cortex activity. *Journal of Affective Disorders, 122*, 76–85.

Part V

Discussion

17 Autobiographical memory in clinical disorders: a final discussion

Dorthe Berntsen

Basic and applied researchers ideally collaborate in a cyclical manner. According to a standard view summarized and discussed by Herrmann (1998): "Basic researchers discover fundamental principles. Applied researchers apply these principles until inadequacies are detected, at which point applied researchers communicate the inadequacies to the basic researchers. Basic researchers then investigate the inadequacies until they find a way to improve the original principle" (p. 17).

However, the cyclical approach is far from (always) the reality in psychology, as pointed out by Herrmann (1998). This is also true for the field of autobiographical memory and psychopathology (see, e.g., McNally, 2003). Of course, this is not just a problem related to applied versus basic approaches to psychology, but rather a general problem of integration and cross-fertilization between subdisciplines in the field. Although the most recent decades have shown a growing exchange of ideas, methods, and findings between clinical and basic approaches to autobiographical memory, as demonstrated by many chapters in this book, there still are points of disagreement that may be rooted more deeply in different traditions than in conflicting evidence. Such points of disagreement are healthy to the extent they stimulate new research aiming at resolving them. Fortunately, this seems to be what is going on.

In the following, I discuss some of the questions that emerge from this collection of chapters. The purpose is not to repeat the many interesting reviews and analyses of these topics in the preceding chapters, but rather to provide some reflections of my own after reading these chapters. My discussion is structured around some of the major themes of this book: overgeneral memories, intrusive memories, and flashback, and the relation between autobiographical events and autobiographical knowledge.

Overgeneral memories

One of the most frequently studied phenomena in the field of autobiographical memory and psychopathology is overgeneral memory, defined as an inability to retrieve memories of specific experiences that took place on a particular day in the past. Because this phenomenon has been so extensively studied over the last decades, it is not surprising that it is analyzed and discussed in many chapters in this book (e.g., Bryant, Chapter 2; Watkins, Chapter 10; Van den Broeck and colleagues, Chapter 11; McNally and Robinaugh, Chapter 12; Rathbone and Moulin, Chapter 14; Brown and colleagues, Chapter 15; and Watson and Dritschel, Chapter 16). An impaired ability to retrieve specific autobiographical events when instructed to do so was originally identified in depressed and suicidal patients by Williams and Broadbent (1986). However, the study of this phenomenon now has branched out to a variety of disorders, such as posttraumatic stress disorder (PTSD) and complicated grief (see McNally and Robinaugh, Chapter 12), borderline personality disorder (BPD; see Van den Broeck and colleagues, Chapter 11 for a review), autism (see Crane & Goddard, 2008; see Rathbone and Moulin, Chapter 14, for a review), and schizophrenia (e.g., D'Argembeau et al., 2008; Riutort et al., 2003; see Rathbone and Moulin, Chapter 14 for a review).

The most commonly cited explanation for the overgeneral memory effect is the CaR-FA-X model, which describes overgeneral memory as the result of an interplay between three factors: (1) capture and rumination processes, (2) functional avoidance, and (3) impaired executive control processes (Williams et al., 2007). This model attempts to integrate clinical insights with a theoretical model of autobiographical memory, the self-memory system, introduced by Conway and colleagues (2000), which assumes a hierarchical organization of autobiographical knowledge with increasing levels of abstraction referring to decreasing levels of temporal specificity of autobiographical knowledge. Thus, at the bottom of the hierarchy is concrete episodic knowledge referring to events with a specific location in time and space. At more abstract levels are knowledge of nonspecific events and time periods encompassing more than a single episode (e.g., Conway, 2005; Conway & Pleydell-Pearce, 2000). According to the CaR-FA-X model, overgeneral memories are the result of strategic search processes becoming truncated at nonspecific levels in the autobiographical memory knowledge base, due to rumination, avoidance, or reduced executive control. For that reason, the person is unable to retrieve a memory for a specific event at the time of the task, although such events are likely to be stored in memory and may be accessible at a different time or with more support (e.g., Tulving & Pearlstones, 1966).

Because overgeneral memory has been found in many different disorders, it can be seen as a broad transdiagnostic phenomenon. However, it has attained little attention in this field that reduced episodic specificity is not necessarily a clinical phenomenon per se; it also is a phenomenon observed in healthy aging. In the literature on aging, reduced episodic specificity is often conceptualized as a binding problem or as reduced source memory – that is, an impaired ability to locate an object or an experience to a specific temporal and spatial context in order to form an accurate episodic memory (Johnson et al., 1993). Such problems, which increase with age, are generally attributed to declining frontal functioning (e.g., Glisky, 2001; Glisky et al., 2001). A natural question for future research is whether overgeneral memory as studied in psychopathologies is the same phenomenon as the decline in episodic memory details observed in aging, or whether the two are separate phenomena requiring separate explanations.

One way of approaching this question may be to employ a greater variety of methods in the study of the overgeneral memory in psychopathology, for example, by administering source memory tasks to participants suffering from depression (or suffering from other types of psychopathology showing the overgeneral memory effect). One commonly used test in relation to the decline of contextually specific episodic details observed in aging, which rarely has been used in clinical research, is the Autobiographical Interview, developed by Levine and colleagues (2002). In this test, the reported memory is coded for its relative content of episodic and semantic (nonepisodic) details. Studies have shown that the relative frequency of semantic details is higher among older individuals, whereas young individuals report more episodic details (Addis et al., 2008; 2010; Piolino et al., 2002; Schacter et al., 2013). Although this method also has been used in brain-damaged populations (Levine, 2004; Rasmussen & Berntsen, 2014), the majority of research conducted on overgeneral memory in psychopathological disorders is based on the standard autobiographical memory test, which uses positive and negative cue words to elicit the memories and a categorical coding system to assess whether they are about specific events. This is a robust method with well-documented effects (Williams et al., 2007). Still, it might facilitate further progress to combine this method with some of these more recent developments in the study of episodic memory in aging, and thereby triangulate across different methodologies.

Some of the mechanisms underlying reduced episodic specificity in aging may also be central to overgeneral memories in psychopathological disorders. Obviously, one key candidate would be reduced frontal lobe functioning, consistent with at least one of the three components of the CaR-FA-X model. Through an extensive series of experiments,

Dalgleish et al. (2007) demonstrated how reduced executive control appears to play a key role for the overgeneral memory effect in depression. However, meaning-making processes and rumination (e.g., Watkins, Chapter 10) may be other factors that cut across the overgeneral memory effect as observed both in psychopathology and in aging. Older adults tend to engage more frequently in meaning-making processes than do younger adults by relating individual episodes to other parts of their lives and by providing more contextual information for the narration of individual events (e.g., Habermas et al., 2013). Such (healthy) meaning-making processes are likely to lead to less detailed descriptions of individual events and thus to memory narratives with fewer episodic and more semantic details, as pointed out by Habermas et al. (2013). Although Habermas et al. in their reanalysis failed to find a direct relationship between an age-related increase in meaning-making processes and reduced episodicity in remembering in old age, meaning-making processes may still be part of the reason for the decline in episodic memory details in aging. Similarly, in depression and related disorders maladaptive meaning-making processes in terms of ruminative thinking have been shown to lead to overgeneral memories (Watkins, Chapter 10). As noted by Bluck et al. (2014), meaning-making processes, or life review, can be both functional, by causing integration and reflection, and dysfunctional, when associated with rumination and bitterness revival. In both cases, they may lead to reduced specificity in the memory narratives. In short, future research might explore such potentially shared mechanisms underlying reduced episodic specificity in psychopathology and in aging.

In clinical research, overgeneral memory has been found to predict the development of depression and complicated grief (e.g., Bryant, Chapter 2; Watkins, Chapter 10). Conversely, becoming more concrete and experiential when remembering and imagining personal events is associated with reduced emotional distress in individuals suffering from depression or related disorders (see Watkins, Chapter 10). This suggests that there is something uniquely beneficial about remembering and reliving concrete episodic details and thus mentally traveling through time (Tulving, 2002). This puzzling effect has gone almost unnoticed in basic memory research, although it has been described by several artists. One famous example is the French author Marcel Proust, who in his autobiographical novel *À la recherche du temps perdu* (In Search of Lost Time, or Remembrance of Things Past) lets his narrator describe several instances in which the concrete reliving of a vivid autobiographical memory is associated with a deep feeling of joy. This is not because the original experiences necessarily were happy, but rather because reliving them in the present gives him a sense of transcending his present existence: "Of a truth, the being within me which sensed this impression, sensed what it had in common in former days and now, sensed its extra-temporal character, a being which only appeared then through the medium of the identity of present and past, it found itself in the only setting in which it could exist and enjoy the essence of things, that is, outside Time" (Proust, 1949, p. 216).

We do not know whether such a feeling of transcendence may be a key to understanding the beneficial effects of concretely reliving past events in the present or whether a diversion from rumination is a sufficient explanation. Nonetheless, many people express joy associated with the very act of remembering detailed concrete episodes from their past, although there seems to be no direct utility associated with recollecting the event and its associated sensory details per se (for an illuminating discussion, see Pillemer, 1992). In spite of an accumulating amount of studies on the functions of autobiographical memories (e.g., Bluck et al., 2005; Harris et al., 2014; Pillemer, 2003), this issue has not been examined systematically. This would be an important question for future research.

Intrusive memories and flashback

Not all spontaneous reliving of past events is associated with joy, in contrast to the example from Proust. Intrusive memories also involve intense reliving, but here the accompanying feeling is distress. Intrusive memories and images are a defining symptom of PTSD, but are also common across a range of other disorders (e.g., Bryant, Chapter 2; Ehlers, Chapter 6; Clark and colleagues, Chapter 7; Moulds and Krans, Chapter 8). Clinical studies and observations have shown that intrusive memories are persistent, are often triggered by perceptual details, are highly vivid and emotional, and involve intense reliving (e.g., Ehlers, Chapter 6; Moulds and Krans, Chapter 8). Highly vivid intrusive memories with a strong sense of emotional reliving have been termed "flashbacks." However, disagreements exist as to exactly how the notion of flashback should be defined and whether it constitutes a separate clinical category of memory phenomena (see, e.g., Ehlers, Chapter 6; Clark and colleagues, Chapter 7; Brewin, 2014; Frankel, 1994).

Different research traditions have attempted to explain intrusive memories with diverse approaches. One position takes its starting point in basic research on autobiographical memory and proposes that characteristics of intrusive memories to a large extent can be explained by extrapolating mechanisms underlying everyday autobiographical memories to events characterized by extreme emotion. First, autobiographical remembering generally involves reliving, in the sense of mentally traveling back in time to reexperience the event, which is a defining characteristic of having an autobiographical recollection (Rubin, Chapter 3; Brewer, 1996; Rubin, 2006; Tulving, 2002). Second, autobiographical memories involve visual imagery more so than information from other sensory modalities (e.g., Brewer, 1996). Therefore, it is not surprising that intrusive memories and flashbacks also are dominated by visual imagery. Visual imagery is generally closely connected with emotional arousal (Clark and colleagues, Chapter 7; Daselaar et al., 2008) and predicts the extent to which the memory involves a feeling of reliving the past (e.g., Daselaar et al., 2008; Rubin & Berntsen, 2009). Third, all autobiographical memories have the potential of coming to mind involuntarily in the presence of relevant cues (Berntsen, Chapter 9). In addition, it is a robust finding that emotional events are well retained over time and may be remembered very vividly, albeit not necessarily accurately, even after many years (McGaugh, 2003). This (basic research) position claims that the additive effect of these factors may explain intrusive memories of stressful emotional events in combination with individual vulnerability factors (e.g., Rubin, Chapter 3; Berntsen, Chapter 9).

A second position takes its starting point in clinical research and observations of patients. Although this position also draws on well-established effects in the memory literature, such as priming and cueing mechanisms, its proponents often claim that additional (e.g., trauma-specific) mechanisms are needed to fully account for the distinct phenomenology of intrusive memories in psychopathology. For example, Ehlers (Chapter 9) proposes that certain aspects of the phenomenology of flashback and intrusive emotional reliving of the past are left unexplained by theories rooted in the autobiographical memory tradition (for similar arguments, see Brewin, 2014).

There are also agreements between the two positions. They both agree that the high emotional arousal at the time of the event is central for the development of subsequent intrusive memories, but they have very different accounts of the mechanisms underlying this development. According to the basic research position, the emotional arousal leads to an enhanced encoding and consolidation of the event in memory, which therefore stays highly accessible for both voluntary and involuntary retrieval (see, e.g., Rubin, Chapter 3; Berntsen, Chapter 9; Rubin, 2011). According to the clinical research position, the emotional stress during the event leads to faulty and fragmented encoding of the event. For this reason, the memory of the event is hard to access strategically (voluntarily), while it persistently may come to mind involuntarily. The latter position thus implies a differential effect of emotional stress on voluntary versus involuntary recall of the event, while the first position claims that voluntary and involuntary retrieval are affected in similar ways by emotional arousal at the time of the event.

One might suggest that such disagreements should be resolvable on the basis of relevant empirical studies. Unfortunately, very few studies involving clinical populations have examined both involuntary and voluntary memories as they occur in everyday life (Rubin et al., 2011; Watson et al., 2012). These studies do not provide support for the idea that emotionally distressing events are related differently to involuntary and voluntary recall. First, the frequency of traumatic and stressful material is not higher for involuntary compared with voluntary memories. Second, in these studies, the clinical sample generally reports memories that are rated as more negative and more vivid, emotional, and self-referential. However, this pattern is found across both involuntary and voluntary memories and across memories both with and without a traumatic or stressful content (Rubin et al., 2011; Watson et al., 2012). This is important because this suggests a general tendency among the clinically disturbed participants to react with stronger emotion in response to many different types of autobiographical memories.

The central importance of such dispositional factors has also been noted in many contributions to this book (see Bryant, Chapter 2; Rubin, Chapter 3; Clark and colleagues, Chapter 7; Moulds and Krans, Chapter 8; Habermas, Chapter 13). For example, in Chapter 8, Moulds and Krans suggest that individual differences in the appraisal of intrusive memories and images play a central role in their effects on the individual and their level of disruption. Bryant in Chapter 2 draws attention to the possible effects of gender differences in the processing and remembering of emotional stimuli. Furthermore, Habermas in Chapter 13 suggests that individuals suffering from PTSD may be more inclined to be dramatic in their description of the events in order to mentally draw the listener into their stressful past, which in turn may cause their memory narratives to appear fragmented. Similarly, Berntsen and Rubin (2014) suggest that the fragmentation of voluntarily retrieved trauma memories that sometimes is observed in individuals with PTSD may reflect a general deficit in strategic retrieval in this population, as reflected in the tendency of PTSD patients to report overgeneral memories in response to cue words (McNally and Robinaugh, Chapter 12; Brown and colleagues, Chapter 15). According to recent findings, such deficits would have stronger effects on voluntary than on involuntary remembering (Watson et al., 2013).

These alternative explanations can be relatively easily differentiated from the notion of trauma-specific mechanisms, as these characteristics would apply broadly across the person's autobiographical memories and thus not be limited to memories of the trauma. Attaining a deeper understanding of individual differences in autobiographical remembering is likely to help to clarify whether there is a need for trauma-specific mechanisms. Methodologically, it is important to include measures of memories of different types of (traumatic and nontraumatic) autobiographical events in studies comparing clinical and nonclinical populations. Only so is it possible to decide whether the characteristics are content or disorder specific (Rubin et al., 2011).

Autobiographical knowledge and autobiographical events

Memories of individual events are always nested in a larger organization of knowledge (Neisser, 1986). This organization develops dynamically as new events are added and integrated, changes when our lives change, and is likely to be affected by clinical disorders.

Many chapters in this book have dealt mostly with memories for individual events. However, a number of chapters have also discussed how discrete event memories are integrated with higher order structures, notably, narrative structures supporting the formation of self and identity (see, e.g., Boals and colleagues, Chapter 4; Watkins, Chapter 10; Habermas, Chapter 13; Rathbone and Moulin, Chapter 14; Brown and colleagues, Chapter 15; Watson and Dritschel, Chapter 16). The interplay between knowledge related to self and identity and concrete episodic knowledge related to particular events is obviously complex. Although memories of individual events are often thought to be building blocks for the stories we construct about our lives, and thus ultimately for our identity (Bluck et al., 2005), some research suggests that the loss of concrete memories (such as in dementia) does not necessarily disrupt a sense of identity (see Rathbone and Moulin, Chapter 14). Based on their review in this book, Rathbone and Moulin conclude that "there is a driving force to achieve personal continuity and this can be supported by either episodic or semantic systems."

Even if the loss or impairment of episodic memory abilities does not necessarily harm a sense of personal identity, it may indeed still be possible that a disturbed and disconnected life story and sense of identity would reduce the ability to retrieve episodic information and construct coherent memory narratives. Severe disturbances at this level of autobiographical knowledge (such as severe identity disturbances in BPD or in schizophrenia) appear to be accompanied by a reduced ability to construct coherent personal memory narratives (e.g., Bennouna-Greene et al., 2012; Berna et al., 2011; Jørgensen, 2006; Jørgensen et al., 2012). Habermas in Chapter 13 describes a number of ways in which autobiographical narratives may be formed by the psychodynamics associated with different clinical disorders.

PTSD is caused by one or more traumatic events in the past, according to the diagnostic criteria. Therefore, the interplay between memory for this concrete etiological event(s) and the broader conceptual autobiographical knowledge in which this memory is nested has been a topic for research and discussion (see Boals and colleagues, Chapter 4; Alley and colleagues, Chapter 5; McNally and Robinson, Chapter 12; Habermas, Chapter 13; Brown and colleagues, Chapter 15). One question that has received considerable attention is the relation between PTSD symptoms and the importance of the traumatic event for the person's life story and identity.

It is well documented that memories of significant personal events may serve as reference points for the organization of memories of less important events. They have been found to structure our life narratives temporally and thematically by providing turning points, forming beginnings and endings of lifetime periods (e.g., Conway & Pleydell-Pearce, 2000; McAdams, 2001; Robinson, 1992; Shum, 1998), and anchoring and stabilizing our conceptions of ourselves (Pillemer, 1998; Singer & Salovey, 1993). However, consistent with findings on a positivity bias in autobiographical memory (e.g., Walker et al., 2003; see Watson and Dritschel, Chapter 16), it is more common for positive than for negative events to show such centrality in healthy cognition. They thereby become foundation stones for life stories and identities, in part because their roles and strength are reinforced by cultural norms (Berntsen & Rubin, 2004; Berntsen et al., 2011). However, for some individuals who have encountered one or more severe traumas in their lives, a highly aversive event may become central to the organization of a person's autobiographical knowledge and ways of reasoning. When this happens, the temporal and thematic organization of autobiographical knowledge may change radically.

One early observation of this effect was reported by McNally et al. (1995). They found that veterans with PTSD who were still wearing their regalia recorded more memories of their time in Vietnam and more overgeneral (nonspecific) memories in response to both positive and negative cue words than did veterans with PTSD who were not wearing regalia. As wearing regalia indicates persistent identification with the time in Vietnam and with the role as a soldier, the findings from McNally et al. suggest that trauma memories may form reference points for the attribution of meaning to current events and for the generation of future expectations, with the result that the person's current mental life becomes enmeshed with the past traumatic experiences.

In an attempt to examine this effect more systematically, Berntsen and Rubin (2006) introduced the centrality of event scale, which measures the extent to which a highly emotional negative event has become a personal reference point for the attribution of meaning to other events, a salient turning point in the life story, and a central component of a person's identity and self-understanding. These three characteristics are highly correlated, although recent research suggests that they form different factors (McNally and Robinaugh, Chapter 12). An accumulating number of studies have shown that people reporting greater centrality of their most negative/traumatic event also score higher on measures of PTSD symptoms (for reviews, see Rubin, Chapter 3; Boals and colleagues, Chapter 4; Berntsen, Chapter 9; Brown and colleagues, Chapter 15). Findings reported by Boals and colleagues (see Boals and colleagues, Chapter 4) suggest that the centrality of the traumatic event is critical also for posttraumatic growth, and thus not simply detrimental to a person's well-being.

The nested organization of autobiographical memory as conceptualized by Conway and Pleydell-Pearce (2000) is often used as a starting point for understanding the relation between the self and concrete autobiographical memories in psychopathology (for a review and discussion, see Watson and Dritschel, Chapter 16). However, the hierarchical structure as described in this particular model with temporally segmented layers of autobiographical knowledge may ignore dimensions in autobiographical memory organization that are based not on a temporal organization, but instead on emotion or knowledge of relationships. Such forms of organization may be especially important in some clinical disorders. For example, psychodynamic theories (e.g., Horowitz, 1988) have been concerned with the kinds of schemata we develop for relationships with concrete individuals, a topic closely associated with attachment (see Alley and colleagues, Chapter 5). Horowitz (1988) introduced the notion of person schemata, which depict individual relationships with significant others, including anticipations for these relationships in the future. The schemata "summarize past interpersonal experience into integrated, generalized, and modular forms against which incoming information is measured and reorganized for 'goodness-of-fit'" (Horowitz, 1988, p. 13). Such schemata may also strongly influence the organization of autobiographical memory; that is, how we segment our experiences and nest them into higher order structures may be influenced by our relationships with significant others. As noted by Linton (1986), some memories may contain information that is highly indicative of our relationship with particular others and may be used as reference points for how we understand this relationship. She observed that "sometimes my whole relationship with people spanning years or decades seems encapsulated in a series of such fragments" (p. 53).

On a similar note, it is likely that organization according to the emotional tone of events (e.g., whether pleasant or unpleasant) may become more dominant in disorders with a tendency for black and white thinking. In extreme cases, a division into positive (good) and negative (bad) occurs, which is known as "splitting" in the psychodynamic literature (Habermas, 2012). This primitive defense mechanism, which may be often found in personality disorders, such as BPD, may obscure more emotionally sophisticated and reflective organization and integration of individual events into broader structures of autobiographical knowledge (e.g., Berntsen & Rubin, 2012; Jørgensen, 2006). This may render the life stories of individuals with such problems temporally and thematically fragmented. Also, a different type of autobiographical memory organization may be found in disorders characterized by delusional self-beliefs (for examples, see Rathbone and Moulin, Chapter 14).

The basic point is that we know relatively little about how the organization of autobiographical memory may change dynamically as a consequence of the phenomenology of different mental disorders, although promising work is budding (for reviews, see Rathbone and Moulin, Chapter 14; Watson & Dritschel, Chapter 16). Attaining a deeper understanding of such possible differences and disorder-related changes is an important topic for future research. A unique developmental approach to this question is found in the research carried out by Goodman and colleagues (see Alley and colleagues, Chapter 5). Among other things, this line of research examines how coping with childhood maltreatment influences the development of autobiographical memory and may cause dysfunctional emotion regulation strategies. This underscores the importance of viewing the role of the effects of trauma in a broader, life story perspective and in relation to attachment. For further discussions on the interaction between self-knowledge and memories of specific traumatic or negative events, see Habermas, Chapter 13; Brown and colleagues, Chapter 15; and Watson and Dritschel, Chapter 16.

Future directions

From forming a relatively exclusive field consisting of a handful of innovative and far-sighted psychologists, who wanted to attain a deeper understanding of the overgeneral memory effect in depression, the field of autobiographical memory in clinical disorders has grown enormously to now include a variety of disorders and a large selection of different memory phenomena. In addition to the overgeneral memory effect, other research topics now include the visual perspective of the reported memories (e.g., Bryant, Chapter 2), the level of subjective reliving (e.g., Rubin, Chapter 3), the narrative structure of memory reports (e.g., Habermas, Chapter 13), and the content and frequency of intrusive memories (e.g., Ehlers, Chapter 6; Clark and colleagues, Chapter 7; Moulds and Krans, Chapter 8). One insight from this wide range of research is that many disturbances of autobiographical memory appear to be present across different disorders rather than being disorder-specific. To move the field forward, it will be important to identify which autobiographical memory disturbances are specific to particular disorders and which are general. For example, some research suggests that the phenomenon of flashback may differentiate PTSD from other disorders (e.g., Bryant et al., 2011). If this indeed is the case, it seems pertinent to arrive at a clearer definition of what exactly constitutes a flashback experience (for a similar point, see Brewin, 2014).

Even though many disorders have gained attention from autobiographical memory research, this research tends to be dominated by studies on autobiographical remembering in depression and PTSD. More research is needed on autobiographical memory disturbances in other psychopathologies, such as eating disorders, anxiety disorders, bipolar disorder, schizophrenia, autism, and personality disorders, to further develop the budding research already existing in these areas.

The ability to remember personal events is at the heart of what defines an individual as a person with obligations, roles, and commitments in a given society (Berntsen & Rubin, 2012). It is likely to have evolved to allow us to participate in complex social systems. It is therefore not surprising that disturbances of autobiographical memory are found in many clinical disorders. Establishing the causal relation between such autobiographical disturbances and the development and maintenance of the disorders is an important topic for future research. Not only will this allow us to attain a deeper understanding of the disorders as well as of autobiographical memory, it may also facilitate the development of new psychological treatments that are more efficient than those available today.

Acknowledgments

Thanks to Lynn A. Watson for suggestions to the content of this chapter and to Tine Bennedsen Gehrt for her assistance. Thanks to Müge Özbek for comments to a previous version of the chapter; I am especially indebted to her for drawing my attention to the possible relation between meaning-making processes and reduced memory specificity. Thanks to Danish National Research Foundation for funding (DNRF93).

REFERENCES

Addis, D. R., Wong, A. T., & Schacter, D. L. (2008). Age-related changes in the episodic simulation of future events. *Psychological Science*, 19(1), 33–41.

Addis, D. R., Musicaro, R., Pan, L., & Schacter, D. L. (2010). Episodic simulation of past and future events in older adults: evidence from an experimental recombination task. *Psychology and Aging*, 25(2), 369–376.

Bennouna-Greene, M., Berna, F., Conway, M. A., Rathbone, C. J., Vidailhet, P., & Danion, J.-M. (2012). Self-images and related autobiographical memories in schizophrenia. *Consciousness and Cognition*, 21, 247–257.

Berna, F., Bennouna-Greene, M., Potheegadoo, J., Verry, P., Conway, M. A., & Danion, J. M. (2011). Impaired ability to give a meaning to personally significant events in patients with schizophrenia. *Consciousness and Cognition*, 20, 703–711.

Berntsen, D., & Rubin, D. C. (2004). Cultural life scripts structure recall from autobiographical memory. *Memory and Cognition*, 32, 427–442.

(2006). The Centrality of Event Scale: a measure of integrating a trauma into one's identity and its relation to post-traumatic stress disorder symptoms. *Behaviour Research and Therapy*, 44, 219–231.

(2012). Understanding autobiographical memory: an ecological theory. In D. Berntsen & D. C. Rubin (eds.), *Understanding Autobiographical Memory: Theories and Approaches* (pp. 333–355). Cambridge: Cambridge University Press.

(2014). Involuntary memories and dissociative amnesia: assessing key assumptions in PTSD research. *Clinical Psychological Science*, 2, 174–186.

Berntsen, D., Rubin, D. C., & Siegler, I. C. (2011). Two versions of life: emotionally negative and positive life events have different roles in the organization of life story and identity. *Emotion*, 11, 1190–1201.

Bluck, S., Alea, N., Habermas, T., & Rubin, D. C. (2005). A TALE of three functions: the self-reported uses of autobiographical memory. *Social Cognition*, 23, 97–117.

Bluck, S. Alea, N., & Ali, S. (2014). Remembering the historical roots of remembering the personal past. *Applied Cognitive Psychology*, 28, 290–300.

Brewer, W. F. (1996). What is recollective memory? In D. C. Rubin (ed.), *Remembering Our Past: Studies in Autobiographical Memory* (pp. 19–66). Cambridge: Cambridge University Press.

Brewin, C. R. (2014). Episodic memory, perceptual memory, and their interaction: foundations for a theory of posttraumatic stress disorder. *Psychological Bulletin.* 140, 69–97.

Bryant, R. A., O'Donnell, M. L., Creamer, M., McFarlane, A. C., & Silove, D. (2011). Posttraumatic intrusive symptoms across psychiatric disorders. *Journal of Psychiatric Research*, 45, 842–847.

Conway, M. A. (2005). Memory and the self. *Journal of Memory and Language*, 53, 594–628.

Conway, M. A., & Pleydell-Pearce, C. W. (2000). The construction of autobiographical memories in the self-memory system. *Psychological Review*, 107, 261–288.

Crane, L., & Goddard, L. (2008). Episodic and semantic autobiographical memory in adults with autism spectrum disorders. *Journal of Autism and Developmental Disorders*, 38(3), 498–506.

Dalgleish, T., Williams, J. M. G., Golden, A.-M. J., Barnard, P. J., Au-Yeung, C., et al. (2007). Reduced specificity of autobiographical memory and depression: the role of executive processes. *Journal of Experimental Psychology: General*, 136, 23–42.

D'Argembeau, A., Raffard, S., & Van der Linden, M. (2008). Remembering the past and imagining the future in schizophrenia. *Journal of Abnormal Psychology*, 117, 247–251.

Daselaar, S. M., Rice, H. J., Greenberg, D. L., Cabeza, R., LaBar, K. S., & Rubin, D. C. (2008). The spatiotemporal dynamics of autobiographical memory: neural correlates of recall, emotional intensity, and reliving. *Cerebral Cortex*, 18, 217–229.

Frankel, F. H. (1994). The concept of flashback in historical perspective. *International Journal of Clinical and Experimental Hypnosis*, 42, 321–336.

Glisky, E. L. (2001). Source memory, aging, and the frontal lobes. In M. Naveh-Benjamin, M. Moscovitch, & H. L. Roediger III (eds.), *Perspectives on Human Memory and Cognitive Aging: Essays in Honor of Fergus Craik* (pp. 265–276). New York: Taylor & Francis.

Glisky, E. L., Rubin, S. R., & Davidson, P. S. R. (2001). Source memory in older adults: an encoding or retrieval problem? *Journal of Experimental Psychology: Learning, Memory, and Cognition*, 27, 1131–1146.

Habermas, T. (2012). Identity, emotion, and the social matrix of autobiographical memory: A psychoanalytic narrative view. In D. Berntsen & D. C. Rubin (eds.), *Understanding Autobiographical Memory: Theories and Approaches*. Cambridge: Cambridge University Press.

Habermas, T., Diel, V., & Welzer, H. (2013). Lifespan trends of autobiographical remembering: episodicity and search for meaning. *Consciousness and Cognition*, 22, 1061–1073.

Harris, C. B., Rasmussen, A. S., & Berntsen, D. (2014). The functions of autobiographical memory: an integrative approach. *Memory*, 22(5), 559–581.

Herrmann, D. J. (1998). The relationship between basic research and applied research in memory and cognition. In C. P. Thompson, D. J. Herrmann, D. Bruce, J. D. Read, D. G. Payne, & M. P. Toglia (eds.), *Autobiographical Memory: Theoretical and Applied Perspectives* (pp. 13–28). Mahwah, NJ: Lawrence Erlbaum.

Horowitz, M. J. (1988). Person schemas. In M. J. Horowitz (ed.), *Person Schemas and Maladaptive Interpersonal Patterns* (pp. 13–31). Chicago, IL: University of Chicago Press.

Johnson, M. K., Hastroudi, S., & Lindsay, D. S. (1993). Source monitoring. *Psychological Bulletin, 114*, 3–28.
Jørgensen, C. R. (2006). Disturbed sense of identity in borderline personality disorder. *Journal of Personality Disorders, 20*, 618–644.
Jørgensen, C. R., Berntsen, D., Bech, M., Kjølbye, M., Bennedsen, B., & Ramsgaard, S. B. (2012). Identity-related autobiographical memories and cultural life scripts in patients with borderline personality disorder. *Consciousness and Cognition, 21*, 788–798.
Levine, B. (2004). Autobiographical memory and the self in time: brain lesion effects, functional neuroanatomy, and lifespan development. *Brain and Cognition, 55*, 54–68.
Levine, B., Svoboda, E., Hay, J. F., Winocur, G., & Moscovitch, M. (2002). Aging and autobiographical memory: dissociating episodic from semantic retrieval. *Psychology and Aging, 17*, 677–689.
Linton, M. (1986). Ways of searching and the content of memory. In D. C. Rubin (ed.), *Autobiographical Memory* (pp. 50–67). New York: Cambridge University Press.
McAdams, D. P. (2001). The psychology of life stories. *Review of General Psychology, 5*, 100–122.
McGaugh, J. L. (2003). *Memory and Emotion: The Making of Lasting Memories*. New York: Columbia University Press.
McNally, R. J. (2003). *Remembering Trauma*. Cambridge, MA: Harvard University Press.
McNally, R. J., Lasko, N. B., Macklin, M. L., & Pitman, R. K. (1995). Autobiographical memory disturbance in combat-related post-traumatic stress disorder. *Behavioral Research and Therapy, 33*, 619–630.
Neisser, U. (1986). Nested structure in autobiographical memory. In D. C. Rubin (ed.), *Autobiographical Memory* (pp. 71–82). Cambridge: Cambridge University Press.
Pillemer, D. B. (1992). Remembering personal circumstances: a functional analysis. In E. Winograd & U. Neisser (eds.), *Affect and Accuracy in Recall: Studies of "Flashbulb" Memories* (4th ed.) (pp. 236–264). Emory Symposia in Cognition. New York: Cambridge University Press.
  (1998). *Momentous Events, Vivid Memories*. Cambridge, MA: Harvard University Press.
Piolino, P., Desgranges, B., Benali, K., & Eustache, F. (2002). Episodic and semantic remote autobiographical memory in ageing. *Memory, 10*(4), 239–257.
Proust, M. (1949). *Remembrance of Things Past*, vol. 12: *Time Regained*. Trans. Stephen Hudson. London: Chatto & Windus.
Rasmussen, K., & Berntsen, D. (2014). Autobiographical memory and episodic future thinking after moderate to severe traumatic brain injury. *Journal of Neuropsychology, 8*(1), 34–52.
Riutort, M., Cuervo, C., Danion, J. M., Peretti, C. S., & Salamé, P. (2003). Reduced levels of specific autobiographical memories in schizophrenia. *Psychiatry Research, 117*(1), 35–45.

Robinson, J. A. (1992). First experience memories: context and functions in personal histories. In M. A. Conway, D. C. Rubin, H. Spinnler, & W. A. Wagenaar (eds.), *Theoretical Perspectives on Autobiographical Memory* (pp. 223–239). Dordrecht: Kluwer Academic.

Rubin, D. C. (2006). The basic-systems model of episodic memory. *Perspectives on Psychological Science, 1,* 277–311.

(2011). The coherence of memories for trauma: evidence from posttraumatic stress disorder. *Consciousness and Cognition, 20,* 857–865.

Rubin, D. C., & Berntsen, D. (2009). The frequency of voluntary and involuntary autobiographical memories across the lifespan. *Memory and Cognition, 37,* 679–688.

Rubin, D. C., Dennis, M. F., & Beckham, J. C. (2011). Autobiographical memory for stressful events: the role of autobiographical memory in posttraumatic stress disorder. *Consciousness and Cognition, 20,* 840–856.

Schacter, D. L., Gaesser, B., & Addis, D. R. (2013). Remembering the past and imagining the future in the elderly. *Gerontology, 59,* 143–151.

Shum, M. S. (1998). The role of temporal landmarks in the autobiographical memory processes. *Psychological Bulletin, 124,* 423–442.

Singer, J. A., & Salovey, P. (1993). *The Remembered Self: Emotion and Memory in Personality.* New York: Free Press.

Tulving, E. (2002). Episodic memory: from mind to brain. *Annual Review of Psychology, 53,* 1–25.

Tulving, E., & Pearlstone, Z. (1966). Availability versus accessibility of information in memory for words. *Journal of Verbal Learning and Verbal Behavior, 5,* 381–391.

Walker, W. R., Skowronski, J. J., & Thompson, C. P. (2003). Life is pleasant – and memory helps to keep it that way! *Review of General Psychology, 7,* 203–210.

Watson, L. A., Berntsen, D., Kuyken, W., & Watkins, E. R. (2012). The characteristics of involuntary and voluntary autobiographical memories in depressed and never depressed individuals. *Consciousness and Cognition, 21,* 1382–1392.

(2013). Involuntary and voluntary autobiographical memory specificity as a function of depression. *Journal of Behavior Therapy and Experimental Psychiatry, 44*(1), 7–13.

Williams, J. M. G., & Broadbent, K. (1986). Autobiographical memory in suicide attempters. *Journal of Abnormal Psychology, 95,* 144–149.

Williams, J. M. G, Barnhofer, T., Crane, C., Hermans, D., Raes, F., Watkins, E., & Dalgleish, T. (2007). Autobiographical memory specificity and emotional disorder. *Psychological Bulletin, 133,* 122–148.

Index

aboutness, in PTSD. *See* intentionality, in PTSD
abstract thinking style, 144
Acceptance and Commitment Therapy (ACT), 70–1
active memory storage, 181
acute stress disorder, 123
adrenergic agonists, arousal and, 21
affect without recollection, 111–12
agency, in narratives, 272–3
agoraphobia, 154
  narratives with, 281–2
alien abduction, false autobiographical memories of, 254–6
Alzheimer's Disease
  anosognosia with, 309
  selfhood with, 296
AMI. *See* Autobiographical Memory Interview
amnesia
  AMI for, 298
  selfhood with, 297–300
AMQ. *See* Autobiographical Memory Questionnaire
AMT. *See* Autobiographical Memory Test
anchor events, 74
anosognosia, 309
anxiety
  event centrality and, 69
  rumination and, 200
anxiety disorders. *See also specific disorders*
  narratives with, 281–3
arousal
  adrenergic agonists and, 21
  glucocorticoid systems and, 22
  intrusive memories and, 21
  stress hormones and, 22
  trauma and, 21–3
ASD. *See* autism spectrum disorder
associative learning processes, 115–16
attachment theory
  autobiographical memory and, 93–4
  childhood abuse and, 93–4, 98
  defensive exclusion in, 93–4
  emotional regulation and, 98
attention. *See* narrowed attention
autism spectrum disorder (ASD)
  memory impairment with, 303–5
  OGM with, 247
  selfhood with, 303–6
  self-images with, 306
  SRE with, 304
autobiographical memory. *See also* false autobiographical memories; heightened autobiographical memory; impaired autobiographical memory; overgeneral memory; posttraumatic stress disorder
  acute stress disorder and, 123
  alterations of, 1
  attachment theory and, 93–4
  autonoetic awareness and, 111–12
  Bartlett on, 2
  basic system model for, 45–7
  behavioral results of, 48–50
  bottom-up disorders and, 8–9
  CaRFAX model of, 18, 205–6, 235
  CBM with, 143
  change in, 45–6
  childhood abuse and, 95–8
  clinical disorders and, 1
  in clinical psychology, 1–2
  cognition and, 67–8
  cognitive psychology and, 1
  construction of, 41, 43–7
  core structures, 88
  emotional, 87–8
  emotional regulation in, 95
  Freud on, 2
  as function of psychopathology, 1, 6–7
  functions of, 1

378 Index

autobiographical memory. (cont.)
　hierarchical organization of, 318–19
　identity and, 10–11, 30–2
　intrusive memories and, 160
　involuntary, 184–7
　across lifespan, 293–4
　loss of narrative reason in, 48
　multiple dimensions of, 54–5
　narratives and, 267–8
　negative cues and, 6
　neurobiological perspectives on, 87–9
　neuroimaging literature on, 48
　neuropsychological effects of, 47–8
　organization of knowledge for, 368–71
　positive cues and, 6
　psychological well-being and, 10–11
　reconstructive nature of, 32
　retrieval of specific memories, 6
　the self within, 338–40
　self-discrepancy and, 340–1
　selfhood and, 481.90
　SMS and, 338–40
　special mechanisms of, 55–8
　stability of, 45–6
　top-down cognitive models of, 8–9
　trauma and, 7–8
　for twins, 43–4
　uniqueness of, 185–6
　voluntary, 184
　working self in, 319
Autobiographical Memory Interview
　　(AMI), 298, 363
Autobiographical Memory Questionnaire
　　(AMQ), 49–50
Autobiographical Memory Test (AMT),
　　204, 221
　for BPD, 224–5, 231–4
　for CG, 256–7
　CSA and, 249
　for PTSD, 244–5
　for war veterans, 244–5
autobiographical narrators, 273
autonoetic awareness, 111–12
avoidant coping, 95

Baddeley's model, of working memory,
　138
Bartlett, Frederic C., 2
basic system model, for autobiographical
　　memory, 45–7
　component system in, 46
　event memory system in, 46–7
　search-and-retrieval system in, 46–ENF
basolateral nucleus of the amygdala (BLA),
　21

bipolar disorder
　intrusive memories, 154
　mental imagery with, 141–2
BLA. *See* basolateral nucleus of the
　　amygdala
borderline personality disorder (BPD)
　AMT characteristics in, 224–5, 231–4
　comorbidity with, 223
　diagnostic status and, 224–31
　emotional regulation with, 235–6
　etiology of, 222–3
　memory specificity with, 229–30, 232
　narratives with, 284–5
　OGM and, 224–33
　rumination and, 235
　severity of, 224–31
　socio-demographics of, 231–3
　stress reduction with, 236
　symptoms of, 224–31
bottom-up disorders, autobiographical
　memory and, 8–9
BPD. *See* borderline personality disorder
brooding, 277–8. *See also* rumination
bundle theory, of self, 336

Capture and Rumination, Functional
　　Avoidance, and Executive Function
　　(CaRFAX) model
　of autobiographical memory, 18, 205–6,
　　235
　mnemonic interlock process and, 206
　OGM and, 18, 205–6, 235, 362–4
category fluency tasks, 203–4
CBM. *See* cognitive bias modification
CBT. *See* Cognitive Behavioural Therapy
Centrality of Events Scale (CES), 68, 370
　for childhood abuse, 246
　for recall of trauma memories, 177–9
　for self-identity, in PTSD, 322
　for sexual abuse, 246
　for women, 246
CG. *See* complicated grief
childhood abuse. *See also* heightened
　　autobiographical memory; impaired
　　autobiographical memory
　attachment theory and, 93–4, 98
　autobiographical memory and, 95–8
　avoidant coping with, 95
　CES for, 246
　Christianson's model and, 90
　defensive responses in, 92
　depression and, 87
　dissociative disorders and, 86–7, 91–2
　emotional regulation and, 89, 95–8
　OGM and, 92–3, 95

Index

orienting responses in, 92
physical examinations for, 95–6
PTSD and, 86
repression in, 91–2
survival processing in, 90
threat cues and, 91
trauma-related psychopathology and, 95–8
childhood sexual abuse (CSA)
AMT and, 249
depression and, 249–50
DID and, 251–3
memory recall after, 248–9, 251–2
OGM and, 248–53
PTSD and, 249–52
repression after, 248–9
SCEPT and, 250
Christianson's model, 90
cognition
autobiographical memory and, 67–8
PTSD and, 67–8
Cognitive Behavioural Therapy (CBT)
for PTSD, 140
RFCBT, 210–11
cognitive bias modification (CBM)
autobiographical memory and, 143
in clinical studies, 145
mental imagery with, 143–4
positive imagery-based, 145
thinking styles and, 144
cognitive models
of autobiographical memory, 67–8
of PTSD, 67–8
top-down models, 8–9
cognitive psychology, autobiographical memory and, 1
cognitive reactivity, 343–4
cognitive therapy
CT-PTSD, 6–7, 120, 125
imagery re-scripting and, 6–7
imagery rescripting in, 135
Competitive Memory Training (COMET), 212
complicated grief (CG), 256–7
AMT for, 256–7
imagination of future events with, 257
MDD and, 258–9
OGM and, 364–5
WMC with, 257
concrete thinking style, 144
coping styles
avoidant, 95, 221–2
PTG and, 72
self-efficacy and, 328
CSA. *See* childhood sexual abuse

cued-recall test, 27
cues
negative, autobiographical memory and, 6
positive, autobiographical memory and, 6
for self-discrepancy, 343
threat, 91
culture
Eastern, collective model of self in, 349–50
self-identity influenced by, 329, 349–51
Western, individual model of self in, 349

defensive exclusion, in attachment theory, 93–4
defensive responses, 92
depression
bottom-up approach to, 165
cognitive conditions for, 157
CSA and, 249–50
dissociation and, 87
emotional conditions for, 157
event centrality and, 69
intrusive memories and, 154–9
involuntary memories and, 164–5
narratives with, 276–8
OGM and, 364–5
PTSD and, 87
rumination and, 201, 210–13, 277–8
self-appraisals with, 160–1
self-relevance and, 344–6
shame and, 326
top-down approach to, 165–6
trauma film paradigm and, 143
Diagnostic and Statistical Manual of Mental Disorders (Third Edition) (DSM-III), 4
DID. *See* dissociative identity disorder
dissociation
in DID, 251–3
as emotional regulation, 86–7, 96
emotional regulation and, 96
event centrality and, 69
impaired autobiographical memory and, 91–2
panic attacks and, 29
peritraumatic, 66
for PTSD, 42, 56–7
for trauma memories, 29, 42, 56–7
dissociation disorders
childhood abuse and, 86–7, 91–2
depression and, 87
dissociative flashbacks, 111
autonoetic awareness and, 111–12
dissociative identity disorder (DID), 251–3

380   Index

distorted memory. *See* false
    autobiographical memories
distraction hypothesis, for flashbacks, 139
dual representation theory
    PTSD and, 21
    SAM and, 20
    stress response theory and, 177
    trauma and, 19–20, 32

EMDR treatment. *See* eye-movement
    desensitization and reprocessing
    treatment
emotional autobiographical memory, 87–8.
    See also narratives
emotional regulation
    attachment theory and, 98
    in autobiographical memory, 95
    with BPD, 235–6
    childhood abuse and, 89, 95–8
    dissociation as, 86–7, 96
    functions of, 86
    in involuntary memories, 51–2
    OGM as strategy for, 223–4, 230–1
    by the self, psychopathology of, 352
    in voluntary memories, 51–2
emotions
    as evaluation, 269
    homologous structures of, 268–70
event centrality
    ACT principles and, 70–1
    anxiety and, 69
    CES scale for, 68
    construction of, 69–70
    depression and, 69
    dissociation and, 69
    narratives and, 77–8
    posttraumatic cognitions and, 69–70
    PTG and, 72–7
    PTSD and, 68–71, 74–7
    redundancy with other predictors, 70
event memory system, 46–7
everyday involuntary memories, 183–90
    characteristics of, 183–4
    development of, 184–7
explicit memory system, 46–7
extinction learning processes, 116
eye-movement desensitization and
    reprocessing (EMDR) treatment, 140

FA. *See* functional avoidance
false autobiographical memories, 253–6
    of alien abduction, 254–6
    formation of, 254–6
    among war veterans, 253–4
    in war veterans, 253–4

fear network theory, 90–1
females. *See* women
flashbacks
    Baddeley's model of working memory
        and, 138
    dissociative, 111–12
    distraction hypothesis for, 139
    formation of, 137–8
    intrusive memories and, 19, 23, 365–8
    in laboratory, 136–7
    memory activation through, 242
    memory consolidation and, 137–8
    memory-encoding and, 137
    mental imagery and, 134–5
    PTSD and, 19, 23, 86, 134–5
    reduction of, mechanisms of, 138–40
    in trauma film paradigm, 136
fMRI. *See* functional magnetic resonance
    imaging
focus retrograde amnesia (FRA), 297–8
functional avoidance (FA), 221–2
functional magnetic resonance imaging
    (fMRI), trauma film paradigm with,
    141
future events, construction of, 44
    with CG, 257
    with MTT, 321

gender. *See also* males; women
    PTSD and, 24, 66
    rumination by, 200
    trauma memories and, 24–5
glucocorticoid systems, arousal and, 22

heightened autobiographical memory
    Christianson's model and, 90
    fear network theory and, 90–1
    for negative experiences, 89–91
    survival processing in, 90
hippocampal activity, PTSD and, 88
hormones. *See* sex hormones; stress
    hormones

I Am Memory (IAM) Task, 295–6, 482.60
identity
    autobiographical memory and, 10–11,
        30–2
    PG and, 31–2
    trauma and, 30–2
IES. *See* Impact of Event Scale
imagery rescripting, 6–7, 135
Impact of Event Scale (IES), 155
impaired autobiographical memory
    defensive responses in, 92
    dissociation and, 91–2

Index

for negative experiences, 91–3
OGM and, 92–3
orienting responses in, 92
repression in, 91–2
impaired memory. *See* memory impairment
impaired problem solving, 6
insight-oriented psychotherapy, 285–6
intentional recall, of trauma memories, 177–80
intentionality, in PTSD, 242–3
intrusive memories, 8–9
  arousal and, 21
  autobiographical memory and, 160
  in clinical conditions, 154
  clinical disorders and, 365–8
  comparison of, with depression, 156–9
  comparison of, with PTSD, 156–9
  defined, 164
  in depression, 154–9
  emotional arousal levels and, 366–7
  everyday involuntary compared to, 183–90
  explanations for, 19
  features of, 187–90
  flashbacks and, 19, 23, 365–8
  IES for, 155
  as involuntary, 86, 162–4
  management of, 159–62
  memory content in, 118–20
  methodological considerations of, 156–9
  MTT and, 366
  peritraumatic processes and states, 156–7
  prevalence of, 155
  PTG and, 75
  PTSD and, 18–19, 154–9
  recurrent nature of, 189–90
  reexperiencing in PTSD and, 110
  self-appraisals of, 160–1
  sensory features of, 159–60
  sex hormones as influence on, 25
  stress hormones and, 22
  stress response theory and, 5
  trauma as influence on, 5, 18–19
  visual imagery and, 366
  visual vantage perspective for, 160
  in women, 25
involuntary autobiographical memory, 184
  development of, 184–7
  uniqueness of, 185–6
involuntary forgetting, 174
involuntary memory, 8–9
  activation of, 166
  behavioral differences in, 54
  centrality of, 50
  characteristics of, 183–4
  construction of, 50–3
  defined, 163–4
  depression and, 164–5
  development of, 172–3
  emotional intensity of, 50
  emotional regulation in, 51–2
  emotionally positive events and, 183
  everyday, 183–90
  evidence of, 174–7
  general model of, 166
  as intrusive, 86, 162–4
  negative stimuli for, 181–2
  origins of, 174–7
  PTSD and, 42, 58
  reliving events with, 183
  retention time for, 183–4
  retrieval of, 3, 50
  as stress response, 174–7
  trauma and, 42, 58
involuntary recall, of trauma memories, 21, 167
  enhanced, 180–2

knowledge, autobiographical memory and, 368–71
  CES and, 370
  splitting and, 371

learning processes. *See* associative learning processes; extinction learning processes
life scripts, 307
life stories, 317–18
long-term memory, memory reconsolidation and, 25

major depressive disorder (MDD). *See also* depression
  CG and, 258–9
  OCD and, 244
  OGM and, 229
  PTSD and, 258–9
males
  intrusive memories in, 25
  PTSD in, 24
  rumination for, 200
  trauma memories in, 24–5
maltreatment. *See* childhood abuse
MDD. *See* major depressive disorder
memory content, with or without PTSD, 118–20
memory disorganization, 121–2
  therapy implications for, 123–4
memory fragmentation
  PTSD and, 21, 42, 57–8

memory fragmentation (cont.)
    recall of trauma memories and, 121
    trauma and, 42, 57–8
memory impairment. *See also* amnesia
    with Alzheimer's Disease, 309
    anosognosia as, 309
    with ASD, 303–5
    with schizophrenia, 301–2
    selfhood and, 291, 296–7
    with TEA, 300–1
Memory Modulation hypothesis, 32–3
memory reconsolidation. *See also*
        rumination
    long-term memory and, 25
    propranolol and, 26
    trauma and, 25–6
Memory Specificity Training (MEST),
        212–13
mental death, 325–6
mental imagery. *See also* trauma film
        paradigm
    in autobiographical memory, 133
    with bipolar disorder, 141–2
    CBM with, 143–4
    clinical implications of, 140–1
    defined, 133
    emotion and, 133
    flashbacks and, 134–5
    functions of, 133
    manipulation of, 146
    memory consolidation through, 137–8
    memory-encoding and, 137
    neural systems for, 134
    in psychopathology, 135–6
    rescripting of, 6–7, 135
    visual, 134, 366
mental time travel (MTT), 321
    intrusive memories and, 366
MEST. *See* Memory Specificity Training
MTT. *See* mental time travel

narcissistic personality disorder, 285
narrative theory, in psychoanalytic
        tradition, 10
narratives, 75
    agency in, 272–3
    with agoraphobia, 281–2
    with anxiety disorders, 281–3
    autobiographical, 273
    autobiographical memories and, 267–8
    with BPD, 284–5
    with depression, 276–8
    development of, 267–8
    direct evaluations in, 273–4
    event centrality and, 77–8
    fragmentation of, 280–1
    functions of, 268–9
    homologous structures of, 268–70
    insight-oriented psychotherapy and,
        285–6
    levels of, 270–5
    listener orientation in, 274–5
    organization of, 267
    overwhelming, 280–1
    panic, 282–3
    with personality disorders, 283–5
    perspectivity within, 271
    in posttrauma outcomes, 77–9
    in psychological disorders, 277
    psychopathological processes in, 276
    with PTSD, 279–81
    reflective evaluations in, 274
    sad, 283
    sequencing in, 271–2
    splitting within, 284
    trauma, 121–2
narrowed attention, 29–30
negative cues, autobiographical memory
        and, 6
negative experiences
    heightened autobiographical memory for,
        89–91
    impaired autobiographical memory for,
        91–3
neuroticism, PTSD and, 78

obsessive-compulsive disorder (OCD)
    MDD and, 244
    OGM and, 244
    PTSD and, 244
overgeneral memory (OGM), 6, 221–2,
        243–8. *See also* borderline personality
        disorder; rumination; self-identity, in
        PTSD
    AMI for, 363
    AMT for, 204, 221, 224–5
    ASD and, 247
    BPD and, 224–33
    CaRFAX model and, 18, 205–6, 235,
        362–4
    CG and, 364–5
    childhood abuse and, 92–3, 95
    childhood sexual abuse and, 248–53
    clinical disorders and, 361–5
    defined, 199
    depression and, 364–5
    development mechanisms for, 199
    discrepancy constructs with, 213–15
    as emotion regulation strategy, 223–4,
        230–1

Index

FA and, 221–2
hierarchy constructs with, 213–15
impaired autobiographical memory and, 92–3
MDD and, 229
mechanisms of, 9–10
OCD and, 244
perceived permanent change and, 122–3
problem solving with, 221
PTSD and, 17–18, 67
retrieval style in, 247–8
rumination as causal influence, 202–7
self-identity in PTSD and, 319–22
SMS for, 221–2
social problem solving and, 17–18
as trans-diagnostic phenomenon, 362–3
trauma as influence on, 17–18
for war events, 244–5
WS and, 222
overwhelming narratives, 280–1

panic attacks, 29
panic narratives, 282–3
perceived permanent change, PTSD and, 122–3
perceptual priming, 116–17
posttrauma, 117
perceptual processing, during PTSD, 117
peritraumatic dissociation, 66
personality disorders. *See also specific disorders*
    narratives with, 283–5
personality traits, PTSD and, 66
perspectivity, within narratives, 271
PG. *See* prolonged grief
phobias. *See specific phobias*
positive cues, autobiographical memory and, 6
possible selves, 328
Posttraumatic Cognitions Inventory (PTCI), 69
posttraumatic growth (PTG)
    anchor event and, 74
    coping styles and, 72
    event centrality and, 72–7
    intrusive thoughts and, 75
    personal growth in, 71
    from PTSD, 71–2
    rumination and, 77
    self-defining memory and, 74
    social support and, 72
    trauma and, 71–2
posttraumatic stress disorder (PTSD). *See also* involuntary memory; overgeneral memory; reexperiencing; self-identity, in PTSD; voluntary memories
    accuracy of memory with, 56
    AMT for, 244–5
    arousal symptoms of, 41
    autonomous orientation with, 351
    avoidance symptoms of, 41, 86
    behavioral differences in, 53–4
    bottom-up approach to, 165
    CBT for, 140
    cognition and, 67–8
    cognitive models of, 67–8
    cognitive therapy for, 6–7, 120
    CSA and, 249–52
    current threats in, 109
    depression and, 87
    diagnosis of, 175
    dissociation models for, 42, 56–7
    dual representation theory of, 21, 67
    elaboration of trauma memory with, 119–20
    EMDR treatments for, 140
    etiology of, 66–7
    event centrality and, 68–71, 74–7
    experimental cognitive psychology methods for, 243
    flashbacks as part of, 19, 23, 86, 134–5
    gender influences on, 24, 66
    hippocampal activity and, 88
    intentionality in, 242–3
    intrusive memories and, 18–19, 154–9
    involuntary memory and, 42, 58
    involuntary recall and, 21
    in males, 24
    MDD and, 258–9
    memory content with, 118–20
    memory fragmentation and, 21, 42, 57–8
    mental death and, 325–6
    multiple dimensions of, 54–5
    narratives with, 279–81
    neuroticism and, 78
    OCD and, 244
    OGM retrieval after, 17–18, 67
    pathogenesis of, 10
    perceived permanent change and, 122–3
    peritraumatic dissociation and, 66
    peritraumatic processes and states, 156–7
    personality traits and, 66
    posttrauma correlates for, 66, 69–70
    predictors of symptoms for, 76
    pre-trauma correlates for, 66
    psychological symptoms of, 65–6
    PTG and, 71–2
    reexperiencing in, 18–19
    rumination and, 77

posttraumatic stress disorder (PTSD). (cont.)
  self-appraisals with, 160–1
  self-representations in, 244–5
  sensory dominance of, 21
  severity scores for, 45
  shame and, 326
  from specific event, 66
  stress response theory and, 5, 175–7
  Stroop interference effect and, 91
  top-down approach to, 165–6
  vantage point and, 28
  verbally-based memories with, 67
  from war experiences, 244–5
  in women, 24
processing modes
  abstract, 207–13
  perceptual, during trauma, 117
  for rumination, 203–5, 207–13
  survival, 90
  theory for, 208
  for trauma, 19–21
  visually-based, 20
prolonged grief (PG), 31–2
propranolol, 26
psychoanalytic tradition, narrative theory in, 10
psychopathology. *See also* emotional regulation; mental imagery
  autobiographical memory as function of, 1, 6–7
  mental imagery in, 135–6
  self-discrepancy and, 341–4, 346–9
  self-identity and, 349–53
  self-relevance and, 344–9
  trauma and, theoretical development of, 4
PTCI. *See* Posttraumatic Cognitions Inventory
PTG. *See* posttraumatic growth
PTSD. *See* posttraumatic stress disorder

recall, of trauma memories, 120–2
  CES for, 177–9
  after CSA, 248–9
  encoding in, 182
  enhanced involuntary, 180–2
  intentional, 177–80
  involuntary, 21, 167, 180–2
  memory disorganization in, 121–2
  memory fragmentation and, 121
  specificity of, 121
  trauma narratives in, 121–2
reexperiencing, with PTSD
  affect without recollection in, 110–12
  associative learning in, 115–16
  clinical implications of, 118
  defined, 110–12
  dissociative flashback in, 111–12
  extinction learning with, 116
  frequency of, 109
  intrusive memories and, 110
  memory content in, 118–20
  negative appraisals of, 124–5
  perceptual priming and, 116–17
  perceptual processing during, 117
  persistence of, 124–5
  without PTSD, comparisons to, 114–15
  recurrent intrusions in, 112
  rumination and, 124–5
  stimuli triggers for, 115
  stimulus discrimination training and, 118
  symptoms of, 109–12
  therapy implications for, 114, 125
  thought suppression and, 124–5
  after trauma, 112–13
  warning signals for, 113
repetitive thinking, trauma as influence on, 4
repression
  after CSA, 248–9
  in impaired autobiographical memory, 91–2
retrieval induced forgetting (RIF), 26–7
RFCBT. *See* Rumination-focused Cognitive Behavioral Therapy
RIF. *See* retrieval induced forgetting
rumination, 18
  abstract processing and, 207–13
  anxiety predictions and, 200
  BPD and, 235
  category fluency tasks and, 203–4
  control theory and, 214–15
  cued-recall test and, 27
  defined, 199–201
  depression and, 201, 210–13, 277–8
  discrepancy constructs with, 213–15
  by gender, 200
  hierarchy constructs with, 213–15
  induction, 200–1
  manipulation of, negative effects from, 200–1
  MEST for, 212–13
  mnemonic interlock process, 206
  OGM influenced by, 202–7
  processing modes for, 203–5, 207–13
  PTG and, 77
  PTSD and, 77
  reexperiencing with PTSD and, 124–5
  RFCBT for, 210–11
  RIF and, 26–7
  SCEPT for, 204

Index 385

self-discrepancy and, 344
    trauma and, 18, 26–8
Rumination-focused Cognitive Behavioral
    Therapy (RFCBT), 210–11

sad narratives, 283
SAM. *See* situationally accessible memory
SCEPT. *See* Sentence Completion for Past
    Events task
schizophrenia
    memory impairment with, 301–2
    selfhood with, 301–3
    self-images with, 302
the self. *See also* self-discrepancy; ; selfhood;
    self-relevance
    within autobiographical memory, 338–40
    bundle theory of, 336
    defined, 336
    in Eastern culture, 349–50
    emotional regulation and,
        psychopathology of, 352
    neural studies of, 337–8, 346–8
    within philosophical realm, 336
    positive information for, 339–40
    role in self-identity, 336
    role of memory in, 337
    schemas for, 337
    self-discrepancy, 340
    SMS and, 338–9
    SRE and, 337
    in Western culture, 349
Self Memory System (SMS). *See also* self-
    discrepancy
    autobiographical memory and, 338–40
    framework for, 221–2, 480.160
    hierarchical organization of memory in,
        318–19
    the self and, 338–40
    self-identity and, 318–19
    WS and, 319
self-appraisals
    with depression, 160–1
    of intrusive memories, 160–1
    negative, reexperiencing and, 124–5
    with PTSD, 160–1
    self-identity and, in PTSD, 324–5
self-defining memory, 74
self-discrepancy
    autobiographical memory and, 340–1
    cognitive reactivity and, 343–4
    cues for, 343
    memory retrieval and, 346–9
    psychopathology and, 341–4
    rumination and, 344
    the self and, 340

self-efficacy
    coping and, 328
    defined, 327
    in self-identity, with PTSD, 326–8
    WS and, 327–8
selfhood
    with Alzheimer's Disease, 296
    with amnesia, 297–300
    with ASD, 303–6
    autobiographical memory and, 481.90
    future conceptualizations of, 309–10
    IAM Task and, 295–6, 482.60
    life scripts and, 307
    memory impairment and, 291, 296–7
    personal continuity as part of, 306–8
    with schizophrenia, 301–3
    through self-images, 293
    with TEA, 300–1
    TST for, 305
self-identity, in PTSD
    attributional style for, 317
    CES for, 322
    culture as influence on, 329, 349–51
    life stories as, 317–18
    mental death and, 325–6
    models of, 317–18
    MTT and, 321
    OGM and, 319–22
    of possible selves, 328
    psychopathology and, 349–53
    the self and, 336
    self appraisals and, 324–5
    self-defining memories as part of,
        323–4
    self-efficacy and, 326–8
    SMS and, 318–19
    trauma centrality and, 322–3
    among war veterans, 320–1, 325–6
    WS and, 327–8
self-images
    with ASD, 306
    with schizophrenia, 302
    selfhood through, 293
self-reference effect (SRE), 337
    with ASD, 304
self-relevance
    memory retrieval and, 346–9
    psychopathology and, 344–6
Sentence Completion for Past Events task
    (SCEPT)
    CSA and, 250
    for rumination, 204
sex hormones
    intrusive memories influenced by, 25
    trauma memories influenced by, 24–5

sexual abuse. *See also* childhood sexual abuse
  women and, 246
shame, 326
situationally accessible memory (SAM)
  dual representation theory and, 20
  neural networks and, 23
  trauma and, 19–20
SMS. *See* Self Memory System
social media networks, 1
social phobia, 154
social problem solving, OGM retrieval and, 17–18
social support, PTG and, 72
specific memories
  retrieval of, in autobiographical memory, 6
  trauma and, 17–18
splitting
  in knowledge organization, within autobiographical memory, 371
  within narratives, 284
SRE. *See* self-reference effect
stimulus discrimination training, 118
stress hormones, 22
stress response theory
  active memory storage and, 181
  BPD and, 236
  dual representation theory and, 177
  intrusive memories and, 5
  involuntary memories and, 174–7
  for involuntary recall, 180–2
  model for, 174–5
  PTSD and, 5, 175–7
Stroop interference effect, 91
survival processing, 90

TEA. *See* transient epileptic amnesia
thinking styles. *See* abstract thinking style; concrete thinking style
thought suppression, 124–5
threat cues, 91
transient epileptic amnesia (TEA), 300–1
trauma, memories and. *See also* involuntary memory; posttraumatic stress disorder; recall, of trauma memories; reexperiencing; stress response theory; voluntary memories
  accuracy in, 56
  arousal and, 21–3
  autobiographical memory and, 7–8
  behavioral differences in, 53
  dual representation theory and, 19–20, 32
  elaboration of memory, 119–20
  gender as influence on, 24–5
  historical examples of, 65
  identity and, 30–2
  incoherence of, 42
  integration model for, 32–3
  intrusive memories after, 5, 18–19
  involuntary memory and, 42, 58
  lifetime exposure rates for, 65
  memory fragmentation and, 42, 57–8
  memory influenced by, 4
  Memory Modulation hypothesis for, 32–3
  memory reconsolidation and, 25–6
  mode of processing for, 19–21
  narratives and, 77–9
  narrowed attention and, 29–30
  neural mechanisms for, 23–4, 87–9
  OGM and, 17–18
  panic attacks and, 29
  perceptual processing during, 117
  PG and, 31–2
  positive outcomes from, 42, 56–7, 71–2
  psychopathology and, theoretical development of, 4
  PTG and, 71–2
  reexperiencing after, 112–13
  repetitive thinking influenced by, 4
  rumination and, 26–8
  SAM and, 19–20
  sex hormones as influence on, 24–5
  specificity of, 17–18
  VAM and, 19
  vantage point and, 28
  visually-based processing in, 20
trauma film paradigm
  adaptations to, 141–2
  depression and, 143
  flashbacks in, 136
  fMRI with, 141
  laboratory studies with, 141
  memory consolidation after, 137–8
  memory-encoding and, 137
trauma narratives, 121–2
Twenty Statements Test (TST), 305
twins, autobiographical memory for, 43–4

uniqueness, of autobiographical memory, 185–6

VAM. *See* verbally accessible memory
vantage point, PTSD and, 28
verbally accessible memory (VAM)
  neural networks and, 23
  trauma and, 19
verbally-based memories, 67

veterans. *See* war veterans
visual mental imagery, 134
   intrusive memories and, 366
voluntary autobiographical memories, 184
voluntary memories
   centrality of, 50
   construction of, 50–3
   emotional intensity of, 50
   emotional regulation in, 51–2
   emotionally positive events and, 183
   reliving events with, 183
   retention time for, 183–4
   retrieval of, 3, 50

war veterans
   AMT for, 244–5
   false autobiographical memories in, 253–4
   mental death for, 325–6
   MTT for, 321
   OGM and, 244–5
   PTSD and, 244–5
   self-identity for, with PTSD, 320–1
well-being, psychological, 10–11
WMC. *See* working memory capacity
women
   CES for, 246
   intrusive memories in, 25
   PTSD in, 24, 66
   rumination for, 200
   sexual abuse against, 246
   trauma memories in, 24–5
working memory, Baddeley's model of, 138
working memory capacity (WMC), 257
working self (WS)
   in autobiographical memory, 319
   OGM and, 222
   self-efficacy and, 327–8
   self-identity in PTSD, 327–8
   in SMS, 319

For EU product safety concerns, contact us at Calle de José Abascal, 56–1º,
28003 Madrid, Spain or eugpsr@cambridge.org.

www.ingramcontent.com/pod-product-compliance
Ingram Content Group UK Ltd.
Pitfield, Milton Keynes, MK11 3LW, UK
UKHW011327060825
461487UK00005B/398